Applying Cultural Anthropology
READINGS

Gary Ferraro
University of North Carolina at Charlotte

Wadsworth Publishing Company
I(T)P® An International Thomson Publishing Company

Belmont, CA • Albany, NY • Bonn • Boston • Cincinnati • Detroit • Johannesburg • London • Madrid
Melbourne • Mexico City • New York • Paris • Singapore • Tokyo • Toronto • Washington

Anthropology Editor: Denise Simon
Editorial Assistant: Angela Nava
Marketing Manager: Chaun Hightower
Print Buyer: Karen Hunt
Cover: Bruce Kortebein/Design Office
Cover photographs: © Reagan Bradshaw (background); © Robb Kendrick/Material World (foreground)
Compositor: Lorrain and Jim Sargent/Pacific Publications
Printer: Courier Companies, Inc./Kendallville

Printed in the United States of America
4 5 6 7 8 9 10

For more information, contact Wadsworth Publishing Company, 10 Davis Drive, Belmont, CA 94002, or electronically
at http://www.thomson.com/wadsworth.html

International Thomson Publishing Europe
Berkshire House 168-173
High Holborn
London, WC1V 7AA, England

International Thomson Editores
Campos Eliseos 385, Piso 7
Col. Polanco
11560 México D.F. México

Thomas Nelson Australia
102 Dodds Street
South Melbourne 3205
Victoria, Australia

International Thomson Publishing Asia
221 Henderson Road
#05-10 Henderson Building
Singapore 0315

Nelson Canada
1120 Birchmount Road
Scarborough, Ontario
Canada M1K 5G4

International Thomson Publishing Japan
Hirakawacho Kyowa Building, 3F
2-2-1 Hirakawacho
Chiyoda-ku, Tokyo 102, Japan

International Thomson Publishing GmbH
Königswinterer Strasse 418
53227 Bonn, Germany

International Thomson Publishing Southern Africa
Building 18, Constantia Park
240 Old Pretoria Road
Halfway House, 1685 South Africa

ISBN 0-534-53324-8

Preface

Over the past several decades there has been an appreciable increase in the number of cultural anthropologists whose work has focused on the solution of societal, rather than purely theoretical, problems. Without getting into the distinction between "applied" and "practicing" anthropologists, suffice it to say that these more pragmatic anthropologists have been bringing their theories, methods, and insights to bear on a wide variety of social, economic, and technological problems, both at home and abroad. Since the 1970s we have witnessed a marked acceleration in the number of anthropologists conducting research and/or becoming involved in policy implementation in a wide variety of areas, including, medicine, international development, education, business, substance abuse, housing, law, agriculture, criminal justice, housing, and conflict resolution among others. However we may choose to measure it, there has been a significant transformation within anthropology in recent decades toward greater concern for the solution of human problems.

This reader is a logical outgrowth of that transformation going on within the profession. The reader offers a selection of 39 articles written in the words of those cultural anthropologists who are making their discipline useful. The readings are organized into five major sections—medicine, business, education, government and law, and economic development—reflecting those areas that are benefitting from the practice and application of cultural anthropology. Realizing that many other articles could have been included, the categories, and the articles contained within them, are meant to be suggestive rather than exhaustive. The reader can be used effectively as a supplement to any introductory textbook in cultural anthropology. Moreover, the readings would be appropriate for undergraduate level courses in applied anthropology.

The intent of this reader is twofold. First, it is to provide undergraduate anthropology student with a wide range of examples as to how the discipline is making meaningful contributions to the mitigation of human problems. And second, we hope to convey, through the words of the practicing anthropologists themselves, some of the challenges and rewards involved in making cultural anthropology useful.

Acknowledgments

The editor and Wadsworth Publishing Company wish to express their sincere gratitude to the many journals that permitted us to reprint their articles. We are indebted to Doreen Eisner and Donna Schlatter who served as research assistants to the editor and to Lorrain and Jeff Sargent of Pacific Publications who typed and produced the camera-ready pages for this reader.

About the Editor

Gary Ferraro is a professor of anthropology and the director of the Intercultural Training Institute at the University of North Carolina at Charlotte. In addition to publishing in a number of journals, he is the author of THE TWO WORLDS OF KAMAU (1978), THE CULTURAL DIMENSION OF INTERNATIONAL BUSINESS (1990, 1994, 1998), CULTURAL ANTHROPOLOGY: AN APPLIED PERSPECTIVE (1992, 1995, 1998), ANTHROPOLOGY: AN APPLIED PERSPECTIVE (1994).

Contents

Section IV: Government and the Law

Section V: Economic Development

Section I
Medicine

Despite the remarkable advances in the technical and biological aspects of medicine in recent years, many physicians continue to overlook the cultural context of curing and healing. While it is true that certain antibiotics will fight infection in similar ways in all of the world's people, the (culturally produced) attitudes that patients bring with them often impact the delivery of health care services. Why people alter their diets, follow the advice of traditional healers, or prefer one remedy over another is the result of their cultural environment, and thus must be taken into consideration. Helman reminds us that medical anthropology is more than the dabbling into exotic cultures, but rather provides insights into the very nature of medical practice.

Medicine and Culture: Limits of Biomedical Explanation

By Cecil G. Helman

Over the past century, most branches of medicine have made impressive advances in preventing disease and improving health care. However, certain aspects of the modern medical model limit the efficacy with which it can deal with contemporary health issues in different cultures.

Medical anthropology is the study of how people in different cultures and social groups explain the causes of ill-health, the types of treatment they believe in, and to whom they turn if they do get ill. The scope of medical anthropology also extends to how these beliefs and behaviours relate to biological and psychological changes during both health and disease.[1] Anthropologists have adopted a holistic approach based on "ethnography" (participant observation and open-ended interviews) or other qualitative research methods originally developed for work with non-literate societies, where questionnaires and techniques involving measurements were not practicable.[2] Anthropology is still "concerned with meanings, rather than with measurements, with the texture of everyday life in communities, rather than formal abstractions."[3]

Medical vs. lay perspectives

Medical anthropology has focused on the widening gap between medical and lay perspectives on ill-health. That is, between "disease"—the biomedical model with emphasis on physiological data, which is seen as more real than social or psychological data—and "illness", the subjective experiences of the patient and the meanings that are given to such experiences.[4]

Modern biomedicine tends to regard "diseases" as universal entities, irrespective of the context in which they appear. Physiological measurement, although an essential aspect of medicine, only gives one view about the complexity of human illness. Many attributes of an individual, such as personality, experience, culture, social class, family, and religion together with their fears, beliefs, behaviour, and the meanings they give to their ill-health, cannot be understood with the aid of diagnostic technology alone. The importance of patients' health beliefs should not be underestimated, especially since non-medical health care from family and friends still copes with most symptoms in the community.[5] Doctors need to know what patients believe about the cause, significance, and appropriate treatment of their condition, since this will influence self-treatment strategies and the sort of help that they seek.[6] The same sudden, severe infection, for example, may be blamed on witchcraft, divine punishment, "fate", or cold, draughts, and invisible "germs".

Health beliefs are also important because of the physical and psychological effects of belief itself. Thus the placebo effect is often dismissed as a peripheral event by some doctors, because it cannot easily be explained, measured, or predicted in an individual. However, the placebo response remains a key component of any therapeutic relationship, medical or nonmedical, and is of special interest to medical anthropologists. Litigation against doctors is a further reflection of modern health beliefs. In some cases such action may be seen as a modern form of witchcraft

Reprinted by permission of The LANCET 337(8749), May 4, 1991, pp. 1080-83

accusation: other people (but never physiology, ageing, "fate", or "bad luck") are judged responsible for most of one's afflictions, unhappiness, or failure to recover from ill-health.

Research on lay health beliefs

Medical anthropology may be especially helpful in answering some of the 'Why?' questions posed by modern health care.

> Why, for example, do the members of one cultural group reject one form of medical treatment, but accept another?[7]
>
> Why do some groups of patients follow their doctors advice while others do not?[1]
>
> Why do some people prefer traditional or alternative healers for some conditions, but not for others?
>
> Why does one ethnic group have higher rates of alcohol use compared with another?[8]
>
> Why do some people change their diet during illness, pregnancy, or lactation in ways harmful to their health?
>
> Why are some conditions regarded as "diseases" in one culture but not in another?[1,7]
>
> Why is behaviour that is thought to be "bad" in one group seen as "mad" in another?[7]

These issues have contemporary relevance—e.g., in understanding and controlling the spread of viral infections such as human immunodeficiency virus and hepatitis B.[9]

My own research has been largely concerned with lay health beliefs. In a north London suburb, I sought patients' beliefs about minor viral illnesses, summarized in the phrase, "feed a cold, starve a fever".[10] Older patients thought that "chills" and "colds" were due to penetration of environmental cold or damp through skin. Once inside the body, the illness might move from the head, to the chest or stomach. These conditions were deemed to be one's own fault, caused by going outdoors in cold weather from a warm house, or after a hot bath. Younger patients, born since the advent of antibiotics, blamed their colds on "bugs", viruses, or "germs". They thought themselves to be less responsible for their illness than their elders, and often demanded unnecessary antibiotics for mild viral infections.

I have also studied the symbolism that patients attach to their long-term use of benzodiazepines.[11] Many women saw the drug as a "fuel" without which they could not function

socially, maintain relationships, or meet the expectations of others, especially within the family. Other patients described their drug as a "tonic"; something to give them more energy, to be taken only occasionally; some even saw it as a "food" without which they could not survive.

How patients believed to have psychosomatic illness in Massachusetts view their own bodies and emotions has also been an interest of mine.[12] Several individuals described themselves as completely healthy and took little responsibility for either their illness or its treatment. They blamed their condition on organs of their body that they described as unreliable, uncontrollable, and even hostile towards them, such as a "nervous stomack", "irritable colon", or "weak chest".

Body image

Lay theories of anatomy and physiology may influence how people interpret and respond to physical symptoms. In south Wales in 1970, a group of women described their menstrual blood as "bad" or "toxic", and therefore welcomed a monthly "good clearance".[13] This belief system is found in many parts of the world and may have important clinical implications. Some women might ignore menorrhagia. Others might unnecessarily fear the menopause, amenorrhoea (post pill or post partum), or the lighter menses that sometimes result from oral contraceptive use.[14]

Industrial society has helped to create a new image of the human body.[15] Patients may believe from both their doctors and the media, that their bodies are repairable machines that can be diagnosed, measured, monitored, and even kept alive by other machines. This new body image is reflected in language: "nervouse breakdown", "blow off steam", "recharge batteries", or "reprogramme myself". Some patients, as a result, regard their doctors as mechanics, plumbers, electricians, or carpenters, rather than as healers. Some women feel strongly that many obstetricians see childbirth in these mechanistic terms, as a technical procedure, rather than as an important emotional and social event for the mother.

Medical institutions

Medical anthropology is also concerned with the social organization and culture of biomedicine, and how these relate to delivery of health care. The hospital is a tiny self-contained city, with its own history, hierarchies, uniforms, rituals, and slang. A hospital has its own workers, cleaners, guards, bureaucrats, technicians, as well as a temporary and involuntary population of patients.

Anthropologists have pointed out that such large institutions have their own culture, their own unique view of the world with implicit and explicit rules of behaviour.[16] This idea also extends to each medical school, ward, clinic, or family practice. These microcultures can influence the attitudes of medical staff towards both patients and other health-care professionals.

Admission to a modern hospital commonly involves a process of depersonalisation, where patients are stripped of many of the markers of their social and individual identity. They are removed from the familial, cultural, and religious contexts in which they spend most of their lives. Then they are sub-divided by gender, age, type and severity of condition, and reduced to a numbered case among a ward of strangers with a uniform of pyjamas or bathrobe (fig 1). Privacy is often limited, and even physiological functions are tightly controlled by the daily cycles and rituals of the ward.

The culture of biomedicine

A system of health care, irrespective of its basis in scientific empiricism, is always embedded in a specific historical, cultural, political, and economic context. The system is shaped by, and in turn influences, some of the values and ideologies of the society from which it arises.[17] Divisions, inequalities, and prejudices based on gender, social class, or ethnic criteria are often reproduced.[18]

In each country, medical professionals form a privileged subculture, with their own language, rituals of healing, and use of powerful symbols, such as the white coat. A health-care system is shaped not only by economic factors, such as health insurance or reimbursement schemes, but also by cultural factors. Differences are found between industrialised countries for rates of caesarean section,[19] prescribed treatments, [20] and diagnostic categories.[21] For instance, bouffees delirantes (transitional delusional states) and delires chroniques (chronic delusional states) in French psychiatry,[21] as well as categories of physical illness such as spasmophilia and crise de foie (French), or Herzinsuffizienz and Kreislaufkollaps (German), have no exact parallel in other European countries.[22] In addition, differences have been reported between the diagnostic behaviour of British and American psychiatrists,[23] while some forms of treatment, such as spas and hydrotherapy in Germany (the kur) and in France (la thermilisme), are largely unknown in the English-speaking world.

These cross-national differences in health care cannot be explained simply by economic factors, availability of medical resources, or the health of their respective populations. The cultural values of the doctor, patient, and the society in which they live are also important influences.

These culture-bound aspects of western biomedicine limit the universal applicability of its philosophy and techniques. This is especially true in the developing world, where attempts to import expensive, overspecialised, high-technology, and curative aspects of biomedicine to countries with few doctors, and limited resources, have often been unsuccessful.

In other cases, medical aid programmes have foundered on communication difficulties between aid workers and indigenous communities, partly because of different perspectives on the origin, nature, and management of ill-health. Oral rehydration therapy (ORT), although a life-saving treatment for infant diarrhoeal diseases is sometimes refused on cultural grounds.[24] Mothers from rural Pakistan reported that infantile diarrhoea was "normal" and did not require treatment; others blamed it on the "evil eye" (nazar), malevolent spirits (jinns), or on a folk illness called sutt (fallen fontanelle). They did not consider ORT appropriate for these conditions, and children were given home remedies or taken to a traditional healer instead.

Medical anthropologists can contribute to the adaptation of western medicine for specific local contexts, cultures, and health needs. In a British Council link programme begun in 1989, in which I am involved, Brazilian anthropologists are studying the delivery of primary health care in Porto Alegre (figs 2 and 3), southern Brazil, and community responses to it. They are also researching women's attitudes to contraception, mothers recognition of infant malnutrition, and the selection and training of lay community health workers from the local favelas, or urban shanty towns.

Consideration of community, as well as individual, health issues and needs,[26] is an increasingly common approach in medical aid programmes to developing countries. Such an approach moves away from more mechanistic and reductionist aspects of western medicine towards a preventive health strategy combined with greater community participation.

REFERENCES

1. Helman CG. Culture, health and illness. London: Wright, 1990.
2. Peacock JL. The anthropological lens. Cambridge: Cambridge University Press, 1986.
3. Keesing RM. Cultural anthropology. New York: Holt, Rinehart and Winston, 1981.
4. Eisenberg L. Disease and illness: distinctions between professional and popular ideas of sickness. Cult Med Psychiatry 1977; 1: 9-23.
5. Elliott-Binns CP. An analysis of lay medicine: fifteen years later. J R Coll Gen Pract 1986; 36: 542-44.
6. Helman CG. Disease versus illness in general practice. J R Coll Gen Pract 1981; 31: 548-52.
7. Kleinman A. Patients and healers in the context of culture. Berkeley: University of California Press, 1980.
8. Greeley AM, McCready WC. A preliminary reconnaissance into the persistence and explanation of ethnic subcultural drinking patterns. Med Anthropol 1978; 2: 31-51.
9. Brabin L, Brabin BJ. Cultural factors and transmission of hepatitis B virus. Am J Epidemiol 1985; 122: 725-30.
10. Helman CG. 'Feed a cold, starve a fever': folk models of infection in an English suburban community, and their relation to medical treatment. Cult Med Psychiatry 1978; 2: 107-37.
11. Helman CG. 'Tonic', 'fuel', and 'food': social and symbolic aspects of the long-term use of psychotropic drugs. Soc Sci Med 1981; 15B: 521-33.
12. Helman CG. Psyche, soma and society: the social construction of psychosomatic disorders. Cult Med Psychiatry 1985; 9: 1-26.
13. Skultans V. The symbolic significance of menstruation and the menopause. Man 1970; 5: 639-51.
14. Good BJ. The heart of what's the matter: the semantics of illness in Iran. Cult Med Psychiatry 1977; 1: 25-58.
15. Helman CG. Dr Frankestein and the industrial body: reflections on 'spare part' surgery. Anthropology Today 1988; 14: 14-16
16. Goffman E. Asylums. Harmondsworth: Penguin, 1961.
17. Lock M, Gordon D, eds. Biomedicine examined. Dordrecht: Kluwer, 1988.
18. Stacey M. Sociology of Health and Healing. London: Unwin Hyman, 1988.
19. Vayda E, Mindell WR, Rutkow IM. A decade of surgery in Canada, England and Wales, and the United States. Archh Surg 1982; 117: 846-53.
20. O'Brien B. Patterns of European diagnosis and prescribing. London: Office of Health Economics, 1984.
21. Pichot P. The diagnosis and classification of mental disorders in French-speaking countries: background, current views, and comparison with other nomenclatures. Psychol Med 1982; 12: 475-92.
22. Payer L. Medicine and Culture. London: Gollancz, 1989.
23. Cooper JE, Kendell RE, Gurland BJ, Sartorius M, Farkas T. Cross-national study of diagnosis of the mental disorders: some results from the first comparative investigation. Am J Psychiatry 1969; 125 (suppl): 21-29.
24. Weiss MG. Cultural models of diarrhoeal illness: conceptual framework and review. Soc Sci Med 1988; 27: 5-16.
25. Mull JD, Mull DS. Mothers' concepts of childhood diarrhoea in rural Pakistan: what ORT program planners should know. Soc Sci Med 1988; 27: 53-67.
26. Kark S. The practice of community-oriented primary care. New York: Appleton-Century-Crofts, 1981.

Questions:

1. What is the difference between disease and illness?

2. Why have programs of oral rehydration therapy in rural Pakistan been unsuccessful?

3. What are some of the areas of research that medical anthropologists are conducting at Porto Alegre in southern Brazil?

The answer section begins on page 243.

In this selection applied medical anthropologist Eric Bailey discusses the role that he played in the development of health fairs in predominantly African-American neighborhoods in Detroit and Houston. By conducting ethnographic research on the target population, Bailey was able to design the health fairs in a way that took maximum advantage of the socio-cultural realities of the neighborhood. Bailey's work is an excellent example of how applied anthropologists need to share their anthropological insights and strategies with a wide range of other professionals (including medical staff, public health officials, and neighborhood residents) if they are to contribute to the improvement of health care services.

The Medical Anthropologist as Health Department Consultant

By Eric J. Bailey

Medical anthropology is often poorly understood by those who are not a part of the discipline. When working with other health care professionals, medical anthropologists are commonly asked to explain what their field is, what they do, and how they can assist clinicians and public health officials in appropriating better health care for their patients/clients. Many assume that medical anthropologists are always on excavations like archaeologists or that we are very similar to biologists. To counteract such misconceptions and misinterpretation, we need to develop practical applications of our work so that others can benefit from our expertise, and we need to market our skills better. In sum, practical strategies are needed in *applied* medical anthropology in order to justify our existence in economic and sociopolitical terms with various health organizations.

Trained as an applied medical anthropologist at Wayne State University, I felt that my academic training was transferable to the real world. I thought that I could use my skills, if necessary, to get a job outside of academia—for example, as a consultant or program director of a major health care project. Although at the time my role was perceived more as student than consultant, I had had the chance to collaborate with a local health care organization for my dissertation research.

The United Health Care Organization had been co-sponsoring annual health fairs throughout metropolitan Detroit for the previous twenty years with a great deal of success. Interestingly, however, the organization had had little success in African American communities. In fact, African Americans participating in the annual health fairs had declined from 20 percent in 1976 to a mere 6 percent in 1984. As an African American, resident in Detroit and trained as an applied medical anthropologist, I felt I could be of help in this "practical" and real life health care situation. In order to show the organization's administrators my commitment to this project, however, I had to "sell" or "market" my idea that I could improve the Annual Free Health Fair.

I addressed one major question: What had United Health Organization been doing wrong in the African American communities? To provide an answer and practical suggestions, my strategy consisted of the following:

1. To conduct cultural-historical background research on Detroit's African American population;
2. To engage in informal observations in the local communities where the screening sites existed;
3. To carry out informal interviewing of key informants in the African American communities; and
4. To implement formal quantitative and qualitative data collection.

My cultural-historical research revealed that many institutions which had provided health care for African Americans through the 1950s

Reprinted by permission of PRACTICING ANTHROPOLOGY, 16 (1), Winter, 1994, pp. 13-15.

were in decline by the 1970s. Those institutions currently accessible to African Americans tended to be large teaching hospitals with a high turnover of medical staff. Many African Americans, especially the elderly accustomed to the medical institutions of the fifties, reported feeling a lack of trust and rapport in the facilities available to them in the eighties. Consequently, they often avoided seeking medical care until a health problem had grown serious.

When I went into communities in which United Health Care Organization had been holding annual health fairs and asked people why they had not frequented them, they often told me they were not aware of the fairs. Those who were aware of them often saw the fairs as an occasion for outside organizations to do something for their own benefit, and not really for the benefit of the local population. Key informants also indicated that health screening staff failed to work "with" the local residents; it only worked "for" them. This difference has important psychological implications. When African Americans perceive a health service as strictly a "hand-out," they believe that the service is of poor quality and demeaning to the psyche of the individual. This perception caused many not to participate in the local health screenings.

Local residents and key informants also observed that the staff at the health fairs were not of the same ethnic background as the local population, their promotion materials were not culturally sensitive, and their advice was not in tune with the realities of life in these communities. The health screenings provided only a tentative diagnosis; those with possible health problems were told, "See your physician," ignoring the fact that most had no physician and no regular access to the health care system. Health fair organizers also failed to recognize that people who have multiple economic and social problems may not want to know about as yet imperceptible health problems. To attract more participants, some health fairs had been held in shopping malls. People found the setting incongruous, however, and told me, "I didn't come to the mall to find out that something else is wrong with me!"

At the conclusion of my research, I recommended the following:
1. utilize more local community leaders;
2. locate influential community leaders to endorse the program;
3. incorporate other community services into the health fairs;

4. include work site screenings;
5. create incentives with local businesses; and
6. advertise and educate through innovative means.

To what degree United Health Organization actually used my recommendations, I cannot state, since I left the area at the end of the internship. Nonetheless, this experience provided me with the incentive to develop my skills as a consultant to various public health organizations.

The opportunity to use my skills as a consultant or program director did not present itself at graduation, so I took an assistant professor's position at the University of Houston. I taught the normal course load for a junior faculty member and participated in a number of academic activities. Of course, being a junior faculty member and an African American at a major university meant that much of my professional time centered around university service activities and functions. As each day passed, my identity as an academic professional became more solidified.

Yet my desire to do applied work and to work with "real" people and "real" issues continued. In order to do applied anthropology at a non-applied anthropology department, I sought out opportunities to volunteer with local health and social organizations in the Houston area. Fortunately, in 1989 I became associated with the Houston Health Department. I first served on an advisory board at the Riverside Health Center to assist with development of a health fair. Once the planning phase started, I was elected chairman of the 1989 Riverside Health Fair.

My job was to organize, coordinate, and direct all operations of the health fair. The prospect of organizing this event while also maintaining my academic duties at the University of Houston was a bit intimidating. Nonetheless, I accepted this job because I knew that it would be a very good learning experience for me and that a successful health fair would have a direct impact on the health status of the local African American community.

I felt that it was critical to conduct some basic field work and background research on the community surrounding Riverside Health Center. Cultural-historical documents and health department statistics led to identification of the following socioeconomic factors in the Riverside area (Houston's Third Ward):
1. Riverside's population totaled nearly 70,000. Blacks accounted for 77.5 percent of the

population, whites for 12.9 percent, Hispanics for 7.5% and others for 2.1 percent.

2. The average age of the population as a whole and of blacks fell within the 25-29 year age group. The average age of Hispanics and others was within 20-24 years, and whites had an average age within the 30-34 year age group.

3. Socioeconomic indicators listed 24 percent of families as under the poverty level and 36 percent of households as headed by single females. The median household income for 1989 was $15,666.

To find out more about Riverside's African American community, I established a working dialogue and association with three key informants in this area: Shannon Jones (Riverside Medical Director), Dr. Brobbey (Riverside Medical Director), and Mrs. Helen Hall Kinard (President of the Advisory Board for the Riverside Health Center). These three informants provided substantive qualitative data about Houston Health Department's program procedures and Riverside residents' needs.

As in Detroit, by 1989 the African American health care system that developed in Houston during the period of segregation had all but disappeared. Of the four African American hospitals still operating in the city in 1970, only two, Riverside General Hospital and Charles Drew Hospital, were still open. In an effort to improve the health care available to African Americans and other ethnic populations, the city of Houston's Department of Health and Human Services had expanded their operation of health clinics.

To get to know more of the personal and health care dynamics of local community residents, I spent many hours at the Riverside health clinic. The information I gathered from those who worked at the clinic and from those who lived in the neighborhood suggested that for the average household the priority placed on maintaining "health" had to be adjusted in light of economic and social needs. I concluded that since unemployment and public safety were major issues affecting most community residents, residents needed information on job opportunities and public safety strategies for the young and elderly as much as they needed traditional health messages.

The advisory board at the Riverside Health Center consisted of local residents, Houston's Health Department officials, and local business leaders. Charged with overseeing the operations of the clinic and developing community programs, the board met once a month. Initially, board members thought that a health fair should offer strictly medical services to local residents. Cholesterol screening, blood pressure screening, vision screening, and height/weight measurements were the "norm" for a public health fair. After much debate, the health fair was finally expanded to include a wider array of health care and social services and was designed as a "community festival." As chairman and acting consultant, I proposed and strongly supported this modification because my background research had shown that the previous model was outdated and not oriented to the needs of the local African American community.

In cooperation with Houston's Department of Health and Human Services and eighteen local agencies, basic tests and preventative health services offered at the health fair were height and weight screening, dental screening, pulmonary function screening, prenatal and child care counseling, law enforcement child identification screening, social service counseling, AIDS counseling, and an AIDS educational play. In addition, this day-long, free community event provided food and prizes to all participants. An initial projection was for seventy participants. To our surprise, well over two hundred local residents of all age groups participated. Approximately 90 percent of the participants were African American, 5 percent Anglo American and 5 percent Hispanic. The proportion of African American participants was even higher than their proportion in the local population.

Advisory board members, staff personnel from the Riverside clinic, local businesses, and community volunteers all contributed to the success of this modified health fair. Yet, ultimately its success depended upon the application of anthropological concepts. Developing a more "culturally oriented" and "culturally sensitive" approach in reaching out to and working with the African American community was responsible for the high rate of participation. This approach consisted of three major steps:

1. Increasing the number of African American health care and social service personnel who could participate in the fair;

2. Promoting the event through African American media; and

3. Educating African Americans in a style and pattern which they could understand and to which they are accustomed.

All agencies were encouraged strongly to have a diversified staff work their booth. This strategy helped many of the participants feel more comfortable asking questions and helped them develop an immediate rapport with the agency's workers. The advisory board also enlisted the services of the local African American radio station not only to announce the health fair on the air but also to bring their special mobile van to play music. In addition, we advertised the health fair in the local, well-established African American newspaper.

The AIDS educational play provided an example of how to educate and to discuss serious health issues with an entertaining and culturally sensitive approach. The playwright was an African American male, and the performers were young adults. Thus, the play had dialogue and issues directly reflecting young African American life-styles.

I also used anthropological concepts and data in working with the Riverside Advisory Board. The ethnographic data and the cultural-historical information helped me show the board that other health, social, and cultural issues are of major importance to the design of a health fair. If health fairs are to be successful in this community, "health" must be defined broadly, and the fair must include local cultural institutions and agencies and local leaders.

From these experiences using anthropology in applied settings, I realized that my skills as a health care consultant are definitely needed, and I have continued to work in the public health area. My association with Detroit's United Health Organization, with Houston's Riverside Health Center, and later with Indiana State Health Department has been very productive, rewarding, and eye-opening. Trained as an applied medical anthropologist, I realized that if one wants to become a consultant, one must learn to modify and adapt skills to the organizational environment in which one works. This does not mean that the applied medical anthropologist disregards his/her approach entirely. What it does mean is that applied medical anthropologists need to appreciate, to understand, and to work with different sociocultural, medical, and public health personnel in order to gradually introduce change from "within" as opposed to demanding change from the "outside." By doing this, more applied medical anthropologists and more public health departments (city and state) can benefit from collaboration.

Questions:

1. Why have the number of African-Americans participating in health fairs declined from 1976 to 1984?

2. Based on his research among people in the Riverside community, what did Bailey learn about the type of information the local people wanted in addition to traditional medical information?

3. What suggestions did Bailey make to increase the number of African-Americans at the health fairs?

The answer section begins on page 243.

3

In the 1980s Washington, D.C. had the highest infant mortality rate of any major city in the United States. Infant mortality, which is closely associated with low birth weights, is particularly prevalent among the Black population in the United States. For eighteen months medical anthropologist Margaret Boone worked at an inner city hospital in Washington gathering data on the sociocultural basis of poor health among Black mothers and their infants. The major significance of Boone's research was that it integrated the medical histories of the Black mothers with their behaviors, their interactions with others, and their values and attitudes. New systems of delivering medical services can only emerge after such studies as this which show how sociocultural factors of certain populations are directly related to poor health.

Practicing Sociomedicine: Redefining the Problem of Infant Mortality in Washington, D.C.

By Margaret Boone

Problem and Client

The problem was death—the highest infant death rate in the United States. In Washington, D.C., babies were dying in their first years of life at the highest rate for any large American city, and nobody could figure out why. In 1979, Washington's high infant mortality rate became a political issue in the campaign of Marion Barry, who promised to appoint a special blue ribbon committee to search for possible solutions. He won his first race and continues to head the city government—although infant mortality has proved to be a more stubborn problem than anticipated.

This chapter describes an unusual research and public policy project in effect from 1979 to 1980 that remains important in today's efforts to reduce teen pregnancy. During these years the Mayor's Blue Ribbon Committee on Infant Mortality actively reviewed the city's policies and programs for pregnant women. My work on the infant mortality problem was funded separately by the National Science Foundation (NSF), so it was first and foremost a scientific research project. However, it also included a strong effort to make research results known to political participants. The result was a shift in the definition of the infant mortality problem away from a strictly medical model and toward a broader framework that included a better understanding of social and cultural behavior.

Infant mortality was a good issue for a Black mayor because Washington has one of the largest, most concentrated Black urban populations in the country. Not only was it the first U.S. city to have a population that was 50 percent Black, but it also was the first big city encountered by north-bound Black migrants from the Carolinas and Virginia during the first sixty years of the twentieth century. Washington has a strong Black middle class that thrives, as do white, in a city that is almost recession-proof because of the federal bureaucracy. Although in many ways it is a model Black city, the indicators for its Black health problems are consistently bad.

Infant mortality in the United States is mainly a Black health problem because of the large and increasing number of disadvantaged Black women—initially Southern and rural but now more often Northern and urban—whose infants are born too soon and weigh too little to have a good chance of survival. The low-birthweight rate for Blacks is the highest of any U.S. racial or ethnic group: Black infants die at almost twice the rate of White infants. Infant mortality is a minority health issue that joins medicine, politics, demography, and health in a powerful, complex web of causation. It has been a subject for research by epidemiologists, clinicians, and sociologists but rarely by anthropologists.

Even during the year of intense effort by the mayor's blue ribbon committee to understand Washington's infant mortality problem, there was

Reprinted by permission of Robert M. Wulff and Shirley J. Fiske (eds.), ANTHROPOLOGICAL PRAXIS: TRANSLATING KNOWLEDGE INTO ACTION. Boulder, CO: Westview Press, 1987, pp. 56-71.

a growing conviction that the city's crisis was essentially unsolvable. This belief was founded on the premise that the problem involved large numbers of disadvantaged Black women whose health status was connected to their socioeconomic condition. No one saw their health behavior as also being culturally based and therefore able to be changed. The question for Washington, D.C., was this: If culture played a role, then what was it?

Who wanted that question answered and why? Who would sponsor complicated and controversial research to discover the possible cultural causes and solutions for infant mortality when it was much easier to continue after-the-fact medical care or social welfare as solutions? The problem was more than money; it was behavior. Who would champion policy and program change directed at behavior? As it turned out, many people favored that kind of change, but they needed solid evidence from a scientist who specialized in cultural behavior. The client who originally sponsored the sociomedical project on infant mortality in Washington, D.C., did so less because of specific concerns about infant mortality and more because of general concerns about the role of science in government decision-making in the mid-1970s.

In February 1979, I called a reporter at the *Washington Post* because I thought that I had found an issue that involved the public understanding of science in an article he had written on the city's infant mortality problem. At the time I was teaching full-time at a university, having graduated two years before with a PhD in cultural anthropology and an emphasis on urban studies and women. I wanted to direct my career into two areas: health and statistics. I reasoned that there would be money in health for at least the rest of this century and plenty of it as the baby-boom generation aged. And, I had found a funding program at the National Science Foundation (NSF) that intrigued me. It gave postdoctoral fellowships to different kinds of scientists to serve in public interest or action groups: for example, a physician in a migrant farmworkers organization in California, a chemist in an environmental group in the Midwest, and an anthropologist in an inner-city hospital.[1] The purpose of the grants was to increases public understanding of issues involving complex scientific information. NSF funded scientists in organizations in which they were not usually found and then encouraged them to make what they knew (or could find out) available to everyone involved in a particular public policy issue. The obligation was to "disseminate results widely." It was not the usual scientific research project; it required outreach.

The *Washington Post* reporter sent me to the new medical director at the city's only public hospital. It had a largely poor, Black service population and was the only acute-care facility required to provide medical care regardless of a patient's ability to pay. On the telephone to the medical director I began, "Now I know I'm calling you clear out of the blue..." But he listened. Later I met with him and we developed a proposal, which was funded that spring by NSF. I spent a year and a half at the hospital trying to understand the sociocultural basis of poor maternal and infant health among inner-city Blacks and brokering that understanding to people in Washington who could change it. I completed a research project that combined a medical record review, statistical analysis (with computer facilities at Georgetown University), interviews with women whose infants had died, and, above all, daily working experience at one of the most important "community centers" for inner-city Black Washingtonians. Toward the end of my residency, the medical director and I testified together before the District Committee of the U.S. House of Representatives on the infant mortality problem in Washington, D.C., and the reporter I had talked to originally covered that hearing. This presentation began for me a long series of public speeches, meetings, reports, and public policy work on the infant mortality problem that continues at this writing. Three years after the residency, I was back at the same hospital in a follow-up study for the U.S. Census Bureau on another public policy issue involving inner-city Blacks: the undercount in the decennial census.[2]

The National Science Foundation funded my research and public service residency at the hospital. However, in the following years the clients, broadly speaking, came to include many units of federal and local government, as well as private groups like the Children's Defense Fund and the National Academy of Sciences. They and many others sought me out as part of their own work to bring down the country's embarrassingly high infant mortality rate—not only among urban Blacks but also among rural Blacks, Mexican-Americans, American Indians, and other minority and refugee groups. Ultimately, the clients for all my activities were inner-city Black women and other minority women at high risk of poor pregnancy outcome, as well as the health care providers who deliver services to them and who are themselves at high risk of chronic burnout, and finally the American taxpayers who shoulder most of the burden for poor minority health.

Process and Players

What did I do every day at an inner-city hospital that served disadvantaged Blacks? I had written a proposal broad enough to support a wide range of activities, with the overall goal of investigating the sociocultural basis of poor maternal and infant health. As I look back, I see that my role as a medical anthropologist was defined more by the requirements of other people than by myself and more by real health policy needs than by any preconceived advocacy stand of my own. Some individuals in city health and at the hospital knew what an anthropologist was; many knew what a social scientist was; and nearly everyone could relate to a college teacher. Many people in the District of Columbia were glad to see the social science perspective represented in the policy review in 1979-1980. Many felt that a sociological examination of Washington's infant mortality problem was needed. However, at that time most people still believed that medical care for newborns was about as good as anyone could do. Social and health programs were considered too expensive to be feasible for more than a handful of women. Yet, they were glad to see that the social science perspective was represented. In a positive sense, I was willingly "co-opted," and my skills were used to the maximum, especially at the hospital. For example:

1. I designed a case/control study[3] and collected all the data for it on women in two equivalent samples. I then statistically examined social, health, and medical care variables familiar to physicians and epidemiologists. I planned interviews with women and conducted them. I supervised the research assistants who helped me. I conducted an in-depth medical record review and scoured charts for quantitative and qualitative information that would give me clues about the origins of poor maternal and infant health.

2. I served on the hospital's Internal Review Board (that year and for four more years), reviewing social and psychological research projects submitted to the hospital, as well as medical research projects on maternal and infant care.

3. I went on rounds and to case presentations with staff psychiatrists and saw some of the effects of chronic alcoholism, poor social support, and mental illness in an inner-city Black community.

4. I spent long hours working in the Obstetrics Service, defining my sample, collecting data, talking to patients, nurses, social workers, and physicians—especially those who worked in the intensive-care nursery.

5. I became a familiar face in the medical records department and worked to maintain good relations with the staff there and with all the other support staff—secretaries, clerks, custodians, and administrative staff.

6. I almost always ate lunch in the hospital's staff cafeteria and usually sat with the physicians and administrators. I learned their problems and attitudes. I enjoyed the mixture of cultures and styles they represented. The medical officers came from all over the world, and they were eager to talk about their own reactions to the inner-city Black community they confronted.

7. Away from the hospital, I met with members of the Mayor's Blue Ribbon Committee on Infant Mortality, its representatives from the Centers for Disease Control, representatives from other hospitals, and other public and private health policy organizations, reporters, and staff at the District of Columbia health commissioner's office and at other city health programs for pregnant women. When my research results began coming in, I gave presentations on my project at the District of Columbia's health commission and the Medical Society and to academic colleagues.

The people who worked at the hospital and the people in city government and health services that I met during that time insisted on placing me within their own familiar frames of reference. In response, I constructed a set of roles—colleague, friend, investigator, teacher, mentor, and information source—that intersected with my own research needs and with my own determination to participate in the policy debate as an expert rather than as a political activist or health advocate. Above all, I remained an anthropologist—a teacher, a researcher, a writer—a scientist like the many other scientists in the hospital. That stance paid good dividends, but the entries in my log still sound like the field notes of any anthropologist going through initial culture shock. In the first month, I wrote:

I do not find the hospital a special world because it is "Black," but because it is a hospital. I am beginning to feel like I am visiting a special village whenever I go over there. But I am beginning to feel comfortable walking down the halls. I got my hair cut. I look different, but do not don the white coat of the physician. I should try that some time just to see what difference it makes...

I also had an office at Georgetown University's Center for Population Research that year, so I was constantly running back and forth between the computer and my research assistants at one end of town and data collection and fieldwork at the other end. Each day I confronted the jarring difference between rich and poor. Less than a week after I wrote the previous comment, I wrote this:

I am finding it a relief to be over here at school for the day. Every day at the hospital is a strain. I feel a stranger, on "my best behavior," and more than anything, pushing to get the data I need... Above all, I am tired. I feel overwhelmed on several fronts. I feel overwhelmed by the research angle to the project, and I feel overwhelmed by the multiplicity of roles at the hospital...

But only through that working experience did I come to understand better the world that disadvantaged Black women face: the frustration, the image of limited good, the good humor and good will in the face of insurmountable obstacles, the importance of friendships with other women, and a certain laissez-faire attitude that was unavoidable sometimes when they just got too tired. These insights gave an invaluable background to the long interviews I had with women whose infants had died.

Results and Evaluation

Some of my results were expected; some were not. Some were controversial and some were not. In many cases, no one had ever thought of asking the questions I asked in the interviews.[4]

As expected, measures of previous poor pregnancy outcome (infant death, miscarriages), absence of prenatal care, smoking, and alcoholism characterized the women who bore low-weight infants or infants who died. However, drug abuse did not because it was high in both samples of women—those with normal-weight infants and those with low-weight infants. Previous abortions did—a controversial finding in light of the high rate of abortion in Washington, D.C. (higher than the live-birth rate in the years of my study) and

the widely—if covertly—acknowledged need to provide abortion as back-up contraception.

Qualitative factors also set apart the women with small infants: psychological distress during pregnancy and hospitalization, evidence of violence (beatings and accidents) in their personal lives, ineffective contraception, and very rapidly paced child-bearing beginning in the teens. Case histories documented a "multiple-abuse syndrome" in which several harmful drugs were used together. Three-quarters of the women in all samples were unmarried at the time of delivery, and the average age for first pregnancy in all samples was eighteen years. The reproductive population was young—thus the later importance of the results in discussions of teen pregnancy.

The results of interviews were disturbing, especially the histories of chronic difficulties in the use of all forms of contraception and the number of times women had been pregnant and failed to deliver because of either miscarriage or abortion. There were no indications of planned pregnancies, although on the surface it seemed that many, many attempts were made in that direction. Attitudes toward men ranged from suspicion and manipulation to outright hostility; yet women remained romantically convinced of the desirability of the conjugal union. Men were very important in their lives for the meager emotional and financial support they managed to give. Surprisingly, mothers of women did not provide the emotional support expected, but girlfriends did. The predominant emotion toward the remembered infant death was disappointment rather than open grief. Women usually became pregnant again soon after an infant death. The attitudes toward physicians and nurses were also disturbing: The women were afraid of doctors and resented nurses who left them alone and handled them roughly.

The result that caused the greatest stir was the strong statistical relationship between alcoholism and prematurity. This finding was headlined in the *Washington Post* the day after the hearing on infant mortality in May 1980. There were many subtle, negative feelings expressed toward this finding by the hospital staff, although nothing overt. To this day, most people are convinced that heroin abuse is far more important in the District of Columbia's infant mortality picture, even though a special alcohol program began at one of the clinics (and has since closed) and public service announcements starting in the early 1980s always mention the dangers of alcohol abuse for pregnant women.

Evaluation of the results of research and public service activities is always difficult when the goals are broadly defined and the definition of achievement is abstract. To determine whether a research project has achieved a practical impact depends on the definition and measurement of "impact." I have previously noted that

> Measuring the results of an individual's or a group's involvement in a health policy issue is extremely difficult because it requires assessment of public sentiment and political trends whose origins are complex. It is easier to trace bureaucratic efforts, such as a decision to change a regulation or fund a program. To a degree, the impact of my participation in the infant-mortality debate in Washington, D.C. can be determined by asking some questions:
>
> Do public health policy makers show any interest in research results? Were congressional testimony and scientific papers picked up by the national and local press? Have any research results sparked public debate and strong reaction? Do privately funded policy reviews quote and publish the results? Do health planning agencies request detailed information for their use in policy recommendations? Is the definition of the problem, as gauged by newspaper coverage and private contacts, changing from a strictly medical model?... The answer to all... is yes. (Boone 1985:120)

More specifically, the change toward a sociomedical redefinition of the infant mortality problem is evident from the comments returned to me on evaluation forms that I sent to major policy participants right after my residency at the hospital in 1981. A physician from the Centers for Disease Control observed that

> The infant mortality problem in the District is well known yet little concerted action has been undertaken. Dr. Boone's work is of high quality and has helped to focus much of the recent discussion concerning possible approaches. She has used the innovative position of an anthropologist on a hospital staff well, both in the quality and impact of her work and in her choice of issues, i.e., one with social, medical and anthropological facets.

A statistician in the District of Columbia's government—who made available to me the city death certificate data so I could track the deaths of infants born at the hospital—noted the following: "Dr. Boone did a very thorough study, made excellent use of the Division's data, and contributed significantly to our understanding of the causes of infant mortality. The anthropological approach was much needed— opened new perspectives." The District of Columbia's health commissioner in 1981 wrote:

> I have been aware of Dr. Boone's efforts and have been most impressed with her enthusiasm and commitment to the project. I believe that her findings will contribute greatly to the formulation of strategies designed to reduce the infant mortality rate in the District of Columbia. In particular, it has surfaced a number of misconceptions that have been widely held pertaining to the specific make-up and behavior patterns of maternity patients at greatest risk.

The chief of psychiatry at the hospital said this:

> Dr. Boone's research at the hospital has been extremely useful in giving the physicians a better understanding of the social characteristics of their patients and thus allowing for a more comprehensive and holistic approach to patient care. Dr. Boone was especially helpful to the Department of Psychiatry as she contributed significantly to the development of our educational program and brought new insights into our understanding of psychopathology and patient care. Dr. Boone's understanding of the social and cultural aspects of normality, pathology, and patient care was appreciated by staff members, psychiatric residents, and medical students, alike.

Equally important was a note written at the bottom of a letter I received five years later in 1986, inviting me to a reception at one of the private programs for maternity care now in Washington, D.C. Its director wrote: "Come see! After all, you helped shape the Program! The head of NICHHD will be another speaker [along with the Mayor]." However, more significant than any of these comments was a statement sent to me by one of the women I interviewed. When asked if she had learned anything in the interview, she wrote: "I learn that Many Dr. or a wear of How uncomfortable I am after Heving 1. Abortions 1. Stillbirths 3. miscarraige one Live son Bore Blue."

The Anthropological Difference

The infant mortality project relied on a broad segment of the literature and a wide range of methods. However, from beginning to end it was based on my background in anthropology. This approach can be seen most clearly in four areas:

1. the design and analysis of the interviews with women who had infant death,
2. the selection of some variables and derivation of others for quantitative and qualitative analysis,
3. the reliance on my working experience at the hospital to understand better the sociocultural basis for infant mortality among inner-city Blacks, and
4. the use of information brokerage to satisfy the requirements of the original client.

The Interview Difference

A broad understanding of natality, human reproduction, population dynamics, and social structures to support pregnant women can all be gained from any good introductory coursework in cultural and physical anthropology. It is surprising that this understanding has not yet been widely applied to the sociomedical problems of the inner-city Blacks—problems such as high rates of infant mortality, childhood disease, teen pregnancy, drug abuse and alcoholism, homicide, and accidents. The best work in practicing anthropology in the maternal and child health area has been carried out among Mexican-Americans in California and Texas and in developing countries. The ethnographic and theoretical work on inner-city Black culture is far from complete, but it is not insubstantial. In fact, two ethnographies are specifically devoted to Washington, D.C., Blacks, mostly males: Liebow 1967 and Hannerz 1969. Fieldwork in other cities such as Chicago has given rise to fascinating, in-depth explorations of Black male ethos (Keiser 1969). Anthropological understanding of Black females is more often restricted to rural or Southern groups, except for the excellent extensive work by Snow (1974, 1977, 1978) and the classic study by Stack (1974).

Using these works and others by sociologists Ladner (1971), Rainwater (1960, 1965, 1966), and Seeman (1959), I developed a large set of YES/NO response items to explore the attitudes and beliefs of women who had suffered infant deaths. I pretested them on obstetric inpatients at the hospital and conducted a final set of interviews with women who had lost their infants. No one had thought of asking them about their feelings of alienation (expressed in familiar idiom), their attitudes toward men and children, their feelings about the rightness or wrongness of

contraception, and their abstract conceptions of birth, death, and lifecycle. I also asked them about their pregnancy histories: each time they had been pregnant, the type of contraception they used between pregnancies, and the outcome of each pregnancy. Questions on their familiarity with contraceptive forms were adapted from the World Fertility Survey, with the substitution of "partner" for "husband." The former term seemed more appropriate in a community where 75 percent of the women are not legally married at the time of delivery. Finally, I asked them about their social relationships and psychological state during pregnancy.

Interview results—in combination with the review of secondary sources and the statistical analysis—gave a historical portrait of the reproductive lives of inner-city Black women. It brought into sharper focus what the medical records had only outlined: the women's rapidly paced pregnancies and chronic difficulty in carrying an infant to term because of abortion, miscarriage, or other poor pregnancy outcome. Taken together their stories were revealing and disturbing, but they had a certain internal consistency. They were understandable in light of the women's histories of poor interpersonal relationships, substance abuse, anxiety and depression, and some of their cultural values and conceptions. For example, the following cultural factors may well play a role in their reproductive lives: a belief in a birth for every death; a high value placed on children; a value on gestation without necessarily any causal or sequential understanding of the children it will produce; a lack of planning ability; distrust of both men and women; and a separation of men's roles from the process of family formation (Boone 1985). The integration of all aspects of their histories within the context of their attitudes and beliefs represents one important element of the anthropological difference in the infant mortality project. The resulting portraits have an ethnographic quality of compelling realism that has been useful in policy-related work.

The power of this type of material in public policy work should not be underestimated, especially if it is presented along with quantitative data and alongside statistical tests of variables that are more familiar to practitioners in the field—in this case, physicians and epidemiologists. Presentation of ethnographic material by itself is not particularly useful in policy-related work because it looks so unusual. It can confuse other practitioners or simply look foolish. Similarly, the use of terms with good, reliable meanings for anthropologists—but emotional overtones for nonscientists—can be counterproductive and "turn off" a non-anthropologist bureaucrat or policymaker. I used terms like "population regulation" and "infanticide" in my congressional testimony but would not use them again in that context. In the infant mortality project, most material—especially the case histories based on interviews, medical records, autopsy reports, and death certificates—had to be presented with a dry, scientific style or it could easily be seen as sensationalist. The right balance between scientific report styles can sometimes be achieved by clearly demarcating (with "boxes" or italicized blocks of text) which sections of writing are reporting and which are ethnographic.

A Difference in Variable Selection

The anthropological difference in the infant mortality project was also evident in more fundamental ways such as the choice of variables for transcription and analysis. A background in anthropology shifted the focus of the infant mortality project from medical care to health and social factors known to be related to health. However, I was careful to use variables that have already been proved to be related to infant mortality, as well as new and more experimental kinds of variables. For example, I took pains to note whether each woman had any prenatal care (from a medical history form in her chart) and how many years of education she had (from the birth certificate worksheet). Both are known to affect pregnancy outcome in the general U.S. population. In this inner-city community, I found that prenatal care was indeed significantly related to pregnancy outcome but years of education were not. Use of these variables made the results appear familiar to physicians and epidemiologists. In this context they were willing to consider other variables based on anthropological and sociological theory.

For example, the concept of a woman's source of social support was operationalized from notes on the responsible person she listed on hospital admission. An analysis of stability of social support was possible by examining the responsible person for three hospital admissions (in the follow-up survey). Similarly, residential stability was analyzed by examining three consecutive addresses over a six to seven year period. The hypothesis that stability of lifestyle and social support affects pregnancy outcomes come directly from studies in the sociology and anthropology of health. The notion that disadvantaged women may receive less support from society during pregnancy comes straight from the theory of social stratification, as well as from physical anthropology, which clearly demonstrates among nonhuman primates that a female's status affects her offspring's chances of survival.

The Difference Experience Makes

No matter how sophisticated the statistical analysis or the construction of the interview instrument, my basic understanding of reproduction in an inner-city Black community comes from daily working experience at the "community center" for birth and death—the hospital. It is a large, complex institution, much like the small society pictured in other anthropological studies of hospitals. It is a symbol for inner-city Black residents, but it also represents the larger society in many of their dealings with it. It serves as a conduit for knowledge and action, connecting disadvantaged Blacks with networks at other levels of medicine and society. Thus, the hospital serves the dual function of community center and cultural broker for the larger society, much the same way that the church and priest serve as brokers for peasants in the villages of developing countries.

Because of the complexity and intensity of the inner-city hospital's functions, I was able to talk with a large number of inner-city Blacks and hospital employees about their experiences and attitudes. Every working day was an experience in classic participant observation—one of the very few sources of ethnographic information. Because of the multicultural nature and multiple social classes of the staff, I was constantly forced to make more than Black/White and rich/poor comparisons. I saw a wide range of styles and mechanisms for coping with fatigue, burn-out, and material shortages and with people from other cultures and classes. Not all of it was attractive or flattering, but it was all comprehensible and it was all set in sharp relief by the inevitable crisis nature of much of the action at an acute-care facility. Among staff, patients, and physicians, an anthropologist in an inner-city hospital can see people at their worst and at their sterling best. My year and a half of experience at the hospital made the largest anthropological difference.

Science Brokerage

Anthropological knowledge of culture and class brokerage confers an enormous advantage in disseminating results widely—the original requirement of my NSF grant. Knowledge of sociocultural sensitivities can aid information exchange by helping an anthropologist know, for example, when to make research results known to the press or to a political leader; when to leak or suggest a result so that more information will be requested officially; when to write a thank-you letter or make a keep-in-touch call with an important information source; and above all, when to keep one's results under wraps. The type of scientific information anthropologists can offer is extremely valuable when couched in terms that are acceptable to the public and to political players. If, as an anthropologist, you become convinced that part of your obligation to society is to disseminate your research results widely, then it makes good sense to use the principles of social interaction that you know to do the best, most helpful job possible in brokering that knowledge.

The Rewards of Successful Practice

Now, seven years after the infant mortality issue emerged in Washington, D.C., medicine seems to have done about all it can. The infant mortality rate has fallen but still remains the highest in the country. The neonatal mortality rate (in the first twenty-eight days of life) has also fallen but principally because of improved care in the newborn, intensive-care nurseries of the city's hospitals. The low-birthweight and fetal death rates—which reflect maternal lifestyle—remain steady and high. So the social scientists and the social engineers are now being listened to as never before. It has been a hard-fought battle to redefine Washington's maternal and infant health problem as sociomedical rather than strictly medical and as sociocultural rather than simply and overwhelmingly socioeconomic. Changes toward this definition of the problem began to speed up back in 1979 but should have begun much sooner. As had been evident for a long time in the lives and health behavior of disadvantaged Black women, socioeconomic status and culture have combined in ways that have hindered health progress.

The results of the project on infant mortality in Washington, D.C., have been good. Policies and programs have changed and sociomedical explanations have been adopted—if only by default after a strictly medical model was exhausted. But the option had been provided. A different, more complicated definition of the infant mortality problem was available and waiting when the overreliance on medical

solutions was finally acknowledged slowly over the past seven years. After high-tech equipment had been provided and staffs trained, the infant mortality and low-birthweight rates were still high, and people were anxious to find other solutions. In Washington, D.C., we are slowly beginning to understand which social and cultural characteristics are connected to poor Black health in the inner city, and from that understanding, service delivery solutions are emerging.

Notes

1. The research and public service project described here was funded as a Public Service Science Residency from the National Science Foundation's Office of Science and Society, Grant No. OSS-7917826. The views expressed in this report are those of the author and do not necessarily reflect those of NSF. The Office of Science and Society is no longer in existence.

2. This was the "Inner-City Hospital Feasibility Study," which I directed at the U.S. Census Bureau in 1983-1984.

3. A case/control study statistically compares cases (usually of a disease, condition, or other health factor) with equivalent controls (which have an absence of the disease, condition, or factor) to determine correlative (and hypothetically causal) factors.

4. A limited number of copies of the Attitudes and Beliefs Section of the interview schedule is available from Margaret S. Boone at GAO/PEMD, Washington, D.C. 20548.

Dr. Boone pursued the activities reported in this chapter from 1979 to 1980 while at the District of Columbia General Hospital, with support from a public service science residency grant from the National Science Foundation, OSS-791726. The views expressed in this chapter are those of the author and do not necessarily reflect those of NSF. Boone conducted a follow-up survey on the same samples of inner-city residents for the U.S. Census Bureau in 1983-1984.

References

Boone, Margaret S. 1982. A Socio-Medical Study of Infant Mortality Among Disadvantaged Blacks. *Human Organization* 41(3):227-236.

_____ . 1985. Social and Cultural Factors in The Etiology of Low Birthweight among Disadvantaged Blacks. *Social Science and Medicine* 20(10):1001-1011.

____. 1985. Policy and Praxis: Anthropology and the Domestic Health Policy Arena. In Carole E. Hill, ed., *Training Manual in Medical Anthropology*. American Anthropological Association Special Publication no. 18, pp. 111-129.

Boone, Margaret S., and S. A. Roman. 1980. Statement Before the Subcommittee on Fiscal Affairs and Health of the Committee on the District of Columbia, U.S. House of Representatives, Ninety-Sixth Congress, 2nd Session, May 7, Serial No. 96-15, pp. 29-32.

Colen, B. D. 1980. Alcoholism, Premature Births, Linked in Study at D.C. General. *Washington Post*, p. B7, May 8.

Hannerz, Ulf. 1969 *Soulside*. New York: Columbia University Press.

Keiser, R. Lincoln. 1969. *The Vice Lords*. New York: Holt, Rinehart and Winston.

Ladner, Joyce A. 1971. *Tomorrow's Tomorrow*. New York: Doubleday.

Leibow, Elliot. 1967. *Tally's Corner*. Boston: Little, Brown.

Rainwater, Lee. 1960. *And the Poor Get Children*. Chicago: Quadrangle Books.

____. 1965. *Family Design*. Chicago: Aldine.

____. 1966. *The Crucible of Identity*. *Daedalus* 95(2):783-791.

Seeman, Melvin. 1959. On the Meaning of Alienation. *American Sociological Review* 24:783-791.

Snow, Loudell F. 1974. Folk Medical Beliefs and Their Implications for Care of Patients. *Annals of Internal Medicine* 81:82-96.

Snow, Loudell F., and Shirley M. Johnson. 1977. Modern Day Menstrual Folklore. *Journal of the American Medical Association* 237(25):2736-2739

Snow, Loudell F., Shirley M. Johnson, and Harry E. Mayhew. 1978. The Behavioral Implication of Some Old Wives' Tales. *Obstetrics and Gynecology* 51(6):727-732.

Stack, Carol B. 1974 *All Our Kin*. New York: Harper and Row.

Questions:

1. In addition to collecting data, what other activities did Boone engage in that provided a broader perspective on her research?

2. What data gathering techniques did Boone use in her research on infant mortality among Blacks in Washington, D.C.?

3. How did medical anthropologist Boone measure the success of her research?

The answer section begins on page 243.

Within the hospital setting no profession has more prolonged contact with patients than do nurses. In addition to the delivery of front line medical care, the role of the nurse also involves brokering the relationships between the patient, other hospital staff, family, and clergy. And since many of these patients bring their own cultural baggage into the hospital with them, there is a particular need for nurses to be culturally sensitive. In this selection, Sandra Sharma provides a brief look at the new sub-specialty area known as "nursing and anthropology." Here she describes her internship and doctoral research conducted while earning her degree in applied anthropology.

Promoting Cultural Sensitivity in Nursing Practice

By Sandra Sharma

Nursing and anthropology have much in common, since both professions aim for a holistic view of their subjects. My interest in health and in culture started in adolescence and continued throughout my nursing career. The doctoral program in applied anthropology at the University of South Florida, in which I used my training as a clinical nurse specialist to meet the requirement for an external specialization, built on these two interests and has had a continuing impact on my subsequent professional career.

I remember writing a paper in high school about wanting to become a nurse and join the Peace Corps so that I could learn first hand about another culture. My plans actually became realities. After graduating from nursing school in 1966, I worked first in psychiatric nursing and later as a surgical nurse for a Cuban physician. I joined the Peace Corps in 1968, serving in India for two and a half years in the area of family planning and maternal-child health. During my experience in India, I lived in the home of an Indian family, learned to speak the language of the area with some facility, followed the dress habits and many other customs, and worked with a number of Indian public health nurses and auxiliary nurse midwives.

The foci of nursing include the assessment of a person's problems, the identification of patient-centered goals and nursing strategies to address the prioritized problems, the implementation of those strategies, and the evaluation of the entire plan. Further education in nursing and my growing specialization in psychiatric nursing reinforced my recognition that sociocultural factors have an impact upon patients' goals and their responses to health care. I eventually became a faculty member at a college of nursing, teaching psychosocial and psychiatric nursing topics and also an elective course on cross-cultural nursing. When applied anthropology became available to me as a specialty for a doctorate, I made the personally logical choice to pursue this path. From the beginning of my doctoral studies in 1984, I knew I wanted to pursue my internship and dissertation research in the area of promoting culturally sensitive health care.

My internship was completed on two medical-surgical units of a large general hospital which served patients from a variety of ethnic groups. My goal was to assist the nursing staff to provide more culturally sensitive care by increasing their knowledge of the cultural beliefs and practices of particular groups and of their individual patients. I obtained permission and support for the project from the hospital's director of nursing education and research and from the head nurses of the two units. The internship spanned two semesters (about eight months) and contained three phases.

In phase one, my objectives were to develop rapport with the nursing staff, to utilize participant observation in order to become familiar with the hospital and unit systems, and to assess the nursing staff's need for cultural information through a needs assessment questionnaire. I also interviewed key informants, such as the two head nurses of the units, the director of nursing education and research, the medical-surgical nursing supervisor, and several staff nurses. The purpose of these interviews was to learn the expected role behaviors of the nursing staff members, the types of constraints under which staff worked, and the general composition and work of the units. In addition, I asked questions aimed at determining the most appropriate techniques to implement the project so as not to increase excessively the staff's workload.

I learned that 51 percent of the nursing staff had not studied cultural aspects of health care before, and that 98 percent felt a need for increased knowledge about a variety of ethnic groups. Interviewing key informants led to scheduling classes at certain times that were usually not so hectic for staff and to limiting each offering to thirty minutes so that staff would not be absent from patient care too long. If the same class were offered twice during a week on each shift, staff who missed the one time might be able to attend the next.

Phase two focused on continued participant observation, on developing and providing educational inservice programs, and on providing consultation to nursing staff concerning the care of particular patients. The educational programs were planned as a series of eight weekly thirty-minute sessions. In the series, topics were planned to build gradually from an increased awareness of the nursing staff's own ethnic backgrounds and feelings toward other ethnic groups to a realization of the need for cultural assessment of their patients. Pertinent concepts, beliefs, and practices related to religion, value orientations, health and illness, verbal and nonverbal communication, and family/lifestyle patterns were included. Examples were drawn from the beliefs and practices of groups that the hospital served. Continuing education credits toward licensing requirements were provided for attendance. In the final evaluation of the project, 95 percent of the staff responded that the classes were helpful and interesting.

Consultation was provided for a variety of patients, including a dying Vietnamese physician with whom I visited frequently. I talked with staff about his diet, the patterns of communication he used, and ways to offer him support. I also assisted with contacting his friend who was helping to take care of his outside financial responsibilities. With these interventions, he communicated more and seemed to find some additional comfort before he died. In another case I worked with a young Hispanic woman whose bowel disorder was mysterious until my interviews uncovered that she had been ingesting large quantities of clay, a pattern not uncommon in her cultural tradition.

In phase three, a patient cultural assessment instrument was developed for use by the nursing staff, its content validity was rated, and the instrument was pilot-tested for a month on the two units by the nurses. In addition, interviews and a questionnaire were used to obtain an evaluation by the nursing staff of the project and the cultural assessment instrument. Participant observation and consultation were also used during that phase. The cultural assessment instrument used check-off and short-answer responses and was designed to be used by nurses in conjunction with their regular assessment of their patients. It included questions concerning the patient's country of birth, length of time in the U.S., ethnicity, religious affiliation, any practices to be observed in the hospital, foods preferred and those disliked or prohibited, usual mealtimes, and whether food might be brought in by family members. In addition, various questions concerning health/illness beliefs and practices, persons with whom the patient lived, which family members should be consulted about decisions, primary and secondary languages of the patient, and the ability to speak, read, and write English were also included. In the final evaluation of the project, 72 percent of the nursing staff responded that they found the cultural assessment helpful. The biggest obstacle they found was the extra time needed for this addition to their assessment.

After earning my Ph.D., I left teaching and entered full-time clinical practice at a veterans' hospital with an ethnically heterogeneous population. I work as a psychiatric clinical nurse specialist in an outpatient mental health clinic providing individual group therapy. The influence of cultural background upon patients' views of themselves and others could be an overlooked aspect of patient assessment if anthropology were not part of my background. It has also been very helpful to consider the influence of military subculture upon veteran patients in understanding their responses in their current civilian situation.

In addition to working as a therapist, I provide educational inservice programs as needed and offer a yearly educational program for health care providers on the cultural aspects of health care. I have presented small workshops on that topic to psychology and social work intern groups within the hospital, and I have also been a requested speaker to area hospitals and collegiate nursing programs. My teaching experience has helped me share anthropological knowledge in structured ways with other health care professionals so that they can later apply it to their own practice.

Health care research is another aspect of my position, with clinical problems and system problems within the hospital (such as, in the referral of patients from one setting to another, in the provision of timely appointments or individualized care, or in the accessibility of services) demand study. Nursing research is generally conducted in clinical settings and is essentially applied research. As an active member of my agency's nursing research committee, I have stimulated interest in qualitative research methods and coordinated workshops and speakers to assist other researchers and myself learn how to utilize particular methods. Nursing and health care practice in general occur in complex natural settings involving multiple variables that are not only impossible to control but are also frequently unidentified when quantitative methods are used

alone. The ability to view these natural settings as cultural systems has been a contribution of anthropology.

My education in applied anthropology has greatly affected my view of patients and the cultural context of their health beliefs and practices. Increased knowledge of anthropology has helped me view my patients in a broader context, and it has helped me understand a little better the complex system within which I work. In retrospect, the internship was a major factor in the development of my role as a nurse-anthropologist. Being able to facilitate the care of patients through the use of cultural knowledge and serving as a broker between patient and staff provided many experiences that increased my ability to apply anthropology to clinical practice.

Obviously, I believe that the practice of applied anthropology in health care is a valid and necessary component of the health care system. Having the knowledge, experience, and role as a health care practitioner has been a very helpful prerequisite for me in applying anthropology in a clinical setting.

Questions:

1. What cross cultural experience had the author had prior to entering her doctoral program in applied anthropology?

2. What practical services was the author able to offer the dying Vietnamese physician under her care?

3. Why was it likely that a nurse-anthropologist (rather than just a nurse) would solve the mysterious bowel problem suffered by the Hispanic patient?

The answer section begins on page 243.

5

Most public health officials consider AIDS to be the most serious health epidemic of the 20th century. Since the disease first appeared as a health threat in the early 1980s, applied anthropologists have made a number of contributions in the fight against the disease. Since there is no medical cure for the disease, the efforts have been toward developing more effective educational programs. Drawing upon traditional anthropological data gathering techniques of observation and interviewing, Dr. Renaud studied how the values and behaviors of legally registered prostitutes in Senegal (West Africa) impacted the educational programs already in place. She concludes that her findings in West Africa have relevance for AIDS education programs in the United States as well.

Applied Anthropology at the Crossroads: AIDS Prevention Research in Senegal and Beyond

By Michelle Lewis Renaud

Describing and responding to the impact of HIV/AIDS on individuals and communities worldwide are invaluable ways in which applied anthropologists can contribute their ethnographic knowledge and skills in the fight against the pandemic. I chose AIDS as the topic of my dissertation primarily because I believed that, if formulated with community needs in mind, the data acquired could be applied by the people with whom I would be working. To me it was also important to conduct research in an area that, while at risk, had a relatively low rate of infection so that my findings could be applied to future efforts to stem the epidemic. Consequently, I selected Senegal, whose rates have remained low in a continent ravaged by AIDS and whose efforts provide lessons applicable the world over.

In this paper I will discuss the roles that I played and the issues affecting my doctoral research in 1991 and 1992. I will explore the ways in which my data have been used—and not used—since the completion of my dissertation. Because I have worked domestically and also internationally, I will also reflect on the ways in which international work has informed my AIDS research in the United States. In this light, I will underline two primary factors that I have found essential in the application of anthropological AIDS research in any venue.

First is the concept of community, defined here as an entity consisting of individuals or groups of individuals, who have a shared interest or commitment, whether it is a geographic area, a livelihood, a common cause or a belief system. The second concept that has become a theme in my work and approach to AIDS research is the importance of having a global perspective that regards what is termed "domestic" and "international" research as points on a continuum rather than as two separate realms. The latter perspective does a disservice to the heterogeneity within each of them and ignores the commonalities between them.

Conducting AIDS Prevention Research in Senegal

In 1991 and 1992 I conducted my doctoral research in Kaolack, Senegal with funding from Fulbright and Family Health International. I chose my research topic and location based on the recommendation of one of Senegal's prominent AIDS researchers, Dr. Souleymane Mboup, who strongly recommended that I evaluate an AIDS education campaign that had been targeting legally registered prostitutes. The campaign was run by a sexually transmitted disease (STD) clinic in Kaolack, the country's third largest town where several major transnational roads intersect. Dr. Mboup and his colleagues were concerned about the extremely high rates of HIV infection among the prostitutes; roughly 40 percent of them were infected, as compared with 10.8 percent of prostitutes nationally and the relatively low rate of approximately 2 percent for the entire

Reprinted by permission of PRACTICING ANTHROPOLOGY 19(1), Winter, 1997, pp. 10-13

population. The researchers suspected the rates among prostitutes in Kaolack were high due to the large number of truck drivers, merchants, and foreigners traveling through the area. However, they had not had the opportunity to uncover the dynamics of HIV transmission between the prostitutes and their clients. More specifically, they wanted to assess whether the AIDS education campaign was making headway in its efforts to convince the women to require their clients and boyfriends to use condoms.

Many Roles for an Applied Anthropologist

From the time I arrived in Senegal until my departure one and a half years later, Dr. Mboup and his colleagues supported my work in many ways. Most important, Dr. Mboup introduced me as a member of the national AIDS research team to the clinic staff in Kaolack, with whom I was to work closely for several months. The clinic staff, in turn, presented me as a team member to the more than three hundred registered prostitutes who attended the clinic for semimonthly examinations, treatment of sexually transmitted diseases and presentations on health issues. It was during these presentations that the clinic's staff educated prostitutes about AIDS prevention, transmission and treatment.

While I have presented information on my methodologies before (in my dissertation and an article in *Practicing Anthropology*, Vol. 15, no. 4, 1993) I prefer to focus here on my approach to working with international funders, national AIDS researchers, clinic staff and prostitutes; the subsequent relationships I formed; and roles I played. Thus, although the clinic staff treated me as a colleague whose work was backed by prominent researchers, I was clearly an "outsider." I was not Senegalese, I was a short-term team member, I was assessing the activities of the staff, and I was providing information about their activities to Dr. Mboup. Consequently, staff did their best to explain their reasons for approaching the campaign as they did and to provide concrete evidence of the impact it had on the women's behavior, attitudes and infection rates. I also talked to prostitutes to learn their perspectives about the education campaign.

In my "researcher" role, I spent most of my first three months at the clinic reviewing the women's records and interviewing clinic staff to better understand their views of their roles and the service that they provide to the prostitutes and other STD patients. Besides talks with the clinic staff, I spoke informally with prostitutes

receiving treatment at the clinic and attended several health presentations. Based on these activities, I developed an interview guide that I used during talks with all women (prostitutes and non-prostitutes) visiting the clinic during a one-month period. I gave all staff members a copy of the interview guide and asked for their opinions regarding content, format and the phrasing of questions in French. Their comments led to a shorter, more focused interview that yielded answers to my own questions as well as those posed by clinic staff and national researchers. Clinic staff helped me test the instrument and conduct the interviews, translating French into Wolof and vice-versa.

The staff's positive response to my emphasis on a team approach showed that they appreciated my recognition of their expertise and that they agreed their help would undoubtedly enhance my work. Additionally, because they always operated as a team—traveling to conferences and giving presentations to the prostitutes as a unit—I believe they saw the strategy as necessary for me in my adaptation to their organizational culture.

For the first interview phase we talked with sixty-eight registered prostitutes and thirty-two other women seeking STD treatment at the clinic. Shortly after that, I began spending more time in the prostitutes' place of work. This gave us a chance to get to know each other before I conducted the second phase of interviews with the translating assistance of a few women who were fluent in French and well-respected in the prostitutes' community. We asked twenty women about their life-styles, life decisions, and world views to understand their perspectives regarding prostitution, gender roles and AIDS prevention. During this process, the women's perceptions of my role changed. Whereas it seems they originally saw me as a staff member to whom they afforded respect, they came to see me as someone who could convey their concerns to clinic staff and to Dr. Mboup and his colleagues. Most notable among their concerns was the shortage of condoms provided them by clinic staff, their perception that clinic staff often treated them in a condescending manner and their fear of growing threats by neighbors who wanted them to work elsewhere.

In my emerging role as outsider-turned-advocate, social problems that I had not anticipated dealing with became important. For instance, I not only described the women's situation to clinic staff and Dr. Mboup, but I made recommendations about how it might be improved. Unlike clinic staff, who were often skeptical of the women's claims that they needed more condoms, I spent enough time with the women to observe that the number of clients they accommodated far exceeded the number of condoms they were provided. Thus, although the women were thankful to receive free condoms, they did not receive enough of them to follow clinic advice to practice safe sex during every encounter.

I also witnessed the mistreatment inflicted upon the prostitutes by their neighbors and sought means to remedy it. Although there was a social worker on staff, he did not see this as his responsibility. But a social worker who formerly worked at the clinic did get involved and asked me to accompany him and the women on visits to the chief of police to explain the situation. Although some of the clinic's staff were of the opinion it was not my role to speak for the women, I saw my role as ensuring that all players knew about the factors affecting the women, whose mental and physical well-being were directly influenced by the social context in which they worked and lived. Attention to the women's work and living environment was as important as educational presentations in perpetuating the clinic's goal of reducing HIV transmission among them. Clearly, knowledge and condoms are insufficient if other concerns and circumstances override the will and capability to engage in safe behaviors.

As I became more aware of the multidimensional nature of relations between clinic staff and prostitutes, I weighed the various outcomes of their interactions and the ethical implications of my role in documenting and questioning them. Thus, when the women complained that staff often treated them unfairly, I was in the position of deciding whether to acknowledge that I had come to the same conclusion. Most notably, the lab technician often provided large amounts of condoms to the women, but only if they would sell them and give him the profits. He was also known to threaten to report that the women had STDs unless they paid him not to. When I carefully spoke with higher ranking staff to assess their awareness of the technician's and others' activities, I discovered they knew of the women's accusations, but had not responded to them although it was clear that the situation directly affected operation of the AIDS education program and the staff's relationships with the prostitutes. However, a few months after I left the field I heard the technician was

no longer in that position, the reasons for which were not clear.

Yet, despite tenuous relations and skepticism, the women also spoke of the emotional and social support they received from the clinic staff and credited them with being the only nonprostitutes in town who understood their situation and the reasons for their participation in this highly stigmatized profession. Most important, I also came to the conclusion that the AIDS education campaign had been very successful. The women were requesting substantially more condoms and were reporting that they required clients to wear them during almost all encounters. Also, clinic staff reported a substantial decrease in STDs and HIV seroconversion rates among the prostitutes. And although the women were quick to complain about staff treatment of them, they did credit the staff with providing them the means and motivation to practice safe sex. This was corroborated when I compared the prostitutes' knowledge, attitudes and practices to those prostitutes interviewed by an American medical student before the advent of the education campaign and to those of women who had not participated in AIDS education presentations at the clinic.

The campaign worked well because the staff had found culturally appropriate ways to educate the women and, through ongoing interventions, had continued to encourage safe sex behaviors. Effective approaches included educating the women in a place and time convenient to them; engaging in an open dialogue with the women, who felt comfortable asking questions and discussing a myriad of issues; acknowledging the importance of children and stressing that concerted efforts were necessary to protect children from infection; and using videos and photographs, which gave the women graphic images of AIDS in a community where no one was willing to admit their illnesses were AIDS-related.

Lessons Learned

In addition to the general finding that the campaign had been successful and could serve as a model for other AIDS education programs in Senegal and elsewhere, many of my seemingly site-specific experiences and findings are applicable to programs and research projects beyond the scope of Kaolack's health clinic. For instance, the concept of community was as central to my approach to research design and implementation as it was to the clinic's approach to HIV prevention and to the prostitutes' views of their daily responsibilities.

An example of this is the clinic's recognition that there are two groups of prostitutes. One group's members are close to each other and work in the same location; this is the group with whom I spent most of my time. The other group's members are not particularly close and work individually in hotels and bars in town. Considering this, clinic staff held separate presentations for the two groups and tailored their topics and AIDS prevention strategies accordingly. They built on the solidarity of the prostitutes who lived and worked together by suggesting that they encourage and monitor each other's requirement of condom use. The women took this seriously and reported colleagues' suspected lapses in safe behavior to each other and to clinic staff. This helped to institutionalize a sense of pride and partnership in AIDS prevention.

The concept of community also played out in prostitutes' relationships with clinic staff, who formed part of their health care and AIDS prevention community. Also, because most of the women who worked and lived together were far from their families of origin, other prostitutes and clinic staff had become their extended family. Thus, despite the tension between the women and staff, they had forged roles in each others' lives, both professional and personal.

The development and implementation of operational policies related to AIDS prevention emerged as a prominent issue as well. Beyond my concern that there was an unequal ratio of condoms to client, I made recommendations regarding the clinic's policy for informing women about their HIV status. Whereas staff had known the women's status for several years, they had not yet informed them prior to my arrival because they did not feel the women were prepared for the news. During my time there, staff developed a protocol for informing them and asked me to develop questionnaires to aid them in assessing the women's potential reactions and identifying the social networks to which they might turn if HIV positive.

After the staff informed the women of their status, the reactions of HIV positive women led to a restructuring of relationships between the women and clinic staff. Not willing to tell fellow prostitutes or their families about their illness, many HIV-infected prostitutes turned to clinic staff for emotional support, often visiting their homes after hours to talk about their dilemmas.

As could be expected, staff were not comfortable with or prepared for the role of counselor. And although staff proposed forming a support group for infected women, the women adamantly refused to attend lest their positive status be discovered. At the time I left the field staff were seeking alternative mechanisms for supporting HIV-infected women.

Responses to the Study

Upon completion of my dissertation in 1993, I provided copies to Dr. Mboup, the USAID office in Dakar and AIDSCAP/Family Health International. In the nearly three years since then, I have heard little about the ways in which my findings were being applied. And because I took a full-time position focusing on domestic issues, playing a continuing role in Senegal's AIDS prevention activities has been difficult. However, because AIDSCAP/Family Health International and other international providers are now becoming more active in Senegal, and because my study is one of the few ethnographies on the pandemic there, I have recently received a number of requests for my dissertation and inquiries about effective and appropriate prevention programs and potential target populations in Senegal. Although I am not in the position to assist full-time in these efforts, it has become clear that the qualitative and quantitative data I collected and the resulting ethnography I produced are useful and serving as a base for future activities. This is due primarily to the guidance and involvement of local researchers, without whom I would not have chosen this topic or been incorporated as fully as a team member.

Conclusions

In closing, I will comment on the ways in which international AIDS research has influenced the AIDS research that I have been doing since returning to the United States. Having internalized the view popular among many colleagues that domestic work and international work have little in common because the former takes place in our own, more "developed" society, it is now clear the skills and experience I gained in Senegal positioned me very well for AIDS work in the United States.

One of my main projects has been to evaluate HIV Prevention Community Planning, an initiative introduced by the Centers for Disease Control and Prevention (CDC) in 1994. The cutting-edge initiative requires that the CDC's sixty-five grantee Health Departments located in United States cities, states and territories form community planing group (CPGs) whose members reflect the current and projected impact of AIDS in their jurisdiction. In brief, a team of consultant researchers, formed by Sociomedical Resource Associates, Inc., and I profiled and evaluated HIV prevention activities in thirteen areas across the country to document the responses to the initiative and to examine the barriers and facilitators affecting its implementation. In-depth interviews, participant observation and close relationships with the CDC and representatives of the jurisdictions evaluated have enabled us to produce rich, collaborative descriptions of community planning and prevention activities and to provide recommendations employed by the sites profiled, the CDC and many others influential in United States HIV prevention policy. Lessons learned in Senegal—particularly about using the community as a unit of evaluating, involving stakeholders in all aspects of the study and giving voice to the often disenfranchised—have been as integral to my work here as it was overseas.

On one level, the community orientation I have had when designing and implementing applied AIDS research projects is based on the tenet that members of any community that is studied or evaluated are stakeholders in the activity or issue examined. This is so regarding the study itself and in the acceptance and reaction to subsequent findings. On another level, there is a need to understand the structure, nature and context of existing communities and to identify the ways in which the formation of an AIDS prevention community unites, and affects the relationship between, various stakeholders in and across communities as they focus on a common cause.

Additionally, a global perspective entails an acknowledgment that methodological and conceptual issues surrounding anthropological research in general, and AIDS prevention research in particular, are applicable and instrumental regardless of geographic location. The often-employed dichotomy of "domestic" work and "international" work misrepresents what I regard as a global continuum of opportunities for applied anthropologists to employ their ethnographic knowledge, sensitivity to context and participatory research methodology in any community.

Questions:

1. What are the two primary factors that the author identifies as being essential in the application of anthropological knowledge to the area of AIDS?

2. What were some of the concerns the Senegalese prostitutes had about the clinics concerning their health needs?

3. What approaches were taken which made the educational campaign successful?

The answer section begins on page 243.

6

Unlike the work of Michelle Renaud in the preceding selection, some medical anthropologists work with culturally different populations in North America. Here medical anthropologist Lance Rasbridge describes his work in Dallas, Texas as a "refugee outreach anthropologist" in which he coordinates the relationship between the medical staff, the refugee clients, and their sponsors and caseworkers. This article is particularly valuable for showing how applied anthropologists need to balance their efforts between research (data gathering) and intervention.

Role Transformation in A Refugee Health Program

By Lance Rasbridge

While all anthropologists go through personal adjustments in the course of the field work enterprise, many of us who work with refugees living within our own society experience special metamorphoses. This is particularly true when one's career evolves from academic research to policy making. In this article, I use my activities as coordinator of a health team to demonstrate aspects of role adjustment which are peculiar to refugee work, as well as some which are common to most applied anthropology. In addition, I outline the health care model developed to meet changing refugee needs in the Dallas area.

As an anthropologist, I have changed over the past decade from a theoretically minded graduate student to an outreach director in applied health. As a researcher, I progressed through the awkwardness of the observer-as-participant stage, not only confused by the culture my respondents brought with them, but also unsure of many of the American social institutions within which they were required to participate. With time I settled into a more balanced participant-observer role, reaching a level of integration into the community where I could participate relatively unobtrusively with my Cambodian friends in day-to-day activities, as well as in special events like Buddhist festivals. Likewise, I learned more about those aspects of American culture which most impacted the Cambodian refugees. Recently I have become more and more a participant; I now influence a small segment of the refugee community's culture, that dealing with health-seeking behavior.

My search for an applied position was in large part a response to the profoundly emotional experience of conducting research with refugees. To become personally familiar with the overwhelming tragedies of the refugee experience and yet remain passively divorced from their plight appears unconscionable to many. Bonding may exist between anthropologists and any subject population, but the situation of refugees particularly demands involvement. Moreover, when the refugees are living in the anthropologist's own society, intervention on their behalf is both more feasible and less ethically suspect than is intervention in a foreign society. Here the anthropologist can help to empower the underdog, in this case the refugee, without risking expulsion from the society or even the state.

Refugee Resettlement in Dallas

Refugee resettlement and its concomitants in health care have changed dramatically over the past fifteen years at both the national and the local level. In Dallas, most initial resettlement during the Southeast Asian crisis of the early 1980s took place in an area known as East Dallas and was coordinated by the three major voluntary agencies in the area. Many social service agencies, including the East Dallas Health Center from which I now work, sprung up around newly arrived Khmer, Vietnamese, and Lao.

Over the years, factors such as the escalating crime rate and the saturation of available housing have prompted resettlement agencies to target several other parts of town. In addition,

Reprinted by permission of PRACTICING ANTHROPOLOGY. 18(1), Winter, 1996, pp 25-27.

the ethnic composition of new arrivals has shifted from Southeast Asian to a broader mixture of Haitians, Cubans, Somalis, Ethiopian, Sudanese, Liberians, Ugandans, Soviet Jews, Armenians, and most recently, Bosnians, Kurds, and Iraqis.

Whereas the health needs of the nucleated Southeast Asian community were met by my centrally located clinic, these newer, scattered, and frequently indigent refugees have turned to Parkland, the main public hospital, for their health care needs. Parkland utilization has often been inappropriate, such as seeking immunizations through the emergency room. It has also been costly in time and money due to the refugees' need for translation and for special care. Furthermore, there was no system for follow-up care, and patients were often lost to the medical community after the initial visit. Finally, there was no system of health surveillance to monitor and treat communicable health problems.

The Applied Team: A Model

The solution implemented in Dallas to meet changing refugee health care needs was to decentralize services to refugees. Regular outreach clinics have been set up in borrowed apartment spaces in the multiple areas of high refugee concentration. This arrangement obviates the need for transportation for clients and proves to be more culturally appropriate than hospital-based care. The clinics are low-tech and are situated in rooms familiar to the refugees, such as English-as-a-Second-Language classrooms. Community leaders are frequently present at the clinic or nearby, and family support is at hand.

The outreach team which I coordinate consists of several physicians, a nurse practitioner, and several bilingual/bicultural medical assistants from the refugee communities. As the health team is small, I rely greatly on mutually beneficial volunteer medical assistance, namely, community health nursing students and their instructor, who use the outreach clinics as a practicum, and also an organization of first- and second-year medical students, who simply want some hands-on experience.

Currently we have three separate, weekly clinics, which can be moved readily as need dictates. We serve about thirty refugees a week for sick care, in addition to screening procedures, such as parasite and tuberculosis skin testing, and immunizations, for about fifty more.

The outreach team works closely with the area refugee resettlement agencies. As a result, caseworkers and sponsors are much more active and better informed concerning their clients health needs. Problems with compliance are minimized and the prospects for follow-up maximized via this coordinated approach. Due to our emphasis on prevention and primary care, we refer refugees to the hospital only rarely for serious problems or occasional diagnostic procedures. The program is cost-effective by keeping the bulk of these patients out of the hospital system.

Anthropologist as Coordinator

To the job title of Community Services Coordinator, which already existed when I was hired, I add Refugee Outreach Anthropologist, three words which did not appear anywhere in the job description. I coordinated both the medical team and the refugee clients and their sponsors and caseworkers, occasionally protecting one from the other, and often mediating between them. My role as a coordinator frequently centers on compromise: sensitizing the agencies, medical providers, and refugees to each other's expectations and limitations.

A common scenario involves sensitizing the medical community to non-Western medical beliefs and practices. For example, dermabrasive techniques such as "coining" and "cupping" are ubiquitously practiced by Southeast Asians, yet typically frowned upon by the U.S. medical establishment. My task is to convince the medical providers that such practices hold tremendous holistic value to the patient and therefore should not be discouraged wholesale, at the risk of alienating the patient from the medical setting. Rather, the most appropriate tact is to provide Western medicines and protocols in conjunction with or couched as supplemental to these more traditional remedies.

As another example, a frequent frustration the health care providers experience is in attempting to medicate Muslims during the fasting month of Ramadan. Many older patients adamantly refuse to take antihypertensives between sunrise and sunset. By working with a religious leader as well as with the health care providers, I have been able to formulate a scheme in which dosage regimens could be adjusted, at least temporarily, to fit the daily dietary practice of the fasting period.

I had learned as a student that what anthropologists are best suited to do in the applied setting is to coordinate. Given sparse funding and inadequate resources, anthropologists working outside academia usually need to do more than just coordinate. Few of us have many concrete services to market independently, but we can learn a little bit about a vast array of subjects when we need to! In my work, I have served as a medical assistant, working up patients, teaching medicine regimens, and even administering tuberculosis skin test injections and performing aspects of phlebotomy. I have also become an expert file clerk, faced with the daunting challenge of organizing hundreds of patients' charts, only recently with a notebook computer. We obtained the computer only after extensive fund-raising efforts, another of my key roles.

In this work, I must constantly guard against burnout on the part of my staff (and myself), a frequent phenomenon in refugee work, stemming from the demands of the health work and the refugees themselves. As survivors, refugees have learned from experience how to get what they need. Rather than being helplessly dependent, refugees often surprise their sponsors by their savvy in manipulating services to maximize their perceived benefits. "Doctor shopping" to acquire as much medicine as possible is a common example in health care. Often times, too, health problems are entwined for refugees with other social issues, complicating the treatment and frustrating health care personnel.

Anthropologist and Power

Even as a student, I was working in a milieu in which I wielded considerable power, unlike the anthropological researcher in a foreign sociopolitical and cultural setting. I was the host, and the refugees were the guests. I was expected to navigate and at times manipulate the system for my refugee respondent; indeed, I frequently felt the need to effect change simply because I could. Helping my friends better their lives fulfilled the need for reciprocity inherent to the research experience. This is not to say that I was any more familiar with the microcosm of a food stamp office or even a public health clinic than were my refugee friends—only that I understood the larger picture more clearly than they did.

There are ethical considerations in such a situation that cannot be resolved through "noninterference" in the name of scientific research. For example, I could report substandard housing conditions in my research findings, and hence put pressure on the landlords. Or, in the course of the research, I could serve as a translator at an agency that did not provide for housing and obtain benefits that the refugees previously did not have. Anthropologists can empower the researchees, and in essence advocate for them, simply by our association, when we work within our own sociopolitical structure.

As an applied anthropologist, I now play the role of refugee health advocate more overtly, both within the vast bureaucracy of a public hospital system, and where this bureaucracy comes in contact with the larger world of resettlement agencies and social service providers. While refugee needs are great, the number of refugees is small, making refugee health needs pale relative to the larger health care crisis in this country. Hence, refugee health needs are too easily bypassed. The anti-immigrant sentiment currently surfacing nationally adds to the challenges of refugee advocacy. Both the concrete needs of refugees and these political challenges can be addressed through a combination of objectivity and cultural relativism, the domains of anthropology.

Conclusions

At one level, the very nature of the refugee experience dictates a metamorphosis in the anthropologist's role over time. The abruptness of change within the resettlement process affects both research problems and palliative solutions. For example, among resettled Southeast Asians acute health problems like parasitism and malnutrition, common upon arrival, have given way to long-range deleterious consequences of resettlement such as chronic alcoholism, depression, high blood pressure, and kidney disease—problems found among a frighteningly high proportion of the population. Meanwhile, waves of refugees from various parts of the world follow one another according to political conditions far away. As we finally gained an understanding of Southeast Asian problems, the Somalis and the Kurds presented us with different customs and different sets of needs. Flexibility in the face of the vagaries of refugee work is vital; close contact with resettlement agencies in order to stay one step ahead affords such flexibility.

In applied anthropology in the home setting, the realities of home and field become blurred. The satisfaction of sharing with a refugee friend some personal aspects of life is most rewarding. On the other hand, the emotional requirement, not to mention the time constraints, of balancing an expanded social network of hundreds of individuals—the births, weddings, family crises, and the like—while maintaining the same within more personal spheres are exhausting and frequently left unfulfilled. For myself, "leaving the field" issues never really arose. Through my clinic position I try to live up to the "patron" status that I took so long to cultivate in the course of research by giving service back to the community.

Questions:

1. What specifically causes problems for the medical establishment when working with refugees?

2. Of what benefit is the outreach team which works with refugee resettlement agencies?

3. What are some ways that anthropologists can aid refugees beyond the scope of the medical system?

The answer section begins on page 243.

This article is based on the premise that women from different cultural backgrounds have different ideas about sickness and healing. Medical care givers need to understand these cultural difference if they are to provide the best possible health care for women from other countries. In this section Kielich and Miller provide a wide array of information about culturally different women (African-American, Latina, Asian/Pacific Islands, and Native American) and how these cultural features impact the delivery of health care.

Cultural Aspects of Women's Health Care

By Andrea M. Kielich and Leslie Miller

To provide optimal health care for female patients, you need to understand their culture of origin, immigration history, and the experience of being a woman in America today.

According to the U.S. Immigration and Naturalization Service, 800,000-900,000 new immigrants are crossing the borders of the United States each year during the last decade of this century. [1] This wave affects even parts of the country that until recently were largely culturally homogeneous.

Each group of new immigrants brings a unique set of cultural beliefs about sickness and health, a vocabulary of medical terms, and, often, a medicine cabinetful of folk remedies, challenging American physicians to use skills not typically taught in medical school. Even people who appear thoroughly Americanized and have a flawless command of English may return to folk customs when faced with a health crisis. Most immigrants don't use their herbs, elixirs, and amulets to the exclusion of western medicine, but, often, only by weaving such beliefs and practices into western treatment can physicians become trusted members of a patient's health care team.

On Being a Female Immigrant

When it comes to the health of immigrant women, experts stress that physicians need to understand the identity and roles that these women are expected to assume in both their communities of origin and their adoptive communities here. Most women are expected to play at least three roles: bearing and raising children, maintaining a household, and generating resources for the household. [2] Such roles differ among cultures and affect health in various ways.

In addition, health care providers need to develop an understanding of how patients with different sociocultural backgrounds and values perceive or define health and illness. Many women of Asian origin, for example, view health as a balance of yin and yang. Women of African, Haitian, Jamaican, and Native American origin may view health as harmony with nature. And women from Spanish-speaking countries often see health as a balance of hot and cold.

In order to reach their target audience, health messages must address the complexity of the relationships among acculturation—the extent to which people assume beliefs and behaviors prevalent in their new location—socioeconomic status, and lifestyle behaviors, as well as cultural values. For example, a Latina woman who is highly acculturated may benefit from virtually the same approaches used for non-Latina women. But a Latina woman who has just recently arrived and who speaks no English requires a different approach.

Becoming American

American women today have adopted more diverse roles than ever before in the history of the United States. Such freedom makes special demands on the health care system. Many women want to be partners in their health care, for instance, while others prefer to be passive recipients of the doctor's wisdom. When treating women of other cultures, consider their degree of assimilation to these and other aspects of American culture (see Table 1).

Reprinted by permission of PATIENT CARE 30(16), October 15, 1996, pp. 60-75. © 1996 Medical Economics.

Table 1
A Guide for cultural assessment of patient

Cultural component	Variables to consider
Communication style	Language and dialect preference Nonverbal behaviors Social customs
Orientation	Ethnic identity Acculturation Values
Nutrition	Symbolism of food Preferences and taboos
Family relationships	Family structure and roles Family dynamics and decision making style Lifestyle and living arrangements
Health beliefs	Alternative health care Health, crisis, and illness beliefs Response to pain and hospitalization Disease predisposition and resistance
Education	Learning style Informal and formal education Occupation and socioeconomic level
Religion	Preference Beliefs, rituals, and taboos

Adapted with permission from Fong CM: Ethnicity and nursing practice. Top Clin Nurs 1985; 7: 1-10.

An unfortunate part of women's experience in America and most other parts of the world is violence. Experts estimate that between one fourth and one third of women in this country, regardless of race, socioeconomic status, or any other factor, have been sexually or physically abused. New immigrant women may be least likely to report abuse to authorities because of fear of the emotional and financial support their partners provide.

The Health of Immigrants and Refugees

Contrary to popular belief, most immigrants arrive here in better health than their U.S.-born counterparts—but their health deteriorates in direct proportion to their length of stay. Relocating, living in poverty, coping with language barriers, striving to become "American," and other stresses contribute to immigrants' adoption of deleterious American habits— smoking, drinking, using illicit drugs, and consuming fat-laden, nutrient-deficient foods.

Physicians have an opportunity to identify and encourage healthy behaviors in newly arrived immigrants before bad habits have a chance to take hold. Other factors that contribute to deteriorating health include the greater affordability of tobacco and cigarettes in this country, occupational exposure to harmful chemicals, and exposure to a whole host of new diseases and bacteria.

Keep in mind too that immigrants and refugees are screened differently when entering the country. Undocumented immigrants have not had an entrance screening, for example, and may not have received all the texts and vaccinations that refugees are required to have. These include a test for tuberculosis and immunization for tetanus, polio, measles, mumps, and rubella.

Whether the patient is an immigrant or refugee, check for parasites and other health problems endemic to her country of origin if she has symptoms. If you're not sure what is endemic, contact the Centers for Disease Control and Prevention, a local travel clinic, or the health department. Keep in mind that even if you successfully treat a patient for one of these conditions, a visit to recently arrived relatives or friends or a vacation at home may re-expose the patient and require re-treatment. Also stay alert to signs of posttraumatic stress disorder, particularly in refugees, and signs of depression. See "Eight bridges that cross the cultural chasm," for other practical tips on caring for women of other cultures.

Finally, remember that vast differences exist among subgroups of the women discussed later in this article—among Mexican, Puerto Rican, and Peruvian Latina women, for instance—as well as among individual members of every subgroup. Each patient is your own best teacher.

Women of African Descent

In many cultures, women are raised to care for everyone and everything but themselves. This is especially true of black women—African Americans, West Indians, and African Caribbeans. Establishing their own well-being as a priority is essential.

Higher Morbidity and Mortality

Generally speaking, women of African descent carry a greater burden of morbidity and mortality than white women, with higher rates for virtually every major illness. For example, the mortality rate from coronary heart disease (CHD) is 22% higher for black women in this country than for white women, and black women die of heart attacks at a younger age. Mortality associated with hypertension in black women is 21.2% compared with 4.8% in white women, and black women's death rate from stroke is 78% higher than white women's. [3]

More than half—55%—of all women with AIDS in this country are black; black women have a nine times higher risk than white women of mortality from AIDS. [4] While black and Latina women constitute about 21% of the U.S. population, they account for 74% of the AIDS cases in women. [5]

The incidence of breast cancer has been increasing more rapidly in black than in white women; among women younger than 40, the rates are higher in black women than white. [6] However, this pattern reverses at older ages. While some of the differences in cancer incidence and mortality rates have been explained by socioeconomic status and access to and use of health services, these factors do not account for the black-white crossover in breast cancer

incidence rates or the more rapidly rising overall incidence in black women. [6]

One study offers the explanation that black women are less likely than white women to engage in primary prevention behaviors such as exercising and maintaining a favorable weight. [7] At least in this study, however, which contradicts earlier reports, they are more likely to engage in secondary prevention behaviors such as cervical cancer screening and breast examinations.

The rates of smoking among black women and white women are comparable, though black women tend to smoke fewer cigarettes per day than their white counterparts. Blacks are, however, less likely to quit smoking than other ethnic groups; and they smoke more high-tar, high nicotine, and mentholated brands, which may serve to elevate the risk for lung and other cancers, CHD, and cerebrovascular disease. [3]

While obesity is a problem for all groups of women, especially as they grow older, studies show that black women gain more weight than white women across most socioeconomic and age-groups. The studies report that, compared with white women, black women are less likely to diet to lose weight, less likely to perceive themselves as overweight, and less likely to equate beauty with slimness. [8]

Language and Religion

While many black women are native English speakers, language problems can still occur. In South Africa, the word "fanny," for example, is a derogatory term for vagina, so asking a patient to prepare for an injection in the fanny will not be well-received.

And while white Americans tend to refer to each other by first name as a sign of friendliness and equality, using first names with anyone other than close friends is considered inappropriate and discourteous in most cultures. Refer to adult patients of other cultures as Mrs., Miss, Ms., or Mr. unless they invite you to do otherwise.

For many black Americans, religion is an integral part of life. Those who are practicing Muslims pray to Allah five times a day on a prayer rug placed on the floor. Many who are Christian view God as the source of health and illness. To be cured of an illness, one must pray and have faith. Some patients will refuse medical procedures or treatment, believing that if they are meant to be cured, God will take care of it. Involving a local priest or spiritual advisor in such a patient's care may be helpful.

Latina Women

With a population of approximately 22 million (not including undocumented immigrants), Latinos are the largest and fastest growing minority in the United States. The term "Hispanic," meaning "pertaining to ancient Spain," has been used to include all people of Central and South American, Mexican, Cuban, Spanish, and Puerto Rican descent, but many people so classified feel no connection to this term and prefer "Latino." While still frequently seen in the literature, "Hispanic" seems to be declining in usage and has, for example, been barred by the Los Angeles Times.

Portrait of a Latina

Latinos are less likely than almost any other U.S. group to have access to health care. There are more Latinos without health insurance in this country than Anglos—White U.S. residents of non-Hispanic descent. The Latinos' poverty rate is 28% compared with 10% for the general population, and they are less well-educated—13% have fewer than five years of schooling, compared with 2% of the general population. [9]

Mexican Americans fare especially badly. An estimated 30% are without health insurance, and recent studies show they are much less likely to use preventive health services. [9] Emergency departments become the most likely source of primary care.

Compared with other groups of U.S. women, Latina women marry and have children at younger ages, and they have more children. Compared with Anglo women, they more often live in poverty and are more likely to be heads of households and to bear the heaviest burden of caring for the health and well-being of family members. [10]

Many Latinas receive the lowest wages in the country and work in the most hazardous jobs and settings: harvesting crops and working in "maquiladoras" (manufacturing and factory plants). [10] Latinas are twice as likely to be murdered as white women.

In spite of low socioeconomic status, Latinos have a number of better health predictors than whites. For example, Latina women are only 82% as likely to die as Anglo women in a given time period. Latina women are only half as likely as Anglo women to die of breast cancer and lung cancer. Although there are differences among Latinas living in different parts of the country, one study involving Latina women in South Florida found that both white Latina and black Latina women generally have lower rates of most kinds of cancer than their race-specific non-Latina counterparts. [11]

At least one study, however, shows that cancer of the breast, the most prevalent type of cancer in women, is increasing in Latina women at a rate three times greater than for Anglo women and that, compared with their white counterparts, Latina women are less likely to have visited a physician in the past year, less likely to have had a mammogram or Pap smear, and are less informed about cancer warning signs. [12] Latinas also appear to have more misconceptions about the causes of cancer. A recent survey of Orange County, California, women found that Latinas were more likely than Anglo women to believe that breast trauma and breast fondling increase the risk of breast cancer, less likely to know that breast lumps and bloody nipple discharge can be signs of breast cancer, and more likely to believe that mammograms are necessary only to evaluate breast lumps. [13]

Religion and Acculturation

Experts speculate about the roles religiosity—meaning belief in God, degree of religious orthodoxy and commitment to a faith, and perception of religion as a source of strength—and spirituality play in protecting the health of Latinos. [9] Religiosity may translate into health-related attitudes and actions derived from a religion's prescriptions and proscriptions about behavior and may involve individuals in social networks that exert behavioral norms. The behaviors in turn make it more or less likely that a person will become ill or die. Unfortunately, studies show that religiosity and spirituality decline with acculturation, as do their protective effects on health. [9]

Latina women who are religious are more likely to be closely integrated with the women in their immediate and extended families and with women in the community who share their values. This network is made up largely of older women who are more experienced with childbirth and other female health issues. It may be that they serve as teachers to the younger women, providing them with wisdom and support during pregnancy and birth. Or it may be that the traditional forms of prenatal and postnatal care known to women within these communities are superior to the forms available outside the network, or that avoidance of the stress associated with the long waits and less loving care provided at clinics helps to improve outcomes. [9]

The extent to which women identify themselves as connected to their subgroup culture and country of origin also seems to play a role in health. Studies show that women born in Mexico are less likely to give birth to low-birth-weight babies than their U.S.-born counterparts. So are Mexican American women with a predominantly Mexican cultural orientation and preference to communicate in Spanish, when compared with Mexican American women with a predominantly U.S. cultural orientation. [9]

Researchers have found that as Latinas become more acculturated to U.S. ways, their consumption of alcohol increases to match the intake of non-Latina U.S. women. Other studies have found that acculturated pregnant Mexican American teenagers completed more years of schooling than recently immigrated counterparts and pursued earlier prenatal care, but they also were younger when they had sexual intercourse for the first time, less likely to be married at the time of conception, and when married, less likely to have husbands who were employed. [9]

Birth Issues

Although American fathers typically assist mothers in the labor and delivery of children, in Mexico, for example, husbands don't see their wives until the delivery is over and both the mother and child have been cleaned and dressed. This may be related to the extreme modesty of most Mexican women. In Mexico, it is a woman's job—ideally, the mother of the woman giving birth—to attend during labor and delivery.

While western medicine emphasizes the value of colostrum for the newborn, many ethnic groups, including Mexicans, see it as bad or spoiled milk that is not good for the baby. Many women will choose to bottle-feed while in the hospital and then to breastfeed once their milk comes in. Modesty and not wanting to reveal their breasts in so public a place as a hospital may also play a role.

Most Mexicans and many other Latinos are devout Catholics, which can make discussions about birth control, abortion, and sterilization difficult. In addition, in many cultures, masculinity and virility are determined largely by the number of children a man can father, so husbands may refuse to allow wives to use birth control or to receive an abortion or a sterilization procedure, even if their health is at stake.

Asian/Pacific Islander Women

Asia is the only region in the world where men outnumber women; the Indian subcontinent is the only area in the world where the life expectancy at birth is lower for females than for males. [14]

"Wasted Investments"

In a number of Asian countries, the low health status of women is the result of deprivation, limited resources, few role opportunities, and cultural forces that devalue women. In many cultures, particularly those that count descent and inheritance through the male line, women are seen as a liability from birth—a wasted investment since they will eventually leave their families to marry. Girls, therefore, receive less food, medication, and educational resources than boys.

In some places in India, if the dowry that must be provided when a girl marries is not satisfactory to the groom and his family, the new bride may die under highly suspicious circumstances—with it being tacitly assumed that her husband or father-in-law killed her so that a more lucrative marriage arrangement can be pursued. The burden of having a female child is so great that infanticide, often by neglect of the newborn female, and abortion of female fetuses still occur.

Girls in many Asian cultures can still anticipate arranged marriages and do not gain domestic authority until they become mothers-in-law. Once married, women may become a physical part of the husband's family and household and be stripped of the supportive network provided by the women of their own family. In these societies, while boys are assured of power and superiority, most girls are taught to be docile, domestic, innocent, polite, obedient to demands, and submissive to violence.

In many Asian cultures, the husband makes all the health care decisions, including those involving contraception. In addition, he may not allow his wife to be examined by a male doctor or be operated on by a male surgeon.

Communication

Because of the hierarchical nature of many Asian cultures—men are considered superior to women, parents to children, teachers to students doctors to patients—Asians believe it is disrespectful to look a superior directly in the eye. Doing so implies equality. An Asian patient who appears disinterested in what you have to say may be avoiding eye contact out of respect for your "superior status."

Dignity and self-esteem are extremely important to most Asians. They may laugh or nod when given instructions, as though in complete understanding even if they comprehend nothing. They will lose their self-esteem if they admit they don't understand, or, worse, they will cause you to lose your self-esteem for not explaining the matter properly. Ask patients to demonstrate understanding of your instructions by asking them to repeat them back to you.

Because women of many Asian cultures are taught to value accommodation, they may agree to return for follow-up visits when they have no intention of doing so. They may agree because you are an authority figure; refusing would dishonor you. Saying Yes avoids the embarrassment of saying No.

On Pain and Childbirth

Asian patients have a reputation for remaining stoic while in pain. This may be partly because many of them, particularly the Chinese, are taught to value self-restraint. Assertive and individualistic people are considered crude and poorly socialized. Thus your Asian patients may not say they are in pain or ask for pain medication unless specifically asked. And even when pain medication is offered, they may refuse out of courtesy; it is generally considered impolite to accept something the first time it is offered. For these reasons, many Asian women remain stoic during childbirth. They believe women must endure pain and discomfort as part of the process and that to express these feelings would bring shame.

Many Asian cultures adhere to strict practices following childbirth. They believe that health depends on keeping the body in a state of balance. Pregnancy is thought to be a "hot" condition; giving birth causes a sudden loss of heat, which must be restored by eating "hot" (spicy, not necessarily hot in temperature) foods, keeping the room and body warm, having limited contact with and responsibility for the new infant, and not bathing, exercising, or leaving the home. Such practices last from a week to a month.

Such customs may make the jobs of postpartum nurses here in the States more difficult and may explain why Asian patients fail to keep postpartum checkup appointments. However, the customs were started with good reason—women typically performed physical labor in the fields, and the month or so after giving birth was their only time to rest. Furthermore, in many countries the water is full of harmful bacteria. Bathing too soon after childbirth could introduce harmful organisms to the body and cause illness.

While mother-infant bonding is viewed as extremely important by western health practitioners, certain Asian cultures, such as the Vietnamese, believe that spirits are attracted to infants and will steal them (through death). To prevent this, parents avoid attracting attention to their newborns; they do not verbally fuss over them and often dress them in old clothes. This can be misconstrued as neglect when in fact the parents are acting out of profound love and concern for their child.

Another Vietnamese custom that can be mistaken as poor bonding is the delay in naming a child. A newborn's name is often decided upon by the entire family during a naming ceremony held at the parents' house. The custom emphasizes the child's importance as a member of the family.

Folk Remedies

Many Asian cultures believe in the healing abilities of such traditional practice as coin rubbing and cupping. Coin rubbing involves either heating a coin or putting oil on it and rubbing a part of the body vigorously with it. Cupping involves heating a glass and placing it on the body. The vacuum created leaves red welts, as does the rubbing. It is believed that both practices bring illnesses to the surface of the body so they can then be released. Unfortunately, both practices can distract health care professionals from the real cause of the problem or be mistaken for child abuse.

Similarly, many Asian cultures believe in the importance of sweating out high fevers. Instead of removing clothing and blankets and using cool compresses, for example, they will pile on blankets and clothing and consume hot liquids. This can be especially troublesome for febrile infants.

For many Asians, having their blood drawn is seen as a weakening experience that robs the body of vital energy. Have a good reason for wanting a sample in the first place. Combine blood draws whenever possible, and request a wide battery of tests at one time.

Family Before Self

Many Asian groups have strong familial support systems. Patients may live in extended family households and value the family of orientation (the individual, parents, and siblings) over the family of procreation (the individual, spouse, and children). They often take care of each other when ill, so small entourages of family members may accompany a patient to your office or visit her in the hospital.

In such cultures, failure to care for oneself is common, particularly following a debilitating injury or disease. Self-care matters less because independence is less important to Asians than to Americans. A patient's unwillingness to do things for herself, combined with a willingness by immediate family members to do everything for the patient, can impede occupational and physical therapy following injuries and delay recovery.

Native American Women

Approximately 2 million Native Americans, representing more than 500 tribes, reside in the United States today. Before 1950, 90% of Native Americans lived on reservations, and 10% lived in urban areas. By 1990, these numbers had changed to 38% and 62%, respectively. Cultural aspects of care differ depending on where the patient lives.

Native Americans are younger on average—18-19 years old—than the U.S. general population—about 33 years. The number one cause of death among Native Americans is accidents, followed by heart disease, cancer, stroke, cirrhosis, suicide, and homicide. Alcoholism, obesity, and diabetes play major roles in many of these diseases. Smoking is also a tremendous problem among Native American women.

In the 1700s and 1800s, Native Americans were in far better health than the European colonists and Native Americans today. The European diseases brought over by the colonists and the native inhabitants' adoption of colonists' bad health habits caused a steady decline in health from about 1900 onward.

Little Access, Little Data

Most residents of Indian reservations are poor. Homes may be 100 or more miles from Indian Health Service clinics, and without cars, assess to care is greatly hindered. Alaskan natives in the bush country may have only community health representatives in the area, who then communicate by telephone with a remote physician or physician assistant. Most Native Americans on reservations are unemployed.

Good data on Native Americans' health, particularly those living in urban areas and especially females, are scarce. While the Indian Health Service provides health care to residents of reservations, it does not cover care for Native Americans who choose to live elsewhere. Clinics are usually more accessible to those in urban settings, but poverty, distance from public transportation routes, and inadequate child care still provide hurdles. And since most urban Native Americans use community health services that don't identify patients by race, the ability to track them and their health problems is lost.

Another confounding factor is misclassification at the time of death. Numerous studies have shown that although many Native Americans are listed as such at birth, up to 30% are classified as white when they die. This greatly underestimates the incidence of diseases among the Native American population.

Mutual Distrust

Many Native Americans are distrustful of western health care providers—and not only because the legacy of treaties broken by westerners is a long one. From about 1887 to 1978, the federal government made it illegal for Native Americans to practice or use their traditional medicine as part of their health care.

A contributing factor is that physicians working on reservations are often moved after two-year stints. Just as residents begin to trust a physician, the doctor moves on and a new one is installed, who must become familiar with the ways of the people.

Conversely, many western physicians may at least initially be distrustful of Native American patients because they are reluctant to make eye contact. Native Americans consider prolonged eye contact intrusive and insulting. They believe the eyes are the window to the soul. To make direct eye contact can endanger the spirits of both parties. Thus, many Native Americans will look down at their feet, which many physicians mistake for disinterest.

Another custom often mistaken for indifference is slow (by white American standards) response time of many Native Americans. Many tribes value silence. They use it to formulate their thoughts and choose their words carefully since they believe words have tremendous significance. A person who interrupts while someone is speaking is considered immature. Most white Americans, on the other hand, are uncomfortable with silences and tend to fill them with small talk.

Traditional Native American Medicine

To Native Americans, medicine and religion are synonymous. All things in the universe have life and a spirit. When a person is in good health, the physical, mental, and spiritual aspects of life are in balance; illness results from some imbalance. Native American medicine seeks to return the world forces to equilibrium largely through the use of herbs, rituals, and chanting.

In most tribes, traditional medicine is practiced by women. The most respected healers tend to be women, and major decisions regarding health care tend to be made by women.

One of the more common traditional medicine practices is the use of medicine bundles—pouches containing various herbs and substances that are carried or worn by or attached to the clothing of someone who is ill. If a patient shows up wearing one, try not to remove it. If you must do so to perform a medical procedure, explain why to the patient and family, remove the bundle gently and respectfully, and keep it in contact with the patient's body if at all possible.

Also, try to avoid cutting or shaving the hair on a Native American's head. Long, thick hair is a sign of health. To cut or shave it signifies that the person may become sick or die.

Kinship

While only the parents or legal guardians of a child can legally sign an informed-consent form, in some cultures—the Navaho, for instance—a grandparent or maternal uncle might be more appropriate. Native American grandparents commonly raise their grandchildren while parents leave the reservation to work. The role of the maternal uncle is a bit more complicated. American kinship is structured bilaterally, with children related equally to maternal and paternal relatives. Many other cultures are unilinear, however, tracing their descent from either a male or female ancestor. A member of a matrilineal culture, such as the Navaho or Hopi, is a member of the mother's family rather than the father's.

If you live near a certain tribe and treat a number of Native American patients, familiarize yourself with their customs as well as with the history and development of U.S. Indian Health Policy. Join the Native American community in their events, and collaborate with traditional healers in the care of patients. Studies involving alcoholism programs for Native Americans, for example, show that programs incorporating traditional medicine achieve much higher rates of sobriety than those that don't.

If possible, attend a seminar given by one of the three Native American Centers of Excellence in the country, located at the University of Washington, the University of Minnesota, and the University of Oklahoma. Such seminars will teach you how to properly address Native Americans, how to take a history, and how to increase the odds that your instructions will be followed.

References

1. Spector RE: Cultural concepts of women's health and health-promoting behaviors. J Obstet Gyascol Neonatal Nun; 1995 : 24 : 241-245.

2. Wilson D: Women's roles and women's health: The effect of immigration on Latina women. Women's Health Issues 1995; 5 : 6-14.

3. Keller C, Fleury J. Bergstrom DL: Risk factors for coronary heart disease in African-American women. Cardiovasc Nuns 1995; 31 : 9-14.

4. Orr ST, Celentano DD, Santelli J, et al : Depressive symptoms and risk factors for HIV acquisition among black women attending urban health centers in Baltimore. AIDS Educ Pn v 1954; 6 : 230-236.

5. Guinan ME, Leviton L: Prevention of HIV infection in women: Overcoming barriers. J Am Med Wom Assoc 1995, 50 : 74-77.

6. Rosenberg L, Adams-Campbell L, Palmer JR: The Black Women's Health Study: A follow-up study for causes and preventions of illness. J Am Med Wom Assoc 1995; 50 : 56-58.

7. Duelberg SI: Preventive health behavior among black and white women in urban and rural areas. Soc Sci Med 1992; 34 : 191-198.

8. Walcott-McQuigg JA: The relationship between stress and weight-control behavior in African-American women. JNat1MedAssoc 1995; 87 : 427-432.

9. Magana A, Clark NM: Examining a paradox: Does religiosity contribute to positive birth outcomes in Mexican American populations? Health Educ Q 1995; 22 : 96-109.

10. Juarbe TC: access to health care for Hispanic women: A primary health care perspective. Nurs Outlook 1995: 43 : 23-28.

11. Trapido EJ, Chen F, Davis K, et al: Cancer in south Florida Hispanic women: A 9-year assessment. Arch Intern Med 1954; 154 : 1083-1088.

12. Balcazar H, Castro FG, Krull JL; Cancer risk reduction in Mexican American women: The role of acculturation, education, and health risk factors. Health Educ Q 1995; 22 : 61-84.

13. Hubbel FA, Chavez LR, Mishra SI, et al: Differing beliefs about breast cancer among Latinas and Anglo women. West J Med 1596; 164 : 405-409.

14. Becktell PJ: Endemic stress: Environmental determinants of women's health in India. Health Care Women Int 1994; 15 : 111-122.

Questions:

1. Why does the health of immigrants often deteriorate after arriving in the United States?

2. What role does the Mexican-American father play in labor and delivery?

3. What accounts for the fact that Asia is the only region of the world where men outnumber women?

The answer section begins on page 243.

The work of dieticians is to inform people how to stay healthy by eating the proper foods. While most dieticians know (from a biological perspective) which foods should be eaten and which should be avoided, their real challenge comes when they attempt to change people's dietary habits for the better. Working with people from their own cultural background may be hard enough because of personal habits and food preferences. But when working with people from different cultural backgrounds, the problems can increase geometrically. Not only do all people have certain cultural and individual preferences, but most cultures have very strong values associated with certain types of food. Some foods are defined as being healthy and essential, while others are to be avoided at all costs. If dieticians are to be successful in changing people's eating habits, they will first need to know as much as possible about the cultural values these culturally different people attach to certain types of food. In this selection Terry makes a strong case for dieticians to learn how to engage in ethnographic interviewing and participant observation in order to collect culturally relevant information on food preferences, dietary practices, and food prohibitions.

Needed: A New Appreciation of Culture and Food Behavior

By Rhonda D. Terry

Childhood recollections of the morning breakfast ritual of my paternal grandmother are still fresh in my memory. As a farm wife in rural South Carolina, she prepared most foods from scratch. To prepare breakfast, she dumped a generous amount of flour, lard from her own hog, and buttermilk into a wooden bowl; mixed; and patted the dough by hand into biscuits. While the biscuits baked, she fried country ham, probably from the same hog who donated the lard, and scrambled eggs. These foods were eaten with syrup made from local sugar cane and butter purchased from a lady down the road who owned a cow.

My grandmother's breakfast ritual illustrates that complex cultural factors are preeminent determinants of nutritional health. The cultural environment she lived in determined food preferences; procurement patterns; distribution among individuals; preparation behaviors; and consumption, storage, and disposal patterns. Her breakfast, as well as her total diet, was high in fat, sodium, and sugar, but was a significant, meaningful part of her life for more than 80 years. Like my grandmother, all individuals live in households, communities, and regions, and in times and circumstances that determine nutritional health or disease with greater

certainty than access to all the nutrition education and services that dietitians can envision. In short, we are what we eat culturally as well as physiologically.

Dietitians are not unaware that cultural forces shape food intake and other health behaviors. However, the incorporation of cultural factors into dietary assessments and interventions are all too often either neglected or superficial. For example, race, ethnicity, or geographic residence are often inaccurately viewed as synonymous with culture. This misconception leads to stereotypical lumping. One may inaccurately perceive, for example, that all Jews follow orthodox food laws or that all Southerners routinely eat grits, biscuits, and country ham. We cannot rely on the cultural sameness of individuals based on their membership in defined racial, ethnic, geographic, or other groups. Although certain shared beliefs, assumptions, values, and behavior patterns may be found among groups defined by such categories, each subgroup of individuals exhibits a unique range of cultural characteristics that affect their food intake and nutritional health.

Why is culture often so poorly understood and superficially incorporated into dietetics practice? Two reasons immediately come to mind. First, the

Terry, Rhonda D. Needed: A New Appreciation of Culture and Food Behavior. Reprinted by permission of JOURNAL OF THE AMERICAN DIETETIC ASSOCIATION. *94(5), May 1994, pp. 501-03.*

educational background of many dietitians offers little preparation for incorporating cultural concepts into practice. Dietetic educators are all too aware of the barriers that impede incorporating desirable but nonmandated concepts into the dietetics curriculum. Curriculum mandates from the university, the department, and The American Dietetic Association consume virtually all of our teaching time and resources. Therefore, until in-depth cultural training is seen as a necessity for dietetics students, it likely will be included in few dietetics education programs. Second, whereas dietetics is both the science and the art of delivering nutrition services, the scientific, prescriptive, and technical aspects have often been given high prestige, respect, and recognition, while those aspects related to the art of delivery have generally been undervalued. This situation has perhaps become more pronounced as the decrease in health care resources has left many clinical, community, and foodservice facilities severely understaffed. Of necessity, emphasis has often been placed on serving as many clients as possible with the least possible resources, not on adapting services to best meet clients' needs, desires, and lifestyles. The following three steps can be taken to address these two problems, thereby strengthening dietitians' knowledge and skills related to culture.

STRENGTHEN THE ACADEMIC CULTURAL TRAINING FOR DIETITIANS

Cultural training for dietetics students typically consists of a background course in anthropology or a related social or behavioral science, combined with dietetics education about traditional food preferences and associated health problems of certain racial and ethnic groups. Such instruction is valuable for introducing students to basic information, but does not prepare them to incorporate cultural concepts into dietetics practice. In fact, students often are left with the impression that culture consists of "odd" beliefs and behavior patterns of groups radically different from themselves. Dietetics students commonly have a poor understanding of what constitutes culture, what are the cultural patterns in their own environments, and how to gather cultural information.

Several curriculum strategies can be used to strengthen the cultural understanding and skills of dietetics students. First, dietetics educators cannot rely on social and behavioral science classes to provide the cultural knowledge and skills

necessary for quality dietetics practice. Therefore, cultural education related to dietetics practice must be provided in dietetics classes. Students need to understand thoroughly what culture is and how it influences food behavior and the food environment (1,2). After dietetics students have a good grasp of what culture is, they can be taught the skills needed to discover for themselves relevant cultural patterns among clients and communities.

Instead of relying totally on traditional library research, students can become skilled in gathering cultural information about client groups through the techniques of observation, participant observation, and informant interviewing (3,4).

- Observation refers to seeking out and visually noting information about client groups that relates to their food behavior, food environment, and nutritional health. Examples include observing the neighborhoods and homes in which clients live; where they shop for food and the types of food available; and how food is stored, prepared, and eaten in homes.

- Participant observation skills teach students to learn more about client groups by participating in the activities of the groups. For example, students can read the same newspapers, listen to the same radio stations, go to the same community meetings, and shop in the same food outlets as clients.

- Informant interviewing refers to learning more about a client group by interviewing individuals from or closely associated with the group. For instance, a wealth of information about the food and health behaviors of client groups can be gleaned by asking relevant questions of other health care professionals who serve the group, community leaders among the group, and group members themselves.

These qualitative assessment techniques are often taught in conjunction with community nutrition, but are equally important in clinical and foodservice practice. For instance, in this issue of the Journal, Shovic describes how she used qualitative techniques to develop a nutrition exchange list for Samoans. An added benefit of inestimable value that occurs when a dietitian engages in observation, participant observation, and informant interviewing is that he or she not only learns about relevant cultural patterns, but also learns why those patterns exist. In other words, the dietitian learns to appreciate that clients feed their babies in certain ways or shop for foods at certain outlets for reasons that are logical and consistent with their lifestyles and environments. The dietitian develops an in-depth understanding of clients' dietary practices, and these practices no longer appear odd or irrational. This understanding marks the beginning of respect for clients, and is the basis for building culturally sensitive interventions.

EXPAND THE REPERTOIRE OF DIETARY ASSESSMENT AND INTERVENTION METHODS TO INCREASE CULTURAL SENSITIVITY

All groups have unique cultural characteristics, not just groups one perceives as being different from oneself. For example, unique shared beliefs, assumptions, values, and behavior patterns are found not only among groups perceived as culturally novel, such as American Indian families living in a small, isolated reservation community, but also among seemingly typical groups such as residents in a retirement village in Dubuque, Iowa, or families living in an urban housing project in Dallas, Tex. Therefore, regardless of what clients a dietitian serves, the range of cultural traits found among those clients needs to be thoroughly understood.

Textbooks, workshops, and professional articles can provide basic cultural information, but do not provide adequate cultural details for delivering dietetics services. In addition, culture is not static—it is ever-changing, making textbook and other written descriptions quickly obsolete. Consider, for example, the striking, rapid change in the food behavior of many US immigrants. As a result of the availability of new foods, the desire to emulate the dominant culture, and, often, rising economic status, traditional plant-based diets are rapidly replaced by diets incorporating more animal foods and a high percentage of Western refined, prestige, and convenience foods, particularly among youth [5]. Food behavior has also evolved with the recent, profound changes in the character of many US communities; for example, high poverty rates among households with children have resulted in increased childhood malnutrition, high violent crime rates in formerly peaceful neighborhoods have made worries about survival paramount to concerns about food and health, and the dramatic increase in day care for preschool children has resulted in many children learning basic food preferences and skills outside of and different from the family. Therefore, dietitians must be skilled in discovering relevant cultural patterns and cultural changes among the clients and groups they serve,

and need to incorporate a knowledge of these patterns into interventions. Melnyk and Weinstein, in their examination of obesity prevention strategies for black females in this issue of the Journal point out that without cultural assessment as well as culturally sensitive interventions, the nutrition information and services provided may be technically correct but ill suited to the needs, desires, and lifestyles of clients.

AFFIRM THAT THE DELIVERY OF NUTRITION SERVICES IS BOTH A SCIENCE AND AN ART, AND THAT THE TWO ARE OF EQUAL IMPORTANCE

The technical competence of dietitians must be excellent. The basis of dietetics practice is a thorough knowledge of the chemical, biochemical, and physiologic aspects of nutrition and foods. In this sense, delivering nutrition services is a science. However, for most human beings eating is not simply an act of nourishment. Therefore, to be relevant and useful, dietetics services must be designed to meet the needs, desires, and lifestyles of clients. When scientific knowledge is combined with a social commitment to service, the art of delivering nutrition services gains importance. Thus, the cultural assessment of clients becomes not just something nice to do if one has time but, instead, essential to quality practice.

References

1. Bass MA, Wakefield L, Kolasa KA. Foodways, food behavior, and culture. In: Bass MA, Wakefield L, Kolasa KA. Community Nutrition and Individual Food Behavior. Minneapolis, Minn: Burgess; 1979 : 1-20.

2. Terry RD. Delivering nutrition services to the community: assessment, planning, implementation, and evaluation. In: Terry RD. Introductory Community Nutrition. Dubuque, Iowa: William C. Brown; 1993 : 9-26.

3. Gonzalez VM, Gonzalez JT, Freeman V, Howard-Pitney B. Health Promotion in Diverse Cultural Communities. Palo Alto, Calif: Stanford Center for Research in Disease Prevention; 1991.

4. Terry RD. Using anthropological tools in clinical and community dietetics. Topics Clin Nutr. 1991; 5 (2) : 10-14.

5. WHO Study Group. Diet, Nutrition, and the Prevention of Chronic Diseases. Geneva, Switzerland: World Health Organization; 1990.

Questions:

1. Give two reasons why dietitians have generally poor understanding of culture.

2. Other than library research, what other data gathering techniques are available to dietitians for learning more about their culturally different clients?

3. Why do immigrants from non-western cultures sometimes neglect their traditional diets and take up food practices of the dominant culture?

The answer section begins on page 243.

9

As recently as several decades ago the prevailing position among psychiatrists and psychologists was the "psychic unity of humanity," the notion that all mental disorders stem from the same biological features shared by all peoples of the world. Psychiatry, with some prodding from anthropology, is beginning to recognize the importance of culture to their clinical practices. Certain mental disorders are found in some societies but not others. In this article Stix illustrates the relevance of understanding the patients' cultures for the successful diagnosis and treatment of certain mental disorders. He also points out the practical difficulties involved in having the psychiatric profession actually integrate these insights into their clinical practices.

Listening to Culture

By Gary Stix

Last April, a Bangladeshi woman who complained that she was possessed by a ghost arrived at the department of psychiatry at University College London. The woman, who had come to England through an arranged marriage, had at times begun to speak in a man's voice and to threaten and even attack her husband. The family's attempt to exorcise the spirit by means of a local Muslim imam had no effect.

Through interviews, Sushrut S. Jadhav, a psychiatrist and lecturer at the university, learned that the women felt constrained by her husband's demands that she retain the traditional role of housebound wife; he even resented her requests to visit her sister, a longtime London resident. The woman's discontent took the form of a ghost, Jadhav speculated, an aggressive man who represented the opposite of the submissive spouse expected by her husband. By bringing the husband into the therapy, Jadhav made a series of subtle suggestions that succeeded in getting him to relent on his strictness. The specter's appearances have now begun to subside.

Jadhav specializes in cultural psychiatry, an approach to clinical practice that takes into account how ethnicity, religion, socioeconomic status, gender and other factors can influence manifestations of mental illness. Cultural psychiatry grows out of a body of theoretical work from the 1970s that crosses anthropology with psychiatry.

At that time, a number of practitioners from both disciplines launched an attack on the still prevailing notion that mental illnesses are universal phenomena stemming from identical underlying biological mechanisms, even though disease symptoms may vary from culture to culture. Practitioners of cultural psychiatry noted that although some diseases, such as schizophrenia, do appear in all cultures, a number of others do not. More over, the variants of an illness—and the courses they take—in different cultural settings may diverge so dramatically that a physician may as well be treating separate diseases.

Both theoretical and empirical work has translated into changes in clinical practice. An understanding of the impact of culture can be seen in Jadhav's approach to therapy. Possession and trance states are viewed in non-Western societies as part of the normal range of experience, a form of self-expression that the patient exhibits during tumultuous life events. So Jadhav did not rush to prescribe antipsychotic or antidepressive medications, with their often deadening side effects; neither did he oppose the intervention of a folk healer.

At the same time, he did not hew dogmatically to an approach that emphasized the couple's native culture. His suggestions to the husband, akin to those that might be made during any psychotherapy session, came in recognition of the woman's distinctly untraditional need for self-assertion in her newly adopted country.

The multicultural approach to psychiatry has spread beyond teaching hospitals in major urban centers such as London, New York City and Los Angeles. In 1994 the fourth edition of the American Psychiatric Association's handbook, the *Diagnostic and Statistical Manual of Mental*

Stix, Gary, "Listening to Culture" Reprinted by permission of SCIENTIFIC AMERICAN. January, 1996, pp. 16-17.

Disorders, referred to as the *DSM-IV*, emphasized the importance of cultural issues, which are mentioned in various sections throughout the manual. The manual contains a list of culture-specific syndromes, as well as suggestions for assessing a patient's background and illness within a cultural framework.

For many scholars and practitioners, however, the *DSM-IV* constitutes only a limited first step. Beginning in 1991, the National Institute of Mental Health sponsored a panel of prominent cultural psychiatrists, psychologists and anthropologists that brought together a series of sweeping recommendations for the manual that could have made culture a prominent feature of psychiatric practice. Many of the suggestions of the Culture and Diagnosis Group, headed by Juan E Mezzich of Mount Sinai School of Medicine of the City University of New York, were discarded. Moreover, the *DSM-IV*'s list of culture-related syndromes and its patient-evaluation guidelines were relegated to an appendix toward the back of the tome.

"It shows the ambivalence of the American Psychiatric Association (APA) in dumping it in the ninth appendix," says Arthur Kleinman, a psychiatrist and anthropologist who has been a pioneer in the field. The APA's approach of isolating these diagnostic categories "lends them an old-fashioned butterfly-collection exoticism." A Western bias, Kleinman continues, could also be witnessed in the APA's decision to reflect the recommendation of the NIMH committee that chronic fatigue syndrome and the eating disorder called anorexia nervosa, which are largely confined to the U.S. and Europe, be listed in the glossary of culture-specific syndromes. They would have joined maladies such as the Latin American *ataques de nervous*, which sometimes resemble hysteria, and the Japanese *tajin kyofusho*, akin to a social phobia, on the list of culture-related illnesses in the *DSM-IV*.

Eventually, all these syndromes may move from the back of the book as a result of a body of research that has begun to produce precise intercultural descriptions of mental distress. As an example, anthropologist Spero M. Manson and a number of his colleagues at the University of Colorado Health Sciences Center undertook a study of how Hopis perceive depression, one of the most frequently diagnosed psychiatric problems among Native American populations. The team translated and modified the terminology of a standard psychiatric interview to reflect the perspective of Hopi culture.

The investigation revealed five illness categories: *wa wan tu tu ya/wu ni wu* (worry sickness) *ka ha la yi* (unhappiness) *uu nung mo kiw ta* (heartbroken), *ho nak tu tu ya* (drunkenlike craziness with or without alcohol) and *go vis ti* (disappointment and pouting). A comparison with categories in an earlier *DSM* showed that none of these classifications strictly conformed to the diagnostic criteria of Western depressive disorder, although the Hopi descriptions did overlap with psychiatric ones. From this investigation, Manson and his co-workers developed an interview technique that enables the difference between Hopi categories and the *DSM* to be made in clinical practice. Understanding these distinctions can dramatically alter an approach to treatment. "The goal is to provide a method for people to do research and clinical work without becoming fully trained anthropologists," comments Mitchell G. Weiss of the Swiss Tropical Institute, who developed a technique for ethnographic analysis of illness.

The importance of culture and ethnicity may even extend to something as basic as prescribing psychoactive drugs. Keh-Ming Lin of the Harbor-U.C.L.A. Medical Center has established the Research Center on the Psychobiology of Ethnicity to study the effects of medication on different ethnic groups. One widely discussed finding: whites appear to need higher doses of antipsychotic drugs than Asians do.

The prognosis for cross-cultural psychiatry is clouded by medical economics. The practice has taken hold at places such as San Francisco General Hospital, an affiliate of the University of California at San Francisco, where teams with training in language and culture focus on the needs of Asians and Latinos, among others. Increasingly common, though, is the assembly-line-like approach to care that prevails at some managed-care institutions.

"If a health care practitioner has 11 minutes to ask the patient about a new problem, conduct a physical examination, review lab tests and write prescriptions," Kleinman says, "how much time is left for the kinds of cross-cultural things we're talking about?" In an age when listening to Prozac has become more important than listening to patients, cultural psychiatry may be an endangered discipline.

Questions:

1. What is the *DSM-IV* and why is it controversial?

2. What is the reasoning behind classifying *anorexia nervosa* as an American or European disorder?

3. Name (in English) the five different types of depression as perceived by the Hopi.

The answer section begins on page 243.

10

The case of a young Bangladeshi girl's reaction to riots in Birmingham England serves as an example of how anthropological (cultural) information can be helpful in the practice of psychiatry. Physicians frequently diagnose and treat patients on the basis of their own models of health and disease which do not take into account those of their culturally different patients. Here Psychiatrist Roland Littlewood argues persuasively for a "clinical applied anthropology" which, by providing insights into the patient's view of illness, can lead to more effective treatment and better compliance by the patient.

From Disease to Illness and Back Again

By Roland Littlewood

What is the value of medical anthropology? Let me begin by recounting a story.

I was working in Handsworth in Birmingham, UK, at the time of the riots in 1986. The riots were first thought to be directed against the mainly white police force, and against local shops and businesses. One local psychiatrist even argued, in evidence to the Government-initiated Silverman inquiry, that the riots were the work of cannabis-intoxicate young Afro-Caribbean men.[1] However, the inquiry suggested that the rioters were white and Afro-Caribbean men in numbers proportional to the local population. Some women and a few young men of Asian origin were also involved. The eventual consensus was that the disturbances were not racially motivated but were a result of the frustration of unemployed people who lived in a ghetto area and who had destroyed their own neighbourhood in despair.

Four days after the riots ended, I was telephoned by a local (Asian) general practitioner (GP) who asked me—a white male hospital psychiatrist—to visit a 15-year-old girl from Bangladesh. She had been in Britain for two years, lived with her family, spoke English well, and attended the local mixed secondary school. She was, he said briefly, hysterical.

The streets were still full of debris being cleared up. Many shops had been burned down, and those that remained had shutters still up or boards nailed across windows to prevent further looting. Police had withdrawn to a discrete distance, and people were gathering on pavements to assess the damage. Life was cautiously re-establishing its pattern.

Around the corner I found the house. The family warily opened the door. I introduced myself. Hasmat (as I shall call her here) was in the downstairs room lying on the floor, eyes closed, occasionally thrashing about with her arms and legs, and shouting something neither the family nor I could understand. Her parents stood helplessly, placing cushions under her head, holding her hands, and trying to calm her down. Occasionally, she got up and quietly joined the others but seemed oblivious to what was happening. She assured us that she was well, was puzzled by our concern but refused to eat. She would then collapse back onto the floor. Her father told me that she was seriously ill with fits and he was glad I had come to take her to hospital. He was distressed but also, I thought, angry. Her elder brother took me aside and told me that Hasmat "was putting it on" because she had been arguing with her father for months about going out in the evening with her schoolfriends.

After greeting Hasmat, I asked her father what they had done to help her. Reluctantly, he told me that he had taken his daughter to the mosque when she had started talking strangely (the GP had told the father off for such "nonsense"). He said that someone at the mosque had spoken Koranic verses over her to make the spirit leave but this action had failed since she was genuinely ill. Perhaps the spirit had left her sick. Had the family lost anything in the riots? No, and no-one they knew had been hurt. I persisted. Could the riots possibly be the cause of Hasmat's distress? He said no: how can riots,

Reprinted by permission of THE LANCET, Vol 337 (8748), pp. 1013-1016.

however terrible, just by themselves make people have fits?

I thought he was probably right and asked the family to leave. I explained that I wanted to talk with Hasmat alone. Standard medical practice. I told her I guessed she was upset by something. She gazed at me, past me, blankly, detached. I felt uncomfortable, somehow embarrassed. She asked me to promise to keep a secret. I agreed rather reluctantly. If I was a doctor, she said, shouldn't I now examine her? I declined. What had happened? She told how, on the morning after the riots ended, she and her brother's young wife had secretly unpadlocked the door—her father had secured it firmly from the inside when the looting spread down a nearby road—and had gone out to have a look "for fun". Terrified at the devastation, they had returned immediately without anyone else in the family knowing. She had seen a boy from her school and thought he might attack her. Back in the house she had "felt dizzy." That was all. Could I now tell her father that she was sick, but it was not serious, and she could not possibly go to hospital? I invited the family back into the room and told them that Hasmat had become ill because of the awful events locally, but that she would soon be well without any medicine. What was the sickness then? The best that I could come up with was that she was "weak". They looked nonplused. I suggested she now had something to eat and said I would call again the next day with a colleague, a Bengali community worker.

That afternoon I was telephoned by the GP who reported that Hasmat seemed much better after my visit. He had reinforced my advice but the family felt let down because I had not seemed very interested: no treatment, no hospital. He had given her some sleeping tablets to keep everybody happy, "a placebo for the whole family" as he put it. The next day the father left a message for me at the hospital: his daughter was much better and she did not need to see a psychiatrist or community worker again. I tried unsuccessfully to arrange another appointment. The GP subsequently told me that everything was back to normal, and I forgot about the whole business. About two months later I was contacted by the West Midlands poisons unit for details of my patient who had just taken an overdose of tablets.

I am not going to offer a "solution" here. I merely want to illustrate the choices and identifications that are available in different explanatory models of illness and distress, each with their own personal experiences and their own social ideologies. Mine must be included—a white male doctor with my own assumptions about gender and ethnicity, preoccupied with the riots, and involved in and controlling (in some part) the process.

Illness and Disease.

The common approach to an individual such as Hasmat is to reach a formal diagnosis—e.g., hysteria, with a note about "cultural conflict", and some poorly informed speculation about Islamic family values. And then? Either clinical despair or some attempt to persuade the family to accept our interpretation of these events in terms of "depression" or "generational conflict." Doctors may not be inclined to take any of the family's explanations seriously apart from that of the elder brother who suggested that Hasmat was "putting it on."[2]

Is this case merely and example of family tensions that should have been left to sort themselves out? Hasmat herself moved towards a more medical solution, an overdose of medically prescribed drugs with subsequent hospital admission. Some family members suggested that she required skilled biomedical intervention. The cultural and political interpretation of the episode is a product of my own perceptions: should Hasmat have been admitted to hospital straight away with ethnicity, personal preoccupations, and family context ignored?

It is no accident that the greatest interest in social science within medicine is found among psychiatrists. Psychiatry is the most self-doubting specialty: it is concerned with the ambiguities of the social practice of medicine. Extreme clinical presentations such as overdoses or Munchausen's syndrome mark the edges. These instances show our difficulty in distinguishing between an understanding of the patient in "naturalistic" terms—as a physical body, subject to disturbance—that can be interpreted and controlled through methods similar to those used in the physical sciences—or the "personalistic" understandings that we apply to everyday life where we acknowledge personal qualities such as memory, reflection, anticipation, and responsibility.

Medical anthropology provides a rigorous basis for the social interests of psychiatry that have remained a marginal discipline within medicine. Psychiatric assessment involves the taking of an extensive social history followed by interpretations similar to those applied in the social sciences. But it is only in extreme instances that doctors call for a psychiatrist. Most doctors muddle along and assume that a patient's perspective is similar to ours, or that the patient will follow our professional advice. Occasionally, we target undesirable illness-related behaviour, unhealthy diet, or lack of exercise through fragmentary attempts at persuasion. Whether in health education policy or in individual patients, doctors know little about a person's knowledge of sickness and health, in any class or culture. These questions are not asked. If medical anthropology has its own impulse, it is to encourage understanding of patients' own illness experiences, the way in which they view their sickness and health, [3] and the context in which such beliefs originate and continue. If doctors seek to change high-risk behaviours such as driving after drinking alcohol, unprotected sex in an era of AIDS, or cigarette smoking, the need to examine the ways in which risk is perceived, and how wider social values or institutions reinforce or create the way in which choices are made.[4]

Medical Anthropology

Western societies now face striking changes in their patterns of sickness and health. Ironically, the success of biological medicine has produced a patient population who live longer, but who have chronic and non-life-threatening disease. It is doubtful whether these improvements in health over the past century can really be attributed to medical knowledge.[5] What are the cultural and moral understandings of notions such as sickness and mortality? When ill, how do we attempt to answer the question "why me?".

Dissatisfaction with what is popularly regarded as excessive medical emphasis on disease (the biological understanding of sickness) has led increasing numbers of patients to seek health care from complementary medicine, self-help groups, or through overtly political perspectives such as the women's' health movement.[6] Psychotherapy and counseling services have expanded in forms ranging from Californian "New Age" theories and neurolinguistic programming to established psychoanalytical therapy. Increasing numbers of nurses and medical professionals are training in various non-western medical practice—e.g., acupuncture and Naikan—while hospital medicine is now more prepared to recognize the skills of chiropractice and hypnotherapy. Religious movements offer "spiritual" alternatives.

Black and ethnic minorities are often dissatisfied with medical services available to them, notably in the area of mental health where certain illnesses—e.g., schizophrenia—are diagnosed disproportionately among minority groups and where culturally sensitive therapies have yet to be offered.[7] If some minority group members, like Hasmat, are moving towards reframing their experiences in a more medical direction, probably with the encouragement of the medical profession, others may see their illness in political terms. Traditional ideas of family responsibility or illness causation are often met with little sympathy in clinical departments, and health education programmes both in western countries and the developing world are limited by an inadequate understanding of popular beliefs of sickness and health. What do these changes mean for the future? Is our society entering a pluralistic market-place for health care or are there important underlying long-term changes in the patterns of health-care uptake.

Medical anthropologists have become established as a recognised group within social anthropology. They concentrate on individuals' own experience and understanding of illness, and relate these beliefs to society's core values, their symbolic representations of power, chance, and misfortune, and to gender relations, social structure, and values of communities. In summary, medical anthropologist apply a more "holistic" approach.[8]

The traditional emphasis within anthropology on small-scale and non-literate societies has shifted, with a recognition that we live in an inter-connected world. All systems of medicine have powerful and shared symbols and metaphors, whether the white coat and high technology image of modern medicine, or the no less ritualistic equipment of the shaman or Unani practitioner. Both are certainly pragmatic—they are seen to work—but both also embody shared social concerns that make them acceptable.

Clinically Applied Anthropology

We know very little about popular understandings of sickness in any culture. To the doctor, lay explanatory models of sickness are characterised by "vagueness, multiplicity of meanings, frequent changes, and lack of sharp boundaries between ideas and experience." In contrast, professional medical theories presume "single causal trains of scientific logic".[3] However, studies by medical anthropologists suggest that this division is not found throughout clinical practice.[9]

Psychiatrists and primary carers will not be surprised to learn that their own understanding of illness includes "multiple and manifestly contradictory models"—behavioural, biochemical, psychodynamic, and sociological.[10]

Medical anthropology applies data from different contexts to assess social as well as biological causation and can redirect traditional epidemiological research. Ethnographic studies focus on a community lived in by an anthropologist, usually for a year or more, although the term "ethnographic" often refers to any participant observation. Although the field-work approach is often purely qualitative, with enhanced validity but diminished reliability, these studies lead to more epidemiological approaches that use conventional sampling procedures, questionnaires, and rating scales.

Participant-observation studies have looked at how patients understand psychotropic drugs; they have examined patterns of child abuse and relatives' understanding of schizophrenia, and have investigated the pattern of life of chronically ill patients. An anthropologically informed medicine can support the interests of ethnic minorities through collaboration with lay healers or through research initiated at the request of community groups. Doctors know little of the importance of illnesses such as Jocob-Creutzfeldt disease and AIDS-related dementia for groups in which they are more common; or how families with thalassaemia, Huntington's disease, or Tourette's syndrome view their illness and its transmission. How do such families conceive of what we call genetic transmission?

An anthropological viewpoint may help in assessing the lives of institutionalised psychiatric patients who are now being placed in the community, especially since ethnographic studies were originally cited as justification for deinstitutionalisation. Medical anthropologists may act as advocates for the patient's perspective and values. In the US, the clinical work of anthropologists has become part of a move to patient-centered medicine.[11] Detailed accounts of how patients' understand their illness can radically assist patient-doctor negotiation over appropriate treatment. Anthropology is especially valuable in pyschosomatic medicine, where divergence between the explanatory models of patient and doctor are commonplace. An anthropological perspective enables the liaison psychiatrist to reduce staff-patient conflicts by clarifying the meaning of their respective explanatory models.[9] In nursing, anthropology can operationalise such diffuse but powerful notions as empathy and care.[12]

Clinically applied anthropology is helpful to psychiatrists who take part in liaison consultation, individual psychotherapy and cognitive therapy, and group and milieu work on psychosomatic wards. On the psychosomatic ward at University College Hospital each patient completes an "explanatory model questionnaire": the patient's perspective then becomes the basis of negotiation and audit in ward rounds and in individual nurse-patient work. Many of these patients have had a long and tortuous relationship with the medical profession that itself becomes part of their model of responsibility and causality.

Medical anthropology is congenial to doctors because of its interest in clinical practice and biological explanation, and because of its concern with the patients' experience of becoming ill.[13] It is also mercifully almost jargon-free.

And Hasmat? Although I was reluctant to offer a solution, her condition improved once both her and her family's idiom of distress was taken seriously.

REFERENCES

1. Littlewood R. Community initiated research: a study of psychiatrists' conceptualisations of 'cannabis psychosis'. Psychiatr Bull 1988; 12: 486-88.
2. Kleinman A. The illness narratives: suffering, healing and the human condition. New York: Basic books, 1988.
3. Kleinman A. Patients and healers in the context of culture. Berkeley: University of California Press, 1980.
4. Douglas M. Risk acceptability and the social sciences. London: Routledge and Kegan Paul, 1985.
5. McKeown T. The role of medicine: dream, mirage or nemesis. London: Nuffield Provincial Hospitals Trust, 1976.
6. Thomas KJ, Carr J, Westlake L, Williams BT. Use of non-orthodox and conventional health care in Great Britain. Br Med F 1991; 302: 207-10.
7. Littlewood R, Lipsedge M. Aliens and alienists: ethnic minorities and psychiatry. London: Unwin Hyman, 1989.
8. Helman C. Culture, health and illness. 2nd ed. London: Wright, 1990.
9. Good BJ, Good M-JD. The semantics of medical discourse. In: Mendelsohn E, Elkand

Y, eds. Science and cultures: sociology of the sciences, vol 5. Dordrecht: Reidel, 1981.

10. Eisenberg L. Disease and illness: distinctions between professional and popular ideas of sickness. Cult Med Psychiatry 1977; 1: 9-23.

11. Chrisman NJ, Maretzki TW, eds. Clinically applied anthropology. Dordrecht: Reidel, 1982.

12. Holden P, Littlewood J, eds. Anthropology and nursing. London: Routledge, 1991.

13. Littlewood R. From categories to contexts: a decade of the 'new cross-cultural psychiatry'. Br F Psychiatry 1990; 156: 308-27.

Questions:

1. Why did Hasmat's father feel the psychiatrist was disinterested in his daughter's condition?

2. In what ways can applied medical anthropology reduce the ambiguities inherent in psychiatric medicine?

3. In recent years a general dissatisfaction with the medical model of disease has caused patients to seek out alternative forms of healing. Name some of these.

The answer section begins on page 243.

Section II
Business

11

Much has been written in recent years on what it takes to be competitive in the global marketplace. A key to all business relationships—whether we are referring to marketing, management or negotiations—is good communication skills. Sending and receiving clear and unambiguous messages in one's own culture is difficult enough. But when attempting to communicate across cultures in a business setting the problems increase geometrically. In this selection the author, an applied anthropologist, argues that understanding the cultural dimension of international business is absolutely critical for success in the world marketplace. And since cultural anthropology involves the comparative study of cultures, it is anthropology, more than any other discipline, that is in the best position to provide that understanding.

Cultural Anthropology and International Business

By Gary Ferraro

How often do we hear people say "the whole argument is academic"? By this statement they mean that despite the elegance of the logic, the whole line of reasoning makes little or no difference. In other words, the term *academic* has become synonymous with *irrelevant*. And in all of academia it is hard to think of other disciplines generally perceived by the public to be any more irrelevant to the everyday world than cultural anthropology, the comparative study of cultures. The student of biology, for example, can apply his or her skills to the solution of vital medical problems; the student of creative arts can produce lasting works of art; and the political science student, owing to a basic understanding of political dynamics, can become a local, state, or national leader. But according to popular perception, the study of cultural anthropology, with its apparent emphasis on the non-Western cultures of the world, has little to offer other than a chance to dabble in the exotic.

To counter the long-held popular view that cultural anthropology is of little use in helping to understand the world around us, an increasing number of cultural anthropologist in recent years have applied the theories, findings, and methods of their craft to a wide range of professional areas. Whereas professionals in such areas as education, urban administration, and the various health services have been coming to grips, albeit reluctantly, with the cultural environments within which they work, those in the area of international business, although having perhaps the greatest need, remain among the most

skeptical concerning the relevance of cultural anthropology. In fact, one is struck by how little contact there has been between cultural anthropology and the international business sector. According to Chambers, cultural anthropologists have avoided working with the international business community because of "a highly prejudiced ethical stance which associates commercial success and profit taking with a lack of concern for human welfare" (1985:128). Also, Western multinational corporations have not actively sought the services of cultural anthropologists, whom they generally view as serving little useful purpose, other than making university undergraduates somewhat more interesting cocktail party conversationalists by providing them with tidbits of data about the esoteric peoples of the world. In short, both cultural anthropologists and international businesspersons view the concerns of the other as irrelevant, morally questionable, or trivial.

Clearly, this book rests on the fundamental assumption that to operate effectively in the international business arena one must master the cultural environment by means of purposeful preparation ahead of time. Interestingly, a survey of international business people (Kobrin, 1984) concluded that most acquired their international expertise while they were on the job, or as Kobrin put it, "they learned to play with the kids on the street by being there and doing it" (1984:41). And since so many of the international businesspeople surveyed had acquired their international expertise experientially, they also considered

Reprinted by permission of Prentice Hall from THE CULTURAL DIMENSION OF INTERNATIONAL BUSINESS (2nd ed). Englewood Cliffs, NJ: Prentice Hall, 1994, pp. 1-15.

such "hands-on" factors as business travel and overseas assignments to be the most important for future generations of international businesspeople. This survey was particularly noteworthy for the nearly total lack of significance attached by the international businesspeople to such factors as training programs or undergraduate and graduate courses. Although in no way attempting to minimize the value of experiential learning, this book argues that in addition to on-the-job learning (and in most cases, before entering the international marketplace), successful international businesspersons must prepare themselves in a very deliberate manner in order to operate within a new, and frequently very different, cultural environment.

CULTURAL ANTHROPOLOGY AND BUSINESS

Since the 1930s cultural anthropologists have conducted a modest amount of research in industrial and corporate settings, focusing largely on corporate cultures in the United States. For example, the human relations school of organizational research of the 1930s and 1940s produced a number of ethnographies showing how informal cultural patterns could influence managerial goals (see Mayo, 1933; Roethlisberger & Dickson, 1939; Gardner, 1945; Warner & Low, 1947; and Richardson & Walker, 1948). More recent studies of corporate cultures have attempted to show how specific configurations of values contribute to the relative success or failure of meeting corporate goals (see Davis, 1984; Denison, 1990; Kotter, 1992; and Frost et al., 1991).

This body of research is predicated on the understanding that in many important respects business organizations are not unlike those societies studied by traditional anthropologists. For example, corporate members, like people found in small-scale, preliterate societies, engage in rituals; perpetuate corporate myths and stories; adhere to a set of norms, symbols, and behavioral expectations; and use specialized vocabularies. Since business organizations tend to be both differentiated and socially stratified, specific roles and statuses can be identified. Also, business organizations, through dealings with such groups as unions, governments, environmental groups, and consumers, can be said to have external relations with other social systems. Given these similarities, cultural anthropologists have been able to make modest contributions to the understanding of domestic business organizations, and they have the potential for making many others.

The anthropological perspective can be useful in the study of purely domestic business organizations, which frequently are comprised of many social components that come from different backgrounds, hold contrasting values and attitudes, and have conflicting loyalties. It is not at all likely that the company vice president will have much in common with the assembly-line worker, the union representative, the president of the local Sierra Club, the OSHA inspector, the janitor, or many members of that diverse group called the buying public. And yet, if the organization is to function effectively, home U.S. businesspeople equip themselves with vast amounts of knowledge of their employees, customers, and business partners. Market research provides detailed information on values, attitudes, and buying preferences of U.S. consumers; middle- and upper-level managers are well versed in the intricacies of their organization's culture; and labor negotiators must be highly sensitive to what motivates those on the other side of the table. Yet when North Americans turn to the international arena, they frequently are willing to deal with customers, employees, and fellow workers with a dearth of information that at home would be unimaginable.

The literature on international business is filled with examples of business miscues when U.S. corporations attempted to operate in an international context. Some are mildly amusing. Others are downright embarrassing. All of them, to one degree or another, have been costly in terms of money, reputation, or both. For example, when American firms try to market their products in other countries, they often assume that if a marketing strategy or slogan is effective in Cleveland, it will be equally effective in other parts of the world. But problems can arise when changing cultural contexts. According to Senator Paul Simon,

> *Body by Fisher*, describing a General Motors Product, came out "Corpse by Fisher" in Flemish, and that did not help sales.... *Come Alive With Pepsi* almost appeared in the Chinese version of the *Reader's Digest* as "Pepsi brings your ancestors back from the grave."... A major ad campaign in green did not sell in Malaysia, where green symbolizes death and disease. An airline operating out of Brazil advertised that it had plush "rendezvous lounges" on its jets, unaware that in Portuguese, "rendezvous" implied a room for making love. (1980:32)

Insensitivity to the cultural realities of foreign work can lead to disastrous results. Lawrence

Stessin reports on a North Carolina firm that purchased a textile machinery company near Birmingham, England, in hopes of using it to gain entry into the European market. Shortly after the takeover, the U.S. manager attempted to rectify what he considered to be a major production problem, the time-consuming tea break. Stessin recounts,

> In England, tea breaks can take a half-hour per man, as each worker brews his own leaves to his particular taste and sips out of a large, pint size vessel with the indulgence of a wine taster.... Management suggested to the union that perhaps it could use its good offices to speed up the "sipping time" to ten minutes a break.... The union agreed to try but failed.... Then one Monday morning, the workers rioted. Windows were broken, epithets greeted the executives as they entered the plant and police had to be called to restore order. It seems the company went ahead and installed a tea-vending machine—just put a paper cup under the spigot and out pours a standard brew. The pint size container was replaced by a five-ounce cup imprinted—as they are in America—with morale-building messages imploring greater dedication to the job and loyalty to the company.... The plant never did get back in to production. Even after the tea-brewing machine was hauled out, workers boycotted the company and it finally closed down. (1979:223)

Just as inattention to the cultural context can result in some costly blunders in marketing and management, it also can affect seriously the success of international business negotiations. Time, effort, reputation, and even contracts can be lost because of cultural ignorance. Alison Lanier tells of one American executive who paid a very high price for failing to do his cultural homework.

> A top level, high priced vice president had been in and out of Bahrain many times, where liquor is permitted. He finally was sent to neighboring Qatar (on the Arabian Gulf) to conclude a monumental negotiation that had taken endless months to work out. Confident of success, he slipped two miniatures of brandy into his briefcase, planning to celebrate quietly with his colleague after the ceremony. Result: not only was he deported immediately on arrival by a zealous customs man in that strictly Moslem country, but the firm was also "disinvited" and ordered never to return. The Qatari attitude was that this man had tried to flout a deeply-held religious conviction; neither he nor his firm, therefore, was considered "suitable" for a major contract. (1979:160-61)

These are only a few of the examples of the price paid for miscalculating—or simply ignoring—the cultural dimension of international business. The most cursory review of the international business literature will reveal many other similarly costly mistakes. In 1974 Ricks and Arpan published a compendium of international business miscues appropriately entitled *International Business Blunders*. Unfortunately, less than a decade later an entirely new collection has been published (Ricks, 1983), describing only those international business blunders that have occurred since 1974. But the purpose here is not to demonstrate beyond any reasonable doubt the folly and insensitivity of the North American businessperson when operating overseas. Rather, the purpose is to show that the world is changing faster than most of us can calculate, and if American businesspersons are to meet the challenges of an increasingly interdependent world, they will need to develop a better understanding of how cultural variables influence international business enterprises.

THE NEED FOR GREATER AWARENESS OF THE CULTURAL ENVIRONMENT

In recent decades there has been a growing tendency of business and industry to become increasingly more globally interdependent. In order to remain competitive, most businesses, both here and abroad, know that they must continue to enter into international/cross-cultural alliances. The overall consequences of this trend for the 1990s and beyond is that more and more companies will be engaging in such activities as joint ventures, licensing agreements, turnkey projects, and foreign capital investments. The creation of the European Economic Community—with its removal of trade barriers, deregulation of certain industries, and the privatization of others—is making Western Europe once again an attractive place for foreign investment. The international marketplace is growing increasingly more competitive due to the rapid and successful industrialization of such countries a Korea, Singapore, and Taiwan, as well as many third world countries. And of course, the weakening of the U.S. dollar in recent years has brought about a dramatic increase in foreign investments in the United States.

It has become a cliché to say that the world is shrinking or becoming a "global village." Rapid technological developments in transportation and communications in recent decades have brought the peoples of the world closer together in a physical sense. Unfortunately, there has not been a concomitant revolution in cross-cultural understanding among all the peoples of the world. And of course, no one could argue that we have witnessed any degree of cultural homogenization of world populations. What we can agree on, however, is that the world is becoming increasingly more interdependent. Despite George Washington's warnings against "entangling alliances," there is no way that any of us can isolate ourselves from the rest of the world. We are, whether we like it or not, enmeshed in global concerns far beyond the wildest dreams, or nightmares, of our founding fathers.

How well the United States will fare in this increasingly interdependent world in the decades to come is not altogether predictable. If the last several decades are a reliable indicator, the future is not particularly bright for the United States to remain a leader in world economic affairs. During the quarter of a century immediately following World War II, the United States enjoyed unprecedented and unparalleled economic success. Our postwar technologies gave rise to products that the world wanted and we were very willing and able to supply, everything form atomic energy and microelectronics to Levis and Big Macs. The United States, owing to its technology, managerial techniques, and investment capital, was in the enviable position of being the "only game in town." During this period our world market shares were large and we enjoyed a healthy balance of payments. Then, in the early 1970s, the trade surpluses that we had enjoyed for so long disappeared and we began to have trade deficits. Ironically, it was in 1976— our bicentennial year—that our trade accounts moved into a negative imbalance. The substantial trade deficit of over $9 billion in 1976 ballooned to over $100 billion by 1990, with little hope for reducing the imbalance in the immediate future, short of some major efforts on the part of the U.S. government.

American business must realize by now that— despite what may have occurred in the past—the product will no longer sell itself. Since there are so many good products on the market today, the crucial factor in determining who makes the sale is not so much the intrinsic superiority of the product but rather the skill of the seller in understanding the dynamics of the transaction between himself or herself and the customer. Unfortunately because of our relative success in the past, we are not particularly well equipped to

meet the challenges of the international economic arena during the twenty-first century.

Part of the problem lies in the fact that many U.S. companies, particularly middle-sized ones, have not attempted to sustain sales and production by venturing into the international marketplace. While there has been an increase during the 1980s in the number of U.S. firms exporting, it remains that fewer than 1 percent of all U.S. companies is responsible for 80 percent of all U.S. exporting activities. Even though most U.S. corporations have competed successfully in domestic markets, with a unified language and business practices, they have not been very adept at coping with the wide range of different languages, customs, and cultural assumptions found in the international business arena. For many of the firms that do enter foreign markets, success has been inconsistent at best. Nowhere is this better illustrated than in the area of Americans living and working abroad.

Statistics on the premature return rate of expatriate Americans (that is, those returning from overseas working assignments before the end of their contracts) vary widely throughout the international business literature. Estimates of attrition rates in the late 1970s (Harris, 1979:49; Edwards, 1978:42) ran as high as 65 to 85 percent for certain industries. More recent figures, while not as high, still serve to illustrate how difficult it is for Americans to live and work successfully abroad. For example, Caudron (1991:27) cites premature returns of Americans living in Saudi Arabia to be as high as 68 percent; 36 percent in Japan; 27 percent in Brussels; and 18 percent in London, a city that one would expect most Americans to adjust to easily. Regardless of whether we are dealing with attrition rates of 68 percent or 18 percent, the costs are enormous. Considering that it costs a firm between three and five times an employee's base salary to keep that employee and his or her family in a foreign assignment, the financial considerations alone can be staggering (Van Pelt & Wolniansky, 1990:40). And of course, this cost refers only to premature returns. There is no way of measuring the additional losses incurred by those firms whose personnel don't become such statistics. Those personnel who stay in their overseas assignments are frequently operating with decreased efficiency, and owing to their less than perfect adjustment to the foreign cultural environment, often cost their firms enormous losses in time, reputation, and successful contracts.

Our nation's leaders from both the public and private sectors have recognized the seriousness of the trade deficit. In its report of December 1980, the president's Export Council, made up of leaders in American business, government, and labor, recommended that the problem of shrinking world markets must be attacked on a number of fronts simultaneously. The council's major recommendations included (1) increasing national export consciousness by establishing a permanent Export Council and providing more export information and assistance through the Department of Commerce; (2) strengthening the federal government's international trade functions; (3) eliminating such export disincentives as taxation of overseas Americans, foreign application of our antitrust laws, and the Foreign Corrupt Practices Act; and (4) improving U.S. export incentives such as financing, export insurance, tax benefits, and the creation of trading companies. Interestingly, none of the recommendations even remotely alluded to the need for more emphasis on foreign language study and cross-cultural education. Despite this glaring oversight the relationship between expanding exports and stimulating language and cultural studies must not go unnoticed. Since we do not take seriously the study of other languages and cultures, we simply are not getting to know our international customers, and not surprisingly, we are not selling abroad as well as we could.

INTERNATIONAL COMPETENCY– A NATIONAL PROBLEM

The situation that has emerged in the last decade is that as the world grows more interdependent, we Americans can no longer expect to solve all the world's problems by ourselves, nor is it possible to declare ourselves immune from them. If our nation is to continue to be a world leader we must build deep into our national psyche the need for international competency—that is, a specialized knowledge of foreign cultures, including professional proficiency in languages, and an understanding of the major political, economic, and social variables affecting the conduct of international and intercultural affairs.

At the same time that we are faced with an ever-increasing need for international competency, the resources our nation is devoting to its development are declining. This problem is not limited to the area of business. It is, rather, a national problem that affects many aspects of American life, including our national security, diplomacy, scientific advancement, and international political relations, in addition to economics. Future generations of American businesspersons, however, must be drawn from the society at large, and it is this society, through its educational institutions, that has not in the past placed central importance on educating the general populace for international competence.

Given the relatively low priority that international competency has had in our educational institutions in recent years, it is not surprising that those Americans who are expected to function successfully in a multicultural environment are so poorly prepared for the task. If the international dimension is weak in our general education programs today, it is even weaker in our business school curricula. According to a report of the Task Force on Business and International Education of the American Council on Education, "...over 75% of the graduating DBA's (or PhD's in business) have had no international business courses during their graduate studies..." (Nehrt, 1977:3).

While graduate schools in business have increased their international offerings since the 1970s, courses on the cultural environment of international business have received relatively little attention. This general neglect of cross-cultural issues in business education is generally reflected in the attitudes of the international business community. To illustrate, in a study of 127 U.S. firms with international operations, respondents showed very little concern for the cultural dimension of international business. When asked what should be included in the education of an international businessperson, respondents mentioned—almost without exception—only technical courses. There was, in other words, almost no interest shown in language, culture, or history of one's foreign business partners (Reynolds & Rice, 1988:56).

However we choose to measure it, there is substantial evidence to suggest that as a nation our people are poorly equipped to deal with the numerous challenges of our changing world. Whether we are talking about language competence, funding for international education, opportunities for foreign exchange, or simply the awareness of global knowledge, the inadequacies are real and potentially threatening to many areas of our national welfare, including international business in particular. The problem referred to in recent literature as a national crisis has no easy solution. What is required initially is broad public awareness of the problem followed by concerted actions on a number of fronts.

References

Caudron, Shari. "Training Ensures Success Overseas." *Personnel Journal*, December 1991, pp. 27-30.

Chambers, Erve. *Applied Anthropology: A Practical Guide.* Englewood Cliffs, N.J.: Prentice Hall, 1985.

Davis, Stanley, MANAGING CORPORATE CULTURE. Cambridge, MA: Bellinger, 1984.

Denison, Daniel R. *Corproate Culture and Organizational Effectiveness.* New York: Wiley, 1990.

Edwards, Linda. "Present Shock, and How to Avoid It Abroad." *Across the Board*, February 1978, pp. 36-43.

Frost, Peter J., et al. *Reframing Organizational Culture.* Newbury Park, Calif.: Sage Publications, 1991.

Gardner, Burleigh. *Human Relations in Industry.* Homewood, Ill.: Irwin, 1945.

Harris, Philip. "The Unhappy World of the Expatriate." *International Management*, July 1979, pp. 49-50.

Kotter, John P. *Corporate Culture and Performance.* New York: Free Press, 1992.

Mayo, Elton. *The Human Problems of an Industrial Civilization.* New York: Macmillan, 1933.

Nehrt, Lee C. BUSINESS AND INTERNATIONAL EDUCATION, (A report by the Task Force on Business and International Education. Washington, DC: American Council on Education, May, 1977.

Reynolds, J. I., and G. H. Rice. "American Education for International Business." *Management International Review*, 28 (3) (1988), 48-57.

Richardson, Friedrich, and C. Walker. *Human Relations in an Expanding Company.* New Haven, Conn.: Yale University Labor Management Center, 1948.

Ricks, D. A. *Big Business Blunders: Mistakes in Multinational Marketing.* Homewood, Ill.: Dow Jones-Irwin, 1983.

Ricks, D. A., M. Y. C. Fu, and J. S. Arpan. *International Business Blunders.* Columbus, Ohio: Grid, 1974.

Roethlisberger, F. J., and W. J. Dickson. *Management and the Worker: An Account of a Research Program Conducted by a Western Electric Company, Hawthorne Works, Chicago.* Cambridge, Mass.: Harvard University Press, 1939.

Stessin, Lawrence. "Culture Shock and the American Businessman Overseas." In *Toward Internationalism: Readings in Cross Cultural Communications*, pp. 214-25, E.C. Smith and L. F. Luce, Eds., Rowely, Mass.: Newbury House, 1979.

Van Pelt, Peter, and Natalia Wolniansky. "The High Cost of Expatriation." *Management Review*, July 1990, pp. 40-41.

Warner, W. L. and J. Low. *The Social System of the Modern Factory: The Strike, A Social Analysis.* New Haven, Conn.: Yale University Press, 1947.

Questions:

1. Where do most international business people from the United States learn about their foreign business partners?

2. What leads to failure in the international business arena?

3. What does the author mean by the term "premature returns?"

The answer section begins on page 243.

12

Even though they do not advertise for anthropologists in the "classifieds," western corporations are beginning to use cultural anthropologists to gain insights into their corporate cultures. This should not be particularly difficult to understand because business organizations are not unlike those societies studied by traditional cultural anthropologists. Corporate employees, like people in small-scale non-western societies, have their own set of rituals, symbols, myths, and stories; use specialized vocabularies; and adhere to behavioral norms. Since business organizations have both hierarchies and a division of labor, statuses and roles can be identified. In this section, Laabs discusses some of the types of contributions that cultural anthropologists are making in the field of corporate anthropology.

Corporate Anthropologists

By Jennifer J. Laabs

The corporate jungle is full of cultural anomalies. Business anthropologists are helping to solve some of them.

Chances are, an anthropologist wouldn't be the first business expert you'd call if you wanted to build a better mousetrap—or a better HR program. Anthropologists aren't exactly listed as consultants in the phone book between *accountant* and *attorney*. But maybe they should be.

Although calling an anthropologist might seem like an unusual answer to a business dilemma, many companies have found that anthropologists' expertise as cultural scientists is quite useful in gaining insight about human behavior within their corporate digs.

Anthropology, by definition, is "the science of human beings," and studies people in relation to their "distribution, origin, classification, relationship of races, physical character, environmental and social relations and culture" (according to *Webster's Ninth New Collegiate Dictionary*).

Although there are many types of anthropologist (see "They Dig up Rocks, Don't They?" p.82), most people have only heard of the archaeology (stones and bones) variety. But there's much more to them than that.

Anthropologists study many different areas of business, but essentially they're all people-watchers of one sort or another. Business anthropologists have been studying the corporate world for years (since the early 1900s), on such varied topics as how to encourage more creativity or how best to integrate multicultural learning techniques into an organization's training program.

There are only a dozen business anthropologists who actually use the title of *anthropologist*, but there are about 200 currently working in and for corporate America.

Lorna M. McDougall, a staff anthropologist at Arthur Andersen's Center for Professional Education in St. Charles, Illinois, for example, currently is studying why people from some cultures learn best from lectures, although others learn best through interactive learning.

Her background includes linguistics study at Trinity College in Dublin, Ireland, and social anthropological study at Oxford. She also has a specialty in medical anthropology, and has worked in a variety of organizations and universities.

McDougall has been a key player in shaping the firm's Business English Language Immersion Training (ELIT) program, directed by the company's management development group, to which McDougall reports.

The ELIT program builds both a common language skill for communication between people who speak English as a second language (there are approximately 800 million in the world), and an awareness of each culture's unique approach to business encounters. The results of her work have helped instructors, who train Andersen consultants working in 66 countries, be better teachers. They've also helped students become better learners.

Reprinted by permission of PERSONNEL JOURNAL. v. 7(1), Jan. 1992 pp. 81-87.

The center is almost a mini-United Nations, and has many of the same kinds of intercultural opportunities and challenges, but is also a melting pot of sorts in which she studies many types of cultural issues. "We're in a unique position to be able to use people's information and exchange it," says McDougall.

Arthur Andersen's product essentially is its people, and keeping them trained and in top shape to consult alongside other Andersen employees in many different countries is a cultural and business challenge that many global firms are facing these days. Although the company has been global for many years, delivering clear, effective training for consultants continues to be an issue.

McDougall is part of Andersen's corporate strategy, says Pete Pesce, managing director for Arthur Andersen's human resources worldwide. "An anthropologist brings a lot of value to an organization," says Pesce. Although McDougall is the company's first on-site anthropologist and has been with Arthur Andersen only one year, she's going to be even more valuable in the future because of the increasing worldwide scope of the company's operations, says Pesce.

Because the organization has more than 56,000 employees and has spent, for example, 7.4% of its annual revenue in 1990 ($309 million) on training and education, the company is committed to enhancing its education programs using expertise that such disciplines as anthropology can offer.

What is that expertise? "Business anthropology, like all anthropology, is based on observing and analyzing group values and behavior in a cultural context. We focus on what people in a cultural group do, how many of them do it and how what they do affects the individuals in the group," she says.

"Business anthropologists seek to identify the connections between national culture and organizational culture," explains McDougall. Just as other cultural scientists, she helps identify some of the major cultural variables within and between organizations and the various ways that these differences impact:

- Structure
- Strategy
- Operations
- Communications
- Behavior.

From a cross-cultural standpoint, McDougall's job was to analyze what Arthur Andersen instructors (usually partners) and students do in the classroom and how they interpret those events.

"When I came in to study this program, I used an anthropological methodology to take a look at what was happening," she says. She listened in on classroom sessions and conducted many face-to-face interviews. "I then analyzed that data from an anthropological perspective," says McDougall. She noticed, for example, that people from certain cultures are used to two-way communication in the classroom, although others just sit quietly while the "professor lectures." To do otherwise, in their minds, would be disrespectful.

"It isn't necessarily an inherent feature of the human mind that people learn in one way or another," says McDougall. It's more a question of how people have learned to learn, and how the company's training can incorporate all types of learning styles for the best possible retention of the material by everyone. "What we're really doing is facilitating," she says.

Changes were made in the objectives of the training program. For example, another component was added—a cultural orientation module, which helps the company's staff and managers become more aware of multicultural diversity issues and how those behaviors are affecting their business interactions.

As a result of the changes, the "students" have been more cooperative and better learners inside the classroom, explains McDougall. Noticeably more intercultural socializing has taken place outside the classroom as well—something management hadn't anticipated. "It's important to realize that when you're looking at the effectiveness of cross-cultural training, you want to look at the outcome in improved relations between the people involved," she explains.

Pesce, from a human resources perspective, has found that the organizational values are the same throughout the firm's many offices globally because of the company's emphasis on homogeneous training and orientation. "I've traveled around the world and talked to employees," he says. "What I see clearly is that the values of the firm are very, very consistent. When our people talk about our organization, they talk about it in the same light in terms of quality, values, delivering client service and developing our people."

McDougall also teaches some of the management development classes, and is involved in the company's "train the trainers" program. In addition, she presents special classes to the company's human resources managers on cultural sensitivity issues.

"Recently, I was in London meeting with our directors of human resources for our Europe, the Middle East, India and Africa divisions," says Pesce. "Their interest in dealing with working standards is very keen. The challenge is to understand the differences in cultures, and in work and family values—the differences between Spain and Germany, for example. Lorna will be very helpful to us in that whole process."

Other areas she is studying involve such topics as:

- Leadership
- Creativity
- Productivity
- Delegation.

Areas for McDougall's anthropological study have been identified in a variety of ways. Sometimes members of the management development team propose ideas; other times, McDougall identifies them. Some recent topics have included teaching associates the cultural meaning of gestures and selecting colors for computer screens used in training.

"Colors have symbolic connections that are culture-specific," explains McDougall. "For example, in some cultures, white is associated with marriage, but in others it's associated with death. Others associate blue with death. In some cultures pink is considered feminine and in others yellow is."

Another project that McDougall is helping develop is an Experienced Hire Orientation program to help new hires assimilate more rapidly into the company's corporate culture. "We would apply what anthropologists call *oral transmission* of beliefs, practices and values by having established personnel pass on the firm's history and traditions by word of mouth, rather than in writing," explains McDougall.

For now, her work has been centered at the St. Charles facility, but in the future she might travel to the company's other worldwide locations for other research projects.

Anthropology Boosts Creativity

"What good are zero defects, if you aren't even making the right product?" asks Roger P. McConochie, a St. Charles, Illinois-based anthropologist who consults with businesses on a variety of topics.

McConochie asks a thought-provoking question. Some companies are looking to people like him to help answer it, because it opens up the corporate agenda to the bigger picture: What really is a company's business all about?

One business person, who has benefited from the anthropological approach, came to this conclusion: "What is our product? It isn't hardware, and it isn't even customer satisfaction, excellence, quality, TQM, or those other buzzwords from the 80s," says Mark T. Grace, operations development manager for Houston-based Generon Systems (a division of Dow Chemical and British Oxygen Corp). Although the company manufactures nitrogen-separation equipment, Grace says: "We have only one product: innovation."

"Today we're the best in the world at what we do," says Grace, "but if we keep doing things the same way for another two or three years, we'll be out of business. That's how quickly this industry is changing and that's how tough our competition is. Our challenge on a daily basis is to redesign our equipment so that it's more efficient: space efficient, weight-efficient, cost-efficient."

In his business, creativity is everything, he continues. "The problem is putting people into a group and having them freely share their ideas. Each person wants individual credit for his or her ideas, yet the best ideas emerge from interaction." Although the company even has "idea rooms" in which people can draw their ideas and put them up on the wall, Grace explains, "We were stuck. So at one meeting, I said, "We've tried everything else, why not bring in an anthropologist?"

He called McConochie, president of Corporate Research International, for suggestions on how to incorporate culturally correct ways of getting staff to contribute. Since then, McConochie, and his associate, Harvard-educated Anthony Giannini, president of The Corporate DaVinci, Ltd., have been an anthropological sounding board for Grace.

Generon's problem is fairly typical in business. But it isn't the company's fault, say these anthropologists, because today's business people are products of the competitive jungle in which they live and work. Although competition may be good among rivals, it often doesn't work within a single organizational culture, as evidenced by the fact that creativity gets stifled. People have a hard time leaving their cultural imprints at the front door.

To understand present society, anthropologists look to the past. From their perspective, McConochie and Giannini liken successful business strategy to the Renaissance period in Europe (between the 14th and 16th centuries), when such individuals as Leonardo DaVinci were guided by many values, including the aesthetics of beauty and the spiritual and emotional sides of humanity.

"During the Renaissance, new institutions were being formed and reformed and the individual was rediscovered," says Giannini. DaVinci's *The Last Supper*, for example, was the first painting that got away from depicting human figures in a flat and monochromatic way. "You had, for the very first time, real people," he notes.

At that time, there was a blending of many human interests and cultures into almost every facet of life, including work. But that approach, for the most part, was abandoned somewhere along the way.

What was lost? "A concern with the human side of things, a concern with the non-quantifiable," says McConochie. He and Giannini say they think business would benefit from getting back to that holistic approach to thinking. "We believe in numbers; and we believe in measurements, but we also believe that there are elements to life and elements to corporate practice that can't be put into numbers."

Today, compartmentalization of human thinking is rampant, but the challenge of globalization requires businesses to rethink that strategy. Such techniques as "bridging" or "scaffolding" allow workers to use the many facets of their collective conscious to come up with solutions to current problems. It also can help them better understand colleagues from other cultures. Anything less, they say, falls short.

Giannini and McConochie created *The Corporate DaVinci*—a program for corporate Renaissance, in which they help organizations rethink their corporate history and recreate their corporate myths. "In anthropological terms, we would call it an *origin myth*. Every tribe in the jungle has a story of how it came to be," says McConochie. And so do companies. They don't usually think about it but it often helps people remember how they came to be, and how they fit into history.

For example, when Giannini took the program to Ford Motor Co., he began the first session with a brief history of the wheel: From its invention to modern-day transportation. "In just 15 minutes, they had a fresh way of looking at the work they were doing day by day," says McConochie. "It was no longer just going out and pushing cars off the assembly line and selling them to get their sales figures up for the year. They were participating in the human drama."

Why is this so important? Because companies need a clear "ego sense": a continual sense of organizational self over time, says McConochie. Most anthropologists talk in terms of thousands, or even millions, of years. People begin to see that their lives, in the grander scheme of things, last only an instant. They also see, however, that what they do has an impact on the historical continuum and gives workers a feeling of oneness.

"What defines us as human beings is that, despite the differences across cultures, we're all trying to create meaning in our lives," says McConochie. "From my experience in corporations, the people on the shop floor have as much need for meaning in their lives as the people in the boardroom," he explains. "Everybody wants fewer defects at a lower cost. That's fine," says McConochie. "I'm not sure that's enough."

Corporations have been trapped by the concept that all that people on the shop floor need is to sleep, eat and get paid at the end of the week—and if you give them those basics, it's enough to motivate them. This isn't so, explains McConochie, who has consulted with many types of businesses, including aviation companies. Even chief executive officers won't work any harder if you double their salaries. "What you need to do is give them an opportunity to be creative, and an opportunity for challenge and growth," he explains. Creativity also must be supported in corporate culture—in word and deed. "Right at the top of their corporate mission statement, organizations ought to have a special credo that reads 'Beauty in our products and services, and in the creative means of their production, is a corporate goal of the highest order,'" says Gainnini.

Everyone can be creative—they just need some tools to help broaden their thinking. Giannini and McConochie's Corporate DaVinci program includes a segment called *The Aesthetic Audit*, which gives people a guide to use as a springboard into the creative process.

For example, if you went to the hardware store, and picked up a simple screw or nut, you could examine it and ask, "Does it suit its purpose?" Then you'd move on to the other points. Does it demonstrate integrity? If it's corroded, has sharp edges that might cut the person using it, or lacks brilliancy and symmetry, for example, you might round the edges and paint it.

"Typically, I find that executives give low ratings to 60 to 70% of their products and services in at least half of these dimensions," says Giannini. Looking at their own products with *focused eyes*, companies then go on to make better products, and also create new ones. It gives colleagues a set of questions from which to start, so they can work together creatively.

Employees also can benefit from cognitive and cultural training, so they understand where ideas come from and how those ideas vary across societal boundaries. For example, these anthropologists include such topics in their program as:

- Organization of Thought Across Cultures
- The Multicultural Technician
- Cognitive Emotions Across Cultures
- Multicultural Business Thinking in Action.

Can corporations actually blend science with poetry? Production with art? Business with aesthetics? Anthropologists who reach from one culture to another—bringing the best cognitive and cultural artifacts from the past into the present—say it *is* possible, and may be just the bridge that sparks innovation of the future.

Questions:

1. What are the two main accomplishments of the ELIT program?

2. What is the purpose of a cultural orientation module?

3. What led Mark Grace to call in an anthropologist to aid Generon System?

4. According to McConochie what is the one thing that unites humanity, regardless of cultural differences?

The answer section begins on page 243.

13

When cultural anthropologists enter a radically different culture for the purpose of describing it, they are engaging in ethnographic fieldwork. They learn the language, live with the people they are studying, and are willing to spend months on end learning about the culture. Good ethnographers consider their subjects to be teachers while they themselves assume the role of students. By making their informants "expert commentators" (which, of course, they are), the ethnographer is able to learn much about the ideas, attitudes, and behavior patterns found in the culture. In this selection anthropologist David McCurdy shows how the qualitative research of ethnography can be used within a complex business organization to diagnose a management problem.

Using Anthropology

By David McCurdy

Recently, a student, whom I have not seen for fifteen years, stopped by my office. He had returned for his college reunion and thought it would be interesting to catch up on news about his (and my) major department, anthropology. The conversation, however, soon shifted from college events to his own life. Following graduation and a stint in the Peace Corps, he noted, he had begun to study for his license as a ship's engineer. He had attended the Maritime Academy, and worked for years on freighters. He was finally granted his license, he continued, and currently held the engineer's position on a container ship that made regular trips between Seattle and Alaska. He soon would be promoted to chief engineer and be at the top of his profession.

As he talked, he made an observation about anthropology that may seem surprising. His background in the discipline, he said, had helped him significantly in his work. He found it useful as he went about his daily tasks, maintaining his shop's complex engines and machinery, his relationships with the crew, and his contacts with land-based management.

And his is not an unusual case. Over the years, several anthropology graduates have made the same observation. One, for example, is a community organizer who feels that the cross-cultural perspective he learned in anthropology helps him mediate disputes and facilitate decision making in a multiethnic neighborhood. Another, who works as an advertising account executive, claims that anthropology helps her discover what products mean to customers. This, in turn, permits her to design more effective ad campaigns. A third says she finds anthropology an invaluable tool as she arranges interviews and writes copy. She is a producer for a metropolitan television news program. I have heard the same opinion expressed by many others, including the executive editor of a magazine for home weavers, the founder of a fencing school, a housewife, a physician, several lawyers, the kitchen manager for a catering firm, and a high school teacher.

The idea that anthropology can be useful is also supported by the experience of many new Ph.D's. A recent survey has shown, for the first time, that more new doctorates in anthropology find employment in professional settings than in college teaching or scholarly research, and the list of nonacademic work settings revealed by the survey is remarkably broad. There is a biological anthropologist, for example, who conducts research on nutrition for a company that manufactures infant formula. A cultural anthropologist works for a major car manufacturer, researching such questions as how employees adapt to working overseas, and how they relate to conditions on domestic production lines. Others formulate government policy, plan patient care in hospitals, design overseas development projects, run famine relief programs, consult on tropical forest management, and advise on product development, advertising campaigns, and marketing strategy for corporations.

This new-found application of cultural anthropology comes as a surprise to many Americans. Unlike political science, for example, which has a name that logically connects it with practical political and legal professions, there is nothing in the term *anthropology* that tells most Americans how it might be useful.

The research subject of anthropology also makes it more difficult to comprehend. Political scientists investigate political processes, structures, and motivations. Economists look at the production and exchange of goods and services. Psychologists study differences and similarities among individuals. The research of cultural anthropologists, on the other hand, is more difficult to characterize. Instead of a focus on particular human institutions, such as politics, law, and economics, anthropologists are interested in cross-cultural differences and similarities among the world's many groups.

This interest produces a broad view of human behavior that gives anthropology its special cross-cultural flavor. It also produces a unique research strategy, called *ethnography*, that tends to be qualitative rather than quantitative. Whereas other social sciences moved toward *quantitative methods* or research designed to test theory by using survey questionnaires and structured, repetitive observations, most anthropologists conduct *qualitative research* designed to elicit the cultural knowledge of the people they seek to understand. To do this, anthropologists often live and work with their subjects, called *informants* within the discipline. The result is a highly detailed ethnographic description of the categories and rules people consult when they behave, and the meanings that things and actions have for them.

It is this ethnographic approach, or cultural perspective, that I think makes anthropology useful in such a broad range of everyday settings. I particularly find important the special anthropological understanding of the culture concept, ethnographic field methods, and social analysis. To illustrate these assertions, let us take a single case in detail, that of a manager working for a large corporation who consciously used the ethnographic approach to solve a persistent company problem.

The Problem

The manager, whom we will name Susan Stanton, works for a large multinational corporation called UTC (not the company's real name). UTC is divided into a number of parts, including divisions, subdivisions, departments, and other units designed to facilitate its highly varied business enterprises. The company is well diversified, engaging in research, manufacturing, and customer services. In addition to serving a wide cross-section of public and private customers, it also works on a variety of government contracts for both military and nonmilitary agencies.

One of its divisions is educational. UTC has established a large number of customer outlets in cities throughout the United States, forming what it calls its "customer outlet network." They are staffed by educational personnel who are trained to offer a variety of special courses and enrichment programs. These courses and programs are marketed mainly to other businesses or to individuals who desire special training or practical information. For example, a small company might have UTC provide its employees with computer training, including instruction on hardware, programming, computer languages, and computer program applications. Another company might ask for instruction on effective management or accounting procedures. The outlets' courses for individuals include such topics as how to get a job, writing a resume, or enlarging your own business.

To organize and manage its customer outlet network, UTC has created a special division. The division office is located at the corporate headquarters and is responsible for developing new courses, improving old ones, training customer outlet personnel, and marketing customer outlet courses, or "products" as they are called inside the company. The division also has departments that develop, produce, and distribute the special learning materials used in customer outlet courses. These include books, pamphlets, video and audio tapes and cassettes, slides, overlays, and films. These materials are stored in a warehouse and are shipped, as they are ordered, to customer outlets around the country.

It is with this division that Susan Stanton first worked as a manager. She had started her career with the company in a small section of the division that designed various program materials. She had worked her way into management, holding a series of increasingly important positions. She was then asked to take over the management of a part of the division that had the manufacture, storage, and shipment of learning materials as one of its responsibilities.

But there was a catch. She was given this new management position with instructions to solve a persistent, although vaguely defined, problem. "Improve the service," they had told her, and "get control of the warehouse inventory." In this case, "service" meant the process of filling orders sent in by customer outlets for various materials stored in the warehouse. The admonition to improve the service seemed to indicate that service was poor, but all she was told about the situation was that customer outlet personnel complained about the service; she did not know exactly why or what "poor" meant.

In addition, inventory was "out of control." Later she was to discover the extent of the difficulty.

> We had a problem with inventory. The computer would say we had two hundred of some kind of book in stock, yet it was back ordered because there was nothing on the shelf. We were supposed to have the book but physically there was nothing there. I'm going, "Uh, we have a small problem. The computer never lies, like your bank statement, so why don't we have the books?"

If inventory was difficult to manage, so were the warehouse employees. They were described by another manager as "a bunch of knuckle draggers. All they care about is getting their money. They are lazy and don't last long at the job." Strangely, the company did not view the actions of the warehouse workers as a major problem. Only later did Susan Stanton tie in poor morale in the warehouse with the other problems she had been given to solve.

Management by Defense

Although Stanton would take the ethnographic approach to management problems, that was not what many other managers did. They took a defensive stance, a position opposite to the discovery procedures of ethnography. Their major concern—like that of many people in positions of leadership and responsibility—was to protect their authority and their ability to manage and to get things done. Indeed, Stanton also shared this need. But their solution to maintaining their position was different from hers. For them, claiming ignorance and asking questions—the hallmark of the ethnographic approach—is a sign of weakness. Instead of discovering what is going on when they take on a new management assignment, they often impose new work rules and procedures. Employees learn to fear the arrival of new managers because their appearance usually means a host of new, unrealistic demands. They respond by hiding what they actually do, withholding information that would be useful to the manager. Usually, everyone's performance suffers.

Poor performance leads to elaborate excuses as managers attempt to blame the troubles on others. Stanton described this tendency.

> When I came into the new job, this other manager said, "Guess what? You have got a warehouse. You are now the proud owner of a forklift and a bunch of knuckle draggers." And I thought, management's perception of those people is very low. They are treating them as dispensable, that you can't do anything with them. They say the workers don't have any career motives. They don't care if they do a good job. You have to force them to do anything. You can't motivate them. It's only a warehouse, other managers were saying. You can't really do that much about the problems there so why don't you just sort of try to keep it under control.

Other managers diminished the importance of the problem itself. It was not "poor service" that was the trouble. The warehouse was doing the best it could with what it had. It was just that the customers—the staff at the customer outlets—were complainers. As Susan Stanton noted:

> The people providing the service thought that outlet staff were complainers. They said, "Staff complain about everything. But it can't be that way. We have checked it all out and it isn't that bad."

Making excuses and blaming others lead to low morale and a depressed self-image. Problems essentially are pushed aside in favor of a "let's just get by" philosophy.

Ethnographic Management

By contrast, managers take the offensive when they use ethnographic techniques. That is what Stanton did when she assumed her new managerial assignment over the learning materials manufacturing and distribution system. To understand what the ethnographic approach means, however, we must first look briefly at what anthropologists do when they conduct ethnographic field research. Our discussion necessarily involves a look at the concepts of culture and microculture as well as ethnography. For as we will shortly point out, companies have cultures of their own, a point that has recently received national attention; but more important for the problem we are describing here, companies are normally divided into subgroups, each with its own microculture. It is these cultures and microcultures that anthropologically trained managers can study ethnographically, just as fieldworkers might investigate the culture of a

!Kung band living in the Kalahari Desert of West Africa or the Gypsies living in San Francisco.

Ethnography refers to the process of discovering and describing culture, so it is important to discuss this general and often elusive concept. There are numerous definitions of culture, each stressing particular sets of attributes. The definition we employ here is especially appropriate for ethnographic fieldwork. We may define culture as the acquired knowledge that people use to generate behavior and interpret experience. In growing up, one learns a system of cultural knowledge appropriate to the group. For example, an American child learns to chew with a closed mouth because that is the cultural rule. The child's parents interpret open-mouthed chewing as an infraction and tell the child to chew "properly." A person uses such cultural knowledge throughout life to guide actions and to give meaning to surroundings.

Because culture is learned, and because people can easily generate new cultural knowledge as they adapt to other people and things, human behavior and perceptions can vary dramatically from one group to another. In India, for example, children learn to chew "properly" with their mouths open. Their cultural worlds are quite different from the ones found in the United States.

Cultures are associated with groups of people. Traditionally, anthropologists associated culture with relatively distinctive ethnic groups. Culture referred to the whole life-way of a society and particular cultures could be named. Anthropologists talked of German culture, Ibo culture, and Bhil culture. Culture was everything that was distinctive about the group.

Culture is still applied in this manner today, but with the advent of complex societies and a growing interest among anthropologists in understanding them, the culture concept has also been used in a more limited way. Complex societies such as our own are composed of thousands of groups. Members of these groups usually share the national culture, including a language and a huge inventory of knowledge for doing things, but the groups themselves have specific cultures of their own. For example, if you were to walk into the regional office of a stock brokerage firm, you would hear the people there talking an apparently foreign language. You might stand in the "bull pen," listen to brokers make "cold calls," "sell short," "negotiate a waffle," or get ready to go to a "dog and pony show." The fact that events such as this feel strange when you first encounter them is strong evidence to support the notion that you don't yet know the culture that organizes them. We call such specialized groups *microcultures*.

We are surrounded by microcultures, participating in a few, encountering many others. Our family has a microculture. So may our neighborhood, our college, and even our dormitory floor. The waitress who serves us lunch at the corner restaurant shares a culture with her coworkers. So do bank tellers at our local savings and loan. Kin, occupational groups, and recreational associations each tend to display special microcultures. Such cultures can be, and now often are, studied by anthropologists interested in understanding life in complex American society.

The concept of microculture is essential to Susan Stanton as she begins to attack management problems at UTC because she assumes that conflict between different microcultural groups is most likely at the bottom of the difficulty. One microculture she could focus on is UTC company culture. She knows, for example, that there are a variety of rules and expectations—written and unwritten—for how things should be done at the company. She must dress in her "corporates," for example, consisting of a neutral-colored suit, bow tie, stockings, and conservative shoes. UTC also espouses values about the way employees should be treated, how people are supposed to feel about company products, and a variety of other things that set that particular organization apart from other businesses.

But the specific problems that afflicted the departments under Stanton's jurisdiction had little to do with UTC's corporate culture. They seemed rather to be the result of misunderstanding and misconnection between two units, the warehouse and the customer outlets. Each had its own microculture. Each could be investigated to discover any information that might lead to a solution of the problems she had been given.

Such investigation would depend on the extent of Stanton's ethnographic training. As an undergraduate in college, she had learned how to conduct ethnographic interviews, observe behavior, and analyze and interpret data. She was not a professional anthropologist, but she felt she was a good enough ethnographer to discover some relevant aspects of microcultures at UTC.

Ethnography is the process of discovering and describing a culture. For example, an anthropologist who travels to India to conduct a study of village culture will use ethnographic techniques. The anthropologist will move into a community, occupy a house, watch people's daily routines, attend rituals, and spend hours interviewing informants. The goal is to discover a detailed picture of what is going on by seeing village culture through the eyes of informants. The anthropologist wants the insider's perspective. Villagers become teachers, patiently explaining different aspects of their culture, praising the anthropologist for acting correctly and appearing to understand, laughing when the anthropologist makes mistakes or seems confused. When the anthropologist knows what to do and can explain in local terms what is going on or what is likely to happen, real progress has been made. The clearest evidence of such progress is when informants say, "You are almost human now," or "You are beginning to talk just like us."

The greatest enemy of good ethnography is the preconceived notion. Anthropologists do not conduct ethnographic research by telling informants what they are like based on earlier views of them. They teach the anthropologist how to see their world: the anthropologist does not tell them what their world should really be like. All too often in business, a new manager will take over a department and begin to impose changes on its personnel to fit a preconceived perception of them. The fact that the manager's efforts are likely to fail makes sense in light of this ignorance. The manager doesn't know the microculture. Nor have they been asked about it.

But can a corporate manager really do ethnography? After all, managers have positions of authority to maintain, as we noted earlier. It is all right for professional anthropologists to enter the field and act ignorant; they don't have a position to maintain and they don't have to continue to live with their informants. The key to the problem appears to the "grace period." Most managers are given one by their employees when they are new on the job. A new manager cannot be expected to know everything. It is permissible to ask basic questions. The grace period may last only a month or two, but it is usually long enough to find out valuable information.

This is the opportunity that Susan Stanton saw as she assumed direction of the warehouse distribution system. As she described it:

> I could use the first month, actually the first six weeks, to find out what was going on, to act dumb and find out what people actually did and why. I talked to end customers. I talked to salespeople, people who were trying to sell things to help customer outlets with their needs. I talked to

coordinators at headquarters staff who were trying to help all these customer outlets do their jobs and listened to what kinds of complaints they had heard. I talked to the customer outlet people and the guys in the warehouse. I had this six-week grace period where I could go in and say, "I don't know anything about this. If you were in my position, what would you do, or what would make the biggest difference, and why would it make a difference?" You want to find out what the world they are operating in is like. What do they value. And people were excited because I was asking and listening and, by God, intending to do something about it instead of just disappearing again.

As we shall see shortly, Stanton's approach to the problem worked. But it also resulted in an unexpected bonus. Her ethnographic approach symbolized unexpected interest and concern to her employees. That, combined with realistic management, gave her a position of respect and authority. Their feelings for her were expressed by one warehouse worker when he said:

> When she (Susan) was going to be transferred to another job, we gave her a party. We took her to this country-and-western place and we all got to dance with the boss. We told her that she was the first manager who ever tried to understand what it was like to work in the warehouse. We thought she would come in like other managers and make a lot of changes that didn't make sense. But she didn't. She made it work better for us.

Problems and Causes

An immediate benefit of her ethnographic inquiry was a much clearer view of what poor service meant to customer outlet personnel. Stanton discovered that learning materials, such as books and cassettes, took too long to arrive after they were ordered. Worse, material did not arrive in the correct quantities. Sometimes there would be too many items, but more often there were too few, a particularly galling discrepancy since customer outlets were charged for what they ordered, not what they received. Books also arrived in poor condition, their covers ripped or scratched, edges frayed, and ends gouged and dented. This, too, bothered customer outlet staff because they were often visited by potential customers who were not impressed by the poor condition of their supplies. Shortages and scruffy books did nothing to retain regular customers either.

The causes of these problems and the difficulties with warehouse inventory also emerged from ethnographic inquiry. Stanton discovered, for example, that most customer outlets operated in large cities, where often they were housed in tall buildings. Materials shipped to their office address often ended up sitting in ground-level lobbies, because few of the buildings had receiving docks or facilities. Books and other items also arrived in large boxes, weighing up to a hundred pounds. Outlet staff, most of whom were women, had to go down to the lobby, open those boxes that were too heavy for them to carry, and haul armloads of supplies up the elevator to the office. Not only was this time-consuming, but customer outlet staff felt it was beneath their dignity to do such work. They were educated specialists, after all.

The poor condition of the books was also readily explained. By packing items loosely in such large boxes, warehouse workers ensured trouble in transit. Books rattled around with ease, smashing into each other and the side of the box. The result was torn covers and frayed edges. Clearly no one had designed the packing and shipping process with customer outlet staff in mind.

The process, of course, originated in the central warehouse, and here as well, ethnographic data yielded interesting information about the causes of the problem. Stanton learned, for example, how materials were stored in loose stacks on the warehouse shelves. When orders arrived at the warehouse, usually through the mail, they were placed in a pile and filled in turn (although there were times when special preference was given to some customer outlets). A warehouse employee filled an order by first checking it against the stock recorded by the computer, then going to the appropriate shelves and picking the items by hand. Items were packed in the large boxes and addressed to customer outlets. With the order complete, the employee was supposed to enter the number of items picked and shipped in the computer so that inventory would be up to date.

But, Stanton discovered, workers in the warehouse were under pressure to work quickly. They often fell behind because materials the computer said were in stock were not there, and because picking by hand took so long. Their solution to the problem of speed resulted in a procedure that even further confused company records.

> Most of the people in the warehouse didn't try to count well. People were looking at books on the shelves and were going, "Eh, that looks like the right number. You want ten? Gee, that looks like

about ten." Most of the time the numbers they shipped were wrong.

The causes of inaccurate amounts in shipping were thus revealed. Later, Stanton discovered that books also disappeared in customer outlet building lobbies. While staff members carried some of the materials upstairs, people passing by the open boxes helped themselves.

Other problems with inventory also became clear. UTC employees, who sometimes walked through the warehouse, would often pick up interesting materials from the loosely stacked shelves. More important, rushed workers often neglected to update records in the computer.

The Shrink-Wrap Solution

The detailed discovery of the nature and causes of service and inventory problems suggested a relatively painless solution to Stanton. If she had taken a defensive management position and failed to learn the insider's point of view, she might have resorted to more usual remedies that were impractical and unworkable. Worker retraining is a common answer to corporate difficulties, but it is difficult to accomplish and often fails. Pay incentives, punishment, and motivation enhancements such as prizes and quotas are also frequently tried. But they tend not to work because they don't address fundamental causes.

Shrink-wrapping books and other materials did. Shrink-wrapping is a packaging device that emerged a few years ago. Clear plastic sheeting is placed around items to be packaged, then through a rapid heating and cooling process, shrunk into a tight covering. The plastic molds itself like a tight skin around the things it contains, preventing any internal movement or external contamination. Stanton described her decision.

> I decided to have the books shrink-wrapped. For a few cents more, before the books ever arrived in the warehouse, I had them shrink-wrapped in quantities of five and ten. I made it part of the contract with the people who produced the books for us.

On the first day that shrink-wrapped books arrived at the warehouse, Stanton discovered that they were immediately unwrapped by workers who thought a new impediment had been place in their way. But the positive effect of shrink-wrapping soon became apparent. For example, most customer outlets ordered books in units of fives and tens. Warehouse personnel could now easily count out orders in fives and tens, instead of having to count each book or estimate numbers in piles. Suddenly, orders filled at the warehouse contained the correct number of items.

Employees were also able to work more quickly, since they no longer had to count each book. Orders were filled faster, the customer outlet staff was pleased, and warehouse employees no longer felt the pressure of time so intensely. Shrink-wrapped materials also traveled more securely. Books, protected by their plastic covering, arrived in good condition, again delighting the personnel at customer outlets.

Stanton also changed the way materials were shipped, based on what she learned from talking to employees. She limited the maximum size of shipments to twenty-five pounds by using smaller boxes. She also had packages marked "inside delivery" so that deliverymen would carry the materials directly to the customer outlet offices. If they failed to do so, boxes were light enough to carry upstairs. No longer would items be lost in skyscraper lobbies.

Inventory control became more effective. Because they could package and ship materials more quickly, the workers in the warehouse had enough time to enter the size and nature of shipments in the computer. Other UTC employees no longer walked off with books from the warehouse, because the shrink-wrapped bundles were larger and more conspicuous, and because taking five or ten books is more like stealing than "borrowing" one.

Finally, the improved service dramatically changed morale in the division. Customer outlet staff members, with their new and improved service, felt that finally someone had cared about them. They were more positive and they let people at corporate headquarters know about their feelings. "What's happening down there?" they asked. "The guys in the warehouse must be taking vitamins."

Morale soared in the warehouse. For the first time, other people liked the service workers there provided. Turnover decreased as pride in their work rose. They began to care more about the job, working faster with greater care. Managers who had previously given up on the "knuckle draggers" now asked openly about what had got into them.

Stanton believes the ethnographic approach is the key. She has managers who work for her read anthropology, especially books on ethnography, and she insists that they "find out what is going on."

Conclusion

Anthropology is, before all, an academic discipline with a strong emphasis on scholarship and basic research. But, as we have also seen, anthropology is a discipline that contains several intellectual tools—the concept of culture, the ethnographic approach to fieldwork, a cross-cultural perspective, a holistic view of human behavior—that make it useful in a broad range of nonacademic settings. In particular, it is the ability to do qualitative research that makes anthropologists successful in the professional world.

A few years ago an anthropologist consultant was asked by a utility company to answer a puzzling question: Why were its suburban customers, whose questionnaire responses indicated an attempt at conservation, failing to reduce their consumption of natural gas? To answer the question, the anthropologist conducted ethnographic interviews with members of several families, listening as they told how warm they liked their houses and how they set the heat throughout the day. He also received permission to install several video cameras aimed at thermostats in private houses. When the results were in, the answer to the question was deceptively simple: Fathers fill out questionnaires and turn down thermostats; wives, children, and cleaning workers, all of whom, in this case, spent time in the houses when fathers were absent, turn them up. Conservation, the anthropologist concluded, would have to involve family decisions, not just admonitions to save gas. The key to this anthropologist's success, and indeed to the application of cultural anthropology by those acquainted with it, is the ethnographic approach. For it is people with experience in the discipline who have the special background needed to, in the words of Susan Stanton, "find out what is going on."

Questions:

1. Where are the recent PhD.'s in anthropology finding work as compared to past decades?

2. What are some microcultures that the author lists as being a part of our world?

3. What were the problems that Susan Stanton, as the company manager, had to contend with in the warehouse department?

The answer section begins on page 243.

14

It has been estimated that 85% of all people entering the U.S. labor force between 1985 and 2000 are minorities and women. With the work force becoming increasingly more diverse, a major concern of North American business organizations today is how best to manage their diverse employees. In this article applied anthropologist Kanu Kogod describes one approach to managing diversity which assists business organizations to tap into the diverse talents and contributions of all employees. When an anthropological approach is used in diversity training/management it can not only minimize cross cultural misunderstandings, but can help organizations utilize the diverse talents and perspectives that culturally different people bring with them to their workplace.

The Bridges Process: Enhancing Organizational Cultures to Support Diversity

By S. Kanu Kogod

The face of American society in the workplace is rapidly changing in its age mix, gender composition, cultural background, education, and physical challenges. Not only must workers adjust to their work environment, businesses are also learning how to respond to these changes. Previously relied-on human-resources policies and practices, supervisory and management techniques, and interpersonal communications skills are becoming outmoded.

As a result of changing demographic trends and the social, economic, and political forces currently impacting business, now more than ever it is necessary to effectively manage a diverse workforce. I have developed a consulting practice in *managing diversity*. Essentially, our company helps organizations change their organizational cultures to make better use of the talents and contributions of each employee. The concept of organizational culture is essential to managing diversity because diversity is a context issue.

To appropriately manage diversity, the organizational culture must be understood. This includes the systems of values and beliefs that are shaped by life experience, historical tradition, class position, job status, political circumstances, economics and the work setting. When understood in this manner, culture can be investigated, defined, and presented like a map to a new territory. By identifying these forces and the barriers to change, we are able to address them in terms of planned organizational change.

This article describes an organizational development model using anthropological principles to meet these challenges. The article is addressed to anthropologists who are interested in the issue of managing diversity.

My attempt is to answer the questions: What is *managing diversity*? How can anthropologists address diversity by looking at organizational cultures? What is an anthropological approach to managing diversity? For clarity, I will describe a case example describing a process approach.

While our focus is on American businesses in terms of identifying issues and defining problems, it is likely that similar issues confront other high-technology workplaces in the Western world. My purpose is to demonstrate that understanding and managing human behavior in an organization requires both knowledge of organizational culture and application of anthropological principles to change it. Hopefully, the process described and the case example may be helpful to a broader audience.

The Need for Managing Diversity

In 1987, the Hudson Institute released *Workforce 2000*(Hudson Institute 1987), the now-famous study of the workforce of the future, commissioned by the U.S. Department of Labor. In it, they made predictions about the demographic composition of the U.S. population and workforce until the year 2000.

Among the startling findings were the following projections: Of the 25 million people

Reprinted by permission of Ann T. Jordan (ed.), PRACTICING ANTHROPOLOGY IN CORPORATE AMERICA: CONSULTING ON ORGANIZATIONAL CULTURE. Napa Bulletin #14 (published by the National Association for the Practice of Anthropology, a section of the American Anthropological Association.)

who will join the workplace between 1985 and 2000, 85 percent will be minorities and women. White males will account for only 15 percent of the net additions to the labor force; the remainder will be comprised of white females, and immigrants and minorities (of both genders) of various black, Hispanic, and Asian origins. The Hispanic and Asian populations will each grow by 48 percent, the black population will grow by 28 percent, and the white population will grow by only 5.6 percent. In fact, it is projected that sometime in the next century, non-Hispanic whites will no longer retain their majority status in the United States.

This dramatic shift in the demographic makeup of the population and the workforce has enormous implications for American employers, who have traditionally relied on white males to fill the majority of their positions. The growing number of women, older workers, foreign-born workers, and physically challenged employees have a profound impact on an organization's needs, styles, expectations, and social policies.

Employers know that they will be competing for increasingly scarce talent, of whatever gender, age, race, or ethnicity, and that they want to be able to retain those workers once they have brought them on board. High turnover is a costly and bothersome phenomenon. It therefore behooves them to do what they can to make the workplace a tolerable, if not supportive and satisfying, environment in which culturally diverse individuals (along with those of different ages and sexes) can work together effectively, productively, and—one would hope—comfortably. The following statements illustrate the emerging attitude within the business community about why there is a need to manage diversity.

- It will help "transform fear and ignorance of foreigners into comprehension and cooperative skills."
- "If you start now and build a climate in which all groups feel comfortable, you enhance your recruiting possibilities and your ability to attract talent."
- "Countless hazards are created by communication problems, cultural differences in motivational and value systems, diverse codes of conduct, even differences in orientation to fundamentals such as perception of time and space."
- "Competition requires full utilization of all our resources. If we develop only white males, we're not really developing our resources, and that is a complete waste."

Gradually in the early 1990s, the process of valuing diversity is seen less and less as an avenue for fulfilling affirmative action and legal requirements. On the contrary, valuing diversity is a positive, voluntary, pro-business activity, as opposed to belonging to the legal and regulatory environment in which many equal employment opportunity (EEO) and affirmative action (AA) programs exist. There is a *pull* to fulfilling organizational potential rather than a *push* to comply with requirements.

In the past several years, large businesses have become increasingly savvy about interpreting the diversity issue to a broader audience—one that is more interested in the bottom line. Organizations such as Motorola, Hughes Aircraft, and Northern States Power Company (NSPC) tie diversity to overall business aims.

Anthropological Principles at Work

An anthropological definition for managing diversity (adapted from Thomas 1991:26) that we use is that *managing diversity* means "to enhance processes and implement practices that continually move the organizational culture closer to welcoming multiple perspectives by tapping into the talents and contributions of all employees."

Diversity is a context issue. To capitalize on diversity, the organizational culture must be understood, especially the variety of values and assumptions held by dissimilar people in an organization. Once the variety of values are examined, a set of core shared values can be communicated. The core values help define the culture change. Keep in mind that the result we are after is to create a process that continually moves the organizational culture closer to welcoming multiple perspectives and tapping into the talents and contributions of all employees.

Involving diverse employees in decision making is a primary means for welcoming their contributions. This means managers can no longer issue autocratic demands and expect those at lower levels to carry them out without question. Managers are accountable but not by closely held control. Instead, managers need a process by which they can motivate, coach, direct, plan, organize, and lead diverse employees to effectively and efficiently meet their organization's business aims.

Multiple perspectives are encouraged, while still honoring and pursuing the fundamental financial needs of the organization. We must recognize that, in organizations, today's immediate needs may be unimportant tomorrow. Management consultants must be able to facilitate a process approach to changing corporate cultures which will be embraced by those in the organization so that they continue to employ practices that lead them closer to their aims.

As suggested above, there are several layers to addressing diversity, and we must attend to all of them for a long-term change effort to work:

1. Acceptance of one's own identity (and areas of internalized oppression);
2. Ability to be flexible and accommodating to those who are different from oneself in terms of language, culture, and physical appearance;
3. Power and capability to change the current culture and establish an organizational mission that will support diversity goals;
4. Capacity for implementing strategies that involve employees in the culture change process.

Organizations that offer training alone address the first two layers of diversity. The second two layers address the overall organization. These are the areas of culture change that we seek to address.

As anthropologists, we have long recognized that culture is not suddenly created, nor is it easily changed. Culture is the (permeable) boundary that limits infinite possibilities (Joe Duffy, personal communication, November 1992). When working with client organizations, the definition of *culture* that we use is "a shared design for living; based on the values and practices of a *society*, a group of people who interact together over time. People imbibe culture through the early process of socialization in the family, and then this process carries over to the ways people perceive themselves and the world."

We explain the importance of understanding culture in the following manner: Because we learn to perceive our world through our cultural glasses, it becomes essential to get as clear a prescription as possible. When we uncover our shared mental models (Senge 1990: 174-204) along with those that differ from our own, we are in a much better position to *anticipate* and *interpret* events that we experience from a culturally relative point-of-view.

The attitude we promote to clients on the interpersonal level is *cultural relativism*, the attempt to understand another's beliefs and behaviors in terms of that person's culture. While each individual in the organization is different

and each presents a unique perspective, what is shared is the organization. That includes understanding an organizational culture in terms of its values, traditions, rituals, myths, and so forth.

An *organizational culture* is a learned product of group experience shared over time. When appropriate, we use Schein's definition of *organizational culture*:

> a pattern of basic assumptions—invented, discovered, or developed by a given group as it learns to cope with its problems of external adaptation and internal integration—that has worked well enough to be considered valid and therefore, to be taught to new members as the correct way to perceive, think, and feel in relation to those problems. [1991:9]

While it exists within a larger host culture, an organizational culture can, nevertheless, strongly shape one's *worldview*—a simplified model of the world that helps us make sense out of all we see, hear, and do.

In our training workshops, we define *worldview* and *values*: How do we know if our view of the world makes sense? When our worldview is in line with our society's values and our ability to anticipate and interpret events we experience. Values are the standards we use to determine if something is right or wrong, okay to do. Often values are the unexamined assumptions, never fully articulated, that guide our actions. Values vary from organization to organization and, even more so, from culture to culture.

Again, usually these ideas are implicit; they range from seemingly inconsequential rules for anything from when to hand out a business card to who sits with whom at lunch. In particular, power relationships, work habits, and language special to the organization are examined for their impact on managing diversity. Just as these rules provide guidelines for appropriate behavior, they also color our interpretation of the behavior of others. When our clients understand that these "implicit" cultural assumptions either inhibit or promote expressions of diversity, they, too, become fascinated with the dynamics of culture. They want to understand their own organizational culture better.

An anthropological approach to managing diversity emphasizes that each organization must clarify for itself and consolidate values that guide the performance of those who work together. Understanding the dynamics of culture provides a useful framework for interaction no matter to which cultural group others belong.

Studying organizational culture today is especially interesting to practicing anthropologists because it is an open system in constant interaction with many expanding environments and is composed of a multiplicity of groups, with a variety of interests and skills (frequently at cross-purposes), arranged in hierarchies and associated in networks with anywhere-from-weak-to-strong ties.

The ideal result of applying anthropological principles to managing diversity? Ongoing support for creating an organizational culture that develops systems that support the talents and contributions of all employees. When management and employees seek and choose the practices and goals that will enhance characteristics of the work setting, achieving results makes the fruit of success that much sweeter—and that much more viable.

Table 1. The Bridges Process (SM): A 12-Step Approach.

Used by permission of Bridges in Organization, Inc.

1. Analyze current reality and define the issues.
2. Create a clear and widely agreed upon vision of future reality.
3. Identify the stakeholders who must be involved in the planning and implementation process.
4. Distinguish what prevents realization of the vision by comparing the current situation to the ideal situation.
5. Conduct a *Barriers Analysis*, an integration of challenges to the organization's vision. It includes specific constraints in organizational structure, operations, and human resources which are contrary to supporting diversity.
6. Create a whole picture of the people involved, tasks to consider, and systems for implementing change.
7. Assess potential impact on the whole organization if all these strategies are set in motion.
8. Develop an action plan for agreed-upon management strategies and training implementation.
9. Implement management strategies and training.
10. Monitor and refine the training and the new strategies by eliciting perceptions of all those involved.
11. Evaluate the training process by analyzing the pre- and postassessments.
12. Provide feedback on utility and effectiveness of new management strategies in a written report of the findings presented to top management.

The Process We Use

In order to build multicultural bridges at work, a broad framework for identifying behavioral and social processes must be provided—the holistic approach. Both information about a particular ethnic group or factor, and also generalizable guides to meet any and all situations, are used in the culture-sensitive approach to improving performance in the workplace. Teamwork is stressed in communications, goal-setting, meetings, and coordination within the team. Aids and guides such as the feedback review can be used in clarifying the relationship of cultural values to performance objectives.

We have applied the principles of anthropology in a framework for guiding organizational culture change (see Table 1). This 12-step process provides direction for introducing the valuing and managing of diversity in large organizations. Like the approach of other management consultants, it is used to promote the new paradigm of diversity—to value all differences and welcome multiple perspectives.

Currently in corporate America, the most-sought-after remedy for addressing diversity is training managers and implementing awareness workshops for employees. For our clients, we promote focusing on the process that will make training meaningful and carry over to real change in the workplace. The process captures the standard method for developing training:

- analysis
- design
- development
- implementation
- evaluation.

It also goes beyond to provide feedback systems, management strategies, and new resources to support organizational transformation. The uniqueness of this process is the focus on both the organization and individual employees in a two-way exchange that is supported by the system. Many people have opportunities to provide meaningful contributions.

The aim of a process approach is to meet the challenges of cultural diversity and its influences on behavior both internal and external to the organization over time. Merely training to elicit overt behavior—politeness and sensitivity—will not accomplish support for the valuing of diversity on an ongoing basis.

In order to support an organizational culture that will attract and retain service-oriented staff and management, there must be a clear, inspiring, and widely agreed upon "vision." The organizational setting should be characterized as genuinely caring about the professional growth and development of each person.

What we are after is a process approach, one that values the end results but also recognizes that any reformation of policies and practices must be coherent with the actual day-to-day practices. A process approach is based on an anthropological view of organizations. It takes into account the considerable time and thought it takes to introduce this type of change in an organization.

Feedback systems are linked through the manager's active involvement in the change process. (Managers are not just told and then expected to carry out orders; likewise, they are not just judged and then expected to listen to the judgment.) Management effectiveness relies on the skill and attitudes of individual managers, as well as the capacity of the organization to support them. Feedback and rewards for good performance help to shape the desired environment. Good performance for all encourages innovation, self-development, and leadership abilities.

Our process has 12 steps that make it possible to be consistently aware of a particular organizational culture. It emphasizes the problem-solving capability of the system by encouraging a series of steps in introducing the value of diversity. Without placing the vision of diversity into its context, pursuit of valuing diversity can do more harm than good since it raises employee expectations without hope of being sustained.

Case Example: Green & Black, Inc.

The following example illustrate how the process is applied and how anthropological principles help to guide it. While there are many interesting aspects of the project, our discussion will be limited to relevant issues directly pertaining to anthropological principles. A fictitious company name is used; also other minor descriptors are changed to protect the identity of the client.

Green & Black, Inc., is a small business specializing in providing scientific and other professional services to large companies. The company was founded by two white males, with scientific expertise in their related fields.

In the past 12 years, Green & Black grew from a small, collegial team to a total staff of over one hundred employees with several project teams and five principal lines of business. As the company grew, it became increasingly difficult to become more than superficially acquainted with newcomers, particularly outside one's team. The atmosphere of the workplace changed, and it became necessary to manage. The company has been moving from an entrepreneurial operation to one that is professionally managed.

While white males own the company, three women sit on the 12-member executive committee. About 25 percent of the total census is comprised of African Americans, Filipino Americans, and other Asian American groups mostly in scientific areas and administrative support. Ages are concentrated between young employees in their twenties and those between 40 and 50 years old. About half the company is female.

Green & Black, Inc., prides itself on the organization's overall cooperation, but some recent newcomers have had a more difficult time "fitting in." Complaints about subtle discrimination began to surface. Perceptions of "bending over backward to please those who are culturally different" raised concerns about reverse discrimination.

The staff providing direct services was composed of myself, a white female, and two African American management consultants, Rick and Katy. We were initially hired to address the diversity issue by "adopting policies and practices that support the value of diversity in the workplace...to introduce various strategies (particularly training) to support the value of diversity in all levels of the firm—from the owners to senior associates to the professional and administrative staff" (from proposal to Green & Black, September 1990, by Bridges in Organizations, Inc.).

Our approach was explained to the client from the outset and was a selling point as far as they were concerned. At our initial introduction, we emphasized a "valuing differences" approach based on changing the culture to support the people in it. We explained that we do not see diversity as a problem but rather a learning opportunity and that this process would be a "learning process." We went on to say that we have no recipe for success and that we cannot even point to another organization as a role model for having attained all their diversity goals. "Nevertheless," we said, "the process we use will guide you to realizing the vision you set for yourselves."

As emphasized above, the client follows the steps in The Bridges Process (SM). While step one (current reality), step five (barrier analysis), step seven (impact), and step twelve (findings and written report), are the primary responsibilities of the consultants, the client has the option of proceeding independently. At any time during the process, other sessions are scheduled upon request. Telephone support is available throughout the duration of the project.

At the initial meeting, we addressed a diversity committee and explained our process to them. In the session, we went over each step in our guideline including the major outputs: developing management strategies and training to support diversity. We explained that the process involves people from all levels in the organization. Nonetheless, for change to be both positive and acceptable, the process must begin at the top. The list below describes our initial deliverable services and projects that support various steps in The Bridges Process (SM). The list outlines the primary responsibilities of Bridges in Organizations, Inc.

- Provide *executive briefing* sessions to provide information and guidelines to top management, which allows the leadership to clarify their current reality, future goals, and the disparity between the two.
- Conduct five days of *ethnographic inquiry*: structured interviews, focus groups, collection of critical incidents, and content analysis of past complaints. The purpose of the *ethnographic inquiry* is to collect data about perceptions, complaints, values, and implicit influences affecting the organization. This data is used in the *barriers analysis*. Management strategies and training objectives are all influenced by the results of the data-analysis phase.
- Complete a systematic *barriers analysis*, in order to create a succinct listing of specific internal and external influences that inhibit support for diversity in the workplace. When critically examining problems, it is often easy to jump to solutions. The analysis helps to determine how the issues are connected and the impact of change before introducing the change.
- Offer individual management assessments of the leadership using the *Hartman Value Profile*. The profile identifies specific strengths and weaknesses of an individual; interpretive feedback targets areas

considered important to success in a given organization.

Unlike any other assessment instrument, the Hartman Value Profile (HVP) describes the way a person thinks. It is based on the research of Robert S. Hartman, the founder of modern axiology, the science of values. Hartman constructed a method for measuring value concepts which allows us to relate potential biases, values, and the clarity of one's perceptions of themselves and the world around them. Essentially, the HVP describes mental models.

- Present findings of *barriers analysis* and *big picture* (where we are so far) to top management in a management retreat. Establish *benchmarks*, outputs that demonstrate the organization's movement closer to realization of the vision.
- Continue to guide the process as deemed necessary by project staff. The project coordinator plays multiple roles according to the task. The roles are:
  - objective observer
  - fact finder
  - process counselor
  - joint problem solver
  - culture broker
  - trainer
  - informational expert

One of the roles of the consultant is to act as a joint problem solver. By offering alternatives and participating in decisions related to action plans, we ensure success of the project. However, the level of consultant activity in this role is determined by the client.

- Conduct three one-day training sessions, "Cultural Encounters in the Workplace," for all staff. Elicit *action plans* from each participant. These plans allow participants to commit to one action that they can personally accomplish according to their interest and level in the organization.
- Prepare a *participant's manual* to guide the training sessions. The manual includes worksheets for supporting the workshop activities, readings for understanding diversity, and resources for gaining more information.
- Assess potential impact on the whole organization if all the strategies proposed by management and in training sessions are set in motion. Include *potential impact of changes* in final report. Action plans that were

developed by the project staff and in the management retreat are combined with the action plans submitted by participants in the training. Once again, if all the suggested actions were implemented, what would be the *impact* on the organization? Specific strategies are endorsed.

- Present a written report to top management on effectiveness of new management strategies.

Once the project was underway, it became apparent that people, especially top managers, were confused about the focus of the project and the definition of diversity. Did this mean the company wanted to adopt new AA/EEO promotion and recruitment policies? Did it mean prejudice-reduction training? Was the aim to provide touchy-feely training so everyone got along better?

The project was renamed the Corporate Culture Management Project (CCMP—the company loves acronyms) so that the emphasis would remain on the culture itself and the activities we proposed would make sense to the organization.

We began the project with several sessions of the company's executive committee. The outcome was the development of the following vision to inspire the desired goals for Green & Black:

Green & Black is a business committed to quality where everyone is motivated to serve our customers. People from different backgrounds with different personal values are appreciated and rewarded for contributing to the company's success. We work together in an environment of creativity, openness, trust and respect.

To describe *current reality*, we conducted an ethnographic study: structured management interviews, focus groups, analysis of critical incidents, and observation. In general, the *barriers analysis* is developed from the findings of the current-reality description, in comparison with themes derived for the vision. The barriers analysis represents an integration of challenges to supporting diversity at Green & Black. The *barriers* are gleaned from the management's findings, the focus group's findings, and the consultant's observations. In this case, the barriers were then categorized according to the four related themes derived from the vision statement:

- Quality, motivation, and service;
- Diversity, rewards, and recognition;
- Teambuilding;
- Climate setting, work environment, and corporate climate.

Here is a sample of barriers related to the theme of "quality, motivation, and service."

- Not enabling others to act on their own stifles innovation and creativity; both staff and managers need to be both held accountable for their own mistakes and also recognized for their extraordinary efforts. People have expressed intense desire for credit for their work and acknowledgment for their contribution to the organization.
- While many people enjoy working with their colleagues on specific projects, people (in general) do not express a strong sense of loyalty or stake in the success of the whole company.

Here is a sample of barriers related to the theme of "diversity, rewards, and recognition":

- Diversity is of interest to many, but they are not sure what it means to them and to Green & Black. Of greater concern are those who deny differences, with statements like "Everyone is the same to me but some I like more than others," or "I don't care what somebody is. I treat everyone the same." These statements reflect a lack of exposure to diversity and greater comfort with people who are similar to oneself.
- Several well-meaning people express like and respect for individuals who are different, but they seem to be surprised by competence. Others feel diversity means that quality standards will be compromised. These perceptions are a detriment to valuing diversity.
- There is lack of awareness of gender issues. "Lack of fit" at Green & Black is often due to an inability to adapt to a predominantly male style of speech. Male styles tend to be direct; listening is neutral, and small talk includes banter and one-liners. Women tend to listen with affirmation and to seek connections. Women who get ahead at Green & Black adopt male listening and speech styles. The men who are better liked (including one well-noted leader) are more responsive to female styles of speech.

The barriers analysis also included *positive findings supportive of diversity*. Below are several examples:

- Green & Black is profitable.
- People at all levels are aware of the opportunities for growth and economic success.
- Green & Black's image and reputation in the community and with clients is positive.
- The level of talent, technical skill, and expertise amassed at Green & Black is top-notch.

It was these activities—data collection, analysis of current reality, and presentation of the findings—that utilize the special talents of the anthropologist studying organizational cultures. These are the areas of special contributions to our clients. But anthropology also helps us to conduct ourselves as management consultants.

Anthropologist as Management Consultant

While I have had a great deal of experience working with organizations, this project contained new elements that were of great challenge to me. For one, most of my other work had been with government, social-service, and nonprofit agencies. Other projects for larger corporate organizations were clearly defined up front. This was one of the first projects that allowed me to be an "anthropologist." The principles described above helped me to determine how to make decisions about the project—especially in terms of its challenges.

One of the first obstacles I hit as project coordinator was timing. The start of the project was delayed for two months due to travel schedules and other business priorities. By insisting on commitment up front, we had to assure that all 12 executive-committee members would attend the executive briefings. Scheduling activities and rescheduling activities continued to be a timing problem through the project, and so the project schedule was continually being modified.

The *principle of timing* states that planning for change must follow the rhythmic pattern of the group. Thus, it was up to me to be flexible and accommodating. While that sounds good, in reality its difficult to practice when *time* is basically what management consultants are selling. To resolve the issue early on, we came to an agreement that any rescheduling of appointments or activities needed to take place 48 hours before an event; otherwise the time would be billed.

Next came my struggle with defining the identity of my client. Was my client the managing partner (Tom)? the owners? the executive committee? or the organization as a whole? Having sworn fealty years ago to the "powerless" in a group, my struggle was intensified by the fact that, without Tom's authority, there would be no project at all. On the other hand, I felt that I could be a spokesperson and perhaps an advocate for changes that many people expressed to me as needed. Many of these changes in policy fell well beyond the scope of the project, but my first inclination was to help on all counts.

The client-identity question almost stymied the whole project after several head bashings with Tom over the scope of the project. In plain jargon, this was his baby, and he wanted to call the shots. He wanted to keep it limited to the objectives originally described; I wanted to add on other activities that would enhance the overall success of the project. The essence of the struggle is reflected in a memo (an oxymoron, since it turned out to be 12 pages long) that I sent to the two owners. The following is an excerpt from this memo:

MEMORANDUM

Subject: Corporate Culture Management Project

The activities and events shared so far in this project have maintained high quality standards and warm interpersonal communications—the values that are so important to Green & Black and Bridges. This has made the project exceptionally rewarding for Rick, Katy, and me....

In order to achieve success with the project and support you in meeting your management challenges, we would like to meet with you to explore the interrelationship between the project and your current management needs. You can, if you choose, do this as part and parcel of the CCM Project and The Bridges Process.

To be more specific, Rick, Katy, and I recognize the relationship between the mission of the Corporate Culture Management Project and the challenges you now face as you redefine the management culture of your firm. Certain themes and assumptions (most of which you are aware) continue to be issues in the firm, and these themes are cross-purposes for the results we hope to achieve. Although we continue to reaffirm your ownership of the process and we don't intend to resolve all the issues at this time, we are aware [that] in order to achieve success in the project, we must identify the assumptions and plan for change....[*Themes and assumptions were listed.*]

INPUTS

Factors working in our favor are:
- Strategic planning—as the need for employee satisfaction has become a goal, so [has] the understanding that satisfied employees help us achieve our business objectives.
- The possibility that managing diversity will promote the ability to compete in the international market as well as teach consultants to value marketing and sales in the 1990s.
- The recognized need to support the move from being an entrepreneurial organization to being an organization of professional managers.

Factors working against our favor are:
- The narrow focus of the CCM Project as currently defined. A single-focus program that primarily targets interpersonal relations without getting at real business objectives will have a transitory effect on the overall organization.
- The lack of role clarity and expectations between the consultants and the Green & Black client. Is our client Green & Black, and within that is our client the chief operating officer, the owners, or the 12 top managers?

To collaborate means to discuss how the stages of consultation will be carried out, on all aspects of the problem.

Areas of collaboration include: planning how to inform the organization of the project, interpreting the results of the diagnosis, deciding how to make a change.

Our assumption is that our specialized knowledge, along with management's understanding of the organization, allows for joint problem solving. Joint attention is given to technical information and human interactions. Communication is two-way. Implementation responsibilities are determined by discussion and agreement.

The question of client identity was finally answered—Tom, the managing partner, was my client. As a result of the memo, our various roles were clarified. Thus, I came to clearly respect Tom's control and the *principle of authority* and how power affects incorporation of change into the system. Again, without his sanction, there would be no project. On the other hand, as a result of my clarity in the memo about our roles, Tom finally accepted me as a collaborator.

Furthermore, the memo proved to be of great benefit in other ways. It went on to state various suggestions for enhancing the project. Tom and the other top managers who read it were very impressed with the depth of perception and knowledge of the company's real issues. Some felt it was a marketing piece; others felt that it communicated issues too close to home and should be stashed away.

The primary outcome was much greater trust, commitment, and understanding between Green & Black and Bridges. The *principle of feedback* states that the system is continuously recharged by feedback on what the system has done.

Another early challenge was Hartman Value Profile. The assessment piece brought up skepticism and vulnerability for the executive-committee leadership: how could this task give them any meaningful information and what was the purpose of looking at their management potential? The resistance was expressed by not returning the forms on time, not properly competing them and so on.

In spite of this resistance, I kept on selling the assessment to the recipients. Finally, each person had an individual feedback session. Insight gained by such a tool incorporates the *principle of worldview*. To successfully incorporate a new element in an organizational culture, it is necessary that it also became a part of the worldview. By showing them that I had an understanding of their *mental models*, I was able to have an influence on their actions.

When the group composite HVP was presented, we had our first success at team building. People began to really understand what we meant by "welcoming multiple perspectives." The *principle of initial success* was applied to an almost easily achieved goal. This initial success in terms of the overall project, however, was very important in paving the way to commitment for future events in the project.

Conclusion

All things considered, being an anthropologist in corporate America is not easy (Zemke 1989). We have a strong, early affiliation with our academic peers, and we have our own mental models of the ecstasy of studying native cultures in long, extended fieldwork settings. Consequently, we have to shift our awareness in the way we view our contributions, and we have to perform a major transfer of skills to all kinds of settings—some of which we may have strong biases about. For me, meeting this challenge has been both personally and professionally rewarding.

Currently in corporate America, diversity is at the forefront of organizational issues. Many larger organizations are going beyond awareness training to hiring in-house "diversity" professionals. While many have strong management skills and familiarity with the issues of diversity, few of these professionals have a cohesive plan for facilitating organizational-culture change that ties into their strategic plan and/or other organizational initiative such as total quality management (TQM). Both diversity and quality initiatives advocate organizational-culture change to be successful. In-house diversity professionals need guidance (especially from anthropologists) to link these as organizational development processes.

We, as anthropologists, are able to apply our holistic, analytical techniques to describing the themes and compelling forces that support or diminish the welcoming of multiple perspectives. This can be a great boon to corporate leaders who are truly willing to embrace the changes bringing us closer to the 21st century.

References Cited

Hudson Institute
1987 Workforce 2000: Work and Workers for the Twenty-first Century. Indianapolis: Hudson Institute.

Schein, Edgar
1991 Organizational Culture and Leadership. San Francisco: Jossey-Bass.

Senge, Peter M.
1990 The Fifth Discipline: The Art and Practice of Learning Organization. New York: Doubleday.

Thomas, Roosevelt
1991 Beyond Race and Gender. New York: AMACOM.

Zemke, Ron
1989 Anthropologists in the Corporate Jungle. Training 26(4): 48-54.

Questions:

1. What is the purpose of the author's "managing diversity" consulting practice?

2. Demographically, in what ways will the work force change in the near future?

3. Currently what is corporate America doing to address the question of diversity?

4. What were two of the obstacles the author, as an anthropologist, faced as management consultant to Green & Black, Inc?

The answer section begins on page 243.

15

As we move toward the 21st century, the distinction between international and domestic business has almost disappeared. Ford automobiles are manufactured by German workers in Europe while BMWs are made by South Carolinians. We see many examples all over the world of corporate cultures bumping up against national cultures, where managers from one country are supervising workers from another. Often times in such situations misunderstandings occur, hostilities are generated, motivations are reduced, and organizational efficiencies are sacrificed. While not an anthropologist, author Robert Friday is from the allied discipline of intercultural communications. In this selection Friday discusses differences in communication behavior between German and North American managers and how these differences can lead to cross cultural misunderstandings in a business setting. He ends with some practical recommendations for addressing the potential problems of cross cultural misunderstandings between German and North American managers.

Contrasts in Discussion Behaviors of German and American Managers

By Robert A. Friday

AMERICAN MANAGERS' EXPECTATIONS

Business Is Impersonal

In any business environment, discussion between colleagues must accomplish the vital function of exchanging information that is needed for the solution of problems. In American business, such discussions are usually impersonal.[1] Traditionally the facts have spoken for themselves in America. "When facts are disputed, the argument must be suspended until the facts are settled. Not until then may it be resumed, for all true argument is about the meaning of established or admitted facts" (Weaver, 1953) in the rationalistic view. Much of post-WWII American business decision making has been based on the quantitative MBA approach which focuses on factual data and its relationship to the ultimate fact of profit or loss, writing strategy plans, and top-down direction. After all of the facts are in, the CEO is often responsible for making the intuitive leap and providing leadership. The power and authority of the CEO has prevailed in the past 40 years, with no predicted change in view (Bleicher & Paul, 1986, p. 10-11). Through competition and contact with West Germany and Japan, the more personal approach is beginning to enter some lower level decision-making practices (Peters & Waterman, 1982, pp. 35-118).

Another reason for the impersonal nature of American business is that many American managers do not identify themselves with their corporations. When the goals and interests of the corporation match up with those of the American manager, he or she will stay and prosper. However, when the personal agenda of the American manager is not compatible with that of the corporation, he or she is likely to move on to attain his or her objective in a more conducive environment. Most American managers can disassociate themselves from their business identity, at least to the extent that their personal investment in a decision has more to do with their share of the profit rather than their sense of personal worth.

In contrast, "the German salesman's personal credibility is on the line when he sells his product. He spends years cultivating his clients, building long-term relationships based on reliability" (Hall, 1983, p. 67). This tendency on the part of Germans is much like American businesses in the early part of this century.

The cohesiveness of the employees of most German businesses is evidenced in the narrow salary spread. Whereas in the United States the ratio of lowest paid to highest paid is

Reprinted by permission of INTERNATIONAL JOURNAL OF INTERCULTURAL RELATIONS. VOL. 13, 1989, PP. 429-446.

approximately 1 to 80, in Germany this ratio is 1 to 25 (Hall, 1983, p. 74).

GERMAN MANAGERS' EXPECTATION

Business Is Not as Impersonal

The corporation for most Germans is closely related to his or her own identity. German managers at Mobay are likely to refer to "Papa Bayer" because they perceive themselves as members of a corporate family which meets most of their needs. In turn, most German managers there, as elsewhere, have made a lifelong commitment to the larger group in both a social and economic sense (Friday & Biro, 1986-87). In contrast to American post-WWII trends is "the German postwar tradition of seeking consensus among a closely knit group of colleagues who have worked together for decades (which) provides a collegial harmony among top managers that is rare in U.S. corporations" (Bleicher & Paul, 1986, p. 12). Our interviews suggested that many German managers may enter a three-year-plus training program with the idea of moving on later to another corporation. This move rarely occurs.

While a three-year training program appears to be excessively long by American standards, one must understand that the longer training program works on several levels that are logical within the German culture. The three or more years of entry level training is a predictable correlation to the German and USA relative values on the Uncertainty Avoidance index[2] (Hofstede, 1984, p. 122). The longer training period is required to induct the German manager into the more formal decision-making rules, plans, operating procedures, and industry tradition (Cyert & March 1963, p. 119), all of which focus on the short-run known entities (engineering/reliability of product) rather than the long-run unknown problems (future market demand).

On another level the "strong sense of self as a striving, controlling entity is offset by an equally strong sense of obligation to a *code* of decency" (McClelland, Sturr, Knap, & Wendt, 1958, p. 252). Induction into a German company with an idealistic system of obligation requires a longer training period than induction into an American company in which the corporate strategy for productivity is acquired in small group and interpersonal interaction.[3] The German manager who moves from one corporation to another for the purpose of advancement is regarded with suspicion partly because of his lack of participation in the corporate tradition, which could prove to be an unstabilizing factor.

Our preliminary interview results suggested uncertainty avoidance (Hofsted, 1984, p. 130) in everyday business relationships, especially the German concern for security. For example, most of the transfer preparation from the German home office to the USA consists of highly detailed explanations of an extensive benefits package. Since the German manager sees a direct relationship between his or her personal security and the prosperity of his or her company, business becomes more personal for him or her. Similarly, Americans who work in employee-owned companies are also seeing a clear relationship between personal security and the prosperity of their company.

AMERICAN MANAGERS' EXPECTATION

Need to be Liked

The American's need to be liked is a primary aspect of his or her motivation to cooperate or not to cooperate with colleagues. The arousal of this motivation occurs naturally in discussion situations when direct feedback gives the American the desired response which indicates a sense of belongingness or acceptance. The American "envisions the desired responses and is likely to gear his actions accordingly. The characteristic of seeing others as responses is reflected in the emphasis on communication in interaction and in the great value placed on being liked.... American's esteem of others is based on their liking him. This requirement makes it difficult for Americans to implement projects which require an 'unpopular' phase" (Stewart, 1972, p. 58).

For Americans, the almost immediate and informal use of a colleague's first name is a recognition that each likes the other. While such informality is common among American business personnel, this custom should probably be avoided with Germans. "It takes a long time to get on a first-name basis with a German; if you rush the process, you may be perceived as overly familiar and rude....Germans are very conscious of their status and insist on proper forms of address. Germans are bewildered by the American custom of addressing a new acquaintance by his first name and are even more startled by our custom of addressing a superior by first name" (Hall, 1983, p. 57-58). When such matters of decorum are overlooked during critical discussions, an "unpopular phase" may develop.

The need to be liked is culturally induced at an early age and continues throughout life though regular participation in group activities.

> They (Americans) are not brought up on sentiments of obligation to others as the Germans are, but from kindergarten on they regularly participate in many more extracurricular functions of a group nature. In fact, by far the most impressive result in Table 3 is the low number of group activities listed by the Germans (about 1, on the average) as compared with the Americans (about 5, on the average). In these activities the American student must learn a good deal more about getting along with other people and doing things cooperatively, if these clubs are to function at all (McClelland, et al., 1958, p. 250).

This cultural orientation in relation to group participation will be revisited later in the closing discussion on "learning styles, training, instruction, and problem solving."

GERMAN MANAGERS' EXPECTATION

Need to be Credible

The German counterpart to the American need to be liked is the need to establish one's credibility and position in the hierarchy. The contrast between American informality and mobility and German formality and class structure are a reflection of the difference between these two needs. In the absence of a long historical tradition, Americans have developed a society in which friendships and residence change often, family histories (reputations) are unknown, and therefore, acceptance of what one is doing in the present and plans to do in the future is a great part of one's identity. In order to maintain this mobility of place and relationships, Americans rely on reducing barriers to acceptance through informality.

Germans, with their strong sense of history, tradition, family, and life-long friendships, tend to move less often, make friendships slowly, and keep them longer than Americans. Because one's family may be known for generations in Germany, the family reputation becomes part of one's own identity, which in turn places the individual in a stable social position.[4]

The stability of the social class structure and, thus, the credibility of the upper class in Germany is largely maintained through the elitist system of higher education.

> Educational achievement has been a major factor in determining occupational attainment and socioeconomic status in the post-World War II

era. University education has been virtually essential in gaining access to the most prestigious and remunerative positions. Some of the most enduring social divisions have focused on level of education (Nyrop, 1982, p. 113).

A German's education most often places him or her at a certain level which, in turn, determines what they can and can't do. In Germany, one must present credentials as evidence of one's qualification to perform any task (K. Hagemann, personal communication, May-September, 1987). Thus, the German societal arrangement guarantees stability and order by adherence to known barriers (credentials) that confirm one's credibility. In Germany, loss of credibility would be known in the manager's corporate and social group and would probably result in truncated advancement (not dismissal since security is a high value).

The rigid social barriers established by education and credentials stand in direct contrast to the concepts of social mobility in American society. "Our social orientation is toward the importance of the individual and the equality of all individuals. Friendly, informal, outgoing, and extroverted, the American scorns rank and authority, even when he/she is the one with the rank. American bosses are the only bosses in the world who insist on being called by their first names by their subordinates" (Kohls, 1987, p. 8). When Germans and Americans come together in discussion, the German's drive is to establish hierarchy, the American's is to dissolve it.

AMERICAN MANAGERS' EXPECTATIONS

Assertiveness, Direct Confrontation, and Fair Play

In comparing Americans with Japanese, Edward Stewart relates the American idea of confrontation as "putting the cards on the table and getting the information 'straight from the horses mouth.' It is also desirable to face people directly, to confront them intentionally" (Stewart, 1972, p. 52). This is done so that the decision makers can have all of the facts. Stewart contrasts this intentional confrontation of Americans to the indirection of the Japanese, which often requires the inclusion of an intermediary or emissary in order to avoid face to face confrontation and, thus, the loss of face. However, this view may leave the American manager unprepared for what he or she is likely to find in his or her initial discussion with a German manager.

The American manager is likely to approach his or her first discussion with German managers in an assertive fashion from the assumption that competition in business occurs within the context of cooperation (Stewart, 1972, p. 56). This balance is attained by invoking the unspoken rule of fair play.

> Our games tradition, although altered and transformed, are Anglo-Saxon in form; and fair play does mean for us, as for the English, a standard of behavior between weak and the strong—a standard which is curiously incomprehensible to the Germans. During the last war, articles used to appear in German papers exploring this curious Anglo-Saxon notion called "fair play," reproduced without translation—for there was no translation.

> Now the element which is so difficult to translate in the idea of "fair play" is not the fact that there are rules. Rules are an integral part of German life, rules for behavior of inferior to superior, for persons of every status, for every formal situation.... The point that was incomprehensible was the inclusion of the other person's weakness inside the rules so that "fair play" included in it a statement of relative strength of the opponents and it ceased to be fair to beat a weak opponent.

> ...Our notion of fair play, like theirs [British], includes the opponent, but it includes him far more personally...(Mead, M., 1975, p. 143-145).

I am not implying that the American is in need of a handicap when negotiating with Germans. It is important to note however, that the styles of assertiveness under the assumption of American equality (fair play) and assertiveness under the assumption of German hierarchy may be very different. The general approach of the German toward the weaker opponent may tend to inspire a negative reaction in the American, thus reducing cooperation and motivation.

GERMAN MANAGERS' EXPECTATIONS

Assertiveness, Sophistication, and Direct Confrontation

The current wisdom either leaves the impression or forthrightly states that Americans and Germans share certain verbal behaviors which would cause one to predict that discussion is approached in a mutually understood fashion.

> If North Americans discover that someone spoke dubiously or evasively with respect to important matters, they are inclined to regard the person thereafter as unreliable, if not dishonest. Most of the European low-context cultures such as the French, the Germans, and the English show a similar cultural tradition. These cultures give a high degree of social approval to individuals whose verbal behaviors in expressing ideas and feelings are precise, explicit, straightforward, and direct (Gudykunst, & Kim, 1984, p. 144).

Such generalizations do not take into account the difference between *Gespräch* (just talking about—casually) and *Besprechung* (discussion in the more formal sense of having a discussion about an issue). *Besprechung* in German culture is a common form of social intercourse in which one has high level discussions about books, political issues, and other weighty topics. This reflects the traditional German values which revere education. Americans would best translate *Besprechung* as a high level, well evidenced, philosophically and logically rigorous debate in which one's credibility is clearly at stake—an activity less familiar to most Americans.

The typical language of most Americans is not the language many Germans use in a high level debate on philosophical and political issues.

> In areas where English Immigrants brought with them the speech of 16th and 17th century England, we find a language more archaic in syntax and usage than [sic] present-day English. Cut off from the main stream, these pockets of English have survived. But the American language, as written in the newspapers, as spoken over the radio (and television),...is instead the language of those who learned it late in life and learned it publicly, in large schools, in the factory, in the ditches, at the polling booth....It is a language of public, external relationships. While the American-born generation was learning this public language, the private talk which expressed the overtones of personal relationships was still cast in a foreign tongue. When they in turn taught their children to speak only American, they taught them a one-dimensional public language, a language oriented to the description of external aspects of behavior, weak in overtones. To recognize this difference one has only to compare the vocabulary with which Hemingway's heroes and heroines attempt to discuss their deepest emotions with the analogous vocabulary of an English novel. All the shades of passion, laughter close to tear, joy tremulous on the edge of revelation, have to be summed up in such phrases as: 'They had a fine time.' Richness in American writing comes from the invocation of objects which themselves have overtones rather than from the use of words which carry with them a linguistic aura. This tendency to a flat dimension of speech has not

been reduced by the maintenance of a classical tradition (Mead, 1975, pp. 81-82).

Since many Americans tend not to discuss subjects such as world politics, philosophical and ethical issues with a large degree of academic sophistication, a cultural barrier may be present even if the Germans speak American style English. In a study of a German student exchange program, Hagemann observed that "it was crucial for the Germans, that they could discuss world-politics with their American counterparts, found them interested in environmental protection and disarmament issues and that they could talk with them about private matters of personal importance.... If they met Americans who did not meet these demands the relationships remained on the surface" (Hagemann, 1986, p. 8).

This tendency not to enter into sophisticated discussions and develop deeper relationships may be a disadvantage for many Americans who are working with Germans (see Figure 1). In addition, in a society in which one's intellectual credibility [5] establishes one's position in the group and thus determines what one can and can't do, *Besprechung* can become quite heated—as is the case in Germany.

FOCUS: WHEN BESPRECHUNG AND DISCUSSION MEET

The management style of German and American managers within the same multinational corporation is more likely to be influenced by their nationality than by the corporate culture. In a study of carefully matched national groups of managers working in the affiliated companies of a large U.S. multinational firm, "cultural differences in management assumptions were not reduced as a result of working for the same multinational firm. If anything, there was slightly more divergence between the national groups within this multinational company than originally found in the INSEAD multi-national study" (Laurent, 1986, p. 95).

On the surface we can see two culturally distinct agendas coming together when German and American managers "discuss" matters of importance. The American character with its need to remain impersonal and to be liked avoids argumentum ad hominem. Any attack on the person will indicate disrespect and promote a feeling of dislike for the other, thus promoting the "unpopular phase," which, as Stewart indicates, may destroy cooperation for Americans.

American	focus	German
Impersonal—act as own agent—will move on when business does not serve his/her needs or when better opportunity arises	Relationship to Business	Not as impersonal—corporation is more cohesive unit—identity more closely associated with position, and security needs met by corporation
Need to be liked—expressed through informal address and gestures	Personal Need	Need for order and establishment of place in hierarchy—expressed through formal address and gestures
Short-term—largely informal—many procedures picked up in progress	Orientation to Corporation	Long-term training—formal—specific rules of procedure learned
Based on accomplishment and image—underlying drive toward equality	Status	Based on education and credentials—underlying drive toward hierarchy
Assertive, tempered with fair play—give benefit of doubt or handicap	Confrontation	Assertive—put other in his/her place
Discussion about sports, weather, occupation: what you do, what you feel about someone. Logical, historical analysis rarely ventured. Native language sophistication usually low.	Common Social Intercourse	Besprechung—rigorous logical examination of the history and elements of an issue. Politics favorite topic. Forceful debate expected. Native language sophistication high.

FIGURE 1
Development of Discussion Behavior At a Glance

In contrast, the German manager, with his personal investment in his position and a need to be credible to maintain his or her position, may strike with vigor and enthusiasm at the other's error. The American manager with his lack of practice in German-style debate and often less formal language, education, and training, may quickly be outmaneuvered, cornered, embarrassed, and frustrated. In short, he or she may feel attacked. This possible reaction may be ultimately important because it can be a guiding force for an American.

Beyond the question of character is the more fundamental question of the guidance system of the individual within his or her culture and what effect changing cultural milieu has on the individual guidance system. I define guidance system as that which guides the individual's actions. In discussing some of the expectations of German and American managers, I allude several times to what could be construed as peer pressure within small groups. How this pressure works to guide the individual's actions, I will argue in the next section, has great implication for developing programs for American success in Germany.

Viewed as systems of argumentation, discussion and *Besprechung* both begin a social phase even though Americans may at first view the forcefulness of the Germans as anti-social (Copeland and Griggs, 1985, p. 105). However, a dissimilarity lends an insight into the difference in the guidance systems and how Germans and Americans perceive each other.

American discussion, with the focus on arriving at consensus, is based on the acceptance of value relativism (which supports the American value of equality and striving for consensus). The guidance system for Americans is partly in the peer group pressure which the individual reacts to but may not be able to predict or define in advance of a situation. Therefore, some Americans have difficulty articulating, consciously conceiving, or debating concepts in their guidance system but rather prefer to consider feedback and adjust their position to accommodate the building of consensus without compromising their personal integrity.

German *Besprechung*, with the focus on arriving at truth or purer concepts, rejects value relativism in support of German values of fixed hierarchy and social order. The German *Besprechung* is argumentation based on the assumption that there is some logically and philosophically attainable truth. The guidance system for Germans is composed of concepts which are consciously taken on by the individual over years of formal learning (a la Hal) and debate. While a German makes the concepts his/her own through *Besprechung*, his/her position is not likely to shift far from a larger group pressure to conform to one hierarchical code.

The peer pressure of the immediate group can often become a driving force for Americans. The irony is that many Germans initially perceive Americans as conformists and themselves as individualist, stating that Americans can't act alone while Germans with their clearly articulated concepts do act alone. Americans, on the other hand, often initially perceive Germans as conformists and themselves as individualists stating that Germans conform to one larger set of rules while Americans do their own thing.

LEARNING STYLES, TRAINING, INSTRUCTION, AND PROBLEM SOLVING

Education and Training

The ultimate function of group process in American corporations is problem solving and individual motivation (being liked). For Germans motivation is more of a long term consideration such as an annual bonus or career advancement. Problem solving for Germans is more compartmentalized and individualized.

The contrasting elements discussed earlier and outlined in both "At a Glance" summaries (Figure 1 and 2) indicate that considerable cultural distance may have to be traveled by Germans and Americans before they can be assured that cooperation and motivation are the by-products of their combined efforts. The contrasting elements are, of course, a result of the organization and education—the acculturation—of the minds of Germans and Americans. In this section I will examine the different cultural tendencies from the perspective of Hall's definitions of formal and informal culture and discuss some implications for intercultural training and education.

The first level of concern is general preparation for the managerial position. As an educator I must take a hard look at the graduates of our colleges and universities as they compare to their German counterparts. I am not attempting to imply that Germans are better than Americans. All cultural groups excel in some area more than other cultural groups.

American	focus	German
Peer pressure of immediate group—reluctant to go beyond the bounds of fair play in interaction—backdrop is social relativism	Guidance system	Peer pressure from generalized or large social group—forceful drive to conform to the standard—backdrop is consistent and clearly known
Generally weaker higher education—weak historical perspective and integrated thought-focus is on the future results—get educational requirements out of the way to get to major to get to career success	Education	Higher education standards generally superior, speak several languages, strong in history, philosophy, politics, literature, music, geography, and art
More group oriented—social phase develops into team spirit—individual strengths are pulled together to act as one	Problem Solving	More individualized and compartmentalized—rely on credentialed and trained professional
Informal awareness—get the hang of variations—often unconscious until pointed out	Learning	Formal awareness—specific instruction given to direct behavior—one known way to act—highly conscious

FIGURE 2
Manager Background At a Glance

Germans are better trained and better educated than Americans. A German university degree means more than its U.S. equivalent because German educational standards are higher and a smaller percentage of the population wins college entrance. Their undergraduate degree is said to be on par with our master's degree. It is taken for granted that men and women who work in business offices are well educated, able to speak a foreign language, and capable of producing coherent, intelligible, thoughtful communications. German business managers are well versed in history, literature, geography, music and art (Hal, 1983, p. 58).

Americans tend to focus on the present as the beginning of the future, whereas Germans tend to "begin every talk, every book, or article with background information giving historical perspective" (Hall, 1983, p. 20). While Hall makes a strong generalization, a contrary incident is rare. American college graduates are not known for having a firm or detailed idea of what happened before they were born. While some pockets of integrated, sophisticated thinking exist, it is by no means the standard. Indeed, many American college students are unable to place significant (newsworthy) events within an over-all political/philosophical framework two months after the occurrence.

In contrast, college educated Germans tend to express a need to know *why* they should do something—a reasoning grounded in a logical understanding of the past. Compared to the rigorous German theoretical and concrete analysis of past events, Americans often appear to be arguing from unverifiable aspirations of a future imagined. While such vision is often a valuable driving force and the basis for American innovation and inventiveness, it may not answer the German need to explicitly know why and, thus, may fall short (from a German perspective) in group problem solving when these two cultures are represented. From the educational perspective, one must conclude that more than a few days of awareness training is needed before successful discussions can result between German and American managers, primarily because of what is not required by the American education system. The contrary may also be true in the preparation of Germans to work with Americans. Tolerance for intuitive thinking may well be a proper focus in part of the German manager's training prior to working with American managers.

Formal and Informal Culture

The unannounced and largely unconscious agenda of small group process among Americans is usually more subtle than the German formal awareness but equally as important. American individuals come together in the initial and critical social phase, "size up" each other, and formally or informally recognize a leader. In a gathering of hierarchical equals the first to speak often emerges as the leader. At this point the embers of team spirit warm once again. As the group moves through purpose and task definition, members define and redefine their roles according to the requirements of the evolving team strategy.

Fired with team spirit, inculcated through years of group activity and school sports, the group produces more than the sum of their individual promises.

"In the United States a high spontaneous interest in achievement is counterbalanced by much experience in group activities in which the individual learns to channel achievement needs according to the opinions of others.... Interestingly enough, the American 'value formula' appears to be largely unconscious or informally understood, as compared to the German one, at any rate" (McClelland et al., 1958, p. 252). Though this observation is 30 years old, it still appears to be quite accurate. The use of modeling (imitation) as a way of acquiring social and political problem-solving strategies is also a way of adjusting to regionalisms. In taking on different roles, Americans become adept at unconsciously adjusting their character to meet the requirements of different situations. In short, says Hall, "Compared to many other societies, ours does not invest tradition with an enormous weight. Even our most powerful traditions do not generate the binding force which is common in some other cultures.... We Americans have emphasized the informal at the expense of the formal" (Hall, 1973, p. 72).

The German learning style is often characterized by formal learning as defined by Hall (Hall, 1973, p. 68). The characteristics of German frankness and directness are echoed in Hall's example of formal learning: "He will correct the child saying, 'Boys don't do that,' or 'You can't do that,' using a tone of voice indicating that what you are doing is unthinkable. There is no question in the mind of the speaker about where he stands and where every other adult stands" (Hall, 1973, p. 68). German formal awareness is the conscious apprehension of the detailed reality of history which forms an idealistic code of conduct that guides the individual to act in the national interest as if there was no other way.[6]

American informal awareness and learning is an outgrowth of the blending of many cultural traditions, in an environment in which people were compelled to come together to perform group tasks such as clearing land, building shelter, farming, and so on. The reduction of language to the basic nouns and functions was a requirement of communication for the multilingual population under primitive conditions. Cultural variations will always be a part of the vast American society. Americans have had to "get the hang of

it" precisely because whatever *it* is, *it* is done with several variations in America.

In a sense, the informal rules such as 'fair play' are just as prescriptive of American behavior as the system of German etiquette is prescriptive of much of German social interaction, including forms of address (familiar *Du* and the formal *Sie*). Even the rules for paying local taxes, entering children in schools, or locating a reputable repair person vary by local custom in America and can only be known by asking.[7] The clear difference is that the rules are not overtly shared in America.

The American expectations or informal rules for group discussion are general enough to include the etiquette of American managers from different ethnic backgrounds. As long as notions of equality, being liked, respect, fair play, and so on guide behaviors things run smoothly. "Anxiety, however follows quickly when this tacit etiquette is breached.... What happens next depends upon the alternatives provided by the culture for handling anxiety. Ours includes withdrawal and anger" (Hall, 1973, p. 76). In the intercultural situation, the American who participates informally in group behavior may feel that something is wrong but may not be able to consciously determine the problem. Without the ability of bringing the informal into conscious awareness, which is a function of awareness and education, many Americans may flounder in a state of confusion, withdrawal and anger.

CONCLUSION

What should become apparent to intercultural trainers working with companies that are bringing German and American personnel together is that they are working with two populations with distinct learning and problem-solving styles. The American is more likely to learn from an interactive simulation. Within the situation the American can "get the hang of" working with someone who has a German style. Trainers and educators of American managers know that the debriefing of the role play, which brings the operative informal rules in to conscious awareness, is the focus of the learning activity. The short-term immersion training so often used today can only supply some basic knowledge and limited role-play experience.

What must never be forgotten in the zeal to train American managers is that their basic guidance system in America is a motivation to accommodate the relative values of the immediate group. While the general cultural awareness exercises that begin most intercultural training may make Americans conscious of their internal workings, much more attention must be given to inculcate an understanding of German social order and the interaction permitted within it.

Knowledge of the language and an in-depth orientation to the culture for the overseas manager and spouse should be mandatory for American success in Germany and German success in the United States. "The high rate of marital difficulties, alcoholism and divorce among American families abroad is well known and reflects a lack of understanding and intelligent planning on the part of American business" (Hall, 1983, p. 88). In our pilot program we became quite aware of the fact that German spouses require much more preparation for a sojourn to America. American short-term planning is in conflict with the long-term preparation needed for most Americans who are going to work with Germans. In Germany the role of the spouse (usually female) in business includes much less involvement than in the United States. We suspect this has much to do with the lack of attention to spouse preparation that we have observed thus far.

RECOMMENDATION

Long-term programs should be established that provide cultural orientation for overseas families at least three or four years before they start their sojourn with beginning and increasing knowledge of the language as a prerequisite for entry. Such programs should

- attend to the general instructional deficiencies of Americans in the areas of history, philosophy, and politics as studied by Germans,
- prepare Germans to expect and participate in an informal culture guided by value relativism in a spirit of equality,
- incorporate cultural sharing of German and American managers and their families in social settings so the sojourners can come together before, during, and after their individual experiences to establish a formal support network.

Segments of such programs could be carried on outside the corporate setting to allow for a more open exchange of ideas. In America, colleges and universities could easily establish such programs. Many American colleges and universities which have served as research and development sites for business and industry are also developing alternative evening programs to meet the educational needs in the community. Also, corporate colleges are an ideal setting for extended in-house preparation. In such learning environments, professors can come together with adjunct faculty (private consultants and trainers) to produce a series of seminars which combine lecture instruction, small group intercultural interaction, networking, media presentations, contact with multiple experts over time, and even a well planned group vacation tour to the sojourner's future assignment site.

Part of the programs should be offered in the evening to avoid extensive interference with the employee's regular assignments and to take advantage of the availability of other family members who should be included in intercultural transfer preparation. Cost to the corporation would be greatly reduced in that start-up funds could be partly supplied through federal grants, travel costs would be lessened, and program costs would be covered under regular tuition and materials fees. As a final note, I strongly recommend that such programs for American managers be viewed as graduate level education since they will be entering a society in which education is a mark of status.

REFERENCES

Bleicher, K., & Paul, H. (1986). Corporate governance systems in a multinational environment: Who knows what's best? *Management International Review*, 26, (3), 4-15.

Copeland, L., & Griggs, L. (1985). *Going international: How to make friends and deal effectively in the global marketplace.* New York: Random House.

Cyert, R. M., & March, J. G. (1963) *A behavioral theory of the firm.* Englewood Cliffs, NJ: Prentice-Hall.

Dubos, R. (1972) *A god within.* New York: Charles Scribner's Sons.

Friday, R. A., & Biro, R. (1986-87). [Pilot interviews with German and American personnel at Mobay Corporation (subsidiary of Bayer), Pittsburgh, PA]. Unpublished raw data.

Gudykunst, W. B., & Kim, Y. (1984). *Communicating with strangers: An approach to intercultural communication.* Reading: Addison-Wesley.

Hagemann, K. (1986). *Social relationships of foreign students and their psychological significance in different stages of the sojourn.* Summary of unpublished diploma thesis, University of Regensburg, Regensburg, Federal Republic of Germany.

Hall, E. T. (1973). *The silent language*. New York: Doubleday.

Hall, E. T. (1983). *Hidden differences: Studies in international communication--How to communicate with the Germans*. Hamburg, West Germany: Stern Magazine Gruner + Jahr AG & Co.

Hofstede, G. (1984). *Culture's consequences: International differences in work-related values*. Beverly Hills: Sage Publications.

Kohls, L. R. (1987). *Models for comparing and contrasting cultures*, a juried paper, invited for submission to National Association of Foreign Student Advisors, June, 1987.

Laurent, A. (1986). The cross-cultural puzzle of international human resource management. *Human Resource Management*, 25, 91-103.

McClelland, D.C., Sturr, J. F., KNAPP, R. N., & Wendt, H. W. (1985.). Obligations to self and society in the United States and Germany. *Journal of Abnormal And Social Psychology*, 56, 245-255.

Mead, M. (1975). *And keep your powder dry*. New York: William Morrow.

Nyrop, R. F. (Ed). (1982). *Federal republic of Germany, a country study*. Washington DC: U.S. Government Printing Office.

Peters, T., & Austin, N. (1985). *A passion for excellence*. New York: Warner Communication.

Peters, T., & Waterman, R. (1982). *In search of excellence*. New York: Warner Communication.

Reynolds, B. (1984). A cross-cultural study of values of Germans and Americans. *International Journal of Intercultural Relations*, 8, 269-278.

Stewart, E. C. (1972). *American cultural patterns: A cross-cultural perspective*. Chicago: Intercultural Press.

Weaver. R. M. (1953). *The ethics of rhetoric*. South Bend, IN: Rengery/Gateway.

FOOTNOTES

Requests for reprints should be addressed to Dr. Robert A. Friday, Department of Communication, Duquesene University, Pittsburgh, PA 15282.

1. Future references to America and Americans should be understood as referring to the North Eastern United States and the citizens thereof, while references to Germany and Germans should be understood as West Germany and the citizens thereof.

2. Actual German values were 65, with a value of 53 when controlled for age of sample, while the actual USA values were 46, with a value of 36 when controlled for age of sample.

3. For a quick overview of how small group and interpersonal communication is related to corporate success in America see Peters, and Austin, 1985, pp. 233-248.

4. These comparative descriptions correspond to the German social orientation and the American personal orientation discussed by Beatrice Reynolds (1984, p. 276) in her study of German and American values.

5. "In Germany, power can be financial, political, entrepreneurial, managerial or intellectual; of the five, intellectual power seems to rank highest. Many of the heads of German firms have doctoral degrees and are always addressed as "Herr Doktor." (Copeland & Griggs, 1985, p. 120). While there may be exceptions to this rule, exceptions are few and hard to find.

6. "Yet this rigidity has its advantages. People who live and die in formal cultures tend to take a more relaxed view of life than the rest of us because the boundaries of behavior are so clearly marked, even to the permissible deviations. There is never any doubt in anybody's mind that, as long as he does what is expected, he knows what to expect from others" (Hall, 1973, p. 75). "In Germany everything is forbidden unless it is permitted" (Dubos, 1972, p. 100).

7. The perplexing problem for German executives who are new in the United States is that in Germany everything is known thus, you should not have to ask to find your way around. But in the USA where change is the watch word, one has to ask to survive.

Questions:

1. What is the primary motivation for North Americans to cooperate or not to cooperate? For Germans?

2. What are the different goals of Germans and North Americans when they come together in discussion?

3. What is the ultimate function of group process in North American corporations?

The answer section begins on page 243.

16

Not only do different languages have their own vocabularies, grammars, and syntaxes, but they also have unique linguistic styles. Some language communities have very formal styles (which acknowledge status differences), while others have very informal styles (which do not make such distinctions.) Some languages, like North American English, are very direct ("tell it like it is!"), while others, such as Japanese, are very indirect and non-confrontational. Culturally induced differences in linguistic style, however, can be seen within cultures as well as between cultures. Often anthropological linguists find differences in linguistic style that are gender based—that is, between men and women. In this selection Deborah Tannen demonstrates how differences in mens' and womens' conversational style in the United States can result in miscommunication in a business setting. By applying the insights and techniques of anthropological linguistics to the world of business, Tannen suggests how we might become better communicators on the job.

TALKING FROM 9 TO 5

By Deborah Tannen

Women and Men Talking on the Job

Amy was a manager with a problem: She had just read a final report written by Donald, and she felt it was woefully inadequate. She faced the unsavory task of telling him to do it over. When she met with Donald, she made sure to soften the blow by beginning with praise, telling him everything about his report that was good. Then she went on to explain what was lacking and what needed to be done to make it acceptable. She was pleased with the diplomatic way she had managed to deliver the bad news. Thanks to her thoughtfulness in starting with praise, Donald was able to listen to the criticism and seemed to understand what was needed. But when the revised report appeared on her desk, Amy was shocked. Donald had made only minor, superficial changes, and none of the necessary ones. The next meeting with him did not go well. He was incensed that she was now telling him his report was not acceptable and accused her of having misled him. "You told me before it was fine," he protested.

Amy thought she had been diplomatic; Donald thought she had been dishonest. The praise she intended to soften the message "This is unacceptable" sounded to him like the message itself: "This is fine." So what she regarded as the main point—the needed changes—came across to him as optional suggestions, because he had already registered her praise as the main point.

She felt he hadn't listened to her. He thought she had changed her mind and was making him pay the price.

Work days are filled with conversations about getting the job done. Most of these conversations succeed, but too many end in impasses like this. It could be that Amy is a capricious boss whose wishes are whims, and it could be that Donald is a temperamental employee who can't hear criticism no matter how it is phrased. But I don't think either was the case in this instance. I believe this was one of innumerable misunderstandings cause by differences in conversational style. Amy delivered the criticism in a way that seemed to her self-evidently considerate, a way she would have preferred to receive criticism herself: taking into account the other person's feelings, making sure he knew that her ultimate negative assessment of his report didn't mean she had no appreciation of his abilities. She offered the praise as a sweetener to help the nasty-tasting news go down. But Donald didn't expect criticism to be delivered in that way, so he mistook the praise as her overall assessment rather than a preamble to it.

The conversation could have taken place between two women or two men. But I do not think it is a coincidence that it occurred between a man and woman. This book will explain why. First, it gives a view of the role played by talk in our work lives. To do this, I show the workings of conversational style, explaining the ritual nature of conversation and the confusion that arises when rituals are not shared and therefore not recognized as such. I take into account the many influences on conversational style, but I focus in particular on the differing rituals that typify women and men (although, of course, not all individual men and women behave in ways that are typical). Conversational rituals common among men often involve using opposition such as banter, joking, teasing, and playful put-downs and expending effort to avoid the one-down position in the interaction. Conversational rituals common among women are often ways of maintaining an appearance of equality, taking into account the effect of the exchange on the other person, and expending effort to downplay the speakers' authority so they can get the job done without flexing their muscles in an obvious way.

When everyone present is familiar with these conventions, they work well. But when ways of speaking are not recognized as conventions, they are taken literally, with negative results on both sides. Men whose oppositional strategies are interpreted literally may be seen as hostile when they are not, and their efforts to ensure that they avoid appearing one-down may be taken as arrogance. When women use conversational strategies designed to avoid appearing boastful and to take the other person's feelings into account, they may be seen as less confident and competent than they really are. As a result, both women and men often feel they are not getting sufficient credit for what they have done, are not being listened to, are not getting ahead as fast as they should.

When I talk about women's and men's characteristic ways of speaking, I always emphasize that both styles make sense and are equally valid in themselves, though the difference in styles may cause trouble in interaction. In a sense, when two people form a private relationship of love or friendship, the bubble of their interaction is a world unto itself, even though they both come with the prior experience of their families, their community, and a lifetime of conversations. But someone who takes a job is entering a world that is already functioning, with its own characteristic style already in place. Although there are many influences such as regional background, the type of industry involved, whether it is a family business or a large corporation, in general, workplaces that have previously had men in positions of power have already established male-style interaction as the norm. In that sense, women, and others whose styles are different, are not starting out equal, but are at a disadvantage. Though talking at work is quite similar to talking in private, it is a very different enterprise in many ways.

When Not Asking Directions Is Dangerous To Your Health

If conversational-style differences lead to troublesome outcomes in work as well as private settings, there are some work settings where the outcomes of style are a matter of life and death. Healthcare professionals are often in such situations. So are airline pilots.

Of all the examples of women's and men's characteristic styles that I discussed in *You Just Don't Understand*, the one that (to my surprise) attracted the most attention was the question "Why don't men like to stop and ask for directions?" Again and again, in the responses of audiences, talk-show hosts, letter writers, journalists, and conversationalists, this question seemed to crystallize the frustration many people had experienced in their own lives. And my explanation seems to have rung true: that men are more likely to be aware that asking for directions, or for any kind of help, puts them in a one-down position.

With regard to asking directions, women and men are keenly aware of the advantages of their own style. Women frequently observe how much time they would save if their husbands simply stopped and asked someone instead of driving around trying in vain to find a destination themselves. But I have also been told by men that is makes sense not to ask directions because you learn a lot about a neighborhood, as well as about navigation, by driving around and finding your own way.

But some situations are more risky than others. A Hollywood talk-show producer told me that she had been flying with her father in his private airplane when he was running out of gas and uncertain about the precise location of the local landing strip he was heading for. Beginning to panic, the woman said, "Daddy! Why don't you radio the control tower and ask them where to land?" He answered, "I don't want them to think I'm lost." This story had a happy ending, else the woman would not have been alive to tell it to me.

Some time later, I repeated this anecdote to a man at a cocktail party—a man, who had just told me that the bit about directions was his favorite part of my book, and who, it turned out, was also an amateur pilot. He then went on to tell me that he had had a similar experience. When learning to fly, he got lost on his first solo flight. He did not want to humiliate himself by tuning his radio to the FAA emergency frequency and asking for help, so he flew around looking for a place to land. He spotted an open area that looked like a landing field, headed for it—and found himself deplaning in what seemed like a deliberately hidden landing strip that was mercifully deserted at the time. Fearing he had stumbled upon an enterprise he was not supposed to be aware of, let alone poking around in, he climbed back into the plane, relieved that he had not gotten into trouble. He managed to find his way back to his home airport as well, before he ran out of gas. He maintained, however, that he was certain that more than a few small-plane crashes have occurred because other amateur pilots who did not want to admit they were lost were less lucky. In light of this, the amusing question of why men prefer not to stop and ask for directions stops being funny.

The moral of the story is not that men should immediately change and train themselves to ask directions when they're in doubt, any more than women should immediately stop asking directions and start honing their navigational skills by finding their way on their own. The moral is flexibility: Sticking to habit in the face of all challenges is not so smart if it ends up getting you killed. If we all understood our own styles and knew their limits and their alternatives, we'd be better off—especially at work, where the results of what we do have repercussions for co-workers and the company, as well as for our own futures.

To Ask Or Not To Ask

An intern on duty at a hospital had a decision to make. A patient had been admitted with a condition he recognized, and he recalled the appropriate medication. But that medication was recommended for a number of conditions, in different dosages. He wasn't quite sure what dose was right for this condition. He had to make a quick decision: Would he interrupt the supervising resident during a meeting to check the dose, or would he make his best guess and go for it?

What was at stake? First and foremost, the welfare, and maybe even the life, of the patient. But something else was at stake too—the reputation, and eventually the career, of the intern. If he interrupted the resident to ask about the dosage, he was making a public statement about what he didn't know, as well as making himself something of a nuisance. In this case, he

went with his guess, and there were no negative effects. But, as with small-plane crashes, one wonders how many medical errors have resulted from decisions to guess rather than ask.

It is clear that not asking questions can have disastrous consequences in medical settings, but asking questions can also have negative consequences. A physician wrote to me about a related experience that occurred during her medical training. She received a low grade from her supervising physician. It took her by surprise because she knew that she was one of the best interns in her group. She asked her supervisor for an explanation, and he replied that she didn't know as much as the others. She knew from her day-to-day dealings with her peers that she was one of the most knowledgeable, not the least. So she asked what evidence had led him to his conclusion. And he told her, "You ask more questions."

There is evidence that men are less likely to ask questions in a public situation, where asking will reveal their lack of knowledge. One such piece of evidence is a study done in a university classroom, where sociolinguist Kate Remlinger noticed that women students asked the professor more questions than men students did. As part of her study, Remlinger interviewed six students at length, three men and three women. All three men told her that they would not ask questions in class if there was something they did not understand. Instead, they said they would try to find the answer later by reading the textbook, asking a friend, or, as a last resort, asking the professor in private during office hours. As one young man put it, "If it's vague to me, I usually don't ask. I'd rather go home and look it up."

Of course, this does not mean that no men will ask questions when they are in doubt, nor that all women will; the differences, as always, are a matter of likelihood and degree. As always, cultural differences play a role too. It is not unusual for American professors to admit their own ignorance when they do not know the answer to a student's question, but there are many cultures in which professors would not, and students from those cultures may judge American professors by those standards. A student from the Middle East told a professor at a California university that she had just lost all respect for one of his colleagues. The reason: She had asked a question in class, and the offending professor had replied, "I don't know offhand, but I'll find out for you."

The physician who asked her supervisor why he gave her a negative evaluation may be unusual in having been told directly what behavior led to the misjudgment of her skill. But in talking to doctors and doctors-in-training around the country, I have learned that there is nothing exceptional about her experience, that it is common for interns and residents to conceal their ignorance by not asking questions, since those who do ask are judged less capable. Yet it seems that many women who are more likely than men to ask questions (just as women are more likely to stop and ask for directions when they're lost) are unaware that they may make a negative impression at the same time that they get information. Their antennae have not been attuned to making sure they don't appear one-down.

This pattern runs counter to two stereotypes about male and female styles: that men are more focused on information and that women are more sensitive. In regard to classroom behavior, it seems that the women who ask questions are more focused on information, whereas the men who refrain from doing so are more focused on interaction—the impression their asking will make on others. In this situation, it is the men who are more sensitive to the impression made on others by their behavior, although their concern is, ultimately, the effects on themselves rather than on others. And this sensitivity is likely to make them look better in the world of work. Realizing this puts the intern's decision in a troubling perspective. He had to choose between putting his career at risk and putting the patient's health at risk.

It is easy to see benefits of both styles: Someone willing to ask questions has ready access to a great deal of information—all that is known by the people she can ask. But just as men have told me that asking directions is useless since the person you ask may not know and may give you the wrong answer, some people feel they are more certain to get the right information if they read it in a book, and they are learning more by finding it themselves. On the other hand, energy may be wasted looking up information someone else has at hand, and I have heard complaints from people who feel they were sent on wild-goose chases by colleagues who didn't want to admit they really were not sure of what they pretended to know.

The reluctance to say "I don't know" can have serious consequences for and entire company—and did: On Friday, June 17, 1994, a computer problem prevented Fidelity Investments from calculating the value of 166 mutual funds. Rather than report that the values for these funds were not available, a manager decided to report to the National Association of Securities Dealers that the values of these funds had not changed from the day before. Unfortunately, June 17 turned out to be a bad day in the financial markets, so the values of Fidelity's funds that were published in the newspapers around the country stood out as noticeably higher than those of other funds. Besides the cost and inconvenience to brokerage firms who had to re-compute their customers' accounts, and the injustice to investors who made decisions to buy or sell based on inaccurate information, the company was mightily embarrassed and forced to apologize publicly. Clearly this was an instance in which it would have been preferable to say, "We don't know."

Flexibility, again, is key. There are many situations in which it serves one well to be self-reliant and discreet about revealing doubt or ignorance, and others in which it is wise to admit what you don't know.

Questions:

1. According to Tannen, what is the primary reason men, in general, do not ask for help?

2. What are two common stereotypes about male and female conversational styles?

3. Can you give examples of "conversational rituals" common among men? Among women?

The answer section begins on page 243.

The United States remains the only country in the world where one can earn a university degree without fluency in a second language. Of the more than ten thousand Americans doing business in Japan, fewer than ten percent speak any Japanese. In fact, the United States has been referred to as the "land of the free and the home of the monolingual." But as this selection points out, there are a number of reasons (that make good business sense) for learning the language of those with whom you are attempting to do business. Here, applied anthropologist Gary Ferraro argues that learning another language can help international business people more effectively meet their professional objectives.

The Need for Linguistic Proficiency in Global Business

By Gary Ferraro

The Need for Linguistic Proficiency in Global Business

Businesses, like other organizations, require effective communication to operate efficiently and meet their objectives. International business firms require effective communication at a number of levels. A company must communicate with its work force, customers, suppliers, and host government officials. Effective communication among people from the same culture is often difficult enough. But when attempting to communicate with people who do not speak English and who have different attitudes, ideas, assumptions, perceptions, and ways of doing things, one's chances for miscommunication increase enormously.

Unfortunately, the literature is filled with examples of what can go wrong when U.S. businesses attempt to market their products abroad with less than an adequate grasp of the local language. Simon (1980) reports that when General Motors described its "Body by Fisher" in Flemish, it came out "Corpse by Fisher," which did not increase sales. Pepsi-Cola's highly successful slogan "Come Alive With Pepsi" almost appeared in the Chinese version of the *Reader's Digest* as "Pepsi brings your ancestors back from the grave." A U.S.-based airline operating out of Brazil tried to lure business people by claming it had plush "rendezvous lounges" in its first-class sections—without realizing that in Portuguese, the word "rendezvous" implies a room for making love.

Recently Susan Parr (1992) reported that the U.S. chicken entrepreneur Frank Perdue decided to translate one of his very successful advertising slogans into Spanish with some unfortunate—results. The slogan "It takes a tough man to make a tender chicken" was translated into Spanish as "It takes a virile man to make a chicken affectionate."

In other instances of imprecise translation, U.S. firms have advertised cigarettes with low "asphalt" (instead of tar), computer "underwear" (instead of software), and "wet sheep" (instead of hydraulic rams.) As amusing as these examples may seem, such translation errors have cost U.S. firms millions of dollars in losses, not to mention the damage done to their credibility and reputations.

If international business people are to be successful, there is no substitute for an intimate acquaintance with both the language and the culture of those with whom they are conducting business. Because of the close relationship between language and culture, it is almost impossible not to learn about one while studying the other. The argument in favor of foreign language competence for international business people seems so blatantly obvious that to have to recount it here causes twinges of embarrassment.

Yet the very fact that so many Westerners enter the international business arena without language competence helps overcome that embarrassment. A survey by James C. Baker (1984) of U.S. firms conducting business in non-English speaking countries revealed that only 31 percent considered a foreign language necessary for doing

Reprinted by permission of BUSINESS HORIZON, May-June, 1996, pp. 39-46.

business abroad, and only 20 percent required their overseas employees to know the local language.

Although an appreciation for language competency has increased in recent years, the vast majority of U.S. business people continue to operate abroad without adequate fluency in the local language. Most of the explanations offered for not learning to speak another language appear transparent and designed to justify past complacency or ethnocentrism. We frequently hear that U.S. firms doing business abroad need not train their overseas personnel in a second language because English is rapidly becoming the international language of business.

After generations of assuming that our goods and services were so desirable that the rest of the world would come to us, we now find ourselves in a highly competitive world market with greater linguistic parity. English is now just one of the major languages of world trade and the mother tongue of only 5 percent of the world's population. Moreover, business people from other language communities have grown weary of the assumption that they are solely responsible for making the effort of speaking English to their American business partners.

Despite these and other arguments, a fundamental precondition of any successful international business enterprise is effective communication. Whether dealing with international sales, management, or negotiations, the monolingual Western business person is at a marked disadvantage. International business, like any other business, must be grounded in trust and mutual respect. What better way to gain that trust and respect than by taking the time and energy to learn someone else's language?

In certain cultures, particularly those in South America, business is conducted at a more leisurely pace than in the United States. In these settings the U.S. business person who is fluent in Spanish and can speak intelligently about local culture will be far more apt to gain both the respect and the business of the foreign partner.

Enhancing rapport should be sufficient to justify second language competence for Western business people. But we can add other persuasive reasons as well. The experience of learning a second language is beneficial in the learning of third and fourth languages, so that the time spent today learning Spanish will facilitate learning Chinese or Arabic in the future. Moreover, learning another language (and culture) is the best way to gain a fuller appreciation of one's own language and culture.

Perhaps the most compelling reason for learning the language of one's international business partner is that it provides considerable insights into that culture. The language provides entrée into the "world view" of another culture; through its structure and vocabulary it reveals the important values found in the culture; it gives insight into how directly or indirectly people in a particular culture communicate with one another; and it reflects social realities, such as status differences, within a culture. It is this special feature of language—its capacity to enable the learner to go inside another culture—that we will explore in greater depth.

Language and World View

Some linguists have suggested that language is more than merely a system of communication that facilitates sending and receiving messages. Languages serve more than a communication function, they would argue, because they establish categories in our minds that force us to distinguish between objects we consider similar from those things we consider different. Because every language is unique, the linguistic categories of one will never be identical to the categories of any other. Consequently, the speakers of any two different languages will not categorize in the same way, nor will they perceive reality in exactly the same way.

To illustrate, if my language has a single word—"aunt"—that refers to my mother's sister, my father's sister, my mother's brother's wife, and my father's brother's wife, it is likely that I will perceive all of these relatives as genealogically equivalent; consequently, I will behave toward them in much the same way. But whereas this is the case in standard American English, other linguistic communities perceive these four female relatives to be substantially different, label them with different kinship terms, and expect to behave toward them in different ways.

How people categorize or label things differs significantly from one linguistic or cultural group to another, and these different ways of categorizing affect how we perceive the world. As any student of a second language soon realizes, certain ideas and concepts do not translate exactly from one language to another. In some cases, if a language does not have a word for a particular idea, event, or phenomenon, people fail to perceive its existence. Taylor (1990) notes that because the English language lacks a word for the aroma of roasted ground sesame seeds, English speakers fail even to perceive the scent until it is pointed out to them. Yet Koreans, who have a world for that particular aroma, have no difficulty recognizing it when it fills the air.

This notion of language affecting perception, stated in its most explicit form by linguists Edward Sapir and Benjamin Lee Whorf, has come to be known as the Sapir-Whorf Hypothesis. Since its original formulation in the 1930s, a number of ethnolinguists have attempted to test the hypothesis. One very creative test was conducted by Joseph Casagrande (1960) using a matched sample of Navajo-speaking children. Half of the sample, who spoke only Navajo, were matched on all significant sociocultural variables (such as religion, parental education, and family income) with the other half, who spoke both Navajo and English.

Because both groups were identical on all important variables except language, it would be logical to conclude that whatever perceptual differences emerged between the two groups could be attributed to language. Possessing a thorough knowledge of the Navajo language, Casagrande understood that Navajo people, when speaking about an object, are required to choose among a number of different verb forms depending on the shape of the object. When asking a Navajo speaker to hand you an object, for example, you would use one verb form if the object is long and rigid like a stick and another verb form if it is long and flexible like a rope. Based on this Navajo linguistic feature, Casagrande hypothesized that children speaking only Navajo would be more likely to discriminate according to shape at an earlier age than English-speaking children. The latter, it was assumed, would be more likely to discriminate according to other features such as size or color.

This hypothesis was tested by having both groups of children participate in a number of tasks. The children were shown two objects (a yellow stick and a blue rope) and then asked to tell which of these two objects was most like a third object (a yellow rope). In other words, both groups of children were asked to categorize the yellow rope according to likeness with either the yellow stick or the blue rope. Casagrande found the children who spoke only Navajo had a significantly greater tendency to categorize according to shape (yellow rope and blue rope) than the bilingual children, who were more likely to categorize according to color.

Based on the type of experiment conducted by Casagrande, the Sapir-Whorf Hypothesis would appear to have at least a general validity. Though all linguists hardly agree on the extent to which language influences perception, it is generally accepted that because all people are constantly bombarded with sensory stimuli, they need to bring order to all of these incoming sensations. Sapir and Whorf have suggested that language serves as that filtering system by providing a set of lenses that highlight some perceptions and de-emphasize others.

Because language establishes in our minds certain categories that force us to distinguish between like and unlike things, language actually influences people to see the world in different ways. One who understands the language of an international business partner will also understand how that partner organizes the world.

Language Mirrors Values

A language also reveals a culture's basic value structure. For example, the extent to which a culture values the individual, as compared to the group, is often reflected in its language or linguistic style. The value placed on the individual is deeply rooted in the North American psyche. Most citizens of the United States start from the cultural assumption that the individual is supreme and that one not only can, but should, shape one's own destiny. The fact that individualism is highly valued in the United States can be seen throughout its culture—from the love of the automobile as the preferred mode of transportation to a judicial system that goes as far as any in the world to protect the individual rights of the accused. Even when dealing with children, North Americans try to provide them with a bedroom of their own, respect their individual right to privacy, and attempt to instill in them a sense of self-reliance and independence by encouraging them to solve their own problems.

Owing to the close interrelatedness of language and culture, values are reflected in standard American English. One such indicator of how our language reflects individualism is the number of words found in any American English dictionary that are compounded with the word "self." To illustrate, one is likely to find no fewer than 150 such words, including "self-absorbed," "self-appointed," "self-centered," "self-confident," "self-conscious," "self-educated," "self-image," "self-regard," and "self-supporting." This considerable list of English terms related to the individual is significantly larger than one found in a culture that places greater emphasis on corporate or group relationships.

In the U.S., individual happiness is the highest good, whereas in such group-oriented cultures as Japan, people strive for the good of the larger group, such as the family, the community, or the whole society. Rather than stressing individual happiness, the Japanese are more concerned with justice (for group members) and righteousness (by group members). In Japan, the "We" always comes before the "I"; the group is always more predominant than the individual. As John Condon (1984) reminds us, "If Descartes had been Japanese, he would have said, 'we think, therefore we are.'"

An important structural distinction found in Japanese society is between *uchi* (the in-group) and *soto* (the out-group), or the difference between "us" and "them." This basic social distinction is reflected in the Japanese language. For example, whether a person is "one of us" or "one of them" will determine which conversational greeting will be used—either *Ohayo gozaimasu*, which is customarily used with close members of one's in-group, or *Konnichiwa*, which is more routinely used to greet those outside one's inner circle.

Osamu Mizutani (1979) conducted an interesting experiment outside the Imperial Palace in Tokyo, which is a favorite place for jogging. Dressed like a jogger, he greeted everyone he passed, both other joggers like himself and non-joggers, and noted their response. Interestingly, 95 percent of the joggers greeted him with *Ohayo gozaimasu*, whereas only 42 percent of the non-joggers used such a term. He concluded that the joggers, to a much greater degree than the non-joggers, considered him to be an in-group member because he too was jogging.

Group members in Japan do not want to stand out or assert their individuality because according to the Japanese proverb, "The nail that sticks up gets hammered down." In contrast to the United States, the emphasis in Japan is on "fitting in," harmonizing, and avoiding open disagreement within the group. If one must disagree, it is usually done gently and very indirectly by using such passive expressions as "It is said that..." or "Some people think that...." This type of linguistic construction enables one to express an opinion without having to be responsible for it in the event others in the group might disagree. In a study of speech patterns among Japanese and American students, R. Shimonishi (1977) found that the Japanese students used the passive voice significantly more than their U.S. counterparts.

How language is used in Japan and the U.S. both reflects and reinforces the value of group consciousness in the former and individualism in the latter. A main goal of communication in Japan is to achieve consensus and promote harmony, whereas in the United States it is often to demonstrate one's eloquence. Language in Japan tends to be cooperative, polite, and conciliatory; language in the United States is often competitive, adversarial, confrontational, and aimed at making a point. The Japanese go to considerable lengths to avoid controversial issues that might be disruptive; North Americans seem to thrive on controversy, debate, argumentation, and provocation, as is evidenced by the use of the expression "Just for the sake of argument...."

Moreover, the Japanese play down individual eloquence in favor of being good listeners—a vital skill if group consensus is to be achieved. Americans, in contrast, are not particularly effective listeners because they are too busy mentally preparing their personal responses rather than paying close attention to what is being said. All these linguistic contrasts between Japan and the United States express their fundamentally different approaches to the cultural values of "group-ness" and individualism.

Explicit and Implicit Communication

Cultures vary in terms of how explicitly they send and receive verbal messages. In the United States, for example, effective verbal communication is expected to be explicit, direct, and unambiguous. Good communicators are supposed to say what they mean as precisely and straightforwardly as possible. We are expected to "tell it like it is" and not "beat around the bush." Speech patterns in some other cultures are considerably more ambiguous, inexact, and implicit.

Basil Bernstein's (1964) now classic distinction between elaborated and restricted codes provides a conceptual framework to understand the differences better between these fundamentally disparate models of discourse. Restricted codes use shortened words, phrases, and sentences and rely heavily on hidden, unspoken, implicit, contextual cues such as nonverbal behavior, social context, and the nature of interpersonal relationships. Restricted codes are a form of "shorthand" communication that do not rely on verbal elaboration or explication. Elaborated codes, on the other hand, involve verbal amplification and place little importance on nonverbal or other contextual cues.

Like any theoretical distinction, the notions of restricted and elaborated codes are not "either/or" categories. Relatively restricted or elaborated codes often can be found in any speech community, though one or the other is likely to predominate.

Cultures with elaborated verbal codes place high value on words. The Western world, specifically northern Europe and North America, has a long tradition of rhetoric that places central importance on the delivery of verbal messages. An important function of speech in this tradition is to persuade others using the logical and clear expression of one's ideas. By way of contrast, in cultures with restricted verbal codes, words are important, but are only a part of the total communication system. It is not that words are unimportant in such Eastern cultures as China, Japan, and Korea; rather, words are inseparably interrelated to social relationships.

Given this broader view, the purpose of communication in many Eastern cultures is to promote harmony and social integration rather than enhance the speaker's individuality through the articulation of words. Whereas Western cultures tend to place a great deal of power in words, many Asian cultures show a certain mistrust or skepticism of them, or at least have a keen awareness of the limitation of words alone. In societies with restricted codes, this cautious approach to words can be seen in the general suppression of negative verbal messages. Politeness and the desire to avoid embarrassment often take precedence over the truth.

This communication style explains, at least partly, why Eastern cultures have so many indirect or nonverbal ways to say "no" without simply uttering the word. This practice has caused considerable misunderstanding when North Americans try to communicate with Japanese. To illustrate, Japanese in everyday conversation frequently use the word *hai* (yes) to convey not necessarily agreement, but rather that they understand what is being said.

When negotiating with Asians, it is important to understand that "yes" is not always an affirmative response. Before taking "yes" for an answer, one must ascertain whether in fact it was merely a polite response that really meant "no." Asian business people, for example, are not likely to say "no" directly to a proposal, but rather will reply in ways that are synonymous with "no."

Christopher Engholm (1991) cites a number of ways in which Asians say "no" without coming right out and saying it. In response to the question "Has my proposal been accepted?" an Asian is likely to reply in a number of different ways:

- The conditional "yes": "If everything proceeds as planned, the proposal will be approved."
- The counter-question: "Have you submitted a copy of your proposal to the Ministry of Electronics?"
- The question is criticized: "Your question is difficult to answer."
- The question is refused: "We cannot answer your question at this time."
- The tangential reply: "Will you be staying longer than you originally planned?"
- The "Yes, but..." reply: "Yes, approval looks likely, but... (the meaning of "but" could mean "it might not be approved").
- The answer is delayed: "You will know shortly."

In these same societies that rely on restricted codes, it is not unusual to leave sentences unfinished or to tolerate intermittent periods of silence. Whereas most Westerners try to make their point as quickly and straightforwardly as possible, many Eastern cultures value silence as a major element of their rhetorical styles. Most North Americans have been socialized to believe it is wrong not to talk when in a social situation. At cocktail parties, they frequently pick a topic and start talking, largely for the sake of filling up air space. By way of contrast, the Japanese are admired for their modesty, ability to listen, and lack of eloquence. This contrast can be seen in the sheer amount of verbiage found in both societies. Satoshi and Klopf (1975) report that the average American spends approximately seven hours per day in conversation, compared to about three and one-half hours for the Japanese.

Silence can allow Japanese communicators to gain a better feel for their partners. For this reason, they are not reluctant to let long silence develop. As Japanese are likely to turn inward toward their own small, intimate groups, verbal disclosure becomes less necessary. That is, Japanese believe that if two people have close rapport, they do not need to communicate verbally because they already know what the other is thinking. The need to use words, according to the Japanese, implies a lack of understanding.

The radically different meaning of silence in Japan, as compared to the West, is well described by Helmut Morsbach (1982):

> These silences are frequently misunderstood by Westerners, who tend to interpret them as

noncomprehension, and therefore try to shorten the silence by explaining their point once again, or by moving on to the next topic. Well-meaning attempts to make the Japanese partner(s) "speak up" often tend to cause silent frustration and resentment since, from the Japanese viewpoint, the Westerners are often seen as being the culprits who should rather be taught how to "shut up."

Thus, in certain Asian societies rhetorical ambiguity results from restricted codes, and successful communication depends on sensitivity to the nonverbal context.

Other speech communities, such as certain Arabic cultures, are equally imprecise, but for exactly the opposite reason. These cultures engage in over-assertion, exaggeration, and repetition. The Arabic language is filled with forms of verbal exaggeration. For example, certain pronouns often will be repeated to dramatize the message fully; highly graphic metaphors and similes are common; a long list of adjectives is often used to modify a single noun for the sake of emphasizing the point.

On a continuum of understatement and overstatement, Arabic speakers tend toward the "overstatement" polarity. They are considerably more likely than North Americans to overstate their case, and infinitely more likely than the Japanese. What would be an assertive statement to an American might appear to be weak and equivocating to an Arabic speaker. Or a very strongly worded statement in Arabic might seem absolutely fanatical to an American. It is important to bear in mind that in the Arabic world, very strongly worded statements—which have essentially a psychologically cathartic function—are not taken literally as an accurate description of the speaker's real thoughts or intentions. This rhetorical feature of linguistic over-assertion is just another form of verbal ambiguity or inexactness because it fails to send direct, precise messages.

Language Reflects Social Context

The language spoken by a group of people can also provide considerable insights into the nature of their social interactions. People often speak different languages or different forms of the same language depending on the social situation or context in which the speaker may be operating. Bilingualism is the most obvious form of situational language use, for a person many use one language at school, another in the home, and still a third in the marketplace.

As is more often the case, people who are monolingual will speak different forms of the same language, depending on the social situation. To illustrate, the language that a college sophomore might use with a roommate would be appreciably different from that used when talking to a grandparent; or the choice of expressions heard in a football locker room would hardly be appropriate in a job interview.

What is said and how it is said are frequently influenced by such variables as age, sex, and relative social status of the speakers. What can we tell about the social relationships between two people from the language they use with each other? The analysis of terms of address can be particularly useful in this regard. Professor Green, Ma'am, Professor, Ms. Green, Elizabeth, Darling, Doc, Prof, or Beth, depending on who is doing the addressing. One would not expect her mother or husband to refer to her as Ma'am, or her students to call her Beth. Instead, one would expect that the term of address chosen would appropriately reflect the relative social status of the two parties.

In middle-class American society, the reciprocal use of first names indicates a friendly, informal relationship between equals; the reciprocal use of title followed by last name indicates a more formal relationship between people of roughly the same status; and the non-reciprocal use of first names and titles is found among people of unequal social status. We would also expect the same person to use different terms of address for Professor Green in different social situations. Her husband, for example, might call her "Beth" at a cocktail party, "Darling" in a more intimate situation, and "Elizabeth" when engaged in an argument.

In some linguistic communities, every speech situation (not just terms of address) requires the speaker to make choices that reflect the relative social status of the person being addressed. Before a word is uttered in the Javanese language (which is quite typical of other Asian languages), the speaker must choose one of three basic linguistic styles: the plain, the fancy, or the elegant. Moreover, the Javanese speaker can use special terms known as "honorifics," which enable the speaker to express minute gradations of social respect within each of these three styles. As Peter Farb (1974) has noted, the Javanese speaker "has no choice but to inform his listener exactly what he thinks of him—because the style he selects reveals whether he considers the listener worthy of low speech, the middle-ground fancy speech, or elegant speech, with or without honorifics."

Not only is social status reflected in speech patterns, but linguistic differences can be observed between men and women in the same speech community. Often these gender differences are reflected in vocabulary. Some languages have pairs of words (called doublets) that carry the same meaning, but women use one word and men the other. For example, among the Island Carib of the West Indies, reports Hickerson (1980), men use the word *kunobu* to mean "rain" while women use the word *kuyu*. Among the Merina in Madagascar, notes Keenan (1974), speech patterns associated with men, which are indirect, allusive, and formal, are considered both respectable and sophisticated. Merina women, on the other hand, are thought to be ignorant of the subtleties of sophisticated speech and so are considered to be inferior.

Moreover, submissiveness and lack of social power can be observed in female speech patterns in the United States in terms of intonation, loudness, and assertiveness. According to Deborah Tannen (1990), who refers to these gender-based differences in language as "genderlects," women and men in the United States have different linguistic style and communication goals. Women engage in "rapport-talk while men use "report-talk." The language of rapport-talk seeks to establish connections and negotiate relationships, and reflects the tendency to seek agreement. Women's speech is cooperative in that they acknowledge one another's contributions and engage in more active listening.

Report-talk, by way of contrast, represents a male mode of discourse that emphasizes maintaining independence and establishing a place in the competitive hierarchy. Men's conversations, aimed at controlling the flow of talk, are less social and more individualistic. In cross-gender conversations, men tend to dominate women by talking more, interrupting them more frequently, and focusing the conversation on the topics of their own choice.

Learning a second language, particularly in one's adult years, requires time, hard work, and dedication on the part of the learner and a strong sense of commitment on the part of the employer. Even after one masters the vocabulary, grammar, and syntax of a second language, it is still possible to miscommunicate. Often ideas do not translate from one language to another without a certain loss of meaning; some languages rely more heavily than others on nonverbal forms of communication; and to further complicate the communication process, all languages, to some extent, use idioms, slang, and euphemisms.

Despite the formidable challenges that second language learning presents, there are many good reasons for making the effort:

- Learning the host language builds rapport and sets the proper tone for doing business abroad.
- Obtaining the best possible medical care abroad (for oneself and one's family) requires an ability to communicate clearly the nature of a medical problem to local medical personnel who may not speak English.
- Learning a second language facilitates learning other languages.
- Acquiring second language proficiency could prevent injury or death, given the increasing threat of terrorism against U.S. citizens.
- Learning the local language can play a major role in adjusting to culture shock because efficient communication can (a) minimize the frustrations, misunderstandings, and aggravations that face the linguistic outsider, and (b) provide a sense of safety, mastery, and self-assurance.

In addition to all of these cogent reasons, perhaps the best reason for learning a second language is that it enables the learner to get "inside" another culture. Communicating effectively—essential for conducting business affairs—involves more than a proficiency in sending and receiving messages. Effective communication requires an understanding of how people think, feel, and behave. It involves knowing something about the cultural values, attitudes, and patterns of behavior. One of the best ways to gain cultural awareness is through a culture's language.

References

James C. Baker, "Foreign Language and Pre-departure Training in U.S. Multinational Firms," *Personnel Administrator*, July 1984, pp.63-72.

Basil Bernstein, "Elaborated and Restricted Codes: Their Social Origins and Some Consequences," *American Anthropologist* (special issue on "The Ethnography of Communication," J. J. Gumperz and Dell Hymes, eds.), 66, 6 (1964): 55-69.

Joseph Casagrande, "The Southwest Project in Comparative Psycholinguistics: A Preliminary Report," in Anthony F.C. Wallace, ed., *Men and Cultures: Selected Papers of the Fifth International Congress of Anthropological and Ethnological*

Sciences (Philadelphia: University of Pennsylvania Press, 1960): 777-782.

John Condon, *With Respect to the Japanese: A guide for Americans* (Yarmouth, Maine: Intercultural Press, 1984).

Christopher Engholm, *When Business East Meets Business West: The Guide to Practice and Protocol in the Pacific Rim* (New York: John Whiley and Sons, 1991).

Peter Farb, Word Play: *What Happens When People Talk* (New York: Knopf, 1974).

Nancy P. Hickerson, *Linguistic Anthropology* (New York: Holt, Rinehart, and Winston, 1980).

Elinor Keenan, "Norm-makers, Norm-breakers: Uses of Speech by Men and Women in a Malagasy Community," in Richard Bauman and Joel Sherzer, eds., *Explorations in the Ethnography of Speaking* (London: Cambridge University Press, 1974): 125-43

O. Mizutani, *Nihongo No Seitai* [The Facts about Japan] (Tokyo: Sotakusha, 1979).

Helmut Morsbach, "Aspects of Nonverbal Communication in Japan," in Larry Samovar and R.E. Porter, eds., *Intercultural Communication*: A Reader, 3rd ed. (Belmont, CA: Wadsworth, 1982): 300-316.

Susan Parr, "International Education: Don't Leave Home Without It," *Christian Science Monitor,* November 17, 1992, p. 19.

Ishii Satoshi and Donald Klopf, "A Comparison of Communication Activities of Japanese and American Adults," paper presented at the Communication Association of the Pacific, Tokyo, Japan, 1975.

R. Shimonishi, "Influence of Culture and Foreign Language Learning: A Contrastive Analysis in terms of English and Japanese Passive Based on Japanese Culture," unpublished MA Thesis, University of Kansas, Lawrence, 1977.

Paul Simon, *The Tongue-Tied American* (New York: Continuum Press, 1980).

Deborah Tannen, *You Just Don't Understand: Women and Men in Conversation* (New York: Morrow, 1990).

Insup Taylor, *Psycholinguistics: Learning and Using Language* (Englewood Cliffs, NF: Prentice-Hall, 1990).

Questions:

1. What is the Sapir-Whorf hypothesis?

2. How did the author explain the significance of the fact that the English language has over 150 different compound words starting with the term "self?"

3. What are the different goals of language in Japan and the United States?

4. How does Tannen distinguish between "rapport-talk" and "report-talk?"

The answer section begins on page 243.

Since the United States has drawn its population from all over the world, it has often been referred to as the great "melting pot." But many citizens, retaining much of their original ethnicity, have not been homogenized into a standard middle American. More than six of every ten residents of Miami do not speak English as their first language; substantial communities of Chinese and Japanese-Americans live between Seattle and Los Angeles; and many Native American groups continue to maintain their ethnic distinctiveness. These various ethnic enclaves represent not only a substantial segment of the population, but also a substantial segment of the buying public. If companies are interested in penetrating these markets, they will need to know something about their cultural values, behavior patterns, beliefs, and symbols. In this article, anthropologist Alisse Waterston describes the role that anthropology can play in the area of product marketing.

Interpreting Audiences: Cultural Anthropology in Market Research

By Alisse Waterston

INTERPRETING AUDIENCES: CULTURAL ANTHROPOLOGY IN MARKET RESEARCH

A popular topic of discussion these days is "cultural diversity," otherwise known as multiculturalism. There is growing recognition that North American society is no longer dominated, at least demographically, by the stereotypical White Anglo Saxon Protestant Male. Instead, our cities, suburbs, and hinterlands are populated with folks of many colors and cultures.

The latest census information shows tremendous percentage growth of ethnic and racial minorities in the U.S. From 1980 to 1990, the total population grew by 10 percent—white by 6 percent, blacks by 13 percent, Hispanics by 53 percent, and Asians by 108 percent. (The current population distribution is 12 percent black, 9 percent Hispanic, 3 percent Asian or Pacific Islander, 1 percent Native American, 4 percent other, and 80 percent white.) Other census figures show that 20 million U.S. residents were born elsewhere; that since 1960, the number of foreign-born residents has more than tripled from 1.5 million to 5.6 million; and that 25 percent of foreign-born Americans came to the U.S. between 1985 and 1990.

With these demographic changes has come a growing awareness of and attention to various ethnic groups by the media, the public at large, politicians, and private industry. In market research jargon, these groups are called "market segments," and efforts to reach them have become more refined. This is part of a longer-term move from mass marketing to target marketing—first toward young people and women and now toward ethnic groups.

Equipped with this knowledge and trained in sociocultural anthropology, I recently decided to open a research and consulting firm, which I call Surveys Unlimited. Because I have family members already specializing in market research for the cable television industry, it made sense for me to direct my efforts at securing clients in this area.

For the most part, those in the cable television industry (whether networks, programmers, or cable operators) have not made great efforts to reach the potential minority customer. Many companies rely on syndicated studies, which generally present the three main groups—Hispanics, blacks, and Asians—as more or less monolithic and examine broad-based purchasing behavior (i.e., not specific to cable television). Survey research has shown that there is high interest in cable television by Hispanics and blacks, but less product is sold to them; in other words, these "segments" are "under-penetrated."

Reprinted by permission of PRACTING ANTHROPOLOGY 16(2), Spring, 1994, pp. 11-13.

It is surprising that activity in ethnic marketing is so slow since the television industry has seen great success with another segment—teenagers and young adults. At the time that MTV and FOX developed and positioned their product to this targeted segment, industry experts believed they would never secure viewers or advertisers, since traditional targets were white viewers aged twenty-four to fifty-nine. They defied industry skepticism and saw phenomenal success.

Recently, there has been interest by some in the industry in directing programming and marketing efforts to these segments. For example, HBO has hired an ethnic marketing director; a large marketing agency has developed a nationwide direct mail campaign targeting Hispanics and African Americans; and a cable operator in San Diego has developed an in-house research and marketing campaign directed at Hispanic nonsubscribers.

When cable companies and networks commission market research, they look for data on television audiences and cable subscribers. Traditional market researchers provide quantitative and qualitative data which are derived from surveys and focus groups, respectively. While these research techniques do provide "actionable" data for companies and networks—meaning information that can be turned into program development, marketing strategies, and public relations efforts—they have certain limitations. Survey research presupposes categories of respondent thought and behavior. In addition, both survey and focus group research do not get at what people really do but only what they say they do.

The latter limitation has serious consequences for market research. For example, at any focus group session where the topic is television there are always one or two people who insist they never watch TV—but when they do, they *only* watch PBS. Invariably, these are the very same persons who later reveal they have five television sets in their home! A good focus group moderator will elicit these kinds of contradictions. Nevertheless, since television is perceived by many as socially unacceptable (and they therefore report less viewing than may be true), and since the research occurs in an artificial and public setting, focus group results on TV viewing may rest on shaky ground.

Because of these methodological limitations of traditional market research, as well as the changing ethnic/racial composition of the consumer marketplace, I positioned Surveys Unlimited as a "cultural research and consulting company" applying anthropological techniques and analysis to market research. As I met with potential clients, I promoted ethnographic fieldwork as central to the services I offered and advocated using the approach in research on targeted "market segments." Whether over a business lunch or at a midtown office, I described the value of anthropology to potential clients on the programming side of the industry in the following terms:

> In order to produce, develop, and market programming better, networks need to learn more about the who, where, what , and why of audiences and potential audiences. In turn, consumers gain by having their needs and desires better appreciated. A merging of anthropological analysis and research techniques with the best of traditional market research makes for a productive mix and a powerful resource.

Anthropology can address limitations of survey and focus group research and contribute to the knowledge fund in several ways. First, anthropological research is exploratory in the sense that it does not presuppose categories determined by the researcher or rely on the researcher's world view. Second, cultural researchers do fieldwork on informants' home turf, and consumers are observed in their natural environment. Third, exploring issues from the bottom up tunes us into consumers' conceptual systems, and appreciating the subjectivity of consumers in their social and cultural context leads to more accurate findings.

One anthropological approach to audience research would be to examine audiences and their cultural construction of television. As people talk, their metaphors for television indicate the images, attitudes, and beliefs they carry. Moreover, there are various ways television watching may be linked to peoples' everyday lives. For example, television watching may be a solitary or social activity, and people may watch television in repeated, structured ways (i.e., television as ritual). Is there a public/private dichotomy operating whereby watching in the home "counts," but viewing at taverns, the receptionist's desk, or the machine shop is not considered "really" watching TV? In what ways does having a television or subscribing to cable television signify success or "making it" in the U.S.? Answers to these kinds of questions provide insight into how audiences frame and make television-related decisions.

I was very encouraged by the enthusiasm many potential clients expressed to these notions, and I was offered a few opportunities to present a formal proposal. To date, these proposals have not resulted in contracts, however. Perhaps the approach is too esoteric for marketers, who are unable to see how the research translates into "actionable" results.

In addition, there are practical problems in applying anthropological research methods to market research that I had not fully worked out. A successful research company must be able to handle several projects at once, and design, implement, and provide results of the research often in a matter of weeks. How does one generate meaningful data from a short-term research project, and how does one budget an ethnographic study? These questions relate to concerns companies have about anthropology's usefulness in addressing their *immediate* needs.

It became very clear to me that it was necessary to reposition my company. While I continued to use my credentials as a cultural anthropologist, I found it more effective to promote my knowledge and understanding of minority markets while using traditional market research techniques. Our services now include custom market research; cultural, ethnic, and racial group research; community studies; literature searches; and anthropological analysis. Anthrogry's contribution is not limited to research technique (ethnography) but also includes the perspective it brings to bear on the subject.

The following captures my new position as I present it to clients:

Anthropologists, having appreciated cultural diversity for at least a century, can help generate understanding of ethnic identity, symbol systems, cultural values, behaviors, and meanings people attach to specific issues. Since anthropological analysis considers the interplay of class, gender, race, ethnicity, country of origin, regional and global marketplace, etc., it provides context for market research data.

When it comes to ethnic and racial identity, many lapse into static thinking, ignoring history. It is erroneous to assume that ethnic identity simply emerges from static cultural/national heritage or "authentic" tradition. Rather, ethnic and racial group identity reflects social categories and constructions. From this perspective, we can better appreciate that change, contestation, and conflict are a part and parcel of the multicultural landscape.

Marketers often assume that members of each of the three groups, Hispanic, black, and Asian, share the same cultural cues and ethnic values. In reality, there is dissension within ethnic and racial groups on issues of group composition, on what constitutes "heritage," and on the proper emblems of ethnicity. Cultural cues do help consumers connect with a product, but using the wrong symbols may offend and alienate the very consumers being targeted.

The difficulty in arriving at terminology that adequately captures and describes an ethnic group and is acceptable to its purported members illustrates this complex reality. For example, "black" and "African American" are not necessarily interchangeable terms, and the terms "Hispanic" and "Latino" continue to be contested by those in and outside of that social category. Since ethnic identity and its vital symbols are in a state of transition, marketers need to assess and track these issues.

With the shift in the positioning of my services, several potential clients have become *actual* clients. These include networks interested in developing new programming which appeals to specific audiences. Other clients are cable companies, now concerned with new competition from telephone companies and others. These cable operators are becoming more eager to attend to customer needs and wants, and companies operating in central cities are commissioning research on heretofore untapped minority consumers.

A brief description of a study I conducted illustrates the benefit of an anthropologically informed approach. The client, a cable television network interested in targeting Hispanics, wanted to know how far they had to go in creating Spanish-language programming. The marketers assumed that knowledge and use of English would be a marker of Hispanics assimilation into American society and that those Hispanics with less knowledge and use of English would need and want more Spanish-language programming, while English speakers would have less interest and need for such programming.

Three sites, each a major urban center, were chosen in which to conduct six hundred door-to-door interviews. Using traditional market research techniques, I designed a questionnaire which covered a range of issues from awareness and viewership of television programming to migration histories and language use in different contexts. Bilingual field researchers administered the survey. Respondents were also shown mock-ups of different ways the new programming might be provided and asked to vote for the form they would most like to see on television.

At first glance, the findings were confusing. In contrast to the client's assumptions, Hispanic respondents in one city showed very high levels of knowledge and use of English, but indicated their language of preference for television watching as Spanish; they also gave the highest vote to the Spanish-only form of the programming mock-up. On the other hand, Hispanic respondents in the second city, who were more recent arrivals to the U.S. and who showed the lowest levels of knowledge and use of English, indicated no language of preference for television watching and gave the highest vote to a bilingual form of the programming mock-up.

A language model of assimilation could not account for these findings; instead, a broader understanding of ethnicity was needed. Spanish-only programming is important to English-proficient Hispanic respondents in the first city, in which Hispanics constitute a prosperous ethnic enclave. In this site, there are great political, social, and economic advantages to maintaining Hispanic identity and to retaining Spanish, their "native" language. In the second city, the advantages of Hispanic identity are not available to a majority of its Hispanic residents, who also have no need to work at retaining Spanish-language ability. They find bilingual programming more useful, perhaps in part as an aid to learning English.

These interpretations will not only guide the network's strategic program planning, but will also inform the way they market their product to different Hispanic communities around the U.S. In terms of research technique, this study follows in the tradition of market research; the interpretation of results follows in the tradition of anthropology.

As I get more work in this area, I am faced with the ethical dilemma of gathering information on certain populations in order to target them for consumer goods. Will this information be used to meet the real needs and wants of customers, or will it simply be used to recast or reframe what private industry wants customers to want? On the other hand, isn't it a form of redlining when certain groups are ignored?

In my discussions with members of minority groups, many people express resentment at being passed over by marketers. They view attention paid to minority markets as empowering to members of those groups and as providing new work and career opportunities for them. Eager to point out statistics on their buying power and demographic growth trends, minorities in business argue that the time has come for ethnic marketing. In fact, one group has formed the Ethnic Marketing Leadership Council of the American Marketing Association, referring to themselves as "the New Majority." Clearly, the phenomenon of ethnic marketing reflects political and economic processes of ethnic identity formation. It should come as no surprise that exploitation and empowerment are two sides of the coin. The anthropological advantage in market research also involves keeping these issues in sight.

In order to advance my company, I found it necessary to focus on applying an anthropological perspective to market research rather than applying the research techniques of our discipline. I remain hopeful that once clients experience the advantages of anthropology to data analysis, they will be willing to try its methods. My ability to convince a client to experiment with ethnography will most likely depend on how successful I am in demonstrating the advantages of an anthropological perspective.

Questions:

1. What three things have been done to direct programming and marketing efforts to minority segments of the population that have long been ignored?

2. In what ways can anthropology contribute to the knowledge of focus-group research?

3. How did the Hispanic groups from different cities respond to the ideas of a Spanish-only and bilingual form of television programming?

The answer section begins on page 243.

19

In our TV-oriented world that is becoming increasingly more visual, brand images of products are taking on more and more importance. Customers the world over use symbols and images to either reject or identify with certain brand products. And, as the discipline of anthropology informs us, different cultures have different values, myths, and symbols. Thus, marketing strategists need to know about these cultural differences so they will be able to present their products in ways that will be compatible with local cultural perceptions. This selection discusses the role that anthropologists can play in developing culturally relevant brand images for products being marketed around the world. While the author fails to mention the issue, this article does raise an important ethical consideration: that is, what is the responsibility of the anthropologist who provides culturally relevant information to a company that then sells harmful products to local people?

Trends Symbols, and Brand Power in Global Markets: The Business Anthropology Approach

By Jeanne van Rij

"A serious cause of business failure is the common assumption that conditions in foreign markets—market preferences, distribution channels, intellectual property rights and many other things must be what we think they are or at least what we think they should be."—Peter Drucker [1]

Brand image is no longer a marginal dimension of business, but the very core of business identity and strategy. With a world culture evolving, customers everywhere respond to images, myths, and metaphors that help them define their personal and national identities and relationships within a global context of world culture and product benefits.

For most firms, the problem of adopting a global customer strategy or developing the right corporate identity is not only their lack of specific information, but something deeper and more essential—the lack of a mental model that recognizes the power of the external environment to shape customer perception in cross-border marketplaces.

Business anthropology is a new way of thinking about the challenge of keeping up with global change. It tracks the influence of technology-induced trends and cultural symbols on customer standards and perceptions of brand images. Business anthropology provides a set of advanced concepts for market strategy and branding. It can help a firm leverage knowledge of customer perceptions of the environment to enhanced competitive strategy in transnational markets.

Television technology, Hollywood "Dream-Machine" movies, and advertising have created a world culture with implications for brand strategy, market intelligence, and management techniques in every business that becomes international. The subtle messages on worldwide TV are as responsible for the rapid development of the global economy as the expansionist activities of multinational companies. World culture lubricates and intensifies, through brand images, the rapid incorporation of international products into every marketplace.

Customer Perception

About 85 percent of all communication is non-verbal.[2] Customers absorb visual and musical symbols and images from their general environment and from several hours of television viewing each day. Much of the information influencing customers on television (as well as in movies, videos, and CDs) is expressed in coded form. The underlying messages are in images, text and graphics, symbols, myths, and metaphors—stories that come in through the eyes and ears, just as in real life. Customers absorb this coded information intuitively. Intuition is a gut feeling—knowing something and not being conscious of how or why you came to know it. A brand image is like a DNA code or a software icon—it is an encrypted message of benefits and methods of achieving them. The unique goals or vision of a company and its skills are communicated intuitively to customers via these nonverbal symbols.

The image doesn't sell a product, it *is* the product. Brand power and customer loyalty are shaped by the symbols a firm uses and the image it presents in the marketplace. A company image is created in the minds of consumers by a configuration of symbols—its product designs, logos, logotypes, positioning, packaging, advertising concepts, and themes. A brand image is conveyed in messages embedded in a communication style, a configuration of symbols, and content. Customers use the differences between brand images to make their choices among products that are essentially alike in a material sense.

In positioning an international brand, the rapidity of externally induced changes in customer standards is often misunderstood or underestimated. In spite of familiarity with local culture, or perhaps because of it, country managers tend to ignore the massive quantities of nonverbal information in routine, daily life that influence brand perception. To account for the interplay of global and local forces as part of the ongoing reality of markets and as part of a competitive brand strategy, the strategist must see, in a conventional sense, the invisible new world—a world of symbols representing intangible products and intangible benefits.

The U.S. is leading a general world drift to "brain" technologies—the augmentation of brain power and "mind" services. Even our tangible products are increasingly embedded with professional knowledge content as we move out of the older tradition of industrial, "brawn" technologies—the augmentation of muscle power. Our most profitable growth is now based on "mind" benefits. Movies and music, software programs, electronic communication, medical and biotech products, financial services and R&D, all offer more intangible than tangible benefits.

In every marketplace, similar high-quality products and services at or near price parity are available. This drift to intangibles is changing customer perception worldwide. Awash with new goods and services, global and cultural imagery, symbols and metaphors, customers are increasingly making their decisions in the marketplace by applying current ideas, signposts, and icons, rather than by concrete facts alone. Customer needs and desires are no longer limited to "real" benefits. Customers want intangible benefits—the myth and magic that satisfy the mind and imagination. These intangible benefits are undreamed of by managers caught up in the older, more physical and material models of customer expectations. A shift from concrete to abstract, from tangible to intangible value-added products and services has created an altered world in customer standards and perceptions.

To understand what influences foreign customers' perceptions of product and service value, we need to decode the two powerful cultural ecosystems of which we are hardly aware—our own culture and the culture of the global village, born of television.

The World Television Culture

The customer world was once narrowly defined by tradition, neighborhood, culture, and material reality. Now it is defined by a consciousness of world culture as well. Today, decisions are arrived at with the help of symbolic messages, modes of presentation, and patterns of discourse embedded in programs, movies, music, and commercials. Seductive advertising extorts customers to "live their dreams" through the purchase of goods and services. Customer needs, hopes, and expectations explode in a wealth of alternatives created by the self-consciousness induced by a worldwide TV culture.

The influence of worldwide TV culture on the perceptions of foreign customers is enormous. It begins with the profound effect of the visual and auditory images of American culture on the small children of other cultures right in their own living rooms.[3] Through these images and sounds, children of other cultures actively experience the thoughts and feelings conveyed by the images and participate in the messages they bring. Images and symbols, hidden in the subtext of movies, music, and commercials are being diffused without regard to time, geography, or national borders. Worldwide TV culture carries American myths and assumptions around the world, capturing the minds and imagination of people everywhere.

One billion adults have already been raised on worldwide TV culture and the American Dream Machine. They are global consumers in that they have been changed in childhood by television. They learned that independence rather than

111

obedience, initiative and optimism rather than passivity and resignation, bring rewards of mobility and wealth. They learned that products and services create an "experience" or a fantasy of an experience. Particularly in the second- and third-world countries, they learned about "the inalienable right to life, liberty, and pursuit of happiness," the right to choice linked to desire, marriage linked to love and the right to expression of one's identity in the marketplace. American movies and music unite all television-raised consumers in mutually shared beliefs, worldview, and symbol-clusters of desires, images, and expectations.

The human mind, once stretched by a new idea, never regains its original dimensions. The American culture code has successfully invaded half the world by persuading children and teenagers of a new set of beliefs or assumptions about life goals, products, and services. More recent international political events—the breakup of the Eastern European bloc and the modernization of many South American countries—are characterized by an increasing passion for American products, capitalism, and democracy. Multiple scenarios of hope and dreams conveyed through movies and American or American-style commercial television advertising have enlarged possibilities for people all over the globe.

America has acquired power not by outright territorial expansion but by colonizing the future—by defining and monopolizing the modernization process itself. The territorial spread of the American cultural code by means of entertainment content and its half-hidden subtext of beliefs and rules, myth and symbols, is so powerful that it is creating an Americanized world.

The Hidden Depth of Local Culture

In spite of the forces of homogenization, however, consumers also see the world of global symbols, company images, and product choice through the lens of their own local culture and its stage of development and market sophistication. France, among others, has objected to the American invasion of its culture and the replacement of its own cultural code with that of America. French prisoners, for example, keep asking to have their "rights read to them," even though this is not part of the French legal code.

Every national culture has its characteristic myths. These myths are the controlling pattern of a culture—its DNA—and pervade every element

in the system. The myth of the frontier, for example, lives in the mentality of Americans. The physical frontier is closed, but we are excited by the unknown, which for us is the continuation of the frontier. Contemporary Americans see themselves as pioneers on unknown and exciting frontiers. Now the frontiers are "outer space" and "inner space." We are world leaders in "outer space"—the aerospace industry, space research, and now the World Wide Web. We are world leaders in "inner space"—the software and biotech industries, brain research, mental health drugs, and (illegal) recreational drugs. Japan, on the other hand, has a historic tradition of frugality and eye for detail. Its striking talents are expressed in world leadership in miniaturization, product quality control, consumer electronics, and microchip production.

Dr. Joseph Stillman is president of Cognex, the world leader in machine vision technology. Cognex does 50 percent of its business Japan and earns 50 percent of its profits there, with net profit margins running at 30 percent. Stillman says: "If your Japanese customer complains that the boxes in which the product arrived were dented, don't think like an American. When a customer complains about a product in a way that sounds unusual, listen! It may take some time to figure it out, but it is a piece in understanding how [the system] operates. Speak their language. Know their agendas." Stillman doesn't mean speak Japanese—he means you must understand the way a culture operates if you want success in its markets. You have to understand customers' assumptions—their unquestioned beliefs—and figure out the rules that are implied in the local culture.

Difficulties arise because customers have deep and complex commitments to their own national cultural codes as well as the global cultural code. Younger international customers have two lives—the local and the global. The contradictions between them and the exaggeration or over-statement of first one, then the other, are inevitable consequences of the emergence of this new, embracing, powerful American DNA-like code that is embedded in worldwide television programming.

Younger consumers adapt their decision-making to the global code initially, with tentative commitment to a course of action in consumption as a form of self-expression and self-realization. Yet if the ideas implied in a brand identity or corporate brand contradict some valued aspect of the domestic code, a depreciation in the value of the brand may take place, leading to customer confusion, loss of trust, and an unwillingness to buy the product. Global self-consciousness stimulates a new world of customer fantasy and confusion, as customers with destabilized perceptions grapple with old and new loyalties and promises.

As national cultural codes yield to the powerful influence of American films and music, consumers become uncertain. Unable to clearly substantiate differences in products or services and their claims, and focused on country of origin and their own self-identity, younger customers (and increasingly older ones as well) often use brand images to act out alternative fantasies or representations of experience.[4]

Transnational Brand Management

At present, the knowledge most firms have of how best to mange brands and relationships with customers in foreign marketplaces is rudimentary. Better brand management and a better comprehension of customer perception would clearly yield enormous rewards.

Brand power is characterized by the distinctive nature of the brand personality, by the appeal and relevance of its identity, by the consistency of its communication, and by the integrity of its identity.[5] Brand power is evolutionary so as to remain contemporary for each new generation of consumers. The impact of the communications revolution has created a chasm between generations since the '60s, influencing across borders with unimaginable rapidity. Brand power symbols must be simple and dense—that is, complex enough to convey subtly different messages to different groups within the same market and to work in different ways from market to market.

A first TV-connected generation must appear in any country before political and brand benefits can be fully realized. Once that generation emerges, new patterns of consumption, new industries, and new political agendas develop, as happened in Japan and Europe in the '80s.[6] New "ideas spaces" accumulate in each TV-connected generation and are melded into national and local markets as the level of economic expectation and income bring these markets into the circle of "belonging" nations.[7]

Brand power and customer loyalty emerge from a brand image—a DNA with a controlled patter of unique benefits from which every element of the marketing mix is cloned. Successful global brands often use the major themes of Hollywood films—equality, energy, optimism, and irreverence for authority.

Coca-Cola was the first American company to spread the myth of "global belonging"—a symbol of the equality of nations and races and the connection of cultures based on the shared belief in American values. ("I'd like to teach the world to sing in perfect harmony.") This theme is directed to customers under 35—those captured by the code embedded in American media.

Reebok, using this theme in a sports context, can hardly meet the demand of consumers in South Africa reared on African-American success in music and sports. Michael Jackson, Michael Jordan, and Eddie Murphy symbolize the America of freedom and equality, diverse cultures, democracy, consumer culture, upward mobility, and wealth for nonwhite races in second-and third-world cultures.

Benetton's twist is to emphasize equality and irreverence for authority. The ad of two small children chastely kissing—a black boy with an impish smile and small raised horns of hair on his head, and a curly-haired blond girl—brought many complaints from the U.S., as did the one that displayed different colored condoms. Benetton's powerful new photo of thousands of desperate Albanians commandeering ships to take them to the Italian ports of Bari and Brindisi also made Americans uneasy, although it is a variation on an American myth. One reason for this exodus was that the Albanians had been watching Italian television—including commercials for consumer goods such as one in which a cat is served food on a silver platter.

The passage of new "idea spaces" in the minds of consumers moves quickly, and market sophistication evolves more rapidly than many business leaders can believe or even imagine. The excitement of world culture increases demand for added stimulation and becomes more firmly embedded with each TV-connected generation. Consumer expectations and desire for new experiences escalate exponentially. As the world culture enlarges and consolidates via worldwide television, global symbols grow more abstract and complex and circulate more rapidly in the world community, and historic codes of culture alter.

Developing Strategic Insight

Customers in cultures all over the globe are at different stages of evolution and adapting to new conditions. Outdated mental models that ignore meaning and nonverbal communication slow down the process of company adaptation to customer definitions of satisfaction and to patterns in competitor images that influence customers in the immediate marketplace. Brand value in a particular market is determined by customer satisfaction as defined by the customer, not by the company.

Powerful brand identities and corporate branding will be the main engines of continuing international growth. However, building a positive corporate identity is not easy. A firm's identity and use of symbols reflect built-in assumptions about its organization, capabilities, plans, and way of doing business; and its beliefs about the assumptions of its competitors and its customers.

How does a company learn to act upon customers' needs, as the customers themselves perceive them, and effectively communicate its own authentic identity and that of its products at the same time? Obviously, a common organizational perception of company reputation, brand identity, and communication strategy can be better achieved if team members share a common mental model and language for dialogue, just as they do for technical standards and finance.

Management teams may need to learn to extinguish established but unadaptive marketing assumptions and practices, and develop new and different ones. For example, customer-focused, scenario-planning workshops assist in examining alternative customer models of the environment, survival strategies, and priorities of benefits from brand choice as filtered through the influence of their cultures and global influences. These models are biological and organic because they are based on ecological adaptation to new conditions. They challenge conventional wisdom by providing a holistic way of assessing and interpreting the environments to which customers adapt, and they can stimulate widespread discussion. By focusing on the context in which customer decisions are made, managers learn to trust in the logic of the decision-making process.

Business anthropology has developed tools and techniques that enable companies to use myths, metaphors, symbols, and images to address the inherently contradictory needs of global consumers. By identifying customer perceptions of their own and competitors' brands in key cross-border markets, companies can build a competitive advantage. By identifying specific, culture-driven myths and symbols that are important to customers in a local culture, and by identifying worldwide trends that influence customer perceptions, they can create strategic global

advantage. And by viewing customers' need perceptions within a holistic framework, and by examining their own national and corporate culture assumptions, companies doing business around the world can gain the advantage of a vast and useful knowledge base. This knowledge edge can help them forecast believable alternative customer trends, identify market-share opportunities, and develop an unbeatable communication strategy.

Notes and References

1. Peter Drucker, "The Information Managers Truly Need," *Harvard Business Review*, Jan.-Feb. 1995, pp. 54-62.

2. E. T. Hall, *The Silent Language* (New York: Doubleday, 1959); A. Mehrabin, *Silent Messages* (Belmont, Calif.: Wadsworth, 1971); M. Knapp, *Essentials of Non-Verbal Communication* (New York: Holt, Reinhart and Winston, 1980); and the works of Charles Saunders Peirce in Richard J. Parmentier, *Signs in Society: Studies in Semiotic Anthropology* (Indianapolis: Indiana University Press, 1995); John E. Sherry, Jr., ed., *Contemporary Marketing and Consumer Behavior: An Anthropological Sourcebook* (South Salt Lake, Utah: Sage Publications, 1995).

3. Most national requirements demand that "foreign" programs be no more than 49 percent of daily fare. In 1993, the EEC sent out a directive suggesting that each member country try to reduce "foreign" broadcasting— as American broadcasting is euphemistically described—to below the 49 percent level.

4. Jeanne Binstock van Rij. "The New Tokyo Teenager" and "The New Japanese Singles" (the first multi-client anthropological studies of customer cultural psychographics of television-raised customers), McCann-Erickson, Hakuhodo, Tokyo, 1986; also "The New Young Turks," D.A.P., Direkt Marketing, Inc., Istanbul, 1990.

5. Paul Stobart, ed., *Brand Power* (New York: New York University Press, 1994).

6. Prorietary McCann-Erickson comparative studies of younger Japanese and European consumers over a period of ten years; also by Christine Restall, "The New Generation, 1977-1987," McCann-Erickson European Youth Study, 1989.

7. Japanese managers perceived cigarette smoking as a health hazard and unsociable act in business meetings about ten years later

than the U.S. By 1987, business meetings in Japan were smoke-free and women were beginning to smoke, following the pattern set in the U.S. In that same year, Turkey was in rapid industrial development, but managers were smoking at their desks and at meeting and women had not yet begun to smoke. By 1994, however, meetings in business and government were becoming smoke-free and women were smoking as the standards of the "belonging" industrialized economies gained acceptance.

Questions:

1. Based on the new "brain" technologies, where has the greatest profitable growth occurred?

2. According to Dr. Joseph Stillman, what is needed in order for a company to be successful in global markets?

3. What are the four characteristics of brand power?

The answer section begins on page 243.

Traditionally, market research has focused on gathering information on what the general buying public thinks about a certain product. Researchers would conduct interviews in shopping malls, send questionnaires through the mail, or conduct telephone surveys. Some of the more recent, "cutting edge" market researchers, however, feel that asking people what they think is not always the best approach. Rather, they know what any good ethnographer knows: that what people say they do is not always an accurate representation of what they actually do. Thus, ethnographic methods (observing actual behavior) are finding their way into the tool kit of the market research. In this article Posner describes one innovative market research company that uses video cameras, video software, beepers, and disposable cameras to learn—in a first hand, ethnographic way— what people actually do.

Inside a Converted Schwinn Bicycle Factory

By Bruce G. Posner

Inside a converted Schwinn bicycle factory near Chicago's Loop, a team of young social scientists— anthropologists, ethnographers, art historians—is huddled around TV monitors and computer-controlled editing decks. They've been staring for hours at streams of video, sharing their impressions and cataloging thousands of images.

The film is no Academy Award nominee. It is cinema verite—unedited tapes of commuters in three cities pulling into self-service gas stations, filling their tanks, and buying coffee from the convenience store. To these researchers, though, the video is every bit as engaging as the most intricate Hollywood thriller—full of complex patterns, hidden meanings, clues about human behavior. Do people intuitively grasp how to use the pump and where to pay? If not, do they read the instructions or simply fumble around until they get it right?

Welcome to the watchful world of *E.Lab Incorporated*, a small market-research and design firm with big aspirations. The company is only two years old, but it is at the forefront of a growing movement to rethink how companies understand customers and create products that meet their needs. Its clients include some of the best-known names in technology and consumer products: Hallmark Cards, McDonald's, Steelcase, Texas Instruments.

E.Lab's message is as simple as it is subversive. Nearly all the tools of conventional marketing—focus groups, customer surveys, segmentation—are designed to measure what people think. But the secret to breakthrough innovation, E.Lab believes, is understanding how people behave: what they do and how they live.

"It's not 'the product' that matters," says Rick Robinson, 37, an E.Lab cofounder. "People use products to make meaning in their lives and make statements about who they are." Customers often can't articulate those connections, he adds, "because meaning isn't always a matter of conscious belief. You can't just listen to what people say. You have to understand how they interact with their environment and with other people. That's why you have to watch."

"This is new territory," adds John Cain, 33, another E.Lab cofounder. "Marketing is a science. There's syndicated research, data on attitudes and intentions. But something is missing— information about real behavior in real situations. We shoot video to understand patterns of behavior and explore how people actually use things."

What can others learn about the future of marketing by watching how E.Lab watches customers? Consider its work with Thomson, the French company that sells consumer products in the United States under the RCA and GE brands. Thomson recently came to E.Lab with a new technology for storing, accessing, and playing digital music—an innovation both sides believe can become The Next Big Thing. But even the most powerful technology can't guarantee success in a hypercompetitive market like home entertainment. That requires new insights into when, where, and how people interact with music.

It was E.Lab's job to generate those insights. First, the company conducted in-depth interviews with potential users in three cities. Researchers followed people around their homes—from the living room to the laundry room, from the basement to the garage—and carefully noted where they kept their audio equipment and how they organized their music collections. Ethnographers also shot 60 hours of "guerrilla video" in public places—people listening to music on sidewalks and buses, in record stores and malls.

Then it was time to go broader and deeper. E.Lab mailed disposable cameras to potential customers and asked them to photograph the audio equipment in their dens, bedrooms, cars, boats—essentially wherever they listened to music. To understand how listening patterns changed depending on the circumstances, E.Lab provided other people with beepers. Researchers beeped participants as early as 9:00 a.m., as late as 10:30 p.m., and as often as seven times a day. When their beepers sounded, participants took out a company-supplied notebook and answered questions about their listening habits. The questions probed for context (are you alone?), mood (are you feeling happy or sad?), even decision-making patterns (who picked the music?)

Research this exhaustive generates massive amounts of raw data. The challenge is to organize the data in ways that help explain what Robinson calls "the practice of everyday life." Here, too, E.Lab has created a distinctive set of tools. When it comes to analyzing video, researchers can spend as long as one month studying hundreds of hours of images frame by frame. As they watch, they use proprietary software called CAVEAT (Computer-Aided Video Ethnography Analysis Tool) to index the images by activity, environment, type of interaction, and user experience.

Recently, the company worked with Hallmark to investigate why its Showcase stores weren't generating higher sales. E.Lab sent researchers to stores in Pittsburgh, Atlanta, Las Vegas and Kansas City. For three days in each location, ethnographers used five cameras to record customer behavior. The result was 400 hours of tape. Using CAVEAT, researchers sorted through the footage and organized thousands of images into 70 different keywords that became the basis of their recommendations.

"Some people can figure things out through one wicked insight or intuition," Robinson says.

"We're more like inch-worms. We start with the data and slowly aggregate up."

As researchers work with the data, patterns begin to emerge. In the course of analyzing the Hallmark footage, for example, one set of images kept recurring: shoppers would move slowly through the aisles, get discouraged, and leave with only a greeting card. "The store did not do a good job telling people what it was about," Robinson says.

When patterns aren't so clear, E.Lab asks customers to explain their own behavior, a process it calls an "anthropump." The company invites people who've been captured on video to watch their tapes as researchers pose questions about what's happening. E.Lab often videotapes and dissects these follow-up sessions—in effect, analyzing research subjects analyzing themselves.

How have E.Lab's ideas influenced product development? Thomson's hoped-for killer innovation is still in design, but the company says E.Lab's research is shaping its strategy. Hallmark has redesigned its Showcase stores based on E.Lab's critique, using a vocabulary borrowed from city planning. In the new stores, customers navigate "paths" linking "districts" marked by "landmarks" of high-visibility products.

For now, though, E.Lab's most important product is its philosophy for exploring what makes great products. "Too many features can kill a product," warns Robinson. "You don't have to match a competitor feature for feature. You have to give customers what they want. We're trying to help companies go beyond what's possible or what's 'cool' to what resonates with people's needs."

The Telestrator

E.Lab uses a tool dubbed the "Madden Board," after the boisterous football commentator, to examine video footage from multiple points of view. As videotape plays on a giant screen, up to six people, each armed with a telestrator and an electronic pen with different-colored "ink," can highlight important events, diagram how people move around and make decisions, and carefully annotate the tape.

Disposable Cameras

What's in your backpack? To gather data about how junior-high-school students stay in touch with their families and keep track of important information, E.Lab sent disposable cameras—along with $100 per person—to a group of young people.

The kids agreed to photograph the contents of their backpacks as well as all the places in their homes where family members post notices and schedules: the refrigerator door, bulletin boards, the kitchen table.

Video Software

Home-grown software called CAVEAT allows researchers to index video images by activity, environment, type of interaction, and user experience. For example, E.Lab studied a new line of Hallmark gift stores to determine why customers weren't buying more products. After analyzing 400 hours of videotape, E.Lab concluded that the layout was confusing shoppers. The patterns of confusion became so evident that E.Lab researchers could watch video of prospective customers entering the store and predict with uncanny accuracy where they would freeze up and walk away.

Beeper Studies

University of Chicago researchers used beepers to study mood swings among teenagers. E.Lab used them to research home entertainment. "We were looking for data about interactions with music," says John Cain. "When and where do people use it? You can't put enough video cameras in enough places to get that kind of information."

Guerrilla Video

Sometimes the most compelling insights come from the least structured research. Early in most projects, E.Lab sends ethnographers to record "guerrilla video"—handheld taping in a wide range of public settings to frame an initial set of questions. One exercise in guerrilla video documented how often kids, rather than their parents, pushed baby strollers—a finding with obvious implications for product design.

Questions:

1. What makes E.Lab's approach to market research so innovative?

2. How did E.Lab ethnographers use disposable cameras?

3. What was meant by "anthropump?"

The answer section begins on page 243.

Section III
Education

21

Like students from any cultural background, American Indian students bring their cultural values, attitudes, and behavior patterns into the classroom with them. Often these cultural values influence how students learn. Because learning styles differ from culture to culture, educators all too often have seen minority children, including Native Americans, as handicapped or having learning disorders. The problem, however, is more likely to be that teaching strategies are incompatible with certain cultural values that students bring with them. In this selection Wendy Kasten uses anthropological insights to explore the compatibility of many Native American beliefs with the principles of whole language learning, an educational approach which she suggests has relevance for teachers working with Native American children.

Bridging the Horizon: American Indian Beliefs and Whole Language Learning

By Wendy Kasten

The history of educating the Native American student in the United States is long and heartbreaking. A recent special report, *Education Week* (1989), noted that Native American students have the highest dropout rates, suicide rates, and likelihood to be labeled as handicapped or learning disabled of any American minority group. With this high degree of school failure for Indian children, educators must investigate the causal factors that contribute to this situation. It is obvious by now that our schools have not met their needs. Educators have had a tendency, when failure occurs, to think that there is something wrong or lacking in the children. It is time to look at the system that has not been successful for an entire ethnic group.

I wish to explore a relationship which is, for me, a very logical and important one, that is, the relationship between the principles of whole language teaching and learning, especially for elementary-age students, and the culture of many Native American schoolchildren. As I will demonstrate below, whole language philosophy is compatible with many common Native American beliefs and with the way in which American Indian children are typically taught and socialized in their home environment. I will attempt to draw some parallels to demonstrate that compatibility. This is not to suggest in any way that all Native American communities are identical in their belief systems or in the way they raise their children. But there are some commonalities which underlie most Native communities, and which are useful for teachers, especially non-Native teachers, to understand (Locust 1988; Paul 1981). Some Native Americans, caught between their own culture and belief system and the mainstream world, have coined the term "stuck in the horizon" to describe their feelings of dissonance, feeling they are part of neither the Earth nor the sky (*Education Week* 1989). I will attempt to demonstrate how it may be possible to bridge the horizon.

American Indian Belief Systems

Only by being true to the full growth of all individuals who make it up can society by any chance be true to itself. [Dewey 1929]

This quote by John Dewey suggests that every aspect of a human being needs to be considered in his or her education. These aspects must include more than intellectual capability, interests, and developmental issues; they must consider a person's culture as well. Culture, which Heath (1983) describes as ways of thinking, ways of believing, and ways of valuing, has monumental implications in education.

In my earlier work with Native American children on the Tohono O'odham reservation in Arizona (Kasten 1987), I learned that American Indian children may share membership in more than one culture, as they belong to a tribe, to a region of the United States, and to the community of American children. Although this phenomenon of multicultural membership is true for many individuals in the United States, the issues are somewhat more complex when the individual's minority and primary group membership differs drastically from mainstream culture and the culture of many public schools. That is not to suggest that all Native American children share the same culture, even if they share membership in the same tribe, but that their beliefs and values need to be understood by their teachers. In the case of Native American Indians, the values frequently related in school settings not only differ, but are also diametrically opposed to values the children have learned at home.

Carol Locust (1988), a researcher at the University of Arizona, discusses certain beliefs that are common to most American Indian groups, and points out how many are problematic and are often responsible for "wounding the spirit" in traditional classroom settings. For example, community and cooperation are central precepts in many Native American cultures. Working together, maintaining harmonious contacts, and avoiding disharmonious situations are basic values many Native American children assimilate before reaching school age. Avoiding disharmony is desirable because disharmony can result in spiritual unwellness.

A child with these beliefs and values enter a school where systems of reprimands, discipline, or punishment in a traditional classroom often involve confrontation, initiated by a teacher or other adult as part of the management of behavior. Native American children have been taught that confrontation is inappropriate. The children may, for example, believe that to retain their own individual wellness in a situation, they must remove themselves from the situation (Locust 1988). This may take the form of hiding or running away from a classroom or school; a behavior such as this is usually viewed as requiring stiff disciplinary action in most mainstream settings.

Paul (1981) explores certain cultural aspects of Native American students that influence learning and schooling as well. A Native American, Paul describes the cultural dissonance that many Indian children feel upon entering a public school classroom. She mentions several common beliefs that she feels teachers of Native American children need to understand. These include the notion that humans must maintain a harmony with nature and with the Earth, that all humans have value because life is a precious gift

regardless of their age or circumstances, that the extended family is protected and highly esteemed, and that language is a medium through which customs and values are communicated. In contrast, she cites the emphasis that mainstream society places on competition; rushed, precise schedules; orientations that are more future oriented than present oriented; and the "urgency for talk." These more mainstream values may be highly problematic for Indian students. For example, Paul points out that in mainstream culture, people are predictably uncomfortable with silence. Native Americans are not uncomfortable with silence and believe that talk should be purposeful and important, not just used as something to fill an uncomfortable silence. Native American children are sometimes, as a result, mistakenly viewed as shy or reticent by those outside their culture.

Salisbury (1967) tells of the problems of educating local Indian, Aleut, or Eskimo children in the Northwest, and suggests how a typical reading lesson in some older, traditional school materials, such as basal readers, might be viewed by a Native American student. Dick and Jane are a boy and girl who have a father who goes daily to a mysterious place called the "office," and yet he does not bring home any food. There are people dressed in funny clothes called police officers, smiling and helping children cross the street. Native children wonder what may be wrong with these children that they need this special help. Dick and Jane visit their grandparents who are kept on some placed called a "farm," and these grandparents seem very happy to see their grandchildren. Consequently, the Native American children wonder what terrible taboo these grandparents must have broken to be ostracized from their family and kept on a "farm" where there are also animals (Salisbury 1967:4-5).

Terri Tafoya (1981), a Native American and a storyteller from the Northwest, explains adeptly the role of oral tradition in American Indian culture. It is important for teachers of reading and literature to understand this role. Tafoya explains that stories are not strictly for entertainment; they provide the context for the transmission of social structures, patterns, and history of Indian people. Stories are always purposeful, and frequently the time and context in which they are related is purposeful as well. Certain stories are only told in appropriate seasons and in predetermined sequences, so as to fit into a certain cycle that may have an intent, such as to teach a particular important value. Tafoya's insights provide food for thought in considering approaches in the teaching of reading and of literature.

Whole Language and Native American Culture

As I pursued the available literature on Native American schooling, it soon became apparent that particular cultural considerations for Native American students are compatible with, and may be congruent with, basic beliefs about whole language teaching and learning. These proposed compatible precepts will first be listed, and then discussed.

1. Whole language teaching emphasizes process over product, valuing the process, even with mistakes, as part of learning and risk taking. Native American culture is frequently characterized as a process oriented culture that emphasizes life as a journey, and that the journeying is more important than the destination.

In classrooms where a whole language philosophy is being implemented, processes of things are generally considered as important as the product. In reading, for example, the reading process may be highlighted, such as when children are given ample opportunities to read both silently and aloud to their classmates. Children may engage in a variety of activities designed to extend the text, such as artistic representations, dramatized rereadings, or other creative dramatics. In more traditional classrooms, emphases may be placed on exact oral reading and on the responses to questions designed to check comprehension through the students' recall of facts and details.

In writing, in whole language classrooms, work on a particular text typically extends over several days or even weeks, and includes redrafts, peer conferencing and editing, and teacher feedback. This approach takes more time. In more traditional classrooms, assignments are confined to a single period or day, after which a product for evaluation is expected. These products are typically assigned a letter grade with little or no pupil-pupil or teacher-pupil interaction. When American Indians value "journeying through life," it is not unlike the language-rich classroom where students journey through a piece of writing or through a selected story. The emphasis is on savoring the present, enjoying the process, appreciating the moment.

Mainstream cultures are extremely future oriented. Instructional decisions are often made based on next semester's report card, passing on to the next grade, or planning for the next semester.

Adults often plan far in advance, saving money for next summer's vacation, for a new home or a car. This orientation difference is important for teachers of Indian children to understand.

2. Whole language emphasizes group, cooperative working, capitalizing on collaborative learning, and Vygotsky's notion (1978) of a "Zone of Proximal Development." Native American cultures tend to emphasize noncompetitive, cooperative living, with a strong sense of community and extended family.

It is not unusual in traditional classrooms for most of the curriculum to be delivered through teacher presentation. Learning, then, is viewed as the dissemination of information to be absorbed by young minds and subsequently evaluated by an objective assessment tool, such as a multiple choice test. This paradigm allows only minimal student interaction, and, in fact, interaction may be dimly viewed as a form of cheating. Students may hear reminders to "do you own work." There is a considerable emphasis placed on letter or numerical grades, striving for better grades, and even striving to get the best grade in the class.

Whole language classrooms function more like a community, with members of that community learning to share, cooperate, recognize strengths of peers, and use each other's capabilities. Vygotsky (1978) promoted the idea that learners can do more problem solving when they collaborate with peers or with adults than they can accomplish in isolation. He referred to the difference between these two potentials as "the zone of proximal development." In writing, for example, pupils function as a "community of writers" (Kasten 1990), as classmates tackle reference books together, help one other with spelling words and with ideas or feedback about their writing.

In the American Indian way of life, there is typically a similar focus on community and cooperation, where every member of a clan or extended family can have an integral role toward the good of the group. This precept, historically speaking, was essential for survival. Although many things are learned in this community from the elders, the elders are not likely to be didactic or direct in their instruction. A great deal of demonstration takes place, and children make choices about their participation, such as when they will attempt weaving or herding sheep, when they are ready to take risks.

This strong sense of community can be easily misconceived by mainstream teachers and educators when it appears as though Indian children do not desire to achieve. The value of achievement is ingrained in many mainstream cultures, which is characterized by individuals distinguishing themselves. In a classroom, this may take the form of a contest, a chart with stars denoting how much an individual child has completed, for example, in memorizing the mathematical times tables, or how many books each child has read. Many Native Americans do not look favorably upon individuals who seek to distinguish themselves deliberately in this fashion, especially at the expense of others. It is believed that the individual, in such a case, calls bad forces to himself or herself.

3. Whole language learning suggests that the learning of reading and writing are parallel to the learning of oral language. Learning begins from the whole context, with language learners making hypotheses about how language works. The modeling done by adults or older peers in the environment is a strong influential factor. Native American cultures frequently provide learning for children through modeling by elders, including norms of social behavior and specific skills. These skills are learned holistically instead of in small parts or steps. In more traditional practices associated with the teaching of reading, instruction either focuses on producing letter-sound relationships so that pupils will "sound out" the words, or on rote visual learning of "sight words," which, it is assumed, the child will later recognize in context. In primary grades, whole language strategies differ in that entire stories are read chorally, or read aloud by the teacher. These stories, which use predictable and patterned language text to some extent, have great appeal for children. Reading and enjoyment are shared and modeled frequently, providing opportunities for children to experience how written language works. These shared reading experiences (Holdaway 1978) enable children to make hypotheses about language without risking public ridicule or evaluation. Children of varied ability levels can participate in the shared reading and its extended activities, such as dramatization of the story.

Native American children also learn from the whole in their culture, where every skill or lesson is interrelated with other living and learning. Navajo children learn to weave by watching their elders. Among the Tohono O'odham, girls learn to cook fry bread by watching their mothers and grandmothers, and then participating in the preparation and cooking. The opportunities for demonstration occur frequently in Native settings, for both practical skills and social ones. As mentioned earlier, these are not taught in a didactic manner, and a great deal of choice on the part of the child is an element in the learning.

4. Whole language learning places a high value on quality children's literature, including opportunities for self-selected reader choice, culturally relevant literature, and literature related to topics being taught in other subjects. In Native American culture, stories may be purposeful, relevant to the time of year, to events taking place, and are usually intended to teach a value or an important aspect of Indian life or history. In many Native American societies, a story is not simply a source of recreation or entertainment. Stories are part of an oral tradition that serves to record history, teach spiritual aspects of living, instruct youth in appropriate social behaviors, and so on. Stories are nearly always purposeful, told with a particular intent or agenda. Often these stories are told in a particular season, or even in a particular order (Tafoya 1981). For example, among the Tohono O'odham, certain animal stories are only told while those animals are hibernating, considering that it would be inappropriate to talk them while they are awake. Other stories may be told only in conjunction with a particular festival or situation.

Often, in traditional classrooms, the selection of reading material to be read by the teacher and the children is governed by the published materials that are used. Materials are used in the order they are printed in the basal reader. Basal readers are sequenced, based on a controlled vocabulary of most frequently used words (Goodman, Shannon, Freeman, and Murphy 1988). The selection of the stories is decided by vocabulary rather than content or topic. This system of implementing stories could be confusing to a Native American child who has expectations that the stories are supposed to mean something in the greater scheme of things.

However, in classrooms where more whole language learning is implemented, literature is selected by the teacher. If basal readers are used, they are generally used more selectively and purposefully. Whole language classrooms are typically flooded with quality children's literature, frequently integrated and relevant to the content being taught. The way in which stories fit into the larger curriculum in the class is logical and helps students make connections between various aspects of the curriculum.

5. Whole language learning is often taught through content area themes, into which various

aspects of the curriculum, such as math and science, are integrated. Native American culture typically views all aspects of daily living as interrelated. For example, because the physical wellness and spiritual wellness are interrelated, health and religion are often a single word or idea. As stated above, whole language classes in elementary grades are frequently taught either partially or entirely through a thematic approach. For example, a content area topic in science or social studies may form the theme for a period of days, weeks, or even longer. Astronomy, for example, could be a theme around which whole language curriculum might be based.

During this astronomy unit, students would read and write on topics related to stars, planets, the moon, or space travel. Math activities might be related to the calendar, moon phases, speed of travel in space, distances between heavenly bodies, and more. Novels the teachers read aloud to the class might be on space themes, and Native American stories that involve celestial themes might be included. The room would typically be littered with nonfiction books, such as current titles on space exploration, information on NASA, and biographies of astronauts. A great deal of the daily curriculum would fit together instead of being segmented into separate, unrelated periods for math, science, social studies, and language arts. This format more closely resembles life for Native American people, and for all people as well.

6. Whole language teaching incorporates qualitative assessments either in place of, or in addition to, standard quantitative assessments that typically employ a multiple choice format. In Native American cultures, the quick act of choosing from multiple solutions, as is simulated by multiple choice items on a test, is often viewed as irresponsible decision making, since all possibilities are not fully entertained, and there is often more than one possible solution to a problem. Many Native American groups teach that all possibilities among choices need to be given thorough consideration, and that the best solution may be the one that pleases the most people and maintains the strong community. Rhodes (1989a, 1989b) has investigated the high rate of failure by Native American college students on standardized tests. He identified two issues, which he termed product bias and process bias. Product bias involves specific items on standardized tests that represent poor item choices in a culturally diverse society. For example, one test used in his home state of Arizona asked, "Who discovered America?" Another question asked students to identify the first settlement in North America. Native American students typically score incorrectly on both of these items, and for a good reason!

Process bias, according to Rhodes, involves the multiple choice format and the strict time limitations. Rhodes observed that Native American students believe that all items need ample consideration, using a thorough, methodical process for deciding on one answer. Therefore, American Indian students are less likely to be able to complete the test in the imposed time limit. Making rapid choices, such as required items on a multiple choice test, would be considered irresponsible and inappropriate by many Native American people.

In whole language classrooms, teachers recognize the limitations of standardized or objective testing. These procedures are generally deemphasized, with the addition of more qualitative heuristics. "Kid-watching," for example, is one whole language concept that promotes the idea that trained teacher observations and record keeping are worthwhile methods of student evaluation for many areas of curriculum (Goodman 1978, 1989). Whole language teachers explore alternative methods of evaluating students, depending on the needs and issues, with the particular student (Goodman, Goodman, and Hood 1989).

7. Whole language learning typically involves projects that are student initiated, and involve in-depth critical examination instead of focusing merely on facts or information. Native American beliefs value the answer to "why" things are, instead of "how" things are.

Learning in a whole language classroom is active rather than passive. It may be either pupil initiated or teacher initiated, but whichever the case, learning usually becomes fairly involved, with a high degree of student engagement and a great deal of student inquiry. Learning is viewed as exciting, stimulating, and consequently, it generally is. This is far different from curriculum that focuses on information and literal recall of facts. Within the latter curriculum, it is difficult for children to understand the purpose in what they are learning. It often appears as if something is done solely for the sake of schooling, bearing little resemblance to their real world. In whole language settings, children usually have more opportunities to delve deeply into subject areas, exploring the "whys" of living in addition to the "hows" and "whats."

This is similar to the values in many Native American cultures. For example, Rhodes (1989) describes how both Hopi and Navajo children are likely to learn outside of school. He points out that very little, if any, outside learning will be related to books. Children are often assigned duties or chores while adults in their society are busy doing other things. These assignments may be fairly responsible and even beyond expectation of a child's ability by non-Indian standards. For example, a seven or eight year old may be left responsible for a baby, a sheep herd, or meal preparation. If children need instruction or assistance in carrying out the task, they use peers or siblings as resources, but are reluctant to ask adults for help. Thus, they learn to become self-sufficient, self-motivated, and more comfortable initiating or implementing a task without direct adult direction. Rhodes describes this attribute as an emphasis on more full understanding, as a more holistic awareness. He suggests that in-depth projects in classroom settings are useful in that they require active student participation, respect differences in pacing, allow ample observation time for students to learn, and develop pride through teamwork. Rhodes goes on to suggest that although Navajo medicine men encourage the acquisition of knowledge for its own sake, in the real world of the Navajo and Hopi, there is little use for "knowledge which is not immediately practical" (1989:38).

The Miccosukee School

Between the fall of 1988 and the spring of 1990, I had the opportunity to work with the teachers at the Miccosukee Indian School in Miami, Florida. This tribal-run school has both a bilingual and a bicultural mission for the Miccosukee children who choose to attend. After working with the staff for that first year, delivering inservice training specifically designed to implement more whole language teaching and learning, I have begun to see the beginnings of some positive changes.

For example, in the combined kindergarten and grade 1 class, the teacher and I sat down and redesigned the daily schedule. We attempted to make the day move more fluidly, with some areas set up in learning centers where children might work together on art or math. We began each daily schedule with a shared reading experience, where children read chorally while the teacher follows the text with a pointer, using books with both enlarged and predictable or patterned language text. Other activities during the morning were designed to be related to the morning story and current unit of study. Thus, an effort was made to make connections throughout the day between aspects of curriculum, and to remove some of the artificial boundaries between subjects.

There has been at least one observable effect since some of the these changes were implemented. That is the children's positive attitudes toward many of the books used during shared reading. Children appeared eager to spend time with the books on their own, picking them up often in their free time, reading them together, and requesting favorite titles over and over. This enthusiasm for books is the same as Kasten and Clarke (1990) observed in both mainstream and minority preschool and kindergarten settings where whole language strategies were being used on a regular basis.

A second change that was implemented involved the use of more culturally relevant literature. We attempted to obtain copies of every book possible with Native American themes, from authors such as Paul Goble, Tomie de Paola, and others. Teachers tried to develop activities related to the story that would also extend concepts in the story as a part of their curriculum.

A third change involved "webbing" curriculum. Webbing is a technique that begins with one book or topic and attempts to brainstorm, and then plan ways of integrating many or all aspects of the curriculum into one theme. Curriculum is then planned based on the themes and natural extensions of the literature. This small faculty is considering implementing a schoolwide theme for one month of the year to facilitate a great deal of cross-aged tutoring, collaborating, and sharing. One topic under consideration is holidays and celebrations; this topic lends itself nicely to studying the Miccosukee tribal celebrations as well as mainstream holidays such as Christmas and New Year's Day.

Summary

The Miccosukee School realizes the importance of whole language in their school. However, I don't wish to suggest here that implementing whole language is the answer to all problems related to Indian education. Certainly the issues are complex, and the history mixed and largely ineffective. The compatibility between whole language learning and Native American beliefs systems seems too logical to be ignored. Many schools involved with Indian education around the country are reporting success using more whole language with Native students (Fox 1988; Mallett 1977; Pearce and Gilliland 1988).

I believe that implementing more whole language beliefs into curriculum for Native American students will provide an important step toward better serving Indian children. It is hoped that implementing more whole language will result in marked improvements in both the self-esteem of Native American children and in their education. I think it is critically important that educators at all levels realize that the way schools operate and the nature of our schooling is a reflection of the culture of mainstream America.

Schooling reflects the values and beliefs common to the majority population. If schools are to be inviting to all the children we wish to educate, then values and culture need to be taken into consideration. Rather than trying to make children fit into schools as they have been, educators will likely experience more success if the values and heritage of minority children are respected and considered a positive attribute. I think that we should try to do everything possible to bridge the horizon. Sandra Fox, from the Office of Indian Education Programs at the Bureau of Indian Affairs in Washington, D.C., has stated publicly, and willingly granted her permission to be quoted in this article, her support for the positive relationship between whole language learning and Native American culture. An Oglala Sioux, Fox states emphatically (speaking of whole language), "There's an Indian way of teaching, and this is it."

References Cited

Dewey, John. 1929 My Pedagogic Creed. Washington, D.C.: The Progressive Education Association.

Education Week. 1984 The High Cost of Endurance: A Special Report. Washington, D.C.: Editorial Projects in Education, Inc.

Fox, Sandra. 1988 A Whole Language Approach to the Communication Skills. In Teaching the Native American. Hap Gilliland and Jon Reyhner, eds. Pp. 103-112. Dubuque, Iowa: Kendall/Hunt Publishing.

Goodman, Kenneth, Yetta Goodman, and Wendy Hood, eds. 1989 The Whole Language Evaluation Book. Portsmouth, N.H.: Heinemann Educational Books.

Goodman, Kenneth, Patrick Shannon, Yvonne Freeman, and Sharon Murphy. 1988 A Report Card on Basal Readers. New York: R.C. Owen Publishers.

Goodman, Yetta. 1978 Kid-Watching: An Alternative to Testing. The National Elementary School Principal 57(4):41-45.
1989 Evaluation of Students: Evaluation of Teachers. In The Whole Language Evaluation Book. Kenneth Goodman, Yetta Goodman, and Wendy Hood, eds. Portsmouth, N.H.: Heinemann Educational Books.

Heath, Shirley Brice. 1983 Ways with Words. New York: Cambridge University Press.

Holdaway, Don. 1978 The Foundations of Literacy. Portsmouth, N.H.: Heinemann Educational Books.

Kasten, Wendy C.. 1987 Medicine Men, Bethlehem, and Pacman: Writing in a Cultural Context. Anthropology and Education Quarterly 18(2):116-125.
1990 Oral Language During the Writing Process of Native American Children. English Education 23(3-4):149-156.

Kasten, Wendy C., and Barbara K. Clarke. 1988 Reading/Writing Readiness for Preschool and Kindergarten Children: A Whole Language Approach. Research Bulletin, Florida Education Research Council 21(1).

Locust, Carol. 1988 Wounding the Spirit: Discrimination and Traditional American Indian Belief Systems. Harvard Educational Review 58(3):315-330.

Mallett, Graham 1977 Using Language Experience with Junior High Native American Students. Journal of Reading 21(1):25-28.

Paul, Alice. 1981 Cultural Aspects That Affect the Indian Student in Public Schools. Bilingual Resources 4(2-3):32-34.

Pearce, Daniel L., and Hap Gilliland. 1988 Developing Reading Skills. In Teaching the Native American. Hap Gilliland and Jon Reyhner, eds. Pp. 113-122. Dubuque, Iowa: Kendall/Hunt Publishing.

Rhodes, Robert. 1989a Standardized Testing of Minority Students: Navajo and Hopi Examples. Journal of Navajo Education VI(2):29-35.
1989b Native American Learning Styles. Journal of Navajo Education VII(1):33-41.

Salisbury, Lee. 1967 Teaching English to Alaska Natives. Journal of American Indian Education VI(2):1-13.

Tafoya, Terri. 1981 Native Bilingual Education: Oral Tradition and the Teacher. Bilingual Resources 4(2-3):41-44.

Vygotsky, Lev. 1978 Mind in Society. Cambridge, Mass.: Harvard University Press.

Questions:

1. What are some of the major features of Native American values and beliefs?

2. Cite seven characteristics of whole language learning.

3. Give three reasons why whole language learning would be more compatible with Native American cultural values than other teaching methods.

The answer section begins on page 243.

22

Second generation Puerto Rican adolescents in New York City play out their lives in more than one socio-cultural system. Expectations for these teenagers from their parents, their teachers, and their employers are often quite different, and all three are significantly at odds with those who make up the street culture. In this article, educational anthropologists Saravia-Shore and Martinez discuss the findings of an ethnographic study examining the experiences and attitudes of Hispanic adolescents who dropped out of the mainstream school system but subsequently enrolled in a high school equivalency program. By studying the behaviors and attitudes of students both inside and outside of the schools, educational anthropologists are able to make recommendations on how best to meet the educational needs of all students.

An Ethnographic Study of Home/School Role Conflicts of Second Generation Puerto Rican Adolescents

By Marietta Saravia-Shore and Herminio Martinez [1]

Introduction

This chapter[2] reports the findings of an ethnographic study of lower socioeconomic status (SES) second-generation Puerto Rican adolescents in New York City who dropped out of school and subsequently participated in an alternative high school equivalency diploma program. The chapter conveys, in the Hispanic adolescents' own words, their experiences and attitudes toward schooling and the reasons they dropped out and subsequently re-enrolled in the high school equivalency course. A major theme of discussion is their feelings about their dual roles as adults with head-of-household responsibilities outside of school and as adolescents required to follow rules meant for minors inside school walls.

Underlying this duality is the clash between the conflicting value systems of their homes, their peers on the street, and in the social system of the school, which leads to conflicting expectations for Puerto Rican adolescents in these three domains.

Theoretical Framework

The theoretical framework of this study situates schooling within the context of the larger society of which it is a component (Comitas and Dogin 1978). Following the model of the school as a social system described in the ethnographies of Lacey (1970, Rist (1973), and Ogbu (1974), this study seeks to describe the patterns of expectations for adolescent behavior in several social contexts: the home, the street, the workplace, and the school. It also explores the patterns of interaction among teachers and lower SES second-generation Puerto Rican adolescents in a public high school and in an alternative high school setting.

The authors have been guided in their analysis of social interaction in the classroom by the theoretical perspective of Grannis (1967, 1978), who views the school as a model of the larger society. Grannis contends that urban school for lower SES students tend to prepare them for the routinization and close supervision of lower-echelon jobs, whereas suburban schools prepare their students for executive-level, responsible jobs, and hence construct situations where students have more responsibility for their own learning and for decisions about the allocation of their time. One way of constructing such a situation, for example, is the use of contracts for independent or team projects over an extended period of time.

Susan Philips (1972) has documented the effects on student classroom participation of various ways of structuring interaction, which she has termed "participant structures." Grannis (1967) identified several such structures in the classroom that reflect the allocation of resources in the larger society. He points out how student access to such resources as books and materials can be either direct or mediated through the teachers and how control over time, pace of work, and

Reprinted by permission of Marietta Saravia-Shore and Steven Arvizu (eds.) CROSS CULTURAL LITERACY: ETHNOGRAPHIES OF COMMUNICATION IN MULTICULTURAL CLASSROOMS. New York: Garland Publishing, 1992, pp. 227-251.

movement can be either under sole control of the teacher, joint control of students and teachers, or determined entirely by the students. Similarly, task selection or allocation can be controlled in any of these ways.

For the purposes of this paper, the period of adolescence is viewed in a cross-cultural perspective (Mead 1928; Fortes 1938; Firth 1936) as socially and culturally defined. As Firth wrote in his study of the Tikopia:

> Entry into adult life involves the realization of social obligations and the assumption of responsibility for meeting them. What initiation does is to set a time on the way to manhood—often only approximately the time when the parallel physiological changes are due to take place—and by bringing the person into formal and explicit relations with his kindred, confronts him with some of his basic social ties, reaffirms them and thus makes patent to him his status against the days when he will have to adopt them in earnest (Firth 1936:433).

By contrast, in the different sociocultural contexts of the Hispanic home, the ghetto street and the urban school, there are conflicting definitions of adolescence, and thus contradictory expectations of lower SES Hispanic adolescents.

The literature on the socialization of lower SES Hispanics living in large urban ghettos documents the assumption of adult responsibilities by very young children, with vivid examples in such life histories as Piri Thomas's *Down These Mean Streets* (1967) and *Up from Puerto Rico* (Padilla 1958). Older siblings, particularly girls, are expected to act as surrogates for parents who work outside the home or whose large families necessitate this caretaking. A carefree childhood is virtually unknown as adult responsibilities pile up on youngsters, and the harsh realities of life with limited economic resources are all too evident to them on ghetto streets and in overcrowded homes.

Similarly, adolescence brings other adult responsibilities early—for some, the responsibilities of parenthood, for others, self-support or support of younger siblings. At school, however, the situation may be totally different, with no recognition of the students' near-adult or adult status in other settings. One way in which distance, and thus social control (Lacey 1970), is maintained by high school teachers and administrators is to treat adolescents as children in need of close supervision and monitoring through stringent school rules, and to deny them the rights and privileges of adults. It is hypothesized that the resulting role conflicts among adolescent Hispanic students lead either to frustration, aggression and violence, or to their withdrawal from the situation, for example, by dropping out of school.

Another factor to be considered is the Hispanic adolescent's perceptions of the opportunity structure of his or her community and the job market. As documented by Ogbu (1974), adolescents who know of the racial and ethnic prejudices which lead to job discrimination against Blacks and Hispanics and the resulting high unemployment rate in their communities may have little motivation to sustain their participation in school. When they perceive it to be so much more difficult for a member of an oppressed minority group than it is for other persons to obtain a job or even to obtain further education or vocational training to increase the possibilities of employment, dropping out may seem to be a reasonable choice.

Methodology

This study followed an ethnographic approach in which the investigator was an on-site observer in the school and surrounding community. Over a period of ten months, after gaining access to the alternative school, the investigator observed its classrooms and hallways, walked around the immediate neighborhood with some of the students, and hung out in front of the school. Patterns of seating and interaction were recorded in the classrooms and informal conversations were held with the teachers, administrators, and counselors to learn about their perceptions of the students. On the basis of informal discussions with students, an interview schedule was developed and employed among 18 male and 15 female students. The interview elicited student experiences and attitudes toward schooling, sex, work, and family life.

Interviews were conducted in English or Spanish or both, depending on the situation and the student's preference. The interviewer used the interview schedule as a basis for questions but did not strictly adhere to it, since it was important to establish and maintain trust; therefore the interviewer answered questions as well as asked them and shared feelings.

Program Description

The site of this ethnographic study was a community-based organization in a low-income neighborhood in New York City. Of the various youth-oriented programs sponsored by this organization, the General Equivalency Diploma program was selected because of its population and its history of achievement. Interviews were conducted with community members, administrators, teachers, and previous program participants prior to the selection of this particular program.

The requirements for program eligibility included: (1) family income below poverty guidelines, (2) age range between 16-21, (3) application through appropriate channels, and (4) completion of a three-week probationary period. The program is two-fold, including both preparation for a General Equivalency Diploma and part-time work in various non-profit institutions. Students spend 15 hours a week in classroom instruction and 15 hours at work-sites such as hospitals, clinics, and day-care centers. The positions they hold include receptionist, typist, maintenance worker, general office worker, and library worker. Students earn a stipend of $175 every two weeks, representing 30 hours of work per week at the minimum wage.

Classroom Observations

Three classrooms were observed over a period of ten months. Two characteristics of the classroom that were immediately notable were the small size of the groups—from nine to ten students—and the absence of noise. There was task-oriented participation, discussion, and student demonstration of problem-solving in algebra at the blackboard, but there was no "kidding around." This group of former drop-outs was one of the best-behaved groups of high school students the observer had ever seen.

In this alternative school setting, rules, regulations, and restrictions were de-emphasized. Instead, emphasis was placed on the student's goals. These students had enrolled voluntarily to prepare to take and successfully pass the GED exam for a high school equivalency diploma. Thus, the teachers did not demand obedience—"you have to do this homework"—but rather stressed the positive consequence of doing the homework, which would be to reach the student's goal. When students came in late or without their homework, apparently angry and ready to fight the expected put-down or reprimand, their tardiness was ignored and their presence simply acknowledged.

During follow-up interviews, teachers explained that this was a deliberate strategy. They were interested in creating a classroom of adults. The teachers mentioned that their students often had other responsibilities, but that they were also responsible for doing their homework. It was expected that they would do this work, since it was the students themselves who wanted to pass the exam.

In class the teachers would emphasize this goal, which was clear and well defined. There was a lot of talk about the test; for example, "Listen, you've got to get this down pat. They usually have two or three of these problems, and it's worth five points." A student chimed in, "That's right, I missed passing by five points."

One of the students' complaints about their previous schooling was that the work did not lead to a clear goal, that it was "all over the place." It should be noted that these same students were now working diligently on abstract tasks apparently unrelated to their daily lives, such as algebra problems. However, they had made the connection between their learning algebra, passing the algebra component of the exam, and the diploma's significance to their lives.

The classroom's bulletin board featured a list of people who had taken and passed the GED exam. Among these were students from the neighborhood who had attended this alternative school, and everyone knew some of them. All the students in the program, which has a good reputation in the community, had been referred to it by someone who had already gone through it.

The lack of restrictive rules and regulations in the classroom was evident in the following ways: students could get up and walk out of the classroom to go to the bathroom or out for a smoke without asking permission. They could smoke in class; they had direct access to materials and did not have to ask the teacher's permission to obtain them. They were expected to work, but the pace was left up to them. If a student had not had time to do the homework, he or she was nevertheless asked to participate in class by trying to solve the problem rather than being excluded from participation.

If a student missed a day, however, the teacher referred him or her to one of the best students for notes. Thus, rather than being rewarded with extra attention from the teacher, the student was "punished" by being made to ask a better student for assistance. On the other hand, when a student needed further clarification or assistance to understand the process or concept being taught, the teacher would either take class time to assist him or her or make an appointment to do so afterward.

The following observations convey the tone of the class:

- The emphasis on individualized instruction required that each student be actively involved in his or her own work while the teacher worked with other individuals.
- The teacher's presence was not essential to the learning nor to discipline. In several instances, the teacher left the room and the students continued working in absolute silence.
- Students paid attention to instructions with, for the most part, no interruptions. Mutual respect was apparent.
- All the students asked questions at various points.
- There seemed to be great independence regarding behavior. Students smoked, left the room without requesting permission, and exercised their own judgment regarding completion of assignments, selection of some reading material, etc.
- There was a noticeable emphasis on responsibility. After many conversations with teachers, the observer concluded that there is general agreement among them concerning student motivation. One teacher's perceptions of the problems facing adolescents in school may be summarized thus:
- After many years of involvement with the system, she feels that teachers' lack of concern is a real problem. "This sickness has spread to the majority of teachers." There are many reasons for this lack of concern, but they certainly reflect the system's inability to deal with "different students."
- There is a general attitude of low expectations toward Black and Hispanic students. It is assumed that they will never achieve certain goals. The standards of the educational system are therefore constantly lowered, which has a circular effect damaging to the students as well as to the schools.
- "The assumption is that schools which are all Black and Hispanic are inferior!" Therefore, teaching in schools with this population is equivalent to teaching in a setting where learning is severely limited.
- The school plays a more important role in the lives of these students than most people realize. "The school is successful if it can provide the kind of association many of these kids are looking for. If they can find someone to talk to, this usually makes the difference."

According to this teacher, individualized teaching represents

> the only possibility for the successful instruction of inner-city students. You can't just go through the curriculum, or forget that it does exist, but rather there needs to be constant clarification of concepts and building on each student's knowledge. I find myself clarifying concepts that they were taught in high school, but could not understand. Then they gave up or left school. There are many things that have to be clarified before you can move on. Besides, a lot of attention is given to the whole student.

Student Talk

We now turn to the students' interpretations, in their own words, of their experience. These quotations from students have been organized into the following categories:

- Student Attitudes toward the Alternative High School
- Student Perceptions of the Previous School
- Student Perceptions of Being an Adult and Being Treated as a Kid
- Student Comments on Prejudice and the Conditions of Puerto Ricans
- Student Aspirations

Student Attitudes to the Alternative School

There was a consensus among the students that the alternative school they were attending was a good place for them. The teachers cared; the content was more challenging and demanding; and they were learning.

> This place is quite different. You have a lot of students there, but not here, and I like that. Also, the teachers have a real interest in teaching. They care if you pass or not.

> I like it here because they teach you more. I did not know how to do fractions. I could hardly multiply or divide. Here I was doing algebra. My reading is better. My notebooks are filled. Before, they only had drawings and blank pages. I write a lot now. If I am told to study, I do it. I remember things now. Before, I used to forget all the time.

> I like the education here. Each teacher is easier, but they push you. They make believe you are in college. It's training you to be independent in your thinking. They don't let you take breaks and all that.

Students' Perceptions of the Previous School

The students generally evaluated their previous high school experience much less favorably than their current schooling at the alternative high school. Criticisms of the previous schools concentrated on teacher favoritism toward the better students, teachers' lack of respect, care or concern for students, and the repetitiveness of their instruction. The following comments are illustrative of these opinions:

Most of the teachers only cared about the smart kids. Others did not care. They would tell you that you always had an excuse, that you were wrong or something. They would always argue, argue with you, but never listen. I was in-between—I was not very smart—but not too stupid.

I can't think of anything I really liked about school. As I told you, it was very packed and boring. They'll make you take a test, then start the term teaching stuff on the test, then learn it again, then test you again, and on and on.

They never tried to help the bad students. If you fail, it's just too bad. They didn't understand. They had no individual understanding. They tried to get loud and rowdy. Playing the part of super-cool. If you want to learn, fine; if not, fuck you. They only gave attention to two or three; the rest could go to Hell. They cared for the two or three smart ones, the goodies. The rest of us—forget it.

No, I wasn't doing well. When you need help, they [teachers] don't give it to you. They teach you things over and over again.

Before, in a way, I thought it was important to do well. But I gave up.

In a way I didn't care. Now they try to help me so I feel better. I care more. Here they encourage you, they talk to you. Over there, as long as they get paid, they don't care.

I disliked the teachers' attitudes. They don't give a shit and a damn, either you learn or not. I was told a million times, "I get paid, whether you learn or not, as long as I sit at this desk." And that's just what they did many times. If the class was noisy, he just sat behind that desk and did nothing.

They don't respect us. They make believe they are listening, then erase it all from their mind. They don't register a fucking word.

Those guys [the teachers] don't care about the students. In Catholic schools, yes. They were on your back all the time. They wanted you to be somebody. If they had to pull your ear, they did. Even if they had to pull your ear. In high school, if you wanted to do it you did: nobody really cared whether you made it or not. If you could not make it, that was just tough.

They [teachers] don't understand the problems we have. They are into their own generation and the problems that are happening are different now.

Some teachers don't care. But that's only 10%. You can tell the way they treat you, the way they talk to you. They put themselves up there, and you are down here. But we are all human beings.

Most teachers don't respect students, so how can they expect to be respected?

The younger teachers understand the problems of the students. But if they are old, forget it. A lot depends on how they talk. If the words are too hard, then you don't understand what they mean. If they are too easy, then you get angry because you don't want to be treated like a baby. You don't want people to sweet-talk you. You need to talk to people at their level. I like people to talk straight, to tell me the truth without bullshit; because, if they lie to me now, what's going to happen when I grow up?

Some teachers think that we [adolescents] have inferior minds. Maybe we seem that way, but it's the school, the home, the environment. It's like a big puzzle that we have to put together. But teachers don't understand what's going on in our heads.

I quit because it was hard. They had too many unnecessary classes. Gym classes and stuff you don't need for your future. They had all kinds of shops. Then, they told me I needed so many credits. But they put me in classes for half credits. I had passed my courses, but I had been sick. They told me that I had been out too much. I have asthma and I would miss class. It's also a long walk. If you are late three times, you are out. If you are out, you fail the term. I was put into the eleventh grade for two years because I was out. I said I was not going to take gym. They said I had to take it. I argued with the principal and then walked out. They didn't try to stop me.

Those teachers don't give a shit. All they do is check attendance. They never asked you how you were feeling: if you were sick. You know—to make you feel wanted. When I was sick [with asthma]—the teacher would say that every letter was a fraud. He would not accept it; take me to the office, to the counselor; then they would call the hospital. Finally, my doctor got really mad and said to them that he had his work to attend to. What a waste of time!

Students' Perceptions of Being an Adult and Being Treated as a Kid

The students generally expressed annoyance at being treated as kids in their previous high school, while carrying the responsibilities of adults (such as supporting themselves) outside school. A representative selection of such feelings as expressed by the students follows:

I see myself as a young adult. Not completely an adult—because by the government, I am a minor. There are things I can't do because I don't have the schooling or experience.... My boyfriend is a long ways from being an adult. He thinks that everything will always be available to him. I hate to see what will happen when it doesn't. Everything is fantasy. If you don't live in reality, it will pass you. You'll never get anywhere.... Some people see me as an adult. Others don't.... Some people treat me like a kid. When they talk to adults, they do it on a higher level, but when they talk to you so sweet. As I told you, that bothers me. I like to hear things straight. No lying, no bullshit.

It's difficult to say when a man becomes a man. A lot of guys act very young. A woman becomes a woman the day she has a child. She can't come back on it. It is here and is a part of her.... A boy becomes a man around eleven. That's when the system begins to change. But he is not fully until he takes responsibility for himself. As for a woman, this happens when she can take care of herself and keeps her self-respect.

By 18 years, you ought to support yourself, regardless of whether you are a man or a woman.... I am an adult. Since I was 13, I had a lot of responsibility on my self. My mother never told me what to do. I learned all about life—the birds and the bees and all that—in the streets. I went through a lot. That's one thing I will make sure to do with my kids—give them all the advice they need. I want them to learn from me.

My mother, to this day, doesn't see me as an adult. We never talked woman-to-woman. As I told you before, I learned everything on my own and kept it to myself.... Any responsibility makes you grow up. But there are always more responsibilities for the woman. She has to look out for both, for the kids, for the home, to make it work.

I work at a hospital—in the Accounting Department. Before that, I never did anything too serious. I worked at McDonald's, Macy's card shops. I call it more serious because of the responsibility. What you do wrong can have consequences.

I support myself, but my mother gives me room and board. Once I start getting paid there, I want to give her some money.

Everybody—man or woman—should provide for themselves by 15 or 16. In a way I think that I am an adult. I am not in my twenties. But I can do anything an older person can do. I can do a lot of things.

I think that my family sees me as an adult. They don't treat me different from anybody else.

I think that when you are matured, you can take care of yourself. When you can take care of things that get in your way then you are a man or a woman.

A man should be on his own by 18. By 16 he's got to be out there realizing what life is all about. Women at 14 because they mature faster. But both out by 18 to make it by themselves.

Yes, I consider myself an adult. I hope others see me that way. I handle my income, my rent and all that.

I think I'm an adult. I can deal with problems I could not deal with [before]. I use to say "fuck it and let someone else solve it." Now I solve it. If I can't, I ask for help and I learn to solve my problems.

Now that I'm in school they see me as a man. Before, my own family would put me down. I make my own decisions. Now they even ask me my advice on things. Now, they see me as an adult—and my friends too.

When you can deal with a decision, you are an adult. When you can take on something and see it through. It's got nothing to do with work. What separates a kid from a man or woman is the way they handle responsibility.

They [teachers] don't care. They are going to get paid for it no matter what happens to us. She would file her nails and say, "I will get paid—you want to make noise, go ahead." She should have taken the disrespectful people out of the class and taught the others.

Yes, they [students] had freedom. You could leave when you wanted. They didn't care.

They [teachers] treat you like kids. For example, if you don't do a little thing then it's, "I will fail you. I will call your parents, I will send a letter," like that. Here they help you if you want, if you don't want, they don't; they let you be. But you feel the responsibility because they care and it is up to you.

They treat us like kids. The same in the other years when we were small. They don't think that you have problems. But that you need sleep or food or something like that. They can't understand that if your parents fight you don't sleep. They don't want you to talk about it. "You don't sleep—get out of here!"

No, teachers treated us like we were still kids. I remember in one class, they made us fold our hands. And you know—they make you feel dumb, stupid. They call you stupid in a way. They keep saying, "You still don't know this! I taught it five times already." You feel like saying, "Hey if we knew it, we would not be here!" That's why so many kids drop out of Metropolitan. And let me tell you a lot of those—I know them—they are not dumb. They are just tired. Some are dumb, but a lot of them are not. I know.

Student Comments on Prejudice in School

The students' experiences of teacher prejudice directed at Black and Puerto Rican students are expressed below:

A lot of White teachers in that school were against Puerto Ricans and Blacks. In their conversation they always put them down. "The Whites and Chinese are smart, the Blacks and Puerto Ricans dumb." And that's all there is to it.

There was prejudice, but they are careful not to show it. If she would pick a student to do something special, she would pick her nationality, White. That's to do it right. Not give anyone a chance to do things.

I think that they were a bit prejudiced, they knew we were Black and Puerto Rican. They weren't going to kill themselves for us. They are always comparing you to Mr. White, but I am not him.

Some teachers are a bit prejudiced. The Chinese girls got a lot of attention, because they are smart, you know. They would ask them, "Why were you out? Did you understand the work? That's O.K." My biology teacher hated me. My art teacher was nice. Understood.

They would say things like "Do you want to be like the other Puerto Rican women who never got an education? Do you want to be like the rest of your family and never go to school?"

Student Perceptions of the Conditions of Puerto Ricans

The living conditions of Puerto Ricans in the school's neighborhood were perceived as depressed—crime and drug ridden, with unemployment, offering the students little opportunity for any change. Statements illustrating these feeling follow:

The situation of Puerto Ricans is bad. Look at the number without work. It could get better if someone gave them jobs, a place to live, hope. A lot of people complain about teenagers getting high, being on the streets, but they won't help you get a job. I went to many places until I got tired. They tell you "I will call you."

The conditions of Puerto Ricans around here is terrible. No change is possible around here. You have to move away. If they got together like White people, they would come in and tear it down.

I live in *El Barrio*. I like it and I don't. There are lots of good people there, but also muggers. It's terrible how people put up with things, with dirt, the cold, muggings.

The condition of Puerto Ricans is horrible. A lot want a better life but get worn out. I don't think anything will ever change that much. There are too many things keeping us down. I want to make it. I want to move to a nice place uptown. To Park Avenue. Why not?

Yes, I want my kids to stay in school, study a lot, and not live around here. This place is not good for raising kids. There are lots of drugs around here. These kids know about sex and all that before they should. They are learning too fast. That's why there are so many pregnancies.

There is a lot of crime. Not all to get drugs. There is crime for food, medicine, clothes. People don't have enough to put on their back. They feel that it is worth the risk rather than to spend ten years working to get something small. People also rob for food for their stomachs. It's not all for drugs.

A lot of Puerto Ricans came here to the land of opportunity. I would stay in my homeland. By leaving they are not going to be any better here. The situation is bad here. I hope it changes soon. They better do something otherwise overpopulation and crime are going to go up.

Puerto Ricans and Blacks argue. If they got together we would not have this position. Nobody is doing nothing about it. This is a big dumping hole. If we live we live, if we die we die.

Student Perceptions of School

The following interview took place in the hallways of the alternative school. The discussion centered around the student's perception of school and the reasons why he had dropped out of school.

I went in for broadcasting, and they put me into printing. They told me that after the first year I could go into broadcasting because there was no room. After that they told me that there was no room. I didn't want printing. I didn't like it. I was bored.

I was there two years and then I had it. There is a racial problem here. You see a White class and, hey, they are learning and I want to get in it. No chance. I am not getting what I came here for. What should I stay here for? Even if I do all this, it's not what I want and what they accepted me for. I don't want just a certificate. I want a diploma. That's how it was explained to me by my teachers; but people don't want you there. So what the hell are you doing there?

All my teachers were White. Some—one—was poor. We still keep in touch. He is in Albany. He cares. There was something special. He talked to everybody. You don't see that in most teachers. They don't give a damn. That is why you see people dropping out.

What good are counselors? All they talked about is what you passed or failed. And then they tell you to go to night school. When you complain they tell you that you'll find the time.

Finally I brought my mother in. She doesn't speak too well, but I was there. They treated her like a piece of fucking shit, man. I finally got so angry and said, "Hey, that's my mother. You can't treat my mother that way."

I collapsed into tears in the Principal's office. I was going to jump him. Just to have a chunk of him. They were bullshitting me. I was made a fool of. Even my mother said that if I got arrested it would be the only time she would have been on my side.

I am glad I left. Here I am getting a chance. It's not a pretty school. But to me this is better. You know people, their mind, they got a goal. In school there is a lot of competitiveness. Hostility is a way to get attention and get rid of your frustrations.

I had good grades, good references. They want you there. Just to have you there for the rep of the school. I started to play hooky. Then they show they don't give a damn. All they tell you is you are failing, failing, failing. They don't understand.

The same thing more or less happened to all the people there. My brother—they threatened to send him to another school. Then they did. Then he dropped out. He couldn't keep up.

All teachers do is pull pencil on you. They don't treat you like a human being. I deserve more respect. They use power on you. They stick with the ones that are doing O.K. The more they pull pencil on you, the more anger and resentment there is. You are embarrassed. That's why a lot of people yell back at teachers, wave their fingers in their face and all that.

They don't teach. They are always pushing the good one. You got a problem. They tell you to get somebody's notes. Get X to help you. They don't deal with your problems, just tell you how good someone else is and threaten you.

If you try to explain is no good. You feel the pressure of subjects, grade, moving, moving pressure, pressure. This brings violence to the schools. Kids got problems and all they get is more pressure and harassment. Teachers don't care. If you got problems you don't want threats—you won't make it. You will fail. You need understanding and help.

I want to finish and get a job. My parents are going back to Puerto Rico. They just don't understand it here. I want to stay and work so I got to get my diploma and a job.

A girl leaving for Buffalo University brought me here. We all bring each other.

We did not want to say to our parents, forget it. So we played hooky. I did not go to school for a month. Me and my friends use to play basketball and in the winter go to 42nd Street to the movies. We got money from the parents. Some of us had jobs part time. We were going to save money and go to California. One of us had money—his father had a lot of money put away for when he was twenty-one. I think that his father was in organized crime. He had a lot of money in the house.

We were going to take it and go to California. All in one apartment. Taking our time getting there. We were going to take Amtrak. It stops in a lot of cities. We were going to take our time. We wanted a break. His father found out. That was the end of it.

We were not into mugging or stealing. That was not our thing. We just needed enough money to go to the movies in Times Square. They are cheap in the morning.

When people talk about a high school dropout they make you sound sick or something. Did they ever get bored or give up on something? There is a reason for it.

Student Aspirations

Approximately half of the students want to go to college. They would like to earn money than they have thus far and to have easier work. The other half would like to learn a trade that would enable them to earn more money.

Many students realize that a General Equivalency Diploma is not enough to help them make it. This can be very discouraging for them. Many also feel that "The White man always controls, so why bust my ass?" One says, however: "I try to tell them [the other students] that only if we work harder than they [the White majority] did and do can we have some control." Still another has said, "I will be out in the street with a diploma in my hand." These are common feelings among the students; however, they are not prepared by their environment or by the schools for the complexities of the world in which they will have to function.

Implications

An editorial Essay in the April 6, 1981, issue of Time magazine identified a trend: that many parents are putting aside their child-care responsibilities in order to develop an alternative life-style—in effect, reliving their adolescence—while adolescents are becoming more like adults. One in seven adolescents has drinking problems; many adolescents combine concern about jobs and future with cynicism about the way this society works. One adolescent was quoted as saying.

> We've got to look out for ourselves. Nobody else will. The politicians or whatever, those in power are out for themselves. The main thing is taking care of your business, having a job and knowing what to do with the check at the end of the week.

Time posed an interesting question: "Is it possible that society, moved first by alarm about its children and then by disenchantment, has subtly begun the process of disestablishing youth simply by turning everybody to adult ways promptly at puberty?" While we may disagree that "alarm and disenchantment" are the primary factors involved, it seems important to determine whether or not the trend suggested by Time exists—whether adolescence is indeed being "disestablished" and, if so, to what extent and for which group of people. But contemplation of such a study of social change makes it apparent that the baseline itself is not well-understood.

Anthony Burton has suggested, in an article published in Anthropology and Education Quarterly (1978), the need for developing an anthropology of the young. Concerned that the culture of the young may have been ignored in anthropological research concentrating on schooling, Burton suggests an inquiry targeted toward understanding and explaining their lives. He states that anthropology must develop approaches which "regard the young as subjects of their own existence rather than as objects of the efforts of school systems." As can be seen by this chapter, we agree with that suggestion and that a new analysis of the cultural patterns of the young is needed but stress that such an analysis must be sensitive to their varying socioeconomic realities. The cultures of the young differ depending upon their economic class and whether or not they are members of oppressed minority groups as defined by Ogbu (1974).

Burton (1978) has also noted the same phenomenon we found among Puerto Rican adolescents:

> There are many people in state-level industrial societies who are adult in most important senses, but who have not yet completed their school attendance through twelfth grade, under what are often dependent and even humiliating circumstances. It is necessary that they do so because of a technocratically derived cultural norm which specifies that one must survive this quasi-ritual in order to avoid being defined as "young."

Similarly, Glasgow, in The Black Underclass (1980), has suggested that there should be a rethinking of high schools' goals to make them more relevant to the demands of today's society and marketplace:

> It must recognize the special differences of today's inner-city urban youth (who seek earlier marriages, independent functioning, and incomes and who hence need earlier job market entry) and the special obstructions (structural, racial, market constrictions, skills deficits and vocational underexposure) that impede their chances to secure a living. Educational alternatives—such as schools without walls, various work-education combinations, school apprenticeship, earlier technological training and a broad range of differentiated routes to achievement—must be explored (Glasgow 1978:188-189).

We would add that continuing attention must be paid to the racism, sexism, and class biases in our society which are reflected in schooling, in research design as well as in policy implementation. It is equally important to attend to the double and sometimes triple burden of prejudice which must be borne by ethnic and language minority youngsters in a society which often seems to harbor negative attitudes towards its youth. To start where we have may seem obvious, but is in fact rare—by listening to young people, and letting their concerns emerge from their own talk. The lack of such research is perhaps itself some indication of a societal attitude toward our young people.

Some strategies for the educational involvement of minority youth may also be derived from the comments of these Puerto Rican adolescents which reflect the conflicts between those expectations of them expressed at home or in the workplace and those expressed by regular school personnel. Those who participated in our study articulated again and again the importance of being accorded adult freedoms and responsibilities in the school setting. These are to be carefully distinguished from the "freedom" to do what one pleases proffered by teachers who "don't care."

In summarizing the ways in which these students perceived the alternative school as facilitating their learning more fully than did their regular school, the following factors seem to have been most salient:

- The teachers cared about the students and were concerned that they achieve the goal of passing the GED exam.
- The school's social organization emphasized students' decision-making and their responsibility for the ways they spent their time; rules concerning time, such as promptness, were de-emphasized—for example, students did not have to account for being late.
- Goals and tasks were clearly defined, and students and teachers shared them.
- Models of success were in evidence in the form of photographs or lists of previous successful students.

The cultural values of the families of these Puerto Rican adolescents which conflicted with those propagated by their schools may be summarized thus:

- Adult responsibilities are delegated by the parents from an early age.
- Limited-English-speaking parents expect the child to serve as a Spanish/English interpreter to guide them through the rules, regulations and requirements of the English-speaking world.
- The value accorded to intra-family support, which includes the delegation to older siblings of the responsibility for caring for younger ones as parent surrogates, also hastens the process of becoming adult in Puerto Rican families.

To what extent are these family value constellations shared by other immigrant groups and minority groups? How widespread among adolescents of other cultures is this conflict between the parents' expectation that their offspring be an adult and the high school staff's that he or she be a monitored adolescent? These are questions which suggest further ethnographic research concerning adolescents of different cultures.

Endnotes

1. Dr. Marietta Saravia-Shore is Director of the Cross-Cultural Literacy Center, Institute for Urban and Minority Education, Teachers College, Columbia University. Dr. Herminio Martinez is Associate Dean of the School of Education, Baruch College of the City University of New York.
2. This paper was presented at the Annual Meeting of the American Educational Research Association, Los Angeles, California April 16, 1981.

References

Burton, Anthony. 1978 An Anthropology of the Young. Anthropology and Education Quarterly. Washington, D.C.: Council on Anthropology and Education. 9(1). Spring.

Comitas, Lambros, and Janet Dolgin. 1978 On Anthropology and Education: Retrospect and Prospect. Anthropology and Education Quarterly (Washington, D.C.) 9(13).

Firth, Raymond. 1966 We the Tikopia. Boston: Beacon Press.

Fortes, Meyer. 1938 Social and Psychological Aspects of Education in Taleland. London: Oxford University Press.

Glasgow, Douglas. 1979 The Black Underclass. San Francisco: Jossey-Bass.

Grannis, Joseph. 1970 The School as a Model of Society. In The Learning of Political Behavior. Norman Adler and Charles Harrington, eds. Glencoe, Illinois: Scott, Foresman and Company.

1975 Community, Competence and Individuation: The Effects of Different Controls in Educational Environments. IRCD Bulletin. New York: Institute for Urban and Minority Education, Teachers College, Columbia University 10(2). Spring.

Lacey, Colin. 1970 Hightown Grammar: The School as a Social System. Manchester: Manchester University Press.

Mead, Margaret. 1928 Coming of Age in Samoa. New York: W. Morrow.

Ogbu, John. 1974 The Next Generation: An Ethnography of Education in an Urban Neighborhood. New York: Academic Press.

Padilla, Elena. 1958 Up from Puerto Rico. New York: Columbia University Press.

Philips, Susan. 1971 Participant Structures and Communicative Competence: Warm Springs Children in Community and Classrooms. In Functions of Language in the Classroom. Courtney Cazden et al. New York: Teachers College Press.

Rist, Ray. 1972 The Urban School: A Factory for Failure. Cambridge, Mass.: MIT Press.

Thomas, Piri. 1967 Down These Mean Streets. New York: Knopf.

Time. April 6, 1981.

Questions:

1. What major theme underlies the Hispanic adolescents' discussion of their educational experiences?

2. How did the Hispanic students perceive the alternative school as being different from their previous schools?

3. What is the overall implication of this study as suggested by Glasgow in The Black Underclass?

The answer section begins on page 243.

Education in Canada and the United States has never been an ethnically homogenous phenomenon. New York City schools teach large numbers of Puerto Rican children, more than 65 percent of all children in Miami do not speak English as their first language, and Toronto schools are a montage of many ethnic groups from Africa, India, and the Caribbean. A special concern of applied anthropologists is the "ethnography of the classroom"—which involves identifying cultural differences in schools and their implications for teaching and learning. In this selection, educational anthropologist Evelyn Jacob focuses on teachers working with students whose culture and language are different from their own. Jacob's strategy for improving education in muti-cultural classrooms combines the approaches of (a) reflective practice and (b) the application of anthropological principles.

Reflective Practice and Anthropology in Culturally Diverse Classrooms

By Evelyn Jacob

In this article I argue that reflective practice informed by anthropological perspectives offers a strategy that can help educators address their practice-based "puzzlements" and improve educational practice in culturally diverse classrooms. I present anthropological success stories to show (1) that anthropological concepts such as culture, context, social structure, and power provide productive ways of understanding culturally diverse classrooms; (2) that anthropological methods such as observation, open-ended interviews, and artifact analysis can contribute useful information; and (3) that by drawing on anthropological concepts and information educators can develop useful interventions to improve educational practice.

Steve, a new Euro-American teacher, eagerly faced his science classes in suburban Washington, DC. Most of his students were Euro-American middle- and upper-middle-class; the remainder were from Korea and Vietnam. He found the Asian students well-mannered, conscientious, and hardworking.

In mid-September he gave his first science exam, which included math problems, theoretical problems, and some applied word problems. He had tried to make the word problems interesting and relevant to his students. For example, instead of asking students to calculate how far a bullet might travel, he asked them how far a fourth-quarter punt by the school's popular kicker might

travel. He thought he had prepared the students well for the exam and expected all of them to earn high grades. As a result, he was surprised at what he found as he graded the exams. Although the class as a whole did well, his Asian students fell well below the average of their Euro-American counterparts. Steve could have ignored the differences he saw in performance. Or he could have interpreted the lower grades as indicating that the Asian students were not as capable as the Euro-American students. Instead, he wondered whether he might have created their poor performance by relying too heavily in the exam on cultural information unfamiliar to the Asian students. (For whatever reason, Steve apparently did not wonder or examine whether the cultural information in his exams might also be unfamiliar or uninteresting to many of his female students.)

He gathered information about his exam and his students. He studied the students' answers and found that the Asian student did as well or better than the Euro-American students on the problems that were purely mathematical and required little English or cultural knowledge. He also found that the Asian students misunderstood the word problems he had worked so hard to make interesting. In many cases the Asian students had not even attempted the word problems. When Steve examined the backgrounds of his Asian students, he found that they were relatively new

Reprinted by permission of THE ELEMENTARY SCHOOL JOURNAL 95(5), May, 1995, pp. 451-463.

to the United States; none had been here longer than 3 years. Some had just arrived the preceding summer.

Steve then began to consider whether some of the examples he used in class might also present problems for the Asian students. He talked with them privately about this issue, and many indicated that they did not understand his examples.

Steve decided to try to address the problem in both his teaching and his exams. Although he kept his "interesting" applications, he was careful also to provide a more mathematically oriented analog for each application. He also encouraged the Asian students to come to him for help if an example was not clear. During exams he allowed them to use bilingual dictionaries to clarify the meanings of words. As a result, on the second exam, the Asian students' scores improved greatly and did not lag behind their Euro-American counterparts. (This example was derived from Scholla, 1990.)

Teachers who have culturally diverse classrooms (i.e., classrooms with multiple cultural groups) frequently, and increasingly, are responsible for educating students whose lives, cultures, languages, and social statuses are very different from their own, students whom they sometimes do not understand. Teachers with such classrooms sometimes are puzzled by the same kind of situation Steve faced: they have groups of students who perform less well than others in the class. In this article I address the kind of challenge Steve faced—namely, what teachers can do when a cultural group (or groups) of students performs less well than others.

An Alternative Strategy

My approach is different from most discussions of teaching culturally diverse classrooms. Conventional educational theory and research assume that problems of practice fall into easily defined categories and that universally applicable solutions are available for each kind of problem (Schon, 1983). An example of his approach is a booklet published by the U.S.. Department of Education (1986), titled *What Works*. The booklet aims to present universal answers to problems of practice. It represents a top-down approach to teaching, assuming that researchers and theoreticians can tell teachers how to solve the problems in their classrooms. Unfortunately, "what works" has not worked universally. Looking for universal solutions has failed to provide consistent and significant improvement in education.

Many "multicultural" workshops provide general information about the cultures of particular groups. However, broad background knowledge about a cultural group does not necessarily provide answers to teachers' puzzlements. Information about a cultural group in general may not be relevant to a particular local community or a particular group of students, who may vary, for example, by gender, social class, or degree of acculturation. Moreover, presenting *general information* about cultural groups carries the potential of producing or reinforcing stereotypes, especially when only superficial information such as trait lists is presented.

I assume that neither I nor any other professional educator can tell any other teacher what is going to work in his or her own classroom, especially if the classroom is culturally diverse. The teacher, himself or herself, will need to determine what works on a class-by-class basis. However, I can suggest a strategy that should prove helpful to teachers. It combines two existing approaches. The first approach, reflective practice (Schon, 1983, 1987), provides a general framework for teachers to examine their practice critically to determine what works and what does not in their classrooms. The second approach, applying perspectives derived from educational anthropology, provides useful ways to frame puzzlements, alternative methods to gather information, and new ideas for interventions to improve educational practice. A strategy that combines these two approaches can be an especially powerful tool for improving education in culturally diverse classrooms.

In the sections that follow, I elaborate on the strategy of reflective practice informed by anthropological perspectives. I then provide illustrations of how reflective practice, illuminated by understanding of different cultures, can improve education in culturally diverse classrooms.

Reflective Practice Informed by Anthropological Perspectives

Schon's (1983, 1987) reflective practice approach invites teachers to reflect on surprises and puzzlements that they encounter in their classrooms. The first step in reflective practice is to "frame" these surprises, that is, to define the surprise or puzzlement. According to Schon, framing does not necessarily mean pigeonholing a surprise or puzzlement into a conventional category. Instead, he urges teachers to construct their own definition of the problem, derived from their own practice-based knowledge.

According to Schon, competent practitioners of any profession develop tacit knowledge-recurring categories of people, situations, and problems-that informs their practice. As long as practitioners are confronted with the same kinds of people and situations, their "knowing-in-practice tends to become increasingly tacit, spontaneous, and automatic" (Schon, 1983, p. 60), resulting in a certain ease and flow of practice.

However, when practitioners are confronted with new people or new situations in which something fails to meet their expectations (as frequently happens in culturally diverse situations), they may respond in several ways. If the routine of practice is too strong, they may ignore the surprise or force it into preexisting categories. For example, Steve might have concluded, erroneously, that his Asian students were less able than his Euro-American students.

Another way that teachers can respond to surprises is to use them as opportunities to reflect on their practice (Schon, 1987). Reflection may occur before, during, or after action (Elliott, 1991; Schon, 1983). Reflection that occurs before or after action is my focus here, specifically when done consciously and systematically. Systematic reflection on practice, also called classroom research or teacher research, involves several steps: (1) identifying a puzzlement, (2) considering alternative ways to frame the puzzlement and selecting a focus, (3) gathering and analyzing information, (4) developing and implementing an intervention if needed, and (5) monitoring the results of the intervention.

However, reflection by itself does not guarantee that teachers can move beyond their habitual categories and assumptions. Teachers' knowledge-in-practice derives both from their own experience and from discipline-based knowledge in their field of practice (Schon, 1987). In education the discipline of psychology has had a major influence, with the effect that teachers' knowing-in-practice is heavily influenced by psychological categories and concepts. Although psychology undoubtedly will continue to provide valuable insights into classroom practice, it tends to focus attention on individual psychological factors rather than on the social and cultural factors that are especially critical in culturally diverse classrooms.

I suggest that anthropology can likewise provide discipline-based, knowledge pertinent to educational practice, particularly in culturally diverse classrooms, by providing insights into the social and cultural issues that influence education. In particular, anthropology can offer reflective practitioners valuable ways to frame problems, alternative methods for gathering information, and new ideas for solving some educational problems.

Putting the Strategy into Practice

Steve's conduct illustrates this strategy of reflective practice informed by anthropological perspectives. Reflecting on the test results, he was surprised that the Asian students had done less well than other students. This was especially surprising to him because he knew that Asian student have a reputation for doing well in science and math. This is a case in which a stereotype, although positive, could easily have led the teacher astray. If Steve had assumed the stereotype was true, he might have concluded that these particular students were less capable than most Asian students.

However, Steve did not ignore the anomaly, nor did he assume that the students' performance indicated some deficit on their part. Instead, after considering several alternative hypotheses, he framed the issue in cultural terms. He asked whether features of his instruction might be contributing to their poor performance and, in particular, whether culturally based knowledge might be a factor. To answer this question, Steve gathered information about his exam and his students. When it seemed that cultural knowledge might be relevant, he devised and implemented a possible solution, and then he monitored the results of his intervention. Thus, by reflecting on his practice and attempting to understand how cultural assumptions in his test and instruction interacted with the cultures of his students, Steve was able to improve education in his classroom.

Although the literature contains few examples of individual teachers applying this strategy, reports of collaborative work between educators and anthropologists illustrate how the strategy can be used successfully. The reports come from all levels of education. Most of the studies have focused on monocultural or bicultural situations or on individual groups in culturally diverse situations. However, the general principles illustrated in these studies are applicable to educators working without anthropologists in culturally diverse schools.

I organize this discussion around concepts that anthropologists have found to be useful for understanding culturally diverse classrooms: culture, context, social structure, and power. I discuss how teachers could use these concepts to frame their puzzlements and gather information, and I provide examples where the concepts have been used to improve education.

Culture

For anthropologists, culture refers to shared meanings, patterns of behavior, and artifacts. Cultural meanings exert a powerful influence on behavior, and significant regularity exists across individuals within a culture, However, cultural meanings do not *determine* behavior because individuals must decide whether and how to apply cultural guidelines for behavior in specific situations. Moreover, individuals are socialized into cultures in different ways, and individuals belong to different subcultures within their society.

Many people are comfortable applying the notion of culture to national groups (e.g., Japanese culture, Puerto Rican culture) and to ethnic groups within a nation (e.g., African-American culture, Italian-American culture). Anthropologists also apply the concept of culture to smaller groups of people who regularly interact (Goodenough, 1976), for example, a school's culture (Peshkin, 1986), a classroom's culture (Jacob, 1989), or even the culture of a reading group (Eisenhart & Graue, 1993).

Culturally diverse schools can be viewed usefully as sites of cross-cultural encounters. The artifacts and routines of schools and classrooms embody cultural assumptions and values, usually those of the majority Euro-American culture. Teachers (and other educators) bring to classrooms their own cultural meanings and behavior patterns, influenced by their ethnicity, social class, gender, and profession. Students, likewise, bring cultural meanings and behavior patterns from their home and peer cultures, which are influenced by their ethnicity, social class, gender, and degree of acculturation.

Moreover, culture is not static. Educators, parents, and students jointly develop cultures around educational tasks (Eisenhart & Graue, 1993). The culture of an immigrant group is not the same as the culture of the home community it left, and the culture of second-generation children is different from that of their first-generation immigrant parents.

Cultural meanings. Cultural meanings include shared ways of perceiving the world, guidelines for behavior, and standards for judging behavior and artifacts. Two aspects of cultural meanings in schools which may prove useful in framing puzzlements are institutional norms and the meanings of school success to students.

Institutional norms are those shared cultural meanings that extend beyond individual classrooms and pervade a school. Competition is an institutional norm that pervades life in American schools today (Goldman & McDermott, 1987; Smith, Gilmore, Gordman, & McDermott, 1993). The normal curve used in grading is inherently competitive. Students compete in academic games and for positions of honor; they are acutely aware of their ranking in their classes. Most sports, even intramural sports, are competitive. Arts festivals are entered competitively; bands have an elaborate competitive ranking and bumping system. It seems that no area of life in school is free of competition.

Competition in not inherently good or bad, but when the system is set up so that some *must* fail in order for others to succeed, problems arise. Groups (or individuals) with a history of failure may decide to stop trying.

Teachers can identify institutional norms such as competition by examining the school's rituals, activities, publications, slogans, and requirements for grading. Teachers can also observe students' reactions to the results of these norms. In some cases teachers may wish to modify the methods used to achieve institutional norms; in others, they may wish to change the norms.

One area that teachers usually control is the structure of their classrooms. Traditional whole-class instruction comprises a form of competition, "producing conspicuous winners and conspicuous losers in the classroom" (D'Amato, 1993, p. 199). D'Amato (1993) reported that in Hawaiian classrooms where teachers had modified practices so there were not individual winners and losers ("rivalrous approaches to contention"), students were more likely to comply with classroom routines than in classrooms where teachers followed traditional practices in which there were clear individual winners and losers ("overt competition"). The teachers' changes included using "open" interactional structures that permitted students to overlap in their comments and to build on others' statements, implementing small-group instruction, reducing criticisms of task performance, and distributing praise more or less evenly to everyone.

The educational program of a labor union in New York (Goldman & McDermott, 1987; Smith et

143

al., 1993) illustrates a successful attempt to change institutional norms. Most union members had had poor experiences in schools and were afraid of tests. Yet the members needed to pass an extremely difficult examination to become licensed.

Instead of continuing to operate from a competitive norm, the union was committed to teaching its members until all had passed the test. The teachers in the program worked with a reading specialist and an anthropologist to develop a 10-week instructional program based on success. They set up peer teaching with 10 students and two instructors taken from those who had already passed the test. A part of the weekly classes involved taking sample tests. The first tests contained easy questions. Items that everyone got right were put on the test the next week. Soon all the men were doing well on tests with many items. Then the instructors adopted test questions from the manual. During the last 4 weeks students themselves generated questions for the tests. The result was a strong sense of confidence among the students, and "the union went to its next bargaining table with the claim that they were all licensed professionals" (Goldman & McDermott, 1987, p. 297).

Another basic level of meaning is what school in general symbolizes to different adult and student groups. What does school, and particularly succeeding in school, mean to the students and their communities?

Most classrooms are still dominated by Euro-American culture. The content of the curriculum, interactional patterns, and other norms are essentially Euro-American. This association with "white" culture can have clear implications for how the students interpret success in school.

Some students, particularly those from ethic groups that have a history of inferior schooling and discrimination in hiring, may develop a collective oppositional identity that rejects activities, symbols, events, and behaviors that are characteristic of Euro-Americans. These students regard success as inappropriate in areas "traditionally defined as prerogatives of white Americans" (Fordham & Ogbu, 1986, p. 182). For example, a study in a high school in the District of Columbia showed that African-American students often felt that doing well in school meant that they were "acting white" (Fordham & Ogbu, 1986). They saw schooling as diminishing an African-American person's cultural identity rather than as fostering intellectual growth. This viewpoint influenced both underachieving students, who decided (consciously or unconsciously) to avoid "acting white," and high-achieving students; who needed to find ways to cope with "the burden of acting white." A vivid example of this same phenomenon in another cultural group was portrayed in the movie *Stand and Deliver* (1987), when a Hispanic student enlisted his math teacher's help to hide his involvement in the advanced math program.

How can teachers find out what school success means to students? If teachers listen in a nonjudgmental way for cultural meaning in what students say or write, they will learn much. Teachers might interview students either alone or in focus groups. Students might conduct a research project to document peer cultures in the school (e.g., Heath, 1983). Community members and minority educators who are trusted by the students might be helpful in explaining students' viewpoints to educators whose cultural background differ from those of the students.

Jeanette Abi-Nader (1990) documented how a successful college preparatory program for Hispanic students addressed students' cultural meanings. The program helped students to create a vision of the future that "transformed and redressed the past" (p. 49) and to incorporate school success into the group's self-image. The program brought Hispanic college students and professionals to the school to serve as role models and mentors. The teacher who taught in the program continually talked about the successes of the program's graduates and stressed *when* (not *if*) the students would go to college. The teacher helped students develop a more positive self-image "as Hispanics, as learners, and as communicators" (p. 51) He set high standards and expectations, stressed the strengths and contributions of the students' Hispanic heritage, and talked of his own appreciation for and identification with his students. An important theme across all the program's efforts was that the program provided a "family," a supportive community among the students. Programs such as the one described by Abi-Nader can help students see academic excellence as compatible with their cultural identities.

Other successful programs also focus on changing the meaning of school success for minority students. For example, Carl Rowan's Project Excellence provides scholarships to African-American high school seniors for "daring to embrace scholarship" ("For the young," 1992; see also Horwitz, 1992). This program has helped over 300 students receive a college education.

Cultural Behavior. Culture exerts a powerful influence on behavior. Although individuals are aware of some aspects of their culture, they frequently are unaware of other, "implicit" aspects of culture. This is illustrated in Deborah Tannen's (1990) best-seller *You Just Don't Understand,* which showed how social interaction is culturally patterned for girls and boys and for women and men. Before Tannen popularized the relevant sociolinguistic research, most Americans were vaguely aware that members of the opposite gender sometimes did not understand them but had little insight into how differences between male and female cultures influenced social interaction. Culturally based interaction patterns likewise have a profound influence on students' learning in schools (Erickson & Shultz, 1992) and may prove a useful way for teachers to frame some puzzlements.

There is considerable evidence that social interaction patterns in schools differ substantially from those in some students' homes. Conflicts between home and school social interaction patterns can contribute to academic problems (Delgado-Gaitan, 1987; Philips, 1983).

Because social interaction patterns are generally beyond conscious awareness and sometime involve subtle differences, videotape is almost essential for careful examination of these patterns. In examining tapes teachers might look for obvious times when the patterns of teacher and students are not in synchrony. Teachers might also study successful minority teachers to identify interaction patterns they use in their classrooms. (See Erickson & Mohatt, 1982, and Macias, 1987, for discussions of how minority teachers have adapted instruction to their students.) Although examining culturally based social interaction patterns used in students' homes is beyond teachers' resources, they can learn about these from "key informants" in the community.

The Kamehameha program in Hawaii is an example of a successful program that incorporated aspects of culturally compatible social interaction patterns. In Hawaii the majority of native Hawaiian children have done poorly in school (Gallimore, Boggs, & Jordan, 1974). In response to these students' needs, a multidisciplinary team, including anthropologists and teachers, developed a language arts program that incorporated aspects of the children's home culture.

Hawaiian children are given much responsibility at home, often working as part of a cooperating group of siblings. To build on this feature, the team organized classrooms into small-group, teacher-independent learning centers.

The teachers also adapted features of the social interaction styles of Hawaiian children. For example, most interactions between Hawaiian children and adults are mediated through a group of children rather than being one-to-one interactions. Children's immediate interpretation of direct questioning by an adult is that they are in trouble. Building on this knowledge, teachers tries to avoid direct questioning of individual children who had not volunteered. They addressed questions to the whole group and reinforced volunteered responses. They also found that allowing children to engage in overlapping talk, similar to the home cultural pattern of "talk story," also seemed beneficial. The result of these and other adaptations was a successful language arts program (Jordan, 1985; Vogt, Jordan, & Tharp, 1993).

The culturally specific nature of this approach may raise some questions about its usefulness in culturally diverse classrooms. Culturally compatible classroom practices may not be important for every cultural group. D'Amato (1993) suggested that cultural groups who believe that U.S. schools are an avenue to success (i.e., groups who have a "structural rational" for school) may not need culturally compatible practices to succeed. However, he suggested that culturally compatible practices may provide a "situational rationale" for groups who do not have a structural rationale for participating in school.

Cultural artifacts. Artifacts, whether bulletin boards, displays, or texts, reflect and embody cultural meanings and values. There has been much recent discussion of multicultural curricula that include materials beyond those of Euro-American origin (e.g., Banks, 1988; Banks & Banks, 1989). If the culture, achievements, and values of diverse cultural groups are not presented, then the message that is implicitly conveyed is that the achievements of these cultural groups are minimal or not valued. Thus, in exploring their puzzlements, teachers might consider the messages school and classroom convey to students, and whether these messages support students' self-esteem and interest in learning.

Teachers can examine texts (both textual material and pictures), bulletin boards, and other artifacts to see how the cultures of their students are presented. Are the messages consistent, strong, and positive? Or is there merely token attention given at "special" events?

Luis Moll and his colleagues (Moll, 1992; Moll, Amanti, Neff, & Gonzalez, 1992) have documented the extensive "funds of knowledge" that exist in the working-class Latino communities in Tucson. They also report how teachers have explored these funds of knowledge and have incorporated aspects of them into the classroom, with the result of broadening and deepening the curriculum, linking the school to the community, and identifying and drawing on community members as valuable sources of knowledge.

The study by Abi-Nader (1990), discussed above, of the successful college preparatory program for Hispanic students provides another useful example. One characteristic of the program was the inclusion of artifacts that encouraged, supported, and documented students' success. For example, the teacher videotaped students role-playing experiences they would face in college. The tapes of older students were viewed, and students could view their own progress over the 2 or 3 years they were in the program.

Instructional Context

A central principle of anthropology is that all behavior, including students' academic performance, is influenced by the context in which it occurs. Students apply and use their cognitive and linguistic skills differently in different contexts (e.g., Labov, 1982). Thus, different contexts present varying opportunities for demonstrating abilities, and slight changes in contexts can bring out improved performances, as Steve's work in the opening example illustrates. In exploring their puzzlements teachers may consider the role of instructional context in students' performance.

One way to detect whether changing instructional features might help is to observe students in different instructional contexts. The potential results of such comparative information are highlighted in the following example from Moll and Diaz (1993).

Hispanic students in a third-grade English class were reading only at the decoding level. The teacher seemed to interpret their low performance as reflecting the extent of their current ability and responded by only offering the students opportunities for decoding. However, researchers observed that the same students were reading with comprehension in their Spanish class. Thus, although the students could comprehend text, they were not displaying their comprehension skills in their English class. The instructional context did not provide them with an opportunity to display the comprehension skills they did have.

The researchers worked with the English teacher to try some alterations of the context to allow the Hispanic students to display their comprehension skill in their English class. In the first of their modified classes, the researchers instructed students at the beginning to concentrate on understanding the text, thus shifting the focus to comprehension. The researcher read the story to the students to remove all potential decoding problems. They also told the students that they could ask questions in Spanish when needed to clarify meaning in the English text. By the third lesson the researchers required students to read the story on their own and to answer, with some bilingual assistance, grade-level comprehension questions, which students did successfully. This example suggests one way in which the context of instruction can be modified to facilitate higher-level performance. It also suggests that such assistance is not necessarily a permanent feature of a class but can be offered when needed and then removed when no longer needed.

Social Structure and Power

Subgroups in communities are hierarchically arranged and frequently have differential power. Relative power relations between the school and local communities may be a significant factor in students' performance. When minority parents have little influence on their children's education, they often feel powerless even though they may value education for their children (see Cummins, 1986, for a similar argument). In exploring their puzzlements, teachers might consider how power relations in the school and local community might be influencing students' performance. Teachers can gather information on power relations by examining artifacts, as discussed previously. They can also see whether there are community boards with influences and, if so, who holds positions of power. Which parents are able to organize and get what they want for their children? What are parents' perceptions of the school's receptivity to their concern or their power within the school? What is the parents' command of English? What is their knowledge of the culture of the school? What is their relative power within the larger community?

A study by Delgado-Gaitan (1990) in an elementary school in California demonstrated the importance of parental participation and empowerment. At the beginning of her study, teachers complained about the lack of involvement in the school by Mexican parents and interpreted the lack of involvement as reflecting the parents' apathy about their children's education. In interviewing and observing the parents in their homes, Delgado-Gaitan found that the parents did value education highly. Although some of the most educated parents were active, many—the less educated—felt intimidated by the school. They did not understand the culture of U.S. schools. For example, they did not know what the teachers wanted in the homework assignments, and they did not know the appropriate routes to follow to pursue their concerns. In addition, since many held jobs with little flexibility, getting to the school to see teachers was difficult. Moreover, many did not speak English well. The result was that few initiated contact, and few knew how to respond to contacts initiated by the school.

To address these problems, the Mexican parents decided to organize (with the support of the district). They had two goals: to help the school know more about the Mexican families and their culture, and to help the Mexican families know more about how to help their children in school. Although Delgado-Gaitan's book did not report the long-term outcomes of the parent organization, it did report initial success in increasing understanding and communication between the schools and Mexican families. Such understanding and communication could only help the students.

Local control of schools as exemplified in school-based management is ideally suited to address this issue because it provides more direct community control of the school. However, if the Euro-American majority continues to rule, even at the local level, little will have been changed. Ideas for changing power relationships include parent organizations like the one described by Delgado-Gaitan and local community boards with proportional representation.

Discussion

The previous examples suggest how reflective practice informed by anthropological perspectives can enhance education in culturally diverse classroom. The examples illustrated (1) that anthropological concepts such as culture, context, social structure, and power provide productive ways of understanding culturally diverse classrooms; (2) that anthropological methods such as observation, open-ended interviews, and artifact analysis can contribute useful information;

and (3) that by drawing on these concepts and information educators can develop successful interventions.

Although most of the success stories reported here involve collaborations between anthropologists and educators, my work with teachers suggests that they can also apply this approach on their own. By following this strategy teachers become learners. They identify their puzzlements, asking why something is happening. They develop alternative hypotheses about the puzzling behavior, using the concepts of culture, context, social structure, and power. After selecting a likely hypothesis, they gather and analyze information needed to explore their hypothesis. They then develop and implement an intervention, drawing on their pedagogical expertise and on relevant cultural information. Finally, they monitor the results of their intervention based on their new understandings.

What needs to happen for the strategy proposed here to be applied to culturally diverse classrooms? Teachers would need to develop the skill to reflect systematically on their practice, and they would need to learn basic anthropological perspectives to guide their reflection. Teachers could develop these skills and knowledge on their own, or others could facilitate the process.

Programs or courses (whether university- or school-system-sponsored, or collaborative) could be one vehicle to help teachers learn the strategy. Reflective practice, in some form or another, is already widely incorporated into educational courses and programs. Course and programs would also need to incorporate anthropological perspectives. This does *not* mean teaching anthropology in a traditional foundations-type course; rather, it means focusing on the perspectives of anthropology and helping teachers view the world with anthropological perspectives.

The strategy could permeate courses in a program, or it could be taught through one or more separate courses. I teach a university course that combines anthropology and reflective practice. It focuses on helping teachers (1) to identify anthropological perspectives through discussions of anthropological studies, (2) to apply these perspectives to cases that simulate "real-life" dilemmas that teachers face, and (3) to apply the perspectives to their own practice (for a fuller description of the course, see Jordan & Jacob, 1993). Steve's work, reported in the opening example, was conducted as part of this course.

Another way to introduce the strategy is for anthropologists and teachers to work collaboratively in individual schools. In contrast to courses focused on individual teachers, in-school collaboration has the advantages of being school-based and of creating a local learning community. In the past, most school collaborations have involved university-initiated research projects (see Jordan & Jacob, 1993, for a discussion of the range of collaborations between anthropologists and educators). The kind of collaboration I propose is different because the anthropologist would focus on helping educators use the strategy outlined here to address educators' own puzzlements.

No matter what the means for initiating this strategy, some kind of support system would help it continue long-term. Teachers report that they find it difficult to continue systematic reflective practice on their own without some kind of group support. Teachers are more likely to continue using the strategy if a group of like-minded teachers work together to create a community that supports one another in this strategy. An added benefit of such a community is that teachers could help one another identify different ways to frame their puzzlements.

School support would also be critical for the strategy's long-term use. One important requirement would be a recognition of the teachers' professionalism and the need for this kind of strategy. Another would be a principal who supported such efforts, especially by providing time and funds. In such a supportive context, parents and other community members might be enlisted to help provide knowledge of the community and its cultures. Students might be asked to study their own community (e.g., Heath, 1983).

If the strategy presented here is applied widely and the results shared, educators could begin to compile information about strategies that might be applicable to a range of culturally diverse classrooms. Approaches found to be successful in one culturally diverse classroom will not necessarily be successful in others, but the results of other teachers' efforts could provide ideas and guidelines for colleagues to try out in their classrooms, continuing the cycle of reflective practice. This approach presents challenges, but I think it will be more successful in the long run than purported "universal" solutions.

One advantage of using anthropological perspectives to inform reflective practice is that the strategy can help educators identify and build on the strengths of cultures, not just see the "problems" the cultures encounter in interacting with U.S. schools. Cultural variability is significant survival resource for humanity. Just as there is a concern with preserving the range of biological diversity in flora and fauna, preserving cultural diversity may offer important alternative strategies to deal with unanticipated social challenges. United States citizens live in an increasingly global society. People who are bicultural and bilingual, or multicultural and multilingual, are an increasingly important resource to our country.

Cultural diverse classrooms provide educators with major opportunities and challenges. Educators must remember that what currently *is* does not limit what *can* be. Each teacher is responsible for finding ways to bring out the best in all students. The strategy I advocate here provides an avenue to this goal.

Note

Preparation of an earlier version of this article was supported in part by a Lectures Award from the Fund for the Improvement of Postsecondary Education to the American Anthropological Association.

Evelyn Jacob, Barbara K. Johnson, Janell Finley, Jeffrey C. Gurski and Richard Lavine (1996) report their experiences using the approach discussed in this chapter in "One Student at a Time: The Cultural Inquiry Process," Middle School Journal v. 27 no. 4, pp. 29-35. Educational practitioners, drawing on recent approaches to culture, could expand the questions posed about a puzzlement to explore issues such as the ways students or other participants negotiate, produce and transform cultures, and the ways particpants construct identities in relation to existing cultures and structures.

References

Abi-Nader, J. (1990). "A house for my mother": Motivating Hispanic high school students. *Anthropology and Education Quarterly*, 21, 41-58.

Banks, J. A. (1988). *Multiethnic education: Theory and practice* (2d ed.) Boston: Allyn & Bacon.

Banks, J. A., & Banks, C.A.M. (1989). *Multicultural education: Issues and perspectives*. Boston: Allyn & Bacon.

Cummins, J. (1986). Empowering minority students: A framework for intervention. *Harvard Educational Review*, 56(1), 18-36.

D'Amato, J. (1993). Resistance and compliance in minority classrooms. In E. Jacob & C. Jordan (Eds.), *Minority education: Anthropological perspectives* (pp. 181-207). Norwood, NJ: Ablex.

Delgado-Gaitan, C. (1987). Traditions and transitions in the learning process of Mexican children: An ethnographic view. *In G. Spindler & L. Spindler (Eds.), Interpretive ethnography of education: At home and abroad* (pp. 333-359). Hillsdale, NJ: Erlbaum.

Delgado-Gaitan, C. (1990). *Literacy for empowerment: The role of parents in children's education*. Philadelphia and London: Falmer.

Eisenhart, M., & Graue, M.E. (1993). Constructing cultural differences and educational achievement in schools. In E. Jacob & C. Jordan (Eds.), *Minority education: Anthropological perspectives* (pp. 165-179). Norwood, NJ: Ablex.

Elliott, J. (1991). *Action research for educational change*. Philadelphia: Open University Press.

Erickson, F., & Mohatt, G. (1982). Cultural organization of participation structures in two classrooms of Indian students. In G. Spindler (Ed.), *Doing the ethnography of schooling: Educational anthropology in action* (pp. 132-174). New York: Holt, Rinehart & Winston.

Erickson, F., & Shultz, J. (1992). Students' experience of the curriculum. *In P. Jackson (Ed.), Handbook of research on curriculum* (pp. 165-485). New York: Macmillian.

Fordham, S., & Ogbu, J. (1986). Black students' school success: Coping with the "burden of acting white." *Urban Review*, 18, 176-206.

For the young, gifted and black. (1992, May 20). *Washington Post*, p. A22.

Gallimore, R., Boggs, J.W., & Jordan, C. (1974). *Culture, behavior and education: A study of Hawaiian-Americans*. Beverly Hills, CA: Sage.

Goldman, S., & McDermott, R. (1987). The culture of competition in America. In G. Spindler (Ed.), *Education and cultural process* (pp. 282-299). Prospect Heights, IL: Waveland.

Goodenough, W. H. (1976). Multiculturalism as the normal human experience. *Anthropology and Education Quarterly*, 7, 4-7.

Health, S. B. (1983). *Ways with words: Language, life and work in communities and classroom*. Cambridge: Cambridge University Press.

Horwitz, S. (1992, May 13). For area's black students, Project Excellence spells college. *Washington Post*, p. D3.

Jacob, E. (1989, November). *Students creating culture: Cooperative learning in a multi-ethnic elementary school*. Paper presented at the annual meeting of the American Anthropological Association, Washington, DC.

Jordan, C. (1985). Translating culture: From ethnographic information to educational program. *Anthropology and Education Quarterly*, 16, 105-123.

Jordan, C., & Jacob, E. (1993). Contexts of education, contexts of application: Anthropological perspectives and educational practice. In E. Jacob & C. Jordan (Eds.), *Minority education: Anthropological perspectives* (pp. 253-271). Norwood, NJ: Ablex.

Labov, W. (1982). Competing values systems in the inner-city schools. In P. Gillmore & A. Glatthorn (Eds.), *Children in and out of school* (pp. 148-171). Washington, DC: Center for Applied Linguistics.

Macias, J. (1987). The hidden curriculum of Papago teachers: American Indian strategies for mitigating cultural discontinuity in early schooling. In G. Spindler& L. Spindler (Eds.), *Interpretive ethnography of education: At home and abroad* (pp. 363-380). Hilldale, NJ: Erlbaum.

Moll, L. (1992). Bilingual classroom studies and community analysis. *Educational Researcher*, 1(2), 20-24.

Moll, L. C., & Diaz, S. (1993). Change as the goal of educational research. In E. Jacob & C. Jordan (Eds.), *Minority education: Anthropological perspectives* (pp. 67-79). Norwood, NJ: Ablex.

Moll, L., Amanti, C., Neff, D., & Gonzalez, N. (1992). Funds of knowledge for teaching: Using a qualitative approach to connect homes and classrooms. *Theory into Practice*, 31, 132-141.

Peshkin, A. (1986). *God's choice: The total world of a fundamentalist Christian school*. Chicago: University of Chicago Press.

Philips, S. U. (1983) *The invisible culture: Communication in classroom and community on the Warm Springs Indian Reservation*. New York: Longman.

Scholla, S. R. (1990). *Does E = MC^2 in Asia too?* Unpublished paper, George Mason University, Graduate School of Education, Fairfax, VA.

Schon, D. A. (1983). *The reflective practitioner*. New York: Basic.

Schon, D. A. (1987) *Educating the reflective practitioner*. San Francisco: Jossey-Bass.

Smith, D., Gilmore, P., Goldman, S., & McDermott, R. (1993). Failure's failure. *In E. Jacob & C. Jordan (Eds.), Minority education:*

Anthropological perspectives (pp. 209-231). Norwood, NJ: Ablex.

Tannen, D. (1990). *You just don't understand: Women and men in conversation*. New York: Ballantine.

U.S. Department of Education. (1986). *What works: Research about teaching and learning*. Washington, DC: U.S. Department of Education.

Vogt, L. A., Jordan, C., & Tharp, R. G. (1993). Explaining school failure, producing school success: Two cases. In E. Jacob & C. Jordan (Eds), *Minority education: Anthropological perspectives* (pp. 53-65). Norwood, NJ: Ablex.

Questions:

1. What two approaches does Jacobs combine in her strategy for overcoming the challenges facing educators in culturally diverse classrooms?

2. What are the four anthropological concepts the author suggests can be helpful in understanding culturally diverse classrooms?

3. Name three anthropological methods that can be useful for gathering information for the reflective practice.

The answer section begins on page 243.

For most of the 20th century IQ testing has been used in school systems throughout the United States for determining whether students are placed in advanced, intermediate or "slow" classes. By critiquing the book entitled The Bell Curve by Murray and Herrnstein, Cohen shows how these "Intelligence Quotient" tests are inherently culturally biased, tending to favor the children of those segments of the population that construct the text (i.e., PhD psychologists and other upper class people). While giving the appearance of being inherently fair and democratic, IQ tests have, in fact, been responsible for depriving many culturally different children of enriching educational resources. In other words, there is no reason to provide good teachers, challenging curriculum, and enriching experiences for those with low IQ scores (mostly culturally different minorities) because they are, owing to the "low intelligence," incapable of taking advantage of these educational resources. This article, informed by the insights of anthropology, should be required reading of all teachers and administrators who still rely on standardized IQ tests for the sake of predicting who will, and who will not, succeed in the school system.

Anthropology and Race: The Bell Curve Phenomenon

By Mark Cohen

Like many of you, about six months ago, I organized a symposium to discuss the issues of Charles Murray and Richard Herrnstein's book *The Bell Curve* with the students on my campus. The book had burst on the scene without benefit of serious scholarly review, but with the benefit of enormous publicity including lead stories in the *New York Times Magazine and Book Review* and *Newsweek* as well as innumerable talk show appearances by Murray, its surviving author. It purported to demonstrate: (1) that what is commonly called "intelligence" was a single, real (transcultural) *thing* that could be measured on a single scale rather than being a complex amalgam of varied skills and abilities; (2) that IQ tests as constituted through the 20th century could measure it and did measure it fairly; (3) that IQ, the measure of this intelligence, was largely genetically determined; (4) that an individual's IQ could not be modified significantly in that individual's lifetime; (5) that the human "races" were differentially gifted with IQ (although individuals within any race might excel); (6) that IQ was associated as a cause, not as an effect, with economic success or poverty, with class status, with morality and criminality, and with adherence to middle class American, (Christian) "family values"; that the poor were deprived by virtue of their own shortcomings and already had as fair a slice of the country's

wealth as their IQ merited; (7) that attempts to improve IQ by improvements in the learning environment were useless (for the poor/slow, although the authors called for more enriched education for the gifted); (8) that the genetic components of class stratification (via intelligence) were so significant that we were moving inexorably toward a society segregated by biologically determined intelligence; and (9) that government efforts to intercede educationally or economically on behalf of the poor were misguided and doomed to failure. (The authors professed to find the trend toward a society increasingly stratified by IQ distasteful but they did not simultaneously oppose any efforts to reverse the trend.)

The book was well received because it spoke perfectly to American prejudices against minority groups. It justified existing inequalities, and fed cherished beliefs such as the idea that access to success was based purely on merit and open to anyone with sufficient intelligence. It suggested that success, wealth, and high status were clearly deserved, through merit, and therefore easily defended; that failure was the result of individual inadequacy relieving us of social responsibility. It fueled the American dream that held that upward mobility was limited only by one's ability. It suggested that if the "melting pot" were failing, it could only be because some people (disproportionately in some races) were not capable; and by suggesting that efforts to help such individuals "make it" (whether through affirmative action, welfare, or Headstart) were misguided, it fueled conservative visions of government and reduced government expenditure. It helped fuel the current perception that affirmative action is the only barrier to true equality of opportunity. In short, cloaked in a veneer of objective science, it appealed (or even pandered) perfectly to what many Americans wanted to believe.

In response, my associates and I pointed out: (1) that the "races" Murrary and Herrnstein relied on are not recognized by the overwhelming majority of anthropologists as almost any introductory textbook will affirm (They relied heavily on the racial vision of J.P. Rushton.); (2) that the individual traits that make up common racial stereotypes (not to mention myriad other human variations such as blood type) actually vary independently so that expecting a trait like IQ, even if genetic, to run in races, whether defined by color or defined differently by shape of nose or blood type, makes little sense; (3) that there is serious controversy about whether IQ, initially only a kind of average of various test scores, is in fact a "thing" at all rather than a collection of separate abilities or merely a reification of a number (as Stephen J. Gould has argued repeatedly); (4) that there are various reasons to question whether IQ tests measure intelligence fairly in any case as opposed to measuring a kind of cultural literacy (as discussed more fully below); (5) that Murray and Herrnstein's statements about whether IQ is "heritable" are in fact highly questionable on many grounds. They claim that IQ is 60% heritable by which they ultimately mean genetically determined and not modifiable by environmental factors, but they seem not to note that even by their figures, a very substantial environmental component is involved.) The most essential point in this context is that measured "heritability" is only a statistical artifact of a given sample under specific conditions. It varies widely as the conditions change and is never a general, inherent property of IQ itself. Existing estimates are based heavily on twin studies that provide a badly skewed sample and in which the genetic and environmental components are badly confused.

Many of us raised such objections on campuses and in print. My sense is that we have won the battle but are losing the war. Outrage about the book has been so widespread that a great many people now know it is tainted. Murray himself (to judge by a recent performance at Harvard where he was very badly received) has taken to noting publicly that he has become something of a political pariah with whom even conservatives don't want to associate. So *The Bell Curve* itself may have been diffused.

But the overwhelming, "common sense knowledge" of all of this among the public, in which the book fits so well, is still there and it is clearly not getting better, although attempts to give it a scientific patina may have been slowed. People I talk to, including some of my closest non-anthropological friends, listen to me rebut *The Bell Curve* and then say, "yes—but... you can't deny that..." (I have had the most trouble with the professional psychologists on my campus and their students who react as if this were simply a turf battle. IQ tests, it seems, are "their thing," to be protected at all costs, even if racist misuse of the test must be protected as well. No psychologist on my campus has been willing to say forcefully that there are important values to IQ test but that Murray and Herrnstein abused them—or to help explain the limits of the tests or the distinctions between proper and improper use.)

The problem goes much deeper than Murray and Herrnstein and it is partly a failing of ours as anthropologists. We have not spread the message about what human variation actually consists of and what "multiculturalism" really means. I want to focus on the latter point because I think it is the less well understood issue. Well-meaning people around the country are busy celebrating ethnic differences in music, food, dance, and perhaps language under the banner of "multiculturalism," but even they don't get the deeper differences in cultures. It is our collective failure to teach and learn about the real meaning of culture that is at the heart of the problem and the shallow multicultural celebration only fuels it. It seems that no one except professional anthropologists, understands the depth of cultural differences or, more important, the limits of our own cultural assumptions—and we are not getting those points across.

Perhaps the most telling point in *The Bell Curve* is Murray and Herrnstein's contention that the IQ tests are culturally fair (despite widespread criticism) because, they say, minorities don't disproportionately miss the questions with (the most obvious) cultural biases. According to the authors, minorities miss the questions with little cultural bias most closely associated with strict logic, "general intelligence" or "g," their concept of a central (transcultural) core of logical abilities. And therein lies the most important misunderstanding.

Some IQ test, historically, have had egregious examples of overt cultural bias. To cite just three: a question given to South African Blacks in poor, segregated townships asking them to complete a drawing of a tennis court; a question to new immigrants and illiterate farm boys in the U.S. (in an era before widespread radio or television) asking them to identify famous baseball players; a question given to immigrants to the U.S. of varying ancestry asking them to identify a drawing of a Nordic looking man or woman as obviously more pleasing to the eye than a drawing of someone with more nondescript ethnic physiognomy (that in fact resembled many of the immigrants them selves!). (Murray and Herrnstein, although abhorring some of the errors of earlier tests, have no qualms about using those test results to help their case.)

Some more recent tests may have eliminated such obvious biases, *but they often fail to realize the degree and subtlety of cultural differences or the fact that one can live in the United States, Black or White, and still be a member of another culture.* Questions involving an acorn (see *Newsweek* October 1994), a cow, or a single-family house missing its chimney may not seem culturally biased and they still routinely appear on IQ and related tests. But I, for one, have worked with many inter-city children who have never seen any of these items. (Even taking my own college students on archaeological excavations has been a real eye-opener. When we got to Belize several years ago, most had never seen a palm tree, or a picture of one, and did not know what they were; some had never seen a pig before and didn't recognize one!) Moreover, we have to remember that mere exposure to such objects or their pictures is not sufficient to make the tests fair. If the objects have no salience to an individual's own life, they are less likely to be learned well. (Perhaps we could get rid of such culturally loaded items on the tests, although I doubt it. What items would be left?)

Questions involving drawings, of course, also have another layer of bias. It has been pointed out repeatedly that people in nonliterate cultures who know the items on which they are being tested may have difficulty interpreting two-dimensional drawings of those objects—a failure to understand our conventional representation, not ignorance of the objects of their own world. And

we have to remember that drawing conventions vary from culture to culture even among literate groups and even within our own society. One IQ question still used involves noting the fact that a drawing of a cow with three legs is missing the fourth. It is supposed to be a straight-forward question about cows. But we often draw a cow with only two or three legs *showing* depending on perspective and degree of stylization. (Line drawings are by definition very stylized.) So what is actually tested here is the knowledge that *in the drawing convention being employed*, a fourth leg would normally be depicted. But those are cultural rules, not simple logic or even natural knowledge.

But the real problem is much deeper and concerns the deeper meaning of cultural differences.

I recently had occasion to sit through a presentation by a psychologist of the very latest IQ questions offered in defense of IQ testing. Many of the errors above had been expunged and real efforts had been made to make the tests fair—*as long as cultural differences are understood to refer only to the cultural item content of the questions, not to the form of the questions or their underlying presentation, cultural "grammar" or logic.* It is as if we were studying French vocabulary but not grammar, French cuisine or art but not the logic of the thinking of French people. Once we begin looking at the structure of the questions as well as their content, every one can be dissected and layers of bias peeled away like the layers of an onion until nothing is left. (We can do this dissection but have to bear in mind that most of us were reared with many of the same cultural biases and may not notice them because we take them for granted. I recommend that you ask students to dissect the following questions using these examples as a starting point. It would be particularly interesting to get the reactions of minority or foreign students.

Item. One question asks students to identify *either* of two famous, dead scientists, Albert Einstein or G. W. Carver. The question must be "fair" because it has both a Black and a White scientist! But I can think of at least two more levels of cultural bias (and I am sure there are more.) First, the category "scientist" is itself more salient in White American culture than Black American culture (Carver is mostly a White person's Black hero) so a White is more likely to identify a scientist of either race. Second (I am not certain whether this applies to Black/White differences, but it surely applies more broadly), one culture, like ours, might focus more than another on the use of printed pictures as a way of "knowing" as opposed to, say, televised action images, oral traditions, or rap music. (In fact, "knowing" might be altogether less visual in some cultures than in others without implying that people were either less intelligent or even more ignorant of the subject.)

Item. Analogy problems of the type "*acorn* has the same relationship to *seed* as *oak* has to ____ ? that appeared in *Newsweek* (October 1994) are supposed to measure logical ability, but in fact they are based on the way people put things in categories. All analogies, by definition, are based on categorizing. Any anthropologist familiar with Cole and Gay's work on Africa (or who has worked with Mesoamerican populations that employ the famous hot/cold classification) knows that different cultures classify things in different ways or at least focus initially on different (to them) salient properties. But IQ testers and the general public are apparently oblivious to this point. And we, ourselves, of course often classify things in different ways depending on the context. The answer to the acorn problem (*tree*) depends on whether one uses "seed" as an inclusive category containing acorns or whether acorns are "nuts" as opposed to seeds, as archaeologists often use the terms. (Remember that one need not be completely ignorant of a classifying principle to be penalized on an IQ test; one only has to be momentarily confused or slowed by the awareness of alternative possibilities. One's response only has to be less conditioned or automatic.)

Item. Using cartoon figures (that are supposed to be culture-free), students are asked to identify whether two figures viewed at separate times are the same or different. The correct answer in this case is that the two figures are different because the diagonal stripes on their tunics go in different directions. Most of the adults who attended the presentation where these questions were posed missed that one. A child—characterized by the psychologist on this basis as "extremely bright"—got it right. We anthropologists in the audience couldn't help thinking that anyone from a culture that marked gender or class by the direction of their stripes probably got it right. We couldn't help thinking that what was important was not mental ability(s) but cultural differences governing which visual distinctions, like phonemes, we were taught to identify and use, and which distinctions, like other phonetic distinctions, we were simply taught to ignore.

(Most Americans probably pay no attention to whether a man's earring is in his right or left ear; but for some, this is important cultural information that they don't miss and that they remember. Most American men do notice on which finger a woman is wearing a ring, although in culture-free terms, it is a trivial thing.) The child got this question right not because she was "bright," but because she hadn't been socialized yet to ignore what our culture considers extraneous; but she was probably well trained to look for such details by the kind of common tests of sameness/difference that we give children in game books and comic strips.

Most Americans really can't comprehend that there are other systems of thought and they fail to recognize the "blinders" that our own culture imposes, blinders that keep us looking in a common direction and prevent us from seeing alternatives. The people who are trying to make IQ tests "fair"—like the people who are teaching "international business"—apparently have no idea what it actually involves; nor do the people who are sick of affirmative action and who fail to realize the degree to which the status quo—reinforced by the tests is itself affirmative action for the in-group. They don't realize that by relying on tests of cultural literacy for so much of our social placement, we are not only discriminating, we are also straight jacketing our employees and limiting the richness we all might enjoy if we tolerated more cultural diversity in thinking and emotion, not just in food. Other aspects of our lives stand to be enriched as much as our cuisine or music. (Our medicine, for example, is now starting to react constructively to, and be enriched by, the knowledge of other groups.) Even efficiency might well increase through broader cultural tolerance after a period of adjustment. After all, in other areas, we tend to think that efficiency and quality improve as the variety of available options to select from increases.

This is what anthropologist must teach, must sell. Reasonable world order and understanding and cultural enrichment depend on it. We, as anthropologists, have to get beyond our own tendency to celebrate exotic things and practices and to dissolve into esoterica and trivia of the kind that prompted the unfortunate *New York Times* editorial following our last annual meeting. The citation was partly right. Anthropologists need to focus on our central concepts that should be part of everyone's general education. We also have to get beyond our own sense of graduate school intellectual elitism and focus on anthropology as a necessary piece of undergraduate and public education. We have to hammer on the very real importance of anthropology for every-day actions and decisions, not just for visiting remote tribes or digging up ancient relics. And, we have to get the public beyond the sense that "cultural relativism" means a kind of mindless blanket acceptance, abandoning judgment and simply equating all human behavior as the idea is portrayed by our critics. Instead, we need to focus on relativism's two major lessons: that we have to try to understand other people and their actions in context, and that we have to be willing to explore the limits and biases of our own cultural assumptions.

Questions:

1. What did the book entitled *The Bell Curve* purport to demonstrate?

2. What does Cohen have to say about the "blinders" imposed on Americans by their culture?

3. According to Cohen, what are the two major points that we need to keep in mind concerning "cultural relativism?"

The answer section begins on page 243.

25

A fundamental part of educational anthropology deals with the relationship between educational institutions and local cultures. Often, the goals and philosophical assumptions of the formal school system are not compatible with the behaviors and attitudes of local cultures. In such cases either the school systems adapt to accommodate the local cultural realities, or what is more often the case, the local cultures are expected to become more compatible with the educational system. Here an applied anthropologist (Chaudhuri) and an applied sociologist (Deutscher) study some educational problems experienced by the Toto, a local ethnic group from West Bengal, India. Specifically, the authors were interested in examining why the literacy rate among the Toto was so low, particularly in light of the availability of educational resources. By examining a number of culturally relevant educational constraints, the authors are able to make certain recommendations for improving education among the Toto in light of current government policies.

Home Grown Development: The Education of Tribal Peoples

By Sarit K. Chaudhuri and Irwin Deutscher

Like many other developing countries, India seeks a development policy that provides its people with a sense of unity and nationalism. Education plays a key role in this effort to create some homogeneity, some equality, some sense of unity out of a mass of people of varying linguistic, cultural, ethnic, religious, class, caste, tribal, and other backgrounds. We are concerned here with the implementation of this domestic development policy with respect to Indian tribal peoples. Our case study of education among one tribal population illuminates some of the issues involved and suggests at least part of the solution.

The concept of tribal development emerged soon after India achieved independence in 1947, and it received special impetus on the eve of the Fourth Five Year Plan in 1969. Benefits were aimed at scheduled tribes as well as scheduled castes through different development programs. Education is generally perceived in India as a social right and as a major tool for development. Indeed, level of literacy is one of the three major criteria used by the government to identify those tribal groups classified as "primitive" (the other criteria being low population growth rates and pre-agricultural level of technological development). It is not surprising, therefore, that education is prominent among the several well-integrated programs that constitute tribal

development. While the Indian decennial census indicates that literacy among the scheduled tribes has been steadily increasing, from 8.5 percent in 1961 to 11.3 percent in 1971, and finally up to 16.4 percent in the 1981 census, that is less than half of the 36.2 percent literacy rate for India as a whole. Why, after so much organized effort over so long a period of time, does the literacy rate remain so low? What can be done to improve it? These are the central questions around which our study revolves.

Education is, of course, not only a social right and a tool for development; it also helps to protect tribal peoples from unscrupulous exploitation (which is not unknown in India and elsewhere) and opens up alternative work opportunities for those who choose to abandon traditional occupations. Education, and especially literacy, is one of the most important avenues for enabling peoples to move from traditional to modern society with minimal trauma. Although we do not necessarily advocate such a move, we do advocate the right of people to make that choice if they so desire.

In West Bengal there are three tribes identified as "primitive," the Toto, Birhor, and Lodha, each residing in a different district. The senior author engaged in field work among the Toto during the year 1984 and for a short period in 1989. This paper explores educational problems

Reprinted by permission of PRACTICING ANTHROPOLOGY. 15(3), summer, 1993, pp. 25-28.

among the Toto and suggests steps which can help to correct some of those problems within the framework of current government policies.

The Toto: Their World And Education

Today all Toto live in a relatively isolated area known as "Totopara." Totopara is entirely surrounded by rivers, dense forests, and mountains. Wild flora and fauna abound, and they play an important role in the life of the Toto. During the rainy season the area is isolated by the rushing torrents of the rivers Howri and Torsha. Twice a day, when the roads are passable, a private bus connects the center of Totopara, where a small market is located, with the village of Madarihat in the outside world. (Recent ethnographic profiles of the Toto can be found in English in *Tribal Development in India: Problems and Prospects*, edited by B. Chandury [New Delhi: Inter-India Publications, 1982] and *The Meches and the Totos: Two Sub-Himalayan Tribes of North Bengal* by C.C. Sanyal [Darjeeling: The University of North Bengal, 1979].)

The 1901 Indian Census reports the Toto population as 171. We counted nearly 850 Toto people in 1989. Not everyone in Totopara is Toto. In 1984 we counted 25 families from seven other tribal and nontribal groups in addition to 145 Nepali families.

What has been happening to literacy among the Toto? In 1984, interviews with 755 Totos revealed that 60 out of 391 men (15 percent) and 5 of 364 women (1.4 percent) were literate. In 1989 there was no change. The standards adopted to determine literacy in India are very low; if a person can sign his or her name, that person is defined as literate. Ten of our Toto could only sign their names. Thirty-three had completed primary school, thirteen junior high, and only nine had gone beyond that educationally.

As difficult as it may be to believe from these figures, there are extensive educational resources available to the Toto. There is a local primary school handling grades one through four with two teachers, one of whom is also acting headmaster. Nearby there is a junior high school with four teachers. Although now state owned, both of these were originally Swedish Mission schools. Between 1984 and 1989 there was a second primary school; this bamboo school was totally destroyed by a cyclone in 1989. There are also two Anganwadi Centers at Totopara, each with a paid teacher, helper, and cook. These are essentially day care centers where preschool age children are cared for and taught simple rhymes and the like by educated Toto girls.

In addition, there is the Ashram Hostel located in Totopara which houses some of the primary school students. The Ashram Hostels were designed by the Indian Government especially for tribal children. They are somewhat similar (for better or worse) to the American federal boarding schools for children. They provide room and board and all books and school supplies, as well as uniforms for the pupils. The Ashram Hostel, whose superintendent is absent, is run by the headmaster of the nearby primary school. The staff consists of two cooks.

There is also a government-registered library operated by a library officer and an assistant, both of them Toto. It is located in a new and well furnished building and holds about five hundred books. The library has a reasonable budget for the purchase of books based on the choice of members and staff, and it is open six days a week. Of the sixty-five library members, thirty are Totos.

Fifty-two percent of the 142 pupils in the Totopara primary school are Toto, while the junior high enrolls 75 students, of whom only 25 percent are Toto. The distribution of Toto and other pupils in these two schools appears in Table 1. The second primary school had fifty students, of whom five were Toto. Officially, there were thirty pupils at the Ashram Hostel in the 1989-90 school year, all of whom were Toto; actually there were fewer resident pupils. The discrepancy, a product of government regulation threatening withdrawal of funds when an Ashram Hostel's registration falls below thirty, is an open secret discussed by school committee members. The primary schools and the junior high have no minimum registration requirements and therefore no need for such subterfuge. Nevertheless these schools too have fewer pupils in regular attendance than the official figures suggest.

TABLE 1

Number of Toto and Other Pupils Enrolled in Primary School and Junior High School, 1989

Category	Primary (Grades 1-4)	Junior High (Grades 5-8)
Toto	74	19
Other Scheduled Tribes	3	28
Scheduled Castes	13	3
Other (Mostly Nepali)	52	25
Totals	142	75

Educational Constraints

As isolated as Totopara is, the government of West Bengal has managed to make extensive physical facilities available for education of the Toto. It had also enrolled (at least officially) some 98 Toto in 1989. But the enrollment of tribal children in school is only the first step toward education. In the 1962 Report of the Scheduled Area and Tribes Commission (New Delhi: Government of India), the Indian government displays an awareness of the problems of retention and recognizes that "absenteeism, stagnation and wastage are universal problems affecting all educational institutions throughout India particularly at the primary stage of education and these problems are most serious in the tribal areas."

As with religious agricultural peoples elsewhere, there is considerable seasonal variation in attendance at school among the Toto. The labor of children is especially important during harvest and planting seasons. Furthermore, there are numerous feast days and holy days when it would be unthinkable to send a child to school.

In addition, school activities often fail to capture the interest of tribal children. Since there is no script for the Toto language, children cannot be taught in their first language. Although this makes both teaching and learning somewhat more difficult than they would ordinarily be, Toto parents accept the necessity for Bengali as the medium for instruction. What is not necessary is the "Dick and Jane" and "Run, Spot, Run" lifestyle of the educational materials. Textbooks tend to emphasize the urban or plains lifestyles which are difficult for Toto children to relate to.

The recruitment and retention of teachers is nearly as problematic as the retention of pupils. It is most difficult to attract qualified and motivated teachers to such an isolated area, yet the success or failure of the enterprise is dependent upon them. A husband-wife team compose the total teaching staff of the one surviving Totopara primary school. It consists of four grades, two of which are always without a teacher. Furthermore, the headmaster of that school now presides over the administrative unit for the Anchal Panchayet, a position which requires extensive political activity and absences from Totopara. This same headmaster is also acting superintendent of the Ashram Hostel. Toto parents and pupils take note of these complications and tend to become demoralized and disinterested in school as a result.

An additional educational constraint lies in the area of the teacher as role model, motivator, and mentor. When, for example, the headmaster of one primary school leaves under charges of forgery and the headmaster of the other engages in sexual misconduct with a young Toto woman, eventually abandoning his wife to live with the Toto woman, educational chaos is inevitable. In the latter case, angry young Toto men drove the headmaster and the woman from Totopara, and he has not been permitted to return. When the District Magistrate visited Totopara, villagers besieged him with both oral and written complaints and demands for the removal of the headmaster. (Their anger resulted, incidentally, not from the headmaster's abandonment of his wife, but from the rigid Toto taboos against exogamy. For these strictly endogamous people the headmaster could have committed no greater breach of propriety.)

The schools we have described cover only the primary grades (one through four) and junior high (grades five through eight). In the past, several Toto boys did travel to the distant secondary school in the neighboring Coochbehar district. This no longer happens, in part because of the recent ban on missionaries who previously supplemented the stipend provided by the government. There have been no Toto enrolled in secondary classes in recent years.

In addition to the lack of secondary facilities in Totopara, the economic constraints of advanced education are severe for tribal peoples. The Toto view their children as economic assets—as "helping hands." Toto boys are assigned to pasture and tend cows or goats all day long. Female children help with cooking, food preparation, and other household tasks. As soon as children become old enough and strong enough, they participate fully in the agricultural work of the family. Parents find this a more productive use of children's time than formal education. The picture is somewhat different among literate parents who are more aware of the potential economic advantages of education, but only for boys. Even the literate Toto see no advantage in the education of women.

Village Initiatives

Villagers are neither unaware of nor uninterested in educational issues, but they are at a distinct disadvantage when dealing with officials who view them as "primitive" and uninformed. As with many such minorities, they are somewhat in awe of the power and authority vested in the functionaries with whom they must deal, making it difficult for them to act without some timidity. Nevertheless, they do act, not only through direct action (forcibly removing the errant headmaster), but also by participating in the educational hierarchy through the local school committee.

For administrative purposes, the state of West Bengal is divided into districts each headed by a District Magistrate. Districts are subdivided into blocks which are administered by Block Development Officers (BDO). Totopara, under the block Madarihat, has a school committee composed of distinguished citizens who are responsible for overseeing the performance of local schools. Each year this committee meets to review and consider the educational atmosphere. Their first appeal beyond the village level is the BDO, and beyond him is the District Magistrate and the highest state authorities.

In 1989, the Totopara School Committee consisted of three Toto (including the village head), a Nepali "guest member" (the Nepali are the largest group of nontribal people in Totopara), the headmaster of the primary school, a social worker, and the local compounder (roughly equivalent to a pharmacist). They made a series of unanimous recommendations at their 1989 meeting. They asked that something be done to correct the terrible teacher-student ratio. They discussed the errant headmaster and requested that the matter be urgently pursued. They also discussed the situation at the Ashram Hostel and complained about its acting superintendent. Locals repeatedly asked the Block Development Officer to take steps to improve the situation at the Hostel, but failed to get any response. In addition, they noted that the primary school teachers "are not careful at all about the students and urged them to be careful about them." For the American English reader, the intention here is that the teachers literally be more caring.

These actions by local people are indicative of the problems with which the educational system must cope if it is to deal successfully with tribal peoples.

Some Policy Questions and Suggestions

Our study of the Toto is part of a larger study in progress which includes four tribal groups in West Bengal. Eventually, comparisons will be made among those tribes and a report and recommendations submitted to the state government. Based on our study of the Toto alone,

we conclude that the tribal development educational system is seriously flawed. It is not operating as the governments of West Bengal and of India intend. Therefore, we would urge the government of West Bengal to consider a number of policy questions and suggestions.

Professional staffing is clearly in need of improvement. It is not simply a matter of more teachers, but also a matter of better qualified and more caring teachers. Even though there is a surplus of teachers in India with the necessary bachelor's degree, it is difficult to attract them to isolated posts such as Totopara, when adequate housing, schools for their children, entertainment, transportation, and shopping facilities are unavailable. Consideration by the authorities of how to make teaching in Totopara more attractive to better teachers could improve this situation.

The inflation of official statistics on registered students is another problem that needs to be addressed. What is needed is a system which truly provides incentives to induce tribal parents to enroll their children in schools and to induce children to stay there. Poor families need temporary economic assistance to replace the loss of labor by their children.

In addition, education must be made more relevant from the perspective of tribal peoples. This can take the form, in part, of sensitivity to the agricultural and religious calendar in formulating the school calendar. Relevance requires the introduction of teaching materials that make sense to tribal children rather than the current mandated textbooks which depict a world utterly unfamiliar to them. Relevance is also achieved through caring teachers who have had some indoctrination into the tribal lifestyle, including its taboos, deities, feast days, and agricultural activities. A final kind of relevance can be obtained by introducing trade or occupational training into the curriculum along with academics. Job training and followthrough job placement would go a long way toward persuading the Toto of the importance of education.

It may, nevertheless, be necessary to challenge some of the traditional practices of the Toto and induce them to accept new motions. When there are only five literate women, all under age of twenty, it is clear that special attention needs to be paid to the role of female children in Toto society. They should learn that women too can hold productive and rewarding jobs in the outside world, if not in their own traditional society. The economic incentives could be seductive to tribal parents.

It is also important that secondary school become accessible to the Toto. It is not possible for them to reach a school in a neighboring district for which there is no regular transportation. Either a hostel arrangement for students wishing to continue their education or regular dependable transportation needs to be provided.

It is likely that similar questions and suggestions are relevant to some tribal situations elsewhere in India as well as in other parts of the developing world. There are also important similarities between tribal groups and depressed urban classes in India and elsewhere, including problems of school failure, high dropout rates, and poor attendance which occur for the same economic and cultural reasons. At the very best such minority groups are faced with a patronizing attitude on the part of those better placed in the society and wielding greater power. More often these groups are faced with open prejudice and discrimination. Policies analogous to those we have suggested will make sense for many such peoples wherever in the world they may be found.

Questions:

1. What two questions does this study attempt to answer?

2. What are the major educational constraints to literacy among the Toto as described by the authors?

3. What specific policy recommendations do the authors make for the improvement of education among the Toto?

The answer section begins on page 243.

There is general agreement among developmental psychologists that much of what a person learns occurs before the age of five, before the child enters the system of formal schooling. If this is the case, then such areas as child care, pre-school, and early childhood education become critical in the developmental process of youngsters. And since these pre-school practices and institutions are played out in a cultural environment, then it makes sense that cultural anthropology can make significant contributions to the field of child care and early childhood education. In this selection, educational anthropologist Jonathan Green discusses his work in a day care center in which he applied anthropological methods and insights to working with special needs children as well as developing staff development programs.

Who's Watching the Children? Anthropology in Child Care

By Jonathan Green

For the past several years I have been engaged in graduate study in anthropology, with special focus on applied and especially educational anthropology. During this time economics have necessitated my employment outside academia, primarily in the field of child care and early childhood education. Since June 1994, I have worked with one child-care provider in particular: a large, public, for-profit, preschool and day-care company. I began in the Special Needs Program, but recently moved into the position of Training Coordinator. Rather than working directly with the children, I now work with the teachers who work with the children.

While I became involved in child care largely by chance, I have found numerous intersections between my work in child care and early childhood education and my study and research in anthropology. Anthropology has uniquely prepared me for the exigencies of working in a for-profit corporation and soliciting public funds, for the necessity of collaborative effort, and for other aspects of my role as a child-care worker. I am convinced that child-care workers and educators in general could all benefit from a knowledge of anthropological principles.

The Cultural Context

The company for which I work currently serves over three thousand children in four states, and it is continuing to expand. The goal of the company is to provide a profit-generating service which is in high demand: high quality and relatively affordable child care. In metropolitan Phoenix, it runs fourteen centers serving fifteen hundred children and employing three hundred people in education, management, and maintenance.

The child-care field employs mainly women, often young women, and in large urban areas, often women of color. Incidentally, but probably not coincidentally, child care is also one of the lowest paying and least respected professions. Being an older, white male has made me something of an oddity in the child-care business. Issues of gender and ethnic and linguistic background are always implicit in my dealings with fellow child-care workers.

My anthropological training, particularly in participant observation and dealing with cross-cultural situations, has helped me deal sensitively with these issues. I know my position of authority and my gender and ethnic background structure and may even inhibit discourse with other teachers. Hence, when working in a classroom or with a group of teachers in training session, I always first observe the environment and assess the situation. I make a conscious effort to listen carefully to what others say and how they say it and to seek contextual clues to differences in cross-cultural and cross-gender communication. Too often men, especially white men, cut off and devalue the speech of women, especially the speech of nonwhite women. I do my best to allow ample time for others to speak before I engage in discourse.

Each day-care center and each classroom within each center has its own quirks and character—a distinctive culture. Much of the

Reprinted by permission of PRACTICING ANTHROPOLOGY. 18(4), Fall, 1996, pp. 33-36.

former is based on the geographic locale of the center: whether in a low-income, high-minority central urban area or a high-income, low-minority suburban context. It is also a reflection of the orientation of the center directors. Classroom cultures additionally reflect the background and experience of teachers as well as those of the children and their parents.

The central Phoenix location, where most of the training sessions are held, is open twenty-four hours a day, seven days a week, to serve the downtown business community. Many of the children who attend these center are Hispanic or African American, as they comprise much of the downtown population. Many of the staff also come from the surrounding community, and many are Hispanic or African American as well. The Hispanic heritage especially is reflected in classrooms, where materials and decorations (such as alphabet and color charts) are usually in both English and Spanish.

In contrast, the center located at the Phoenix corporate office—where I mainly work—is in an affluent, predominantly Anglo community. Many of the children are dropped off and picked up in expensive vehicles by well-dressed parents who work in the nearby business and office parks. Most of the staff are also Anglo, reflecting the composition of the community around them. Spanish is here a second rather than a primary language (as it often is at the downtown center).

All of the center directors are women, and all but one are Anglo. The primary difference among them, which helps to establish a distinctive culture for each center, is the extent to which each center director is oriented toward business and management rather than early childhood education. This is reflected in how the centers are run, in director-teacher interactions, and in classroom environment and structure.

More business-oriented directors focus more heavily on their center's budgetary concerns and on attracting new, paying clients. They respond more readily to pressure from the corporate office to keep the bottom line in the black. As a consequence the classroom staff at these centers tend to lack support and training from their director. Not surprisingly, directors at these centers often lament that their classrooms and centers do not run as smoothly as they would like.

More education-oriented directors focus more heavily on supporting their staff and overseeing day-to-day classroom functioning. This greatly improves the educational quality of the classrooms and the expertise of the staff. This focus, however, can lead directors to pay less attention to business details, and their centers may even run it the red, resulting in intervention by management. Education-orientated directors lament the lack of money and equipment to run a high quality program.

At all of the centers, the individual classrooms have their own distinctive cultures as well. Young, relatively uneducated and inexperienced teachers tend to run their classrooms based on their own personal styles and not according to principles of early childhood education, developmental appropriateness, and classroom management. When teacher inexperience is coupled with directorial nonintervention, chaotic and disruptive classes are a frequent result. Not surprisingly, one of the most common concerns voiced by teachers is difficulty in getting and keeping a class "under control." On the other hand, teachers who are educated and/or experienced in early childhood education frequently run very well managed and educationally productive classrooms. When this is coupled with positive directorial intervention, smooth running centers are the result.

In addition, the children themselves and their families have a profound impact on classroom culture. At all of the centers, the children come from varied cultural and economic backgrounds, but the cultural variation is greater in the central urban locations, while the economic variation is greater at the suburban ones. At the urban center a number of different ethnic groups are represented, and one often hears teachers and parents conversing in Spanish, rather than English. Teachers and parents at these locations share working-class or middle-class backgrounds and relate well to one another on a personal level. At the suburban locations teachers and parents often come from divergent socioeconomic situations, and parents relate to teachers as both economic and social subordinates.

Mediation and Advocacy for Special Needs Children

The ability to work within these varied cultural settings was key to my effectiveness in the Special Needs Program. The goal of the program is to mainstream or integrate children who have experienced developmental disability (Down syndrome, autism, Attention Deficit Disorder/Attention Deficit Hyperactive Disorder, medically fragility, etc.) into normal or typical classrooms. My primary role was to assist the special needs children in negotiating the classroom environment and in becoming successful members of the classroom culture. I spent much of my time assisting typical children as well in their understanding and acceptance of the atypical children. I also found, much to my dismay, that I had to assist the teachers in understanding and accepting the atypical children.

I first observed and interacted with the special needs children, who came from a variety of ethnic backgrounds and had a variety of disabling conditions, in order to understand the cultural background and individual personality of each. This prepared me to facilitate interaction between the special needs children and both the typical children and the teachers and to advocate on behalf of the atypical children. When typical children asked me why a particular child could not speak, for example, I could explain that the child communicated in other ways, such as through signs or certain sounds and tones of voice. I helped the typical and special needs children to communicate with each other to understand and accept situations of noncommunication.

Many of the teachers initially felt that they should treat the atypical children differently. Labeling and stereotyping by both children and staff is an on-going problem. I explained and modeled to the teachers that they should treat the special needs children the same, though perhaps offering assistance in certain skill areas and adjusting expectations to meet the child's abilities. Sadly, much prejudice towards children with special needs still exists in our society and even within a company that prides itself on working with this population. Countless times I have heard teachers state that the problems in a particular classroom are caused by the special needs child(ren). In working with these teachers and classes I have usually found that the problems are caused by an inexperienced teacher and the inappropriately managed "normal" children.

I also participated in Individual Program Plan meetings and acted as an advocate for the atypical child's needs and abilities with parents and social service workers. This involved brokerage between the worlds or cultures of the typical and atypical children, and also between those of children and adults. I often helped adults to see both strengths and needs in the child's progress. For example, one boy with Down syndrome had difficulty in associating his actions with their natural-logical consequences and caused pain and occasionally injury to others and himself. I helped his father see that some things in life can only be learned through experience and trial and error. We cannot cushion children, with or without disabilities, or pre-educate them to all the good and bad things that may and will happen to them in life.

Designing and Implementing Effective Training

In my new role as Training Coordinator, I still observe, negotiate, mediate, advocate, and broker, but more often with adults. In addition, I am engaged with curricular and pedagogical issues, both as directed towards children and as directed towards adults. In this role I have drawn more on knowledge and skills developed as a student intern and a research assistant, and as a teaching assistant than those developed through academic training.

In designing the training program, I applied principles of adult learning that I had used as a teaching assistant and that are derived in part from ethnographic literature. Three key themes run through these adult learning principles, mirroring themes in current research in education anthropology: empowerment, collaboration, and critical reflection or thinking. (See, for example, *Anthropology and Education Quarterly* 25, 3[1994].)

Empowerment gives child-care workers the skills and confidence that they need to take charge or their situations, to improve their own classrooms and the lives of the children they care for, and additionally, to influence others in their profession. We help create an environment of empowerment in the training session through interactive discussions, acting out of situations, and team-based problem solving. We help teachers sort out the developmental versus idiosyncratic characteristics of particular children and classroom situations, which in turn helps them to deal more objectively and appropriately with personalities and problem behaviors. In essence we encourage the teachers to become ethnographers in their own classrooms, helping them develop the skills to observe, analyze, and solve the problems they encounter on a daily basis.

We create collaboration as well as empowerment in the training sessions by having the participants raise issues of importance to them and work together to solve these problems. One issue that has been raised by the teachers at nearly every training is children's aggression and violence. Teachers, especially those from central urban areas, lament what they see as a steady increase in violence in society at large, which is mirrored, they say, in aggression and even violence by children towards teachers at the day-care centers. This is an issue which we trainers had not seriously thought about previously. In our renewal proposal, we have included in the training contract provisions for new sessions to address more thoroughly this teacher-raised issue.

Critical reflection and thinking are essential ingredients of both empowerment and collaboration, helping teachers develop the skills and abilities necessary to create more successful classrooms and better cared for and educated children. We foster critical reflection and thinking in the training sessions by involving the participants in outlining and discussing the topic and by encouraging them to discuss their own experiences in a critical yet constructive way.

For example, parent communication has been the subject of some lively and thoughtful discussion. Many teachers talk about how parents are often in a rush, or how they look down upon child-care providers as simply "baby-sitters;" in either case, the parents do not listen to what the teachers have to say about their children. As a result, teachers and parents may find themselves working against each other in raising the children, rather than collaborating, causing problems at home and in the day-care setting.

One teacher raised the problem of single fathers (or even married fathers!) "hitting" on them. Other teachers chimed in, many teachers raising their own stories for the first time. This led to a heated discussion of sexual harassment and appropriate provider-client interaction. Needless to say, none of this discussion was on the original agenda for the training session!

I have worked at two of the centers adapting the training modules to an actual classroom setting. Working one-on-one, the teachers and I were able to go beyond the more hypothetical discussion of the training sessions to concrete, practical application, improving their confidence and performance and bettering the education of children. Through this process of collaboration, the teachers developed their critical thinking skills, in turn empowering them in their understanding and application of early childhood principles. This led to a reduction both in their feelings of lack of classroom control and in actual behavior problems and to a much more conducive learning environment.

Dealing with Public Funding Agencies

Another area in which I have applied my anthropological experience is in helping to secure funds for day care and training programs. Some of these funds come from public agencies, such as the Arizona State Department of Economic Security (DES) which receives federal Child Care and Development Block Grant monies, a percentage of which must be used to fund early childhood education and before-and after-school child-care services. Allocation of these funds must give priority to areas of high poverty and either very high or very low population density. To insure that these requirements are satisfied, much statistical and qualitative data must be gathered. This includes both census tract data (supplied by DES) and service needs data. The latter are gathered primarily through interviews with day-care and other service providers.

Before our training contract was approved, we had to document day-care providers' desire and need for additional training. I assisted in designing and administering these questionnaires. We also administer follow-up questionnaires to ascertain how effective the training sessions are and what issues still need to be addressed. I have also designed several forms for use in the training program: classroom observation forms, action plan goals and objectives forms to improve particular classroom situations, and forms for participant evaluation of training sessions.

Training in anthropology prepared me well for the task of gathering and employing quantitative and especially qualitative data in research and practice. While the surveys and forms still contain multiple choice questions, my anthropological training has led me to include open-ended, narrative-response questions through which child-care providers can freely express an epic viewpoint. Although this results in more data to be compiled, it also yields much more contextualized and insightful information. Even the quality and style of language used by respondents reveals much about their background and education, giving me further insight to incorporate into future training sessions.

We have recently prepared and submitted a proposal to the Administration for Children, Youth and Families to implement a family support and service coordination contract and one to the Arizona Early Intervention Program to provide services to infants and toddlers. A central component of both proposed programs is parent education and training classes, utilizing the principles of adult learning. A second focus of both programs is empowerment of parents over their own lives and in the lives of their children. I helped design several forms to be used in the programs—intake forms, Individual Family Service Plan forms, follow-up forms, participant evaluation forms—all based upon anthropological principles of participant observation, open-ended questioning, and native voice inclusion.

In a few months the federally based funding for the DES-supported Special Needs Program will run out. We are therefore employing the not-for-profit arm of our corporation to solicit monies from a myriad of federal, state and private funding agencies and foundations. In essence, we hope to contract out special needs services to our own as well as other outside agencies, rather than receiving funding directly from the government. Ironically, these efforts parallel the goals of the Republican Revolution to have local agencies control monies and their use. They also parallel the applied anthropological practice of collaboration and cooperation, both between agencies and with the population or community to be served.

Conclusions

Anthropology has much to add to the field of child care and early childhood education. A key contribution is awareness of the importance of culture in defining interpersonal interactions and discourse. This is of relevance in trainer-teacher discourse, director-teacher discourse, teacher-child discourse, and provider-parent discourse. Additionally, applied anthropological concepts of intercultural negotiation and collaborative and cooperative effort towards change can contribute to improving the quality of day care. Again, these principles can be applied with groups of teachers in training sessions and also with individual teachers or children in the classroom. Both negotiation and collaborative effort are also key components in garnering funding and in working with other service providers and the families themselves.

Conversely, the field of child care is ripe for anthropological research and study. We have much to learn concerning the contemporary state of early childhood socialization in our society and the nature of adult-child interactions.

How and what we can teach children in the early years of life has immense repercussions for the future of the children and for our society as a whole. I urge anthropologists who have ignored the field of child care and early childhood education to take a look at it. Our child care has much to say about our society, and it is an area in need of qualitative and quantitative anthropological research and anthropologically informed practice.

Questions:

1. What types of anthropological training helped the author deal with issues involving child care?

2. How did author Green serve as a cultural broker?

3. What key themes are common to both adult learning principles and the current research in educational anthropology?

The answer section begins on page 243.

Section IV
Government and Law

Throughout most of the 20th century the term "homeless" referred to the urban underclass—usually male, hard-core unemployed, and often alcoholics. These were the Hobos studies by Anderson in Chicago in the 1920s and the tramps studied by Spradley during the 1970s. For the past several decades, however, the homeless have come to include an increasing number of women and children as well. In this selection, applied anthropologist Anna Lou Dehavenon describes her research on the causes and conditions of homelessness among families in New York City. Her findings led her to conclude that New York City's welfare system, despite recent changes, is still not meeting the needs of the growing number of homeless families. In light of the recent (1996) federal legislation to turn over responsibility for welfare services to the states, it will be interesting to see if the problems of homelessness are exacerbated even further.

Monitoring Emergency Shelter For Homeless Families in New York City

By Anna Lou Dehavenon

"Sleeping on the floor.... Huddled in corners of the structures in the hallway.... Filthy, atrocious bathrooms, no toilet paper or paper towels, mice and cockroaches, sick children, children sleeping in strollers, hot, humid and chaotic conditions; families sleeping on plastic chairs, or on newspapers spread out on the floor; and families with inadequate food and drink." Author's expert witness testimony in McCain vs. Dinkens, 1991.

Since 1979 I have collected and analyzed primary data on the causes and conditions of hunger and homelessness in New York City households with children. The results of my work have been summarized in yearly research reports that include data-based recommendations for changes in welfare programs at the city, state, and national levels. These reports have been sent to the print and broadcast media at the same time they were distributed to legislators, administrators of welfare programs, and other public officials. This annual media coverage has helped draw the attention of decision makers to the reports and their recommendations.

In 1993, hunger and homelessness continued to increase in the city, and the low level of welfare grants contributed to the rise. Welfare grants are the only form of publicly entitled income not linked to the Consumer Price Index. Nationally, the purchasing power of the Aid to Families with Dependent Children payment has declined 45 percent since 1970. Welfare families in New York

State receive the benefit in the form of two grants: a shelter allowance for rent and a "basic" grant for food and all other expenses. (In addition, they receive food stamps, which are periodically adjusted for inflation, to supplement the food allowance in the basic grant.) Since 1969, when welfare grants were first set by family size, the cost of living has increased almost 300 percent in the New York City metropolitan region, while the basic welfare grant has risen only 56 percent!

The welfare rent allowance in 1993 was only half what families needed to rent apartments in New York City's high-cost private housing market. As a result, many homeless welfare families lived doubled up and sometimes moved between temporary double-ups and the public shelter system. A major focus of my recent research has been homelessness and the city's policies and procedures for providing shelter for homeless families.

Ten years ago, the New York State Supreme Court ruled that the state constitution and social services law require the city to place homeless families with children in emergency shelter. In 1986, it ruled further that they have to be placed in shelter on the same day they request it. In 1992, the city and four top officials were found in contempt of court for violation these rules by allowing homeless families to stay overnight in Emergency Assistance Units (EAUs—after-hours shelter intake offices. A new city plan for the

Reprinted by permission of PRACTICING ANTHROPOLOGY 16(4), Fall, 1994, pp. 12-16.

homeless was initiated in 1992, designed to "divert" as many as possible from the public shelter system. Yet in 1993, the city routinely left dozens of families to sleep overnight on the floors, table, and hard plastic chairs of the EAUs.

Under the new city plan, the four EAUs, located in Manhattan, Brooklyn, Queens, and the Bronx—the boroughs with the highest rates of poverty and welfare participation, were to be closed. Applications for emergency shelter would be accepted at welfare centers during working hours and through a toll-free 800 number at other times. Those seeking shelter for the first time at either source would be referred to a new "reception" center. The next morning they would be sent to a welfare center where workers would try to divert them from the shelter system by trying to help them find (or keep) doubled-up or other housing. Failing this, they would be referred for a week to a new "assessment" center where they would be evaluated further.

Despite the new plan, there were more than 5,000 families in the shelter system at any one time in 1993, and another 5,000 spent some time there during the same period. One EAU was closed in June 1993, yet the placement work had not been taken over by the welfare centers or the toll-free number. Rather than diverting most homeless families, the city violated their legal rights to same day placement. In 12,000 instances between November 20, 1992, and October 1, 1993, families were forced to wait one or more nights in the EAUs.

Research Goals and Methods

Since 1989, the Action Research Project on Hunger, Homeless, and Family Health has continued research I first began with the East Harlem Interfaith Welfare Committee. Each group has been a coalition of voluntary agencies which provide social services to families living in the poorest areas of the Bronx, Brooklyn, and Manhattan. In 1993, these agencies were the Citizens Advice Bureau in the South Bronx; the Catholic Charities Family Centers in Bedford-Stuyvesant, Bushwick, and Downtown Brooklyn; the Entitlements Clinic of West Harlem; and the Little Sisters of the Assumption Family Health Services and St. Cecilia's Parish Services in East Harlem.

As in 1991 and 1992, the project's 1993 research report was based on data gathered from two populations:

(1) homeless families in food and housing emergencies who lived doubled up in the community as documented by the collaborating private agencies, and

(2) homeless families who sought emergency shelter from the city. In my role as project director and EAU monitor for the Coalition for the Homeless (the principal advocacy organization for the homeless at local, state, and national levels), I personally observed and interviewed 285 of the latter families between March 15 and September 7, 1993. The experiences of these families are the focus of this paper. (It was the coalition's willingness to go to court if necessary to affirm their right to have a monitor at the EAUs that has been the basis for my access to these offices since 1986.)

Issues examined in 1993 included why families were homeless; why families were at the EAUs and the impact on them of the conditions they experienced there; the impact on families of the city's new homeless plan, with a particular emphasis on the "diversion" effort; and the adequacy for family life of conditions in the double-ups most families left when they sought emergency shelter. I also requested information on the services homeless families received at their welfare centers and those they received at the EAU and whether the welfare centers and other city agencies had referred families to an EAU rather than to a reception/assessment center as called for under the new plan.

My research methods included participant observation and systematic interviewing at the EAUs. On thirteen Monday or Tuesday nights between March 15 and June 15, 1993, I rotated my weekly observations between the EAUs in the Bronx, Brooklyn, and Manhattan. In July, I began working for eight Monday nights only in the Bronx because of the heavy concentration of families there after the closing of the Manhattan EAU in late June.

Beginning at 5:30 p.m., I walked through the waiting areas to count the families who were there and observe the general conditions. By moving around the EAU, I gave the workers an opportunity to approach me—which they had not done in previous years—to tell me how much worse conditions were at the EAU. Moving around also gave me a chance to talk with families I had interviewed before; they recounted their experiences in the interim and explained why they were again in the EAU rather than in a stable shelter or permanent housing.

Between 6:30 and 11:00 p.m. I completed a long-form questionnaire with six families waiting for placement. The sampling procedures I used in 1993 consisted of approaching in sequence each of the families seated in or nearest the extreme right and then the extreme left corners of each waiting area. If one of the families declined to participate, I moved to the family seated nearest them, first on the right and then on the left.

I introduced myself to the family I hoped to interview as an EAU monitor for the Coalition for the Homeless. I gave them my card which identifies me as Director of the Action Research Project and Adjunct Assistant Professor of Anthropology in Community Medicine at the Mt. Sinai School of Medicine (CUNY). I explained that I was doing a study of services families receive at the EAUs and brief histories of their income sources, housing, and health. I told them that I do not work for the city, and that in order to protect their privacy, I would not use their names or welfare case numbers if they participated. Finally, I told them that while I am not an expert on EAU or shelter services, I would try to answer any questions they might have during the interview. I gave each family a copy of *Homeless Families Know Your Rights*, a booklet prepared by the Homeless Family Right Project of the Legal Aid Society. Only three of the families I approached in 1993 declined to participate.

During each interview, I first completed a welfare budgeting worksheet with the family, using a form prepared by the Legal Aid Project to help homeless families verify that the amounts they receive from welfare are correct. I made a few notes on my own and gave the family the completed form to use as needed with their welfare workers. I then interviewed them using a long-form questionnaire which takes forty-five minutes to an hour to complete. When we finished, I told them that if they had any questions later they could call me collect at the number on my card.

In the third phase of each night's research, a short-form questionnaire was completed with ten to twenty other families who were still waiting for placements after 11:00 p.m. I used the same sampling procedures as in the second phase, moving on from those whom I had already interviewed.

In previous years, my methodology had included documenting the time at which the families interviewed with the long-form questionnaire learned of and then left for shelter placements. In 1993, this was not possible because families often had to wait one or more nights, and I could not stay that long. I did, however, sometimes remain over night to observe and document the conditions under which families waited.

Nighttime at an Emergency Assistance Unit

The EAU ambiance in 1993 was a cross between the waiting rooms of a welfare center and a prison. Uniformed guards with a metal detector flanked the entrance. After the persons and belongings of homeless family members were scanned and searched, they were told to "sign in at the window." If the parents had a referral letter, a center worker directed them to slip it through the narrow slot under a circle of small holes in the Plexiglass barrier that separated them. If the letter was in order, they were directed to sit and wait for their names to be called. Typically, families were not given any other information—oral or written—about what to expect, e.g., what services they would receive, how long they would have to wait, where they would spend the night, and whether they could go to work or school the next day.

It was usually hard for newcomers to find a place to sit and put down their belongings. "Holdover" families—those who had waited for placements over the previous night or several nights—already occupied most of the plastic chairs and upholstered couches. Families fashioned makeshift beds by pushing two couches together or lining up six chairs—three facing three. Some of these "homes," as families referred to them, even had mattresses. When there was an infant, a crib or stroller also stood nearby.

Around 7:30 each night, families were directed over the loudspeaker to line up for cold sandwiches, milk, and juice. In spite of the constant noise of over-stimulated children, the blaring loudspeaker, and the harsh glare of the overhead fluorescent lighting, the younger children soon began falling asleep exhausted in their strollers, or sprawled on parents' laps, hard plastic chairs, or the floor. When both parents were present, only one slept at a time so the other could guard the family and its belongings from the violence caused by the severe overcrowding and the emotional stress associated with "holding over." When families left for shelter placements, the more recent arrivals immediately claimed the empty couches and chairs they left behind.

Research Results

A comparison with the city's nightly EAU reports revealed that the 285 families I interviewed on Monday and Tuesday nights between March 15 and September 7 (100 on the long form and 185 on the short form) constituted 18 percent of the 1,564 families the city recorded as present on the 21 nights the research was conducted. The sample families included 407 adults and 515 children. Both parents were present in more of the families than in previous years (60 percent); 38 Percent were headed by a single female, and 2 percent were headed by a female of the grandparental generation. Almost one-third of the families were separated from one or more of their children for lack of a permanent living space. In one-third, there was an infant aged six months or less, of whom 6 percent were under one month. One-quarter of the families included a pregnant woman, 13 percent of whom said they planned to seek an abortion. The median age of mothers and fathers was twenty-five and twenty-seven, respectively. There was a high prevalence of chronic medical problems in the families—especially asthma and protein deficiency anemia.

Despite the city's new plan and the fact that fewer families sought shelter for the first time in 1993 than in the two previous years, conditions in the EAUs were the worst observed by the project since it was first undertaken in 1986. The new reception/assessment centers were soon filled to capacity and unable to send families on to the long-term shelters or to accept new families. Instead, many new families were placed in short-stay hotels which sent them to the EAUs when their time was up. When the welfare centers had problems placing families during the day, their only alternatives were to refuse them shelter or to circumvent the new process by sending them to the EAUs for nighttime placement.

Analysis of other secondary data revealed the two principal reasons the plan did not work. First was the increased shortage of long-stay shelter. Instead of building additional space for the new reception/assessment centers, the city had reduced shelter capacity by converting almost 250 units of its own shelter space into the new facilities. In addition, the city maintained a longer length-of-stay requirement in 1993 before families already in the shelter system became eligible for permanent housing, further reducing the space available for entering families. The shortage of permanent housing was the second reason for the plan's lack of success. The city failed to meet its goal of providing 5,000 apartments for homeless families in 1993; this included failing to find four hundred apartments for which the federal funding was already and to implement the new plan's special subsidy program for providing permanent housing immediately to families whom the assessment process found "housing ready."

Nor were the city's new diversion teams at the EAUs very effective. Early in the 1993 observation period, diversion team members offered EAU families a modest food allowance to remain in their doubled-up living arrangements until they found an apartment. To help them look for the apartment, they gave them a list of real estate brokers, but they did not offer the additional money that they would need to pay market-level rents. Many families saw this as a hoax.

The teams then began offering them an even more curious kind of help, based on the results of a lawsuit brought in New York State Supreme Court by the Legal Aid society on behalf of the city's welfare families. Jiggetts vs. Dowling calls for the state to provide welfare rent allowances that enable families to rent apartments in New York City's private housing market. Pending the outcome of the case, the judged ruled that the state must pay rent arrears and a higher rent allowance to welfare families threatened with eviction for nonpayment of rent in excess of the current allowance.

Based on this ruling, the diversion teams asked homeless EAU families on welfare to identify an employed person who would sign a letter agreeing to help them pay rent for an apartment whose cost was above the welfare rent allowance. The city would give them a check for the first month's rent and the security deposit. When the second month's rent came due and the family couldn't pay, they would be sued for eviction. At this point, families were told, welfare workers would direct them to a private legal or other agency for help in obtaining relief under the Jiggetts ruling. This relief would be in the form of court-ordered monthly welfare rent payments in excess of the rent allowance to prevent them from being evicted. Very few of the families accepted this proposal—either because they did not have a third party to provide the letter, or because they feared running the risk of becoming homeless again through eviction.

These findings—plus the fact that since 1990, 13,000 welfare families facing eviction have received Jiggetts relief—were the basis for two of the project's principal recommendations in 1993:

1) The city and state should permit the Human Resources Administration to apply for Jiggetts relief directly on behalf of welfare families at risk of eviction, rather than requiring them to go through other agencies.

2) The city and state should permit families in the shelter system to relocate to apartments with rents in excess of the welfare shelter allowance. When families have the apartments, they should be able to obtain the Jiggetts-type rental subsidies which are now being provided to homeless families in shelters in Suffolk and Westchester counties.

The implementation of these recommendations would substantially reduce family homelessness at a time when the other principal solutions—increasing the supply of subsidized low-income rental housing and raising the welfare rent allowance for all needy families—have almost no political priority.

Use of Research Results

As in previous years, the project used the results of the 1993 research in efforts to influence public opinion and public policy. First, the report was released to the print and broadcast media, with emphasis on the recommendations; a number covered it (*New York Daily News*, October 21,1993; *New York Newsday*, October 20 and 21, 1993; *New York Times*, October 21,1993; Channel 5 Morning News; and National Public Radio Morning Edition and All Things Considered). On the same day, copies were delivered by hand or express mail to the top elected and appointed officials responsible for welfare programs at the state and city levels. (Experience shows that these individuals are more responsive to the report's findings and recommendations after reading or hearing about them in the media.) Copies of the report and the media coverage were then mailed to more than three hundred public and private agencies whose work relates to hunger and homelessness. Five hundred more copies were distributed to other agencies, coalitions, and individuals who asked for them. In addition, the report's findings and recommendations were the basis for oral presentations at relevant legislative and other public hearings and at meetings with public officials at the city and state levels.

Working for the implementation of the report's recommendations is a long term endeavor. The small changes to which the project's research may have contributed have typically occurred only after a number of years of effort. For example, New York City only implemented the project's recommendations on "churning" (the closing of welfare cases for administrative reasons unrelated to family need) after nine years of annual reports and other project efforts.

Similarly, the project's research findings and data were included in four affidavits and expert witness testimony between 1986 and 1991 in the court case, McCain vs. Dinkins, before the New York State Supreme Court found the city and four of its top officials in contempt of court for leaving homeless families to sleep overnight in the EAUs. (The court's first contempt finding in 1992 cited the project's testimony extensively.) It was only in May 1994—eight years after the first affidavit—that the contempt finding was upheld by the New York State Court of Appeals. As a result, families forced to stay overnight at the EAUs (including ninety-three of my informants in 1991) will receive $50 in damages for the first night, $100 if the city failed to place them by noon the next day, and an additional $100 for every twenty-four-hour period thereafter. The damages for the first 5,000 families covered under this ruling are estimated to be at least $3.5 million.

Conclusion

One of goals of the city's new plan for homeless families was partially fulfilled by the end of 1993: The EAUs in Brooklyn, Manhattan, and Queens were closed. By March 28, 1994, when the project's 1994 data collection began at the one remaining EAU in the South Bronx, a new city administration was taking an even harsher stance against welfare and homeless families. It introduced extensive staff cuts and threatened to close the remaining EAU. A front-page *New York Times* article on May 14, incorporating some of the project's 1994 observations, focused on the new administration's practice of ejecting homeless families from the EAU by 8:00 a.m. in order to maintain the appearance of having placed them in shelter in conformity with McCain vs. Dinkins.

A preliminary analysis of the project's 1994 data collected in interviews with 201 EAU families suggests that the city's plan to place homeless families from their welfare centers during the day is still not working. More than one-third of the families were referred to the EAU by the welfare centers or by other city agencies responsible under the plan for placing them directly in emergency shelter. This finding suggests that if the court permits the city to close the last EAU, a significant number of homeless families with children will be forced to stay in public places. These data were the basis for the project's most recent affidavit in McCain vs. Dinkins, submitted to the court on July 1, 1994.

[The author acknowledges Margaret Boone's contribution as the project's consultant on methodology.]

Questions:

1. Over the past three decades, how have the problems of New York's welfare families become more severe?

2. When conducting research among homeless families in New York City, what research methods did Dehavenon use?

3. In what specific ways did anthropologist Dehavenon use her findings to influence public policy?

The answer section begins on page 243.

28

In recent years anthropologists have been applying their skills and insights to the governmental area of prisons and corrections. In increasing numbers anthropologists are finding themselves in prison. Since minorities represent a disproportionately large segment of the prison population, applied cultural anthropologists are serving as cultural liaisons between incarcerated minorities and the correctional staff who most often represent non-minorities. In this selection anthropologist Elizabeth Grobsmith discusses her extensive experience of working as an applied anthropologist with Native American inmates in Nebraska prisons. She has served as a teacher, an expert witness, a consultant for prison authorities and the parole board, and as a general cultural resource person.

Applying Anthropology to American Indian Correctional Concerns

By Elizabeth S. Grobsmith

Opportunities abound for the application of anthropological methods, techniques, and data in addressing issues relative to incarceration. Over the last sixteen years, I have worked in a variety of capacities with and on behalf of Native American inmates incarcerated in the Nebraska Department of Correctional Services. My roles as teacher, consultant, trainer, and expert witness have evolved over the years in response to the changing concerns of the Indian prisoners.

In Nebraska, Indian inmates represent about 4 percent of the prison population, which is disproportionately high compared to the 1 percent of Nebraska population that is Indian. As their understanding of their rights to religious freedom has increased, so has their demand for anthropological consultation. I receive letters from Indian prisoners throughout the United States who are seeking similar professional expertise. Becoming such a resource person can easily turn into a full-time job. Furthermore, Native Americans are only one of a number of ethnically diverse groups within the prison population that could benefit from the work of anthropologists.

Teaching

My work with Indian prisoners began in 1975 when Native American inmates were awarded a Consent Decree by the U.S. District Court in Nebraska which enabled them to practice their religion and culture behind the walls. One of the first provisions of decree that Indian prisoners wished to implement was access to education, so the prison, in negotiation with the State of Nebraska Indian Commission, provided academic programs in American Indian Studies.

Teaching in such a program is a rather different experience from teaching large groups of undergraduates at a typical college campus. The educational preparation of Indian prisoner students is quite variable; offering a college course may be unrealistic when members of the class are from nonliterate societies and have dropped out of school by the third grade. Indian prisoners are also rather different constituents from ordinary college students in that they may wish to hear more about their own tribal heritage rather than about other traditions, and they are not afraid to say so. This can be an even greater problem when the number of different tribes represented in a single class may be ten or more.

Being a non-Indian anthropologist carries with it some genuine hazards, including being accused of exploitation and having to deal with sensitive, volatile issues such as religious beliefs being presented from the perspective of a non-native outsider. Another challenge was being a female in a maximum security prison. While there were some disrupters, the majority of inmates behaved in a most gentlemanly manner. This included one occasion when all the electricity in the prison went out and I stood in front of fifty maximum-custody male inmates in

Reprintred by permission of PRACTICING ANTHROPOLOGY 14 (3), Summer, 1992, pp. 5-8

complete darkness for twenty minutes. While this might appear to be a very threatening situation, in actuality, the inmates were so desperate for educational services that any outsider offering such a service would have been greatly protected.

Teaching under these circumstances does leave something to be desired, as we are not accustomed to constant criticism, class disruption, and challenges, if not outright disagreement with what we are teaching. After two semesters, I decided that it was time to give someone else the learning experience of teaching Indian prisoners about their history and culture in prison. Though difficult, the role of teacher is extremely important, for prisoners are acutely in need of education, and they stand to profit both from an academic perspective and from the increased self-respect which education affords. Their culture gains credibility by being the subject of a prison college class.

Consulting for Prison Authorities

The Consent Decree led to increased tension between inmates and correctional officers. Indian inmates now had opportunities to conduct religious ceremonies in prison, and guards encountered unusual and therefore suspicious religious paraphernalia and procedures. Sage, cedar, and sweetgrass burned at ceremonies and during private prayer can easily be mistaken for the smell of marijuana by the untrained. The Sacred Pipe, wrapped carefully with special religious articles, requires special protocol in being unwrapped and used and poses a challenge to normal inspection procedures. Healing ceremonies conducted by medicine men and women from outside the prison, sometimes in a totally blackened room as required in Lakota Sioux ceremonies, and the taking of skin sacrifices with scalpels or exacto blades understandably makes guards nervous.

The contribution of the anthropologist can be great here, serving as consultant to correctional authorities and guiding them as to the legitimacy and meaning of these religious practices. Absence of regular training programs and turnover of employees result in ignorance and insensitivity on the part of correctional officers and continual mistakes which prisoners deeply resent. Guards may be unaware of how "count" in prison can be conducted at a sweat lodge and at what points in the ceremony the "doors" (flaps, tarps) to the lodge may—or may not—be opened. Inmates are offended by accusations of drug use at their sacred sweat lodge grounds and would rather refuse a urinalysis and suffer automatic conviction of "guilty" than humiliate themselves by consenting.

Anthropological expertise is of benefit not because the inmates are incapable themselves of explaining their traditions. Rather, use of an "outside expert" or consultant affords legitimacy to the entire process. The consultant attests to the fact that these traditions are real—that they exist outside the prison walls and have not just been invented to inconvenience the prison system. Greater dependence on such consultation could only improve prisoner-guard relations, and it could potentially reduce the involvement of prisons in continual litigation.

Another area in which anthropological consultation can be beneficial is in dealing with alcoholism among the inmate population. Intake procedures normally ask very limited questions about personal histories, and an inmate's criminal record may be but a skeletal overview of involvement in a criminal career. Nebraska prison data estimate that 40 percent of Indian inmates have a chemical dependency problem. On the other hand, my 1986-87 interviews with forty-five inmates in the Nebraska Department of Corrections (a 56 percent sample) revealed that 100 percent of Indian prisoners claimed to be chemically dependent. The actual involvement of alcohol or drugs in offense commission was unknown by correctional authorities for nearly 74 percent of Indian inmates; in my research, I discovered that between 91 and 100 percent of offenses were alcohol or drug-related. (See Elizabeth S. Grobsmith, "The Relationship Between Substance Abuse and Crime Among Native American Inmates in the Nebraska Department of Correctional Service," *Human Organization* 48,4[1989]:285-298.)

These data should have a tremendous impact on the estimate of services required by and for this population. Anthropological consultation on data gathering procedures used during the intake process can upgrade the quality of inmate intake profile data, which in turn can reinforce the prison's request for resources to develop treatment programs.

Anthropological consultation can also improve the design of treatment programs. Underuse of prison programs concerns prison mental health staff who do not understand why their programs are not popular among Native American inmates. Anthropologists have worked extensively with Indian populations, and they recognize the need to accommodate Indian religious and cultural practices in the design of alcohol and drug treatment programs. Native Americans share—or perceive that they share—certain cultural bases for alcoholism; consequently, addressing the causes and cure must reflect an understanding of Indian values and culture. Indian clients in prison express hesitation to self-disclose unless they are assured the safety of relating exclusively to other Indians. Usually this means separate Indian therapy groups, which prisons hesitate to employ. In addition, incorporation of traditional spiritual elements such as the sweat lodge and use of the pipe can have a significant impact on the degree of commitment to rehabilitation Indian inmates are willing to make.

The consequence of ignoring Native American prisoners' needs is the ultimate return of most Indian inmates to incarceration. A follow-up of the forty-five inmates in my original study showed that within three years of their release from prison, two-thirds either had returned to prison or were confined in a city or county-jail following an alcohol-related offense. (See Elizabeth S. Grobsmith and Jennifer Dam, "The Revolving Door: Substance Abuse Treatment and Criminal Sanctions for Native American Offenders," *Journal of Substance Abuse* 2,4[1990]:405-425.)

Consulting for the Parole Board

Anthropological consulting can be even more effective as inmates prepare to seek release from prison. They typically face a parole board which, like the correctional system, has little knowledge of or sensitivity to Indian cultural approaches to rehabilitation. For example, the Nebraska Board of Parole commonly requires that an offender who has a history of substance abuse attend Alcoholics Anonymous (AA), but the general rejection of AA by the Indian prison population makes such a requirement meaningless. While attendance may result, sincere involvement in addressing one's alcoholism cannot take place in an environment which is distrusted.

Native Americans are, once again, far more willing to involve themselves in the therapeutic environment when clients are exclusively Native American, an option which is often available at urban Indian centers. Outpatient therapy available at specific Native American treatment centers is also a far superior option to attending AA in a "generic" group with which Indians fail to identify. Most cities with even small Indian populations have some Indian treatment programs or centers, or at least an Indian counselor. In some cities, Indian AA meetings are available which

incorporate principles of AA but in a less Judeo-Christian way. Anthropologists' understanding of native perspectives on alcohol treatment can be invaluable in helping to implement systems which inmates *will* use and which are more likely to be effective.

One step is to educate the parole board about Native American perspectives. Some members of the Nebraska Board of Parole have been very receptive to such ideas and have even attended Native American prison club functions to discuss the parole process with Indian inmates. I served as liaison in this process, bringing the two parties into the first dialogue they have ever had and giving inmates the opportunity to express their preferences for referrals in the alcohol rehabilitation process.

I have also served as cultural interpreter or broker and have used ethnographic documentation to support Native American requests. For example, an Indian inmate wanted to attend the funeral of his grandfather, but prison and parole regulations prohibit inmates from attending funerals of anyone but an "immediate" family member. Anthropologists can provide cross-cultural perspective on the extended family and the frequency with which Native Americans are raised in extended family networks or by grandparents alone. As another example, Indian prisoners sometimes request to attend rituals such as the Vision Quest or Sun Dance. In Nebraska inmates with minimum custody are eligible to attend ceremonies away from the prison, but permission to attend these activities is normally denied Native Americans. If parole authorities understood that for most American Indians in prison, attending a Vision Quest or Sun Dance is a principal avenue for alcohol rehabilitation, it would hardly seem reasonable that they would deny such access. The provision of ethnographic information to a parole board serves to educate, and also to lend credibility and thus support to inmate requests.

Serving as Expert Witness

When prison authorities continue to refuse Indian inmates access to the religious practices which inmates believe are within their Constitutionally guaranteed rights, they file grievances and lawsuits. In these instances, there are many ways anthropologists can be and are involved. First, and basic to all positive settlements, is the education of attorneys with reference to Indian prison religious practices. All suits filed by Nebraska Indian inmates are reviewed by the

Chief Judge of the U.S. District Court for the District of Nebraska and a law firm appointed by the judge. If they judge deems the grievance relevant to the original Consent Decree and worthy of being litigated, the case is assigned to an attorney. The attorneys have rarely had any experience with Native American inmates, however, and generally know nothing of Indian culture. On the other hand, the Nebraska Attorney General's Office, which always conducts the correctional system's defense, has excellent knowledge of Indian prison practices.

Attorneys who find themselves in this position are desperate for assistance, and they are extremely grateful for anthropological involvement, both to educate them and ultimately to serve as expert witness in the legal proceedings. They gladly petition the court for expert witness fees to help the scholar prepare material in support of the case.

But getting to court is further complicated by the fact that the Indian plaintiff and his or her attorney may not "speak the same language," both figuratively and literally. Not only must attorneys achieve a greater understanding of Indian culture, Indian inmates must also come to understand the legal negotiation process. They must realize that they cannot always win on every point and that settlement and compromise with correctional officials may be the best avenue to making some gains. On one memorable occasion in my work as liaison between plaintiffs and attorneys, an attorney and I were invited to come to prison and smoke an inmate's Sacred Pipe to bless the negotiation and cement our ties.

I have served as expert witness in suits brought by Indian inmates against the prison in seven instances. The role of the anthropologist here is to inform the court of the content and validity of cultural and religious practices. In this vein, I have testified, as have other anthropologists, about the Native American Church and its use of peyote, the Sun Dance, sweat lodges, powwows, hand games, and religious principles in general. This is probably the most significant role the anthropologist can play, for in this environment we submit our credentials for the court's review and, when permitted, offer testimony that explains the historical and cultural bases for Indian religious practices. In one lawsuit success in alcohol therapy was at issue, and my own research data—rather than the ethnographic literature—were presented as testimony in support of the claim that prison data seriously underestimate the extent of alcohol and drug addiction and that the prison is unable to provide suitable therapy for its Indian population.

Ethical Issues

A statement about the role of anthropologists in corrections would not be complete without a comment on ethical dilemmas. Numerous issues surface, not the least of which are reciprocity and safety. Inmates who participate in research also get released from prison and, in the Indian tradition, they expect reciprocal kindness. These are delicate issues for the anthropologist, for one does not want to convey that one is happy to "use" informants *in* prison, and then refuse to associate with them once they have been released. But neither can one allow the expectation that the anthropologist is willing to go to dinner or to park for a quiet, private visit with an ex-offender.

Teaching and/or consulting in prison may carry with it some obligation of continued involvement with Indian prisoners, but the issue is most pronounced for researchers. Ethnographic and interview research brings the investigator and the subject into much closer personal contact. The prisoner who opens up and shares his criminal as well as alcohol or drug history with a researcher is revealing an intimate part of his or her past, and that self-disclosure requires a very high level of trust. The bond which results can easily be misinterpreted by prisoners as personal affection or willingness to do favors; at a minimum such prisoners are likely to feel that since they shared an important and deeply personal reflection of their lives, the researcher has an obligation in turn to be sympathetic. While teaching and consulting also bring prisoners and the service provider into contact, the depth of one-on-one contact is greatly increased in research with personal interviews, particularly where sensitive information is revealed.

Other ethical concerns revolve around discovery of sensitive information in prison and the protection of confidentiality and anonymity for one's informants. Discovery of intended crimes, illicit drug or alcohol use in prison, or information about unsolved crimes all bring the anthropologist's moral decision making into play. From my perspective, anthropologists can make only one choice—that is, to maintain the strictest confidentiality under all circumstances—for without that, informants will withdraw their trust and ultimately refuse to participate in research of any kind. Protection of the confidentiality of data is particularly difficult for researchers whose data are requested in court testimony. Divulgence of one's sources for verification may be requested, but revealing the identity of our research subjects is forbidden according to the ethics of our discipline, and the anthropologist must be prepared to defend the privacy of the research data.

Conclusion

There is a tremendous need for anthropologists in correctional affairs. With the largest number of inmates representing minorities, and correctional staff seldom representative of those same groups, anthropologists are frequently sought as liaisons, cultural resource persons, and simply savvy outsiders who can help minority individuals interact with the complex, legal world in which they live. Correctional authorities benefit from this interaction as well, through improved inmate-staff relations, decreased litigation, and prison accreditation standards which reward institutions that permit and cooperate with research.

For the anthropologist the rewards of this type of involvement are numerous, but they are not primarily financial. While there may be enough work to keep an anthropologist busy full-time, the court is not accustomed to paying for expert witnesses, and the clients are nearly always indigent. Attorneys are appointed to cases by the court and normally receive no compensation for their services. However, in the cases in which I have been involved, attorneys have attempted—sometimes successfully—to obtain a small expert witness fee for the consultant. Anthropologists may then receive a fee for the preparation and delivery of their testimony or service, but it can in no way compensate them for the amount of time that must be expended in preparing for court. Also, the irregularity of litigation would preclude providing such a service on any but a periodic consultation basis.

The rewards of this type of advocacy lie, rather, in sense of accomplishment from the activities conducted and services rendered. Few activities are more satisfying than helping to mend an intercultural communication network that has broken down. The satisfaction of such a role is primarily in the process, for the actual gains often seem few and far between. Those that do occur are extremely gratifying professionally, and they may put the anthropologist in a situation of great demand and generate numerous additional opportunities for applied work.

Questions:

1. What roles did anthropologist Grobsmith play in her work with native American prisoners in Nebraska?

2. What is the main benefit of anthropological expertise in the prison system?

3. When are Native Americans more willing to involve themselves in the therapeutic environment of Alcoholics Anonymous?

4. What is the major ethical dilemma about the relationship between Native American inmates and anthropologists working in prison?

The answer section begins on page 243.

In the previous selection Grobsmith served in a wide variety of roles as an applied anthropologist working with Native American inmates in Nebraska prisons. Working in the capacity of teacher, consultant and expert witness, Grobsmith was, for all practical purposes, an outsider that was providing culturally relevant information to the correctional staff. In this selection, however, anthropologist Jack Alexander uses his anthropological skills and insights as an official of the correctional bureaucracy in the State of New York. As the Assistant Director of Classification and Movement, Alexander worked on classifying inmates, matching them with state resources, and moving them to the appropriate correctional facility. In this article, Alexander describes how an understanding of anthropological principles, methods, and sights contributed to the work of this very important aspect of the corrections process.

Working in a Prison Organization

By Jack Alexander

Applied anthropologists can make a crucial contribution to public sector organizations. Our anthropological training leads us to think about the diversity of human social conditions and therefore to take very little for granted about any particular human social condition. Thus we are well situated to identify and highlight the taken-for-granted assumptions and objectives that operate in organizations. Furthermore, our training in participant observation inclines us to find these assumptions and objectives as they operate within the everyday social interactions of persons in the organization. Articulating the assumptions and objectives of a complex organization as they work themselves out in social relations is necessary within complex organizations. And accountability is the difference between bureaucracy under legitimate authority and the bureaucracy run amok that Weber rightly feared (Bendix 1960:464). The following pages discuss my specific experience in a complex public sector organization and my opportunities to make a contribution as an applied anthropologist.

The Organization and the Job

The New York State Department of Correctional Services (DOCS) is responsible for incarcerating all persons sentenced to prison for a year or more by New York State Courts. It is a large and complex organization with 55 prisons, over 40,000 inmates and 21,000 staff, and a budget of over a billion dollars. The office I work in, the Office of Classification and Movement, is responsible for sorting inmates by their needs, matching them with department resources, and moving them. The department has four classification centers, which received and classified 14,000 inmates last year: one for females, one for young males, and two for adult males. Once inmates have been initially classified they are placed in prisons where they are reviewed every six months by guidance counselors and, when appropriate, reclassified. The classification work of the counselors in the classification centers and the other prisons is reviewed and monitored by the professional staff in our office; this work amounts to about 55,000 decisions all year.

Classification divides into three areas: security needs, medical needs, and program needs (which include such areas as academic and vocational education and substance abuse). There are assessment techniques in each of these areas, and there are procedures for turning these assessments into classification decision.

As Assistant Director of Classification and Movement, I am responsible to the Director for supervising the central office professional classification staff of seven, for monitoring departmental classification, and for identifying problems and developing and implementing solutions to these problems.

The path to my position has been unusual. Positions in the department are usually filled from civil service lists that are established from written and/or oral exams. Applicants are ranked on the basis of their test scores, and one of the top three who are available for a job must be selected. After one year of probationary service, the employee has a permanent hold on the job title. The principles of the system are simple; the practice is, to put it mildly, Byzantine.

In my case, DOCS had received a federal grant for a classification project (to be discussed later), and was looking for a project director at the time I submitted my resume. An administrator was intrigued by the idea of an anthropologist and hired me (probably the first DOCS anthropologist since Dr. H. R. Wey measured criminal skulls at Elmira Reformatory and ran the Physical Culture program from 1866 to 1900 [Grupp 1959]). Despite the common wisdom, my job really did come as a result of that resume.[1]

After three years as director of the research project, the assistant director position was created and I was appointed to it and have occupied it since. In my experience, the key thing in the job world is to get your foot in the door, once in do as good a job as you can, and not worry too much about what you can't do well.

The Environment of the Job

With the foregoing formal description of my job setting and how I got there in mind, let us turn to what happens.

From the outside, public agencies may appear like large, lumbering, and dull behemoths, swallowing vast resources and crushing any human or humane subtleties in their way. From the inside these agencies appear more like precarious, high-wire balancing acts. Much of the art of management consists in transforming persistent crisis into workable routines, or better (but rare), anticipating crisis and creating workable routines in advance. Staff are uneven in their competence and motivation, sick at the wrong time, and swayed by the ups and downs of promotions. Unions, management, legislators, and executive leaders are at cross-purposes, the environment is constantly changing and the behemoth must adapt. These ongoing pressures are increased by prison overcrowding. The population of the state system has increased from 21,000 in 1978 to 40,000 in 1987. Rapid expansion means rapid expansion of staff and rapid promotion of relatively inexperienced supervisory staff, so that training and quality control become more difficult and innovation both more easily accepted and less effectively executed. There are a limited number of responses to increased convictions or longer prison sentences and each of these responses

creates its own problems. One can place more inmates into the same space, increase prison space, or divert committed persons at the front end (alternatives to incarceration) or at the back end (release inmates early). Jurisdictions use many or all of these solutions, though in very different mixes. New York placed more inmates in the same space (though resisting double-celling) and increased space (though at a much slower rate than many jurisdictions), while diverting some inmates at the front end (through increased use of probation) and at the back end (through programs that encourage the parole board to release inmates earlier). Given all the cross-currents, decisions usually appear only after the problems have become pressing. In the meantime, jurisdictions holding sentenced inmates are pressing the state to take them, while the state pleads that it is already overcrowded. In the Office of Classification there is pressure to fill every available bed. Diversion programs all focus on the least dangerous inmates, who are, of course, also most desired by prison staff, who would rather work with easy than difficult inmates. Therefore, Classification and Movement becomes the identifier and arbiter of who is the good inmate and who gets him. At the other extreme, prisons are eager to move the more difficult inmates, frequently for good reason, and Classification must be the arbiter, a task made more difficult when there is nowhere to move an inmate without finding an inmate to trade.

The Daily Work

How then do I spend my time? Here is a recent week. The seven classification analysts and I meet for about an hour on Monday morning. This week we talk about problems we are having with our Separatee System. We must keep apart inmates who are either enemies or who together may cause physical harm to others (such as extortion rings). The system is only as good as the information that is put into it. The analysts have been dissatisfied for some time with the information, provided by facility counselors, that is entered. We discuss the main problems. I have asked one analyst to design a form that will structure the information for counselors. She distributes the form, we discuss it briefly, and I ask the rest to review it, so we can make a final decision at our next meeting. Then we discuss problems we are having with a program to maintain continuity of substance-abuse treatment from prison onto the street for paroled inmates. Inmates who are or have been in a substance-abuse program and who meet security and medical criteria can be transferred near the end of their terms to a prison in New York City for three months, where they continue their treatment program while parole officers link them up with a treatment program to enter when they are released. However, the procedure for referring inmates from the prisons is working poorly, and the program, which is a small one, is not even filled and is consuming too much of our time. We come up with two improvements, which I have to implement.

On Tuesday there is a full-day meeting of an interagency group that is standardizing criminal justice data elements. The group has worked for two years and is about to expand from 5 to over 20 agencies. We work to revise our data collection instrument and to finalize a structure and process that will enable 21 agencies to produce the same results as 5 have.

On Wednesday there is a full-day meeting at one of the classification centers to finalize the classification procedures for a new Shock Incarceration program to be run somewhat like an army boot camp. Legislation limits closely the types of inmates who can be accepted into the program, since inmates who complete the program are likely to be released early. The classification centers have designed a form and procedure; the Office of Research, which is legally obligated to evaluate the program, has also designed a form. The purpose of the meeting is to come up with a single form and procedure that will be as streamlined as possible, while adequately documenting the fact that things have been done properly. By the end of the day, we have made our decisions; now they must be implemented.

Thursday I meet with a group that meets regularly to work on enhancements in our automated information systems. As the department has expanded to double its 1978 size, we have become utterly dependent on automation to get our work done. In the beginning, automated systems were designed and implemented rapidly and independently. As we used these systems, we found problems with each one and with their interrelationships. At first, whenever we found a problem, we would go to Management Information Systems to request a change. These requests were uncoordinated and not thought through carefully enough. Now we have a work group of staff who are experienced both in classification and automated information systems, and we have a structure for thinking through and discussing proposed changes. In Thursday's session we review

and approve changes introduced at our last session, revise and approve enhancements presented at this session, set aside one particularly complex proposal, and agree on the work for the next session.

On Friday I review the classification work of one analyst and discuss it with him, prepare a brief monthly report on our activities for the director, and prepare for a court case the following week in which an inmate charges that a classification decision was arbitrary, capricious, and retaliatory. We are working on a new security classification guideline for female inmates, so the research assistant and I talk about problems we are having in collecting the data on our sample of 200 inmates and the framework for the statistical analysis.

Interspersed throughout the week are phone calls and memos to follow up on a myriad of details, such as a request for equipment for clerical staff and a request for additional staff.

Applied Classification

Where is the applied anthropology in all this? In most of what I do there is none. I do not believe that persons who were trained as anthropologists and now work in a nonacademic job are automatically applied anthropologists. Nor are they applied anthropologists because their training has "sensitized them to social relations," and they now "work with people" or even "work with people of different cultures."

To be applied anthropologists, I think we must systematically apply the accumulated knowledge of the discipline of anthropology to practical problems. In doing so we can sometimes add to that knowledge.

My training particularly qualifies me to analyze the underlying assumptions, or collective representations, people hold as a consequence of being members of a group and to understand how these assumptions work in social life.

I will describe in some detail one project in which I applied my anthropological skills: the development of security classification guidelines. Prison constraints range from a setting in which an inmate can move no more than six feet in any direction and is under constant observation, to a setting in which the inmate is gone all day to work, school, or his family. This range of constraint is divided into four levels: maximum, medium, minimum, and community release. Inmates are classified to a security level when they first enter the system by classification counselors, and then periodically reclassified by guidance counselors in the general confinement prisons. The process of security classification was a problem for three reasons.

First, there are consequences of security classification decisions that affect powerful interests, and the intuitive judgment of individual staff was vulnerable to second guessing by those interests.

Because low-security prisons are populated by inmates relatively near the ends of their terms, their inmates are released more rapidly than inmates in higher security prisons. Consequently there is a constant demand for low-risk inmates to fill reduced-security spaces. This demand is especially great when the prison system is overcrowded. Furthermore, higher security prisons are reluctant to let go of lower risk inmates who fill jobs of trust (such as on a farm outside the prison wall or clerical jobs in the administration building) and who are seen to have a generally calming influence on the prison. The competition over scarce resources (that is, low-risk inmates) often turns into a controversy over security classification (that is, which inmates are low-risk).

Security classification also has consequences for capital expansion. On the one hand, the State Budget Division, with an eye to the cost efficiency of lower security space, looks for signs that the department overclassified inmates. Department staff, on the other hand, with an eye to the consequences of insufficient security (escape and violence), looks for evidence of underclassification.

The security classification decision was for the most part left to the judgment of staff. Staff exercised this judgment on the basis of their intuitive understanding of what sort of inmate presents what sort of risk, and what sort of risk DOCS was willing to live with at what security levels. In the face of conflicts over the consequences of security classification, the process of intuitive decisions by individual staff did not carry enough weight; it was too vulnerable to second-guessing.

Second, changing notions of law and equity in bureaucracy challenged the department's classification process. In an influential book, *Discretionary Justice: A Preliminary Inquiry* (1969), Kenneth Culp Davis pointed to the potential for arbitrary and capricious actions in governmental agencies. For instance, while the process of determining a citizen's guilt or innocence in court is highly structured, there are many decisions in the criminal justice system that cumulatively have a greater impact than the actual trial and have been left to the discretion of criminal justice personnel. Whether a policeman chooses to arrest, a district attorney to indict, a judge to release a defendant awaiting a trial, a probation officer to recommend probation or incarceration, a parole board to release an inmate from prison before the maximum expiration of his term were all decisions that were largely left up to individual discretion.

Davis showed that there are several ways to balance the equity of a society under law with the flexibility an agency needs to apply law to the unique circumstances of each case. He showed that discretion can be structured by "open rules, open findings, open precedents and fair informal procedure" (1969:98).

At the same time that Davis was showing how to structure agency discretion, the courts determined that inmates were entitled to protection against abuses of discretion. In a 1964 Supreme Court decision, inmates gained standing in court, and in a 1974 decision the Supreme Court declared, "There is no iron curtain between the Constitution and the prisoners of this country" (*Wolf v. McDonnell*). Therefore, the department's security classification process was vulnerable to legal challenge, for it is clear that a process of security classification based on individual intuitive decisions fails to meet the standards set by Davis and supported by the courts.

Third, the expansion of the department turned it from a small collection of prisons into an interdependent set of many prisons. In any group— simple or complex, formal or informal—there must be a fair amount of predictability in behavior, and there must be feedback on the consequences of behavior. Where security classification decisions are made within a prison, as they are in deciding, for instance, which inmates should work on the farm outside the prison perimeter, the person making the decision and the person supervising the farm are in interaction and therefore subject to informal mechanisms that tend to maintain a flow of information, feedback, and consequently, consistency. In a complex organization these interpersonal mechanisms must be augmented by formal mechanisms. The intuitive judgements of individual staff members have to be augmented by formal mechanisms to provide predictability and feedback.

To address the three problems with security classification, it was decided that there should be a quantitative instrument that would produce consistent security-classification decisions and explicit reasons for the decisions and that would be authoritative enough to make decisions stick and give management control over decisions. I was hired to develop and implement such an instrument.

There were two techniques available for developing a guideline, and I will describe them to distinguish them from the anthropological approach I used. One technique is to find statistical correlates or predictors of behavior and then construct an instrument with these predictors. Unfortunately, such instruments are generally ignored by the decision makers for whom they are designed, for two reasons. First, even if these instruments have a high rate of predictive efficiency, they do not weigh the costs of incorrect decisions. The fact that murderers have a low rate of recidivism does not incline parole boards to release murderers. Second, decision makers may have goals in addition to correctly predicting prison behavior, such as maintaining order in the prisons. Though behavior in prison has little relation to recidivism, making good behavior in prison a condition of early release aids in managing prisons.

A second technique for constructing a guideline is to find predictors for what the decision makers do, rather than what persons about whom decisions are made do. This technique has proved far more acceptable to decision makers. The predictors are combined into an instrument that can closely replicate decisions and is therefore a model of the decision makers' behavior. The instrument also fits Goodenough's definition of culture: "standards that, taken as a guide for acting and interpreting the acts of others, lead to behavior the community's members perceive as in accord with their expectations of one another" (Goodenough 1970:101). While this technique enables us to replicate behavior, it does not enable us to understand the behavior from the point of view of the actors, which is what I set out to do. I made use of the anthropological study of classification systems, a line of investigation that goes back at least to *Primitive Classification*, originally published in 1903 by Durkheim and Mauss. To my mind a few simple yet crucial principles can be extracted from this line of work.

1. Classification systems should be understood and studied as bringing order to domains of experience. Without them "consciousness.... is only a continuous flow of representations which are lost one in another...." (Durkheim and Mauss 1963:67). Therefore, in the case of security classification we must ask what is the welter of experience that is ordered. Furthermore, we assume that if classification serves such a crucial purpose much will be invested to maintain it.

2. To understand the classification of inmates, as the classification of plants, animals, and colors, a classification system must be studied in its own right as a social fact. While cognitive capacities may influence the properties of classification systems, and the properties of the things being classified may suggest "natural" categories, there remains a very large component of classification systems to be studied as "social facts."

3. A classification system is to be understood not as a collection of categories but as a set of relationships of which the categories are an expression.

4. A classification system can only be understood within its context; it is generated and maintained in social relations and it acts on those relations.

5. Variability, ambiguity, and anomaly in a classification system are significant features of the system, not noise.

6. Classification systems participate in two aspects of social life, labeled variously instrumental/symbolic, technological/moral, or mundane/ritual (Ellen 1979:20-22). Any classification system must be analyzed for the role of both these aspects in its operation.

In the first phase of the research, I observed classification analysts classify inmates and asked them to tell me what they were thinking as they processed cases. I also observed the place of classification in the overall work of the department. In the second phase, research and the design of the guideline were integrated. Through group and individual interviews staff themselves identified the main features of the guideline. I also interviewed inmates to understand their perspective on security classification. In the third phase, I analyzed statistically a random sample of 500 inmates to simulate the effects of different possible guidelines. In the fourth phase, the guideline was implemented.

I organized my collection and analysis of data by focusing on variability. Although inmates were distributed randomly for staff to classify, the distribution of decisions varied significantly between staff persons and over time. Analysis of variability led me to the following conclusions.

The security classification system is conceived as a continuum from high- to low-risk, and this continuum is marked off into the categories of maximum, medium, and minimum (for another classification system with such a structure see Alexander 1978). Each category is identified by a prototype at its center, so to speak, and as one approaches the edges of the category the boundaries get fuzzy. (Rosch [1973] has shown that classification systems consisting of categories identified by prototypes and having fuzzy boundaries are common.) One source of variability then is disagreement over cases that are near the boundaries between security categories.

A second source of variability is that the risk an inmate poses is conceived to be a result of an internal disposition, and it is easy to disagree on internal dispositions. Underling security classification is the search for the "dangerous man," who is an ideal type similar to the "reasonable man" of law. The dangerous man is the man who is more likely than the normal (reasonable) man to resort to the use of violence. He may be either the sort of man whose use of violence is unpredictable or whose use of violence is predictably triggered more easily than the normal person. Staff assume that any person is capable of violence given the appropriate circumstance (such as defense of self, family, or country), and their concern is to identify the persons who are more likely to resort to violence, how likely they are to resort to violence, and how violent they are likely to be. In order to identify the dangerous man, staff place themselves in the circumstance of the crime and ask themselves how much more violence than that of the normal man did the violent man use? Here is a process that, to say the least, leaves much room for variability.

A third source of variability is the nature of the data available to staff. An inmate enters prison with a Pre-Sentence Report. The report is written by a probation officer after the inmate has been found guilty and before he is sentenced. Its prime purpose is to provide the judge with information relevant to sentencing, but a copy must also be sent to the Corrections Department. The report includes a description of the crime for which the inmate has been convicted, as seen by the police, the defendant and the victim, a criminal history, and a social history that covers the inmate's family history, education, employment, and medical history. After the inmate is in the system, the department also gets an official criminal history that includes all recorded arrests and dispositions.

These official records are prone to errors, omissions, and clichés. Errors of fact are common. For instance, in one study the New York City Police and the New York City Corrections Department differed on subjects' addresses in 53 percent of the cases, though they collect the same information within 24 hours of each other (Criminal Justice Agency 1980:64). Official records are almost always incomplete. There are arrests for which there are no dispositions, convictions for which there are no arrests, victims who cannot be found to tell their versions of the crime, and so on. The social histories in the pre-sentence reports abound with clichés: absent fathers, inadequate mothers, and personalities with poor impulse control.

Furthermore, staff believe that an inmate's criminal behavior and criminal record are two different things, so they try to estimate how much fire there is behind the smoke. (This belief has some empirical support. A study of self-reports from 49 inmates incarcerated for robbery in California shows that arrests as a percent of crimes committed ranges form 8 percent to 13 percent except for Aggravated Assault [31 percent] and Rape [100 percent] [Petersila, Greenwood, and Lavin 1978:36].)

Determining "dangerous" inclinations from this information is a slippery business. For instance, if there are many arrests and few convictions, or the convictions are less serious than the arrest, is this because the police overcharged the inmate at arrest or because the burden of court business forced the district attorney to settle for reduced convictions? If the inmate receives an unusually long or short sentence, given the crime and the jurisdiction in which the inmate was sentenced (the same crime tends to get a longer sentence outside New York City than in), the staff person may conclude that the crime was more or less serious than the description suggests. If the inmate attempted to escape from a police car after arrest, was this a "normal" reaction or an expression of a general tendency to run from trouble?

Thus the image of the inmate as a "dangerous man" is a highly constructed one. The staff person reads the official record, he estimates what "really happened," and he then tries to balance his responsibility to determine what "really happened" with his responsibility to stick with what can documented. This process leaves much room for variability.

A fourth source of variability is that staff assess dangerousness along several dimensions.

The inmate who is dangerous on the street may be quite safe in prison and vice versa. So staff distinguish between risk to the public and risk within the prison. Another type of risk is self-risk, the likelihood that an inmate will be victim-prone or suicidal. Still another type of risk is risk to the system. For instance, many persons convicted of murder have lived apparently normal lives jolted by one atypical crime of passion. Such persons are usually very good inmates and have very low rates of recidivism. Yet from the point of view of the public such persons are murderers, and if it is known that such inmates are at reduced security, it is almost impossible to defend against the charge that the prison is failing in its responsibility to protect the public adequately. Placing different weights on these types of risk is an important source of variability.

So far we have discussed security classification as a technical or instrumental activity; the symbolic or moral aspect is also important. Many staff are particularly conscious of the difficulty they have in dealing with sex crimes; these crimes arouse feelings that are difficult for many staff to handle when facing the inmate. (Inmates also take offense at persons who have committed sex crimes. The social organization and roles of inmates can be described without any reference to their crimes, except that sex criminals are at the bottom of the hierarchy [for example, Carroll 1974].) These extreme crimes bring to the surface a dilemma for classification staff. They are assailed daily by a litany of assaults against morality, and they confront the assailants daily. No anthropologist will be surprised to discover that a common term for inmate is "dirt-bag." The pollution of the criminal permeates the task of assessing dangerousness.

Anthropological analysis alerts us to the possibility that pollution beliefs are not only associated with deviance; they may also mark vulnerable cultural dilemmas and ambiguities (Douglas 1968). Classification staff are pulled into the dilemma that the agents of pollution are also persons. Society banishes the "hardened criminal," but the prison staff live with him. His existence as a person is hard to avoid. Staff deal with inmates on such mundane human issues as seeing that relatives and friends can write them and on such issues as their schooling. Furthermore, as staff work to assess the risk by determining the inherent disposition to violence by putting themselves in the place of the inmate at the time

of the crime, more and more of inmate criminal behavior becomes understandable. Less of it becomes due to an alien disposition, until there are only a few emblems, such as sex crimes and vicious crimes, of the moral shock of violation. The inmate as person and as polluter are different from the inmate as risk, and yet these aspects penetrate the security classification process and are a fifth source of variability.

The guidelines I designed and implemented build on the research findings in the following ways. The guidelines distinguish the two main types of risk, public and institutional, separately and make the final decision an interaction of the two. Second, the guidelines measure each type of risk on an ordinal scale in keeping with the continuous nature of the set of categories. Third, the guidelines address in detail the relation between the data staff work with and the "dangerous man" they search for. There are detailed instructions for interpreting the pre-sentence reports and other documents on which the security classification system is based. Finally, the punishment aspect is entirely eliminated.

The guidelines have been very effective in achieving our objectives. Foremost, they have increased accountability. The guidelines are an explicit statement of security classification policy for which the managers are responsible. The individual counselors are responsible for applying the policy to individual cases; when they have completed the guidelines they have stated all the reasons for their decisions. In achieving accountability the guidelines also structure discretion. The guidelines have also stilled controversy over security classification decisions. In combination with monitoring reports, the guidelines also provide a formal mechanism for communication between the different units of our complex organization. As an additional benefit, the guidelines have identified additional reduced-security inmates. Several other states have adapted features of the New York Guidelines.

Potentials for Applied Anthropology

I will briefly mention three other projects in which anthropology could have been applied but was not. Everyday work can always keep you more than busy, and if you're not aggressive about turning your anthropological skills into everyday tasks the opportunities slip by.
1. When the present commissioner took over, he ordered a Five-Year Master Plan and I worked on the staff for the plan. It might be

thought that projects such as master plans are exercises in finding attractive rationalizations for doing what gets done anyway or for finding attractive projects that will never get done. In my experience, the attempt to clarify a direction for the organization is quite serious and has serious consequences. An important part of such a project is to clarify the objectives of the organization. This exercise turns out to be one of partially articulating what the organization actually does and partially what it ought to do. One difficulty with this process is that articulate persons play a dominant role, and they are frequently the least knowledgeable about what really goes on (which they are well aware of). Anthropologists are in an excellent position to give a voice to the less articulate and more knowledgeable members of the organization. We are trained to discover the values that people use, more or less consciously, in their daily social lives.

2. Prison systems must separate inmates who threaten harm to each other or inmates who together threaten harm to other inmates. Therefore, DOCS has a system listing all the inmates to be kept separate, and classification analysts must check the system before authorizing any move. The system is only as good as the information entered into it; and therein lies the problem. Inmates have motives to manipulate the system, either by concealing enemies so they can get at them or by naming enemies who are in prisons they want to avoid. Given uncertain information, staff have motive to err on the side of caution. If persons are apart unnecessarily there are no repercussions for the staff, but if they're not kept apart when they should be, the repercussions may be severe for the inmates involved and for the staff that let it happen. To fully investigate a possible relation is very time-consuming, and to completely eliminate the risk of danger is impossible. Therefore, staff tend to submit every possible separatee relationship. Unfortunately, what is rational from the point of view of the individual staff member—when in doubt, submit names—is irrational from the point of view of the system as a whole, because so many names are entered that they can't all be kept apart or can only be kept apart at the expense of other goals of transfers. The solution to this problem lies in sharing responsibility reasonably. The managers must set standards for defining what types of persons must be kept separate and for determining whether a given person fits one of these types, and individual staff must be responsible for applying these standards to individual cases. If we have a detailed understanding of how inmates and staff perceive and work with the risks involved in separating, we can structure responsibility effectively. Anthropologists are well suited to develop such an understanding.

3. I have been involved in several automated information projects, and there is a lot of work to be done in this area by applied anthropologists. The methodology for the development of automated information systems is well developed both for the technical aspects and for strategic planning (for instance, Martin 1982), but the methodology for relating the system to its everyday use in an organization is, to the best of my knowledge, undeveloped. For instance, one project I have been working on is an interagency project to standardize data elements for the entire state criminal justice system. Data standardization should save money by increasing direct electronic transmission of data between agencies; it should improve the quality of information by enabling each agency to concentrate on the information it collects best, and it should improve policy analysis of questions that involve more than one agency. There is much variation among agencies that follows from their various uses, but there is also much that has no function and follows from the fact that each agency developed its data elements in isolation. The data collection instrument for our project is well developed for what goes on inside the black box (is the information stored on disk or tape, what retention schedule, if any, is there, and so on), but the questions on the organizational context are general and loose. Anthropologists are well suited to tracking down the everyday uses of information in a complex organization.

Conclusion

To conclude, applying anthropology in a public bureaucracy requires, in my experience, several adaptations for those accustomed to academic anthropology.

First, you must be literate in statistics through the intermediate level, and you should be able to use statistics, including different techniques of multivariate analysis. Quantitative analysis has a legitimacy that you must be able to provide both in your own work and in your evaluation of the work of others. Qualitative analysis is acceptable, but at least in my experience, it should be buttressed or decorated with quantitative analysis.

Second, the goal of every project is simplicity, because the more complex a process is, the more ways it can fall apart. It is easy to develop a complex process; the art is in creating simplicity. In academia things are different: the aim is to display the simplicity underlying complexity, and one must therefore start by demonstrating that things are more complex than hitherto suspected. In the bureaucracy we should be quiet about the complexity we have reduced.

Third, life in a public bureaucracy is less isolated than in academia. While ultimately what counts in academia is participation in a community of scholars, in the short run what counts is the production of publications, and publication is a fairly isolated process. In contrast, whatever I get done I get done through other people.

Fourth, at least in my job, there is the satisfaction of having an effect on what happens. If a project is successful people are working more effectively than they were before.

Finally, publications, such as this article, must be approved by your agency. This requirement can have a chilling effect. I think the effect is no more or less than the effect of those in academia on whom one depends for tenure, promotion, and so on.

Note

[1] The greatest bit of resume wisdom I have learned since then is to put your resume on distinctively colored paper; a person I know was hired recently after an employer realized from the buff color of her resume that he had not seen her resume previously.

References Cited

Alexander, Jack. 1978 The Culture of Race in Middle-Class Kingston, Jamaica. American Ethnologist 4:413-435.

Bendix, Reinhard. 1960 Max Weber: An Intellectual Portrait. New York: Doubleday.

Carroll, Leo. 1974 Hacks, Blacks and Cons: Race Relations in a Maximum Security Prison. Lexington, MA: Lexington Books.

Criminal Justice Agency. 1980 Sentenced Inmate Data: A study of Information Transmitted from New York City to the New York State Department of Correctional Services. New York: Criminal Justice Agency. [mimeo]

Davis, Kenneth Culp. 1969 Discretionary Justice: A Preliminary Inquiry. Baton Rouge: Louisiana State University Press.

Douglas, Mary. 1968 Pollution. *In* International Encyclopedia of the Social Sciences. New York: Macmillan

Durkheim, Emile, and Marcel Mauss. 1963 Primitive Classification. R. Needham, Trans. London: Cohen and West. [Original: De Quelques Formes Primitives de Classification: Contribution a L' etude des representations collectives. Annees Sociologique 6:1-72, Paris, 1903]

Ellen, Roy. 1979 Introductory Essay. *In* Classifications in Their Social Context. Roy Ellen and David Reason, eds. Pp 4-32. London: Academic Press.

Goodenough, Ward H.. 1970 Description and Comparison in Cultural Anthropology. Chicago: Aldine.

Grupp, Stanley E.. 1959 Criminal Anthropological Overtones: New York State Reformatory at Elmira. Corrections 24:9-17.

Martin, James. 1982 Strategic Data-Planning Methodologies. Englewood Cliffs, NJ: Prentice-Hall.

Petersilia, Joan, Peter W. Greenwood, and Marvin Lavin. 1978 Criminal Careers of Habitual Felons. Washington, D.C.: National Institute of Law Enforcement and Criminal Justice, Law Enforcement Assistance Administration, U.S. Department of Justice.

Rosch, Eleanor. 1973 On the Internal Structure of Perceptual and Semantic Categories. *In* Cognitive Development and the Acquisition of Language. T.M. More, ed. Pp. 111-144. New York: Academic Press.

Questions:

1. Alexander's job within the state system of corrections involves classifying inmates according to their needs and matching them with departmental resources. On what three criteria are classifications made?

2. What is needed in order for a person to be considered an applied anthropologist?

3. Alexander suggests that applying anthropology to such public bureaucracies as the New York Department of Correction requires working differently than most academic anthropologists. What are three ways in which applied and academic anthropology differ?

The answer section begins on page 243.

Anthropologists conducting field research are often required to deal with host government officials who ultimately have control over whether or not they even receive the appropriate visa to enter the country. We often think government bureaucrats—because of the very nature of bureaucracies—behave in generally the same way the world over. But as anthropologist Elizabeth Eames points out, bureaucratic behavior in Nigeria is very different from that found in North America. In western bureaucracies, at least ideally, decisions are made on the basis of an impersonal set of rules and procedures applied to all people. In Nigerian bureaucracies, however, Eames found that decisions and transactions depended more on the establishment of particularistic social relationships rather than a universally applied set of regulations.

Navigating Nigerian Bureaucracies

By Elizabeth A. Eames

Americans have a saying: "It's not *what* you know, it's *who* you know." This aphorism captures the usually subtle use of old-boy networks for personal advancement in the United States. But what happens when this principle becomes the primary dynamic of an entire social system? The period of three years I spent pursuing anthropological field research in a small Nigerian city was one of continual adjustment and reordering of expectations. This paper discusses a single case—how I discovered the importance personal ties have for Nigerian bureaucrats—but also illustrates the *general process* by which any open-minded visitor to a foreign land might decipher the rules of proper behavior. I was already familiar with Max Weber's work on bureaucracy and patrimony, yet its tremendous significance and explanatory power only became clear to me following the incidents discussed below. Accordingly, the paper concludes with a discussion of Weber's concept of *patrimonial authority*.

I heard the same comment from every expatriate I met in Nigeria—U.S. foreign service officers, U.N. "experts," and visiting business consultants alike: "If you survive a stint in Nigeria, you can survive *anywhere*." The negative implications of this statement stem from outsiders' futile attempts to apply, in a new social setting, homegrown notions of how bureaucratic organizations function. This is indeed a natural inclination and all the more tempting where organizational structure *appears* bureaucratic. Yet in Nigeria, the office-holders behaved according to different rules; their attitudes and sentiments reflected a different moral code. A bureaucratic organizational structure coexisted with an incompatible set of moral imperatives. The resulting unwieldy, inflexible structure may be singled out as one of the British Colonialism's most devastating legacies.[1]

Please bear in mind, the problem of understanding another culture works both ways. Any Nigerian student reading for the first time the following passage by a prominent American sociologist would probably howl with laughter:

> The chief merit of a bureaucracy is its technical efficiency, with a premium placed on precision, speed, expert control, continuity, discretion and optimal returns on input. The structure is one which approaches the complete elimination of personalized relationships and nonrational considerations (hostility, anxiety, affectual involvements, etc.).[2]

Even those well-educated administrative officers who had once been required to incorporate such notions into their papers and exams do not *live* by them.

To many foreigners who have spent time in Nigeria, "the system" remains a mystery. What motivating principles explain the behavior of Nigerian administrative officers? How do local people understand the behavior of their fellow workers? Why do some people successfully maneuver their way through the system while others founder?

Recently I attended a party. As often happens at a gathering of anthropologists, we started swapping fieldwork stories, and meandered onto a topic of our most unpleasant sensation or unsettling experience. That night, I heard tales of surviving strange diseases, eating repulsive foods, losing one's way in the rain forest, being caught between hostile rebel factions or kidnapped by guerrilla fighters. As for me? All that came to mind were exasperating encounters with intransigent clerks and secretaries. I began to ponder why these interactions had proved so unsettling.

My discipline—social anthropology—hinges on the practice of "participant observation." To a fledgling anthropologist, the "fieldwork" research experience takes on all the connotations of initiation into full membership. For some, a vision-quest; for others, perhaps, a trial-by-ordeal: the goal is to experience another way of life from the inside and to internalize, as does a growing child, the accumulating lessons of daily life. But the anthropologist is not a child; therefore, he or she experiences not conversion, but self-revelation.

I came to understand my American-ness during the period spent coming to terms with Nigerian-ness. I found that I believed in my right to fair treatment and justice simply because I was a human being. I believed in equal protection under the law. But my Nigerian friends did not. What I found was a social system where status, relationships, and rights were fundamentally negotiable, and justice was *never* impartial. In the United States, impersonalized bureaucracies are the norm: we do not question them; our behavior automatically adjusts to them. But just imagine spending a year working in a corporation where none of these rules applied.

You see, a Nigerian immigration officer will only sign your form *if* doing so will perpetuate some mutually beneficial relationship of *if* he wishes to initiate a relationship by putting you in his debt. For those unlucky enough to be without connections (this must necessarily include most foreigners), the only other option is bribery—where the supplicant initiates a personal relationship of sorts and the ensuing favor evens matters up.[3]

Hence, Nigeria becomes labeled "inefficient," "tribalistic," and "corrupt." And so it is.[4] Yet this system exists and persists for a profound reason: Whereas in Europe and Asia, power and authority always derived from ownership of landed property, in West Africa the key ingredient was a large number of loyal dependents. Because land was plentiful and agriculture of the extensive slash-and burn variety,[5] discontented subordinates could simply move on. The trick was to maintain power over subordinates through ostentatious displays of generosity. This meant more than simply putting on a lavish feast—you must demonstrate a willingness to use your influence to support others in times of need. Even now, all Nigerians participate in such patron-client relationships. In fact, *all legitimate authority derives from being in a position to grant favors and not the other way around.*

Actually, only a minuscule portion of my time in the field was spent dealing with Nigeria's "formal sector." My research entailed living within an extended family household (approximately a dozen adults and two dozen children), chatting with friends, visiting women in their market stalls, even at times conducting formal and informal interviews. And during the years spent researching women's economic resources and domestic responsibilities, I came to understand—indeed to deeply *admire*—their sense of moral responsibility to a wide-ranging network of kin, colleagues, neighbors, friends, and acquaintances. Even now, I often take the time to recall someone's overwhelming hospitality, a friendly greeting, the sharing and eating together. Such warm interpersonal relations more than made up for the lack of amenities.

The longer I stayed, however, the clearer it became that what I loved most and what I found most distressing about life in Nigeria were two sides of the same coin, inextricably related.

The first few months in a new place can be instructive for those with an open mind:

Lesson One: The Strength of Weak Ties

My first exposure to Nigerian civil servants occurred when, after waiting several months, I realized my visa application was stalled somewhere in the New York consulate. Letter-writing and telephoning proved futile, and as my departure date approached, panic made me plan a personal visit.

The waiting room was populated with sullen, miserable people—a roomful of hostile eyes fixed on the uniformed man guarding the office door. They had been waiting for hours on end. Any passing official was simultaneously accosted by half a dozen supplicants—much as a political celebrity is accosted by the news media. Everyone's immediate goal was to enter through that door to the inner sanctum—so far, they had failed. But I was lucky—I had the name of an acquaintance's wife's schoolmate currently employed at the consulate. After some discussion, the guard allowed me to telephone her.

Mrs. Ojo greeted me cordially, then—quickly, quietly—she coaxed my application forms through the maze of cubicles. It was a miracle!

"What a wonderful woman," I thought to myself. "she understands." I thought she had taken pity on me and acted out of disgust for her colleagues' mishandling of my application. I now realize that by helping me, she was reinforcing a relationship with her schoolmate. Needless to say, my gratitude extended to her schoolmate's husband, my acquaintance. As I later came to understand it, this natural emotional reaction—gratitude for favors granted—is the currency fueling the system. Even we Americans have an appropriate saying: "What goes around comes around." But at this point, I had merely learned that, here as elsewhere, connections open doors.

Lesson Two: No Impersonal Transactions Allowed

Once on Nigerian soil I confronted the mayhem of Muritala Muhammad airport. Joining the crowd surrounding one officer's station, jostled slowly forward, I finally confronted her face-to-face. Apparently I was missing the requisite currency form. No, sorry, there were none available that day. "Stand back," she declared: "You can't pass here today." I waited squeamishly. If I could only catch her eye once more! But then what? After some time a fellow passenger asked me what was the problem. At this point, the officer, stealing a glance at me while processing someone else, inquired: "Why can't you beg?" The person being processed proclaimed: "She doesn't know how to beg![6] Please, O! Let her go." And I was waved on.

A young post office clerk soon reinforced my conclusion that being employed in a given capacity did not in and of itself mean one performed it. Additional incentive was required. Again, I was confronted with a mass of people crowded round a window. Everyone was trying to catch the clerk's attention, but the young man was adept at avoiding eye contact. Clients were calling him by name,

invoking the name of mutual friends, and so on. After some time, he noticed me, and I grabbed the opportunity to ask for stamps. In a voice full of recrimination yet tinged with regret, he announced more to the crowd than to me: "Why can't you greet?" and proceeded to ignore me. This proved my tip-off to the elaborate and complex cultural code of greetings so central to Nigerian social life.[7] In other words, a personal relationship is like a "jump-start" for business transactions.

Lesson Three: Every Case is Unique

Mrs. Ojo had succeeded in obtaining for me a three-month visa, but I planned to stay for over two years. Prerequisite for a "regularized" visa was university affiliation. This sounded deceptively simple. The following two months spent registering as an "occasional postgraduate student" took a terrible toll on my nervous stomach.[8] The worst feeling was of an ever-receding target, an ever-thickening tangle of convoluted mazeways. No one could tell me what it took to register, for in fact, no one could possibly predict what I would confront farther down the road. Nothing was routinized, everything personalized, no two cases could possible be alike.

Lesson Four: "Dash" or "Long-Leg" Gets Results

This very unpredictability of the process forms a cybernetic system with the strength of personal ties, however initiate. *Dash* and *Long-Leg* are the locally recognized means for cutting through red tape or confronting noncooperative personnel. Dash is local parlance for gift or bribe. *Long-Leg* (sometimes called *L-L* or *L-squared*) refers to petitioning a powerful person to help hack your way through the tangled overgrowth. To me, it evokes the image of something swooping down from on high to stomp on the petty bureaucrat causing the problem.

Lesson Five: Exercise Keeps Ties Limber

During my drawn-out tussle with the registrar's office, I recounted my problem to anyone who would listen. A friend's grown son, upon hearing of my difficulties, wrote a note on his business card to a Mr. Ade in the Exams Section. Amused by his attempt to act important, I thanked Ayo politely. When I next saw him at his mother's home, he took the offensive, and accused me of shunning him. It came out that I had not seen Mr. Ade. But, I protested, I did not know the man. Moreover, he worked in exams not the registry. That, I learned, was not the point. I was supposed to assume that Mr. Ade would have known someone at the registry. Not only had I denied Ayo the chance to further his link to Mr. Ade, but ignoring his help was tantamount to denying any connection to him or—more important for me—his mother.

This revelation was reinforced when I ran into a colleague. He accused me of not greeting him very well. I had greeted him adequately, but apologized nonetheless. As the conversation progressed, he told me that he had heard I had had "some difficulty." He lamented the fact that I had not called on him, since as Assistant Dean of Social Science he could have helped me. His feelings were truly hurt, provoking his accusation of a lackluster greeting. Indeed, things were never the same between us again, for I had betrayed—or denied—our relationship.

Lesson Six: Your Friends Have Enemies

Well, I did eventually obtain a regularized visa, and it came through *Long-Leg*.[9] But the problems inherent in its use derive from the highly politicized and factionalized nature of Nigerian organizations, where personal loyalty is everything.

Early on, I became friendly with a certain sociologist and his family. Thereby, I had unwittingly become his ally in a long, drawn-out war between himself and his female colleagues. The disagreement had its origins ten years before in accusations of sex discrimination, but had long since spilled over into every aspect of departmental functioning. Even the office workers had chosen sides, and would perform only for members of the proper faction. More significant, though, was the fact that my friend's chief antagonist and I had similar theoretical interests.

Through in retrospect I regret the missed opportunity, I realize that I was in the thick of things before I could have known what was happening. Given the original complaint, my sympathies should have been with the other camp. But ambiguous loyalty is equivalent to none.

Early in the century, Max Weber, the great pioneering sociologist, articulated the difference between systems of *legal* and *patrimonial domination*. Within systems of legal domination, organized bureaucratically, authority is the property of a given office or position (not an attribute of the person) and is validated by general rules applying to the whole structure of offices. Assignment to an office is based on merit: rights and duties are properties of the office not its incumbent. The system functions according to routine and is therefore predictable and efficient. Great stress is place on making relationships impersonal.

In contrast, patrimonial authority (from the Latin term for personal estate) pertains to the form of government organized as a more or less direct extension of the noble household, where officials originate as household servants and remain personal dependents of the ruler. Note how the following passage summarizing Weber's characterization of patrimonial administration fits with my own observations of Nigerian life:

> *First*, whether or not the patrimonial ruler and his officials conduct administrative business is usually a matter of discretion; normally they do so only when they are paid for their troubles. *Second*, a patrimonial ruler resists the delimitation of his authority by the stipulation of rules. He may observe traditional or customary limitations, but these are unwritten: indeed, tradition endorses the principled arbitrariness of the ruler. *Third*, this combination of tradition and arbitrariness is reflected in the delegation and supervision of authority. Within the limits of sacred tradition the ruler decides whether or not to delegate authority, and his entirely personal recruitment of "officials" makes the supervision of their work a matter of personal preference and loyalty. *Fourth* and *fifth*, all administrative "offices" under patrimonial rule are a part of the ruler's personal household and private property: his "officials" are servants, and the costs of administration are met out of his treasury. *Sixth*, official business is transacted in personal encounter and by oral communication, not on the basis of impersonal documents.[10]

Weber himself believed that bureaucracy would supplant patrimonial authority. He believed that the world was becoming progressively more rationalized and bureaucratized. But there are several different dimensions along which I dispute this connection:

193

Bureaucracy has been invented, declined, and re-invented, several times over the millennia. We have seen how patrimonial ties persisted within a bureaucratic structure of offices in Nigeria. This is also true in America. Within certain organizational structures, personal loyalty remains important, favoritism prevails, connections count, and nepotism or corruption abounds. For instance, urban "political machines" function according to a patrimonial logic. Bureaucracy and patrimonialism may be opposite poles on a continuum (Weber called them "ideal types"), but they are *not* mutually exclusive. Most institutions combine both types of authority structures, with a greater emphasis on one or the other. Personal connections can help in either society, but in America, their use is widely perceived as *illegitimate*.

The system I have outlined is not irrational by any means—but rational actions are based on a different set of assumptions.

Ties of kinship and clientship have an ally in human nature.

By the latter, I mean Weber's ideal types cannot be mutually exclusive for emotional/cognitive reasons: an individual's cognitive understanding of hierarchy is necessarily patterned on the relationship between infant and caretaker. Whatever the form of the earliest pattern (and child-rearing practices vary tremendously between and within cultures), it leaves a residual tendency for personal attachment to develop between authority figures and dependents. Clients in the Unemployment Office naturally wish to be considered individuals and resent cold, impersonal treatment. Each bureaucrat wages his or her own private struggle with the temptation to treat each case on its merits.

This is why most Nigerians' finely honed interpersonal skills stand them in good stead when they arrive in the United States. They easily make friends with whomever they run across, and naturally friends will grant you the benefit of the doubt *if* there is room to maneuver. The psychological need remains, even in our seemingly formalized, structured world, for a friendly, personable encounter. On the other hand, anyone adept at working this way suffers tremendous pain and anxiety from the impersonal enforcement of seemingly arbitrary rules. For instance, a Nigerian friend took it as a personal affront when his insurance agent refused to pay a claim because a renewal was past due.

Once I learned my lessons well, life became much more pleasant. True, every case was unique and personal relationships were everything. But as my friends and allies multiplied, I could more easily make "the system" work for me. As a result of my Nigerian experience, I am very sensitive to inflexible and impersonal treatment, the flip-side of efficiency.

Leaving Nigeria to return to Boston after 2 1/2 years, I stopped for a week in London. I arrived only to find that my old college friend, with whom I intended to stay, had recently moved. Playing detective, I tried neighbors, the superintendent, directory assistance. Tried and bedraggled, I thought of inquiring whether a forwarding address had been left with the post office. Acknowledging me from inside his cage, the small, graying man reached for his large, gray ledger, peered in, slapped it shut, and answered: "Yes,"

"But... what is it?" I asked, caught off guard. He peered down at me and replied: "I cannot tell you. We are not allowed. We must protect him from creditors."

I was aghast. In no way did I resemble a creditor. Noticing my reaction, he conceded:

"But, if you send him a letter, I will forward it."

Bursting into tears of frustration, in my thickest American accent, displaying my luggage and my air ticket, I begged and cajoled him, to no avail. I spent my entire London week in a Bed 'n Breakfast, cursing petty bureaucrats as my bill piled up. "THAT," I thought, "COULD NEVER HAPPEN IN NIGERIA!"

Footnotes

1. One common misunderstanding must be clarified: *bureaucratic organization is not a recent Western invention*. Even during the Han Dynasty (3rd century B.C.), China had developed an efficient bureaucracy based on a system of official examinations. This was the start of a "modern" type of civil service system based on merit. It was almost two thousand years before the West adopted such a system, partly inspired by the Chinese example.

2. Robert K. Merton, *Social Theory and Social Structure* (New York: Free Press, 1969), 250.

3. Bribery exists for several reasons: it initiates a personal relationship, unlike a tip, which terminates all intimacy; if not dedicated to

"duty," a worker must be given added incentive to perform a service; the poor salary scale aggravated by the unpredictable nature of extended kin obligations means everyone is desperately in search of extra cash.

4. Corruption is condemned only in the abstract, when far removed and on a grand scale. But anyone and everyone knows someone "well-placed," and that person is now powerful precisely because he or she has been generous. Moreover, one is more likely to be condemned for going by the book than for corruption. If, for instance, the brother of the man married to one of my cousins (my mother's father's sister's daughter's husband's brother) did not see to it that his colleague signed my tax form with the minimum of fuss, life could be made quite miserable for him indeed!

5. Also known as shifting cultivation or swidden agriculture: small pieces of land are cultivated for a few years, until the natural fertility of the soil diminishes. When crop yields decline, the field must be abandoned. This has obvious implications for the concepts of private property, ownership, and monopoly.

6. It turns out that "begging" means throwing yourself on someone's mercy, rubbing one's hands together, eyes downcast, even kneeling or prostrating if necessary, and literally begging for a favor.

7. Nigerians coming to the United States are always taken aback by our positively inhuman greeting behavior.

8. A few years later, I timed my registration as a graduate student at Harvard. The result: three offices in twelve minutes! Even a foreign graduate student could probably register in less than a day.

9. I never paid *dash* in Nigeria.

10. Max Weber quoted from Reinhard Bendix, *Max Weber: An Intellectual Portrait* (Berkeley: University of California Press, 1960), 245; emphasis added.

Questions:

1. What does the author mean by the term "dash"?

2. What is the distinction Max Weber made between legal domination and patrimonial domination?

3. Why does Eames conclude that the Nigerian bureaucratic system is not irrational?

The answer section begins on page 243.

Whenever we hear the term "government bureaucracies," we usually think of faceless employees whose sole function is to enforce a universally applied set of rules and regulations. As Elizabeth Eames pointed out in the previous selection, we are shocked when we encounter bureaucrats— such as those in Nigeria—whose decisions are made more on personal relationships than on an objective set of rules applied equally to all citizens. But even in certain parts of the United States government employees need to take into consideration the personal, social, and cultural realities of the people they serve. In this reading applied anthropologist Roberta Hammond discusses her role as the director of environmental health in a small rural county in northwest Florida. She found that the best way to carry out her job as the top environmental health official in the county was to be aware of the cultural context of the local people. And the best way to gain that cultural information is through traditional anthropological data gathering techniques such as participant observation, open ended interviewing, and listening to people talk about their attitudes and feelings.

Environmental Health and Anthropology in a County Health Department

By Roberta M. Hammond

I became a participant observer long before I learned much about the academic discipline of anthropology. I have held a variety of unusual jobs over the past twenty years, from working as a deck hand on shrimp boats in Florida to harvesting tobacco in Kentucky. When I enrolled in graduate school, my early experiences in the fishing industry drew me to fisheries issues as they are related to the social sciences, particularly anthropology.

My dissertation field work was performed in a small, rural community of around 8,900 residents on the northwest coast of Florida. Because of its geographical isolation, Franklin County has a frontier-like quality, as exhibited by its independent residents, its relative lack of industrial and land development, and its lack of urban infrastructure such as central sewers and central water systems. During my five and one half years in the county, I supported myself by working first in a bar and then in the field offices of two state agencies.

My job with the Department of Community Affairs provided me with the foundation for my dissertation. When the state legislature deleted my position there, I applied for an opening in the county health department as an environmental specialist. Not only is environmental health a nontraditional field for an anthropologist, it is also a nontraditional field for a woman. Nevertheless, I secured the position.

Environmental health is concerned with the provision of safe and sanitary human needs such as sewage disposal, potable water, and food hygiene. Other programs administered by this section of the health department include rabies surveillance, sanitary nuisance investigations, and sanitary inspections of mobile home parks, group care facilities, and other institutions.

At the time I was hired, I had very little training in this field. Few professional jobs are available in rural areas, and so I felt fortunate to have found any job at all. Having already lived and worked in the county for two and one half years, I knew the geography and many of the local residents including all of the local politicians. For the first two months on the job, I inspected restaurants and institutional kitchens. I also inspected the county's few mobile home parks. It was my introduction to the diplomacy of regulatory field work.

Two months after I began working at the health department, the environmental health director got a promotion and moved to Tallahassee, the state capitol. Because of the county's reputation among state workers for being difficult, cantankerous, contrary, and backward, no one applied for or wanted the position of environmental health director. With my previous local experience in related state programs, I was encouraged to apply. I became the only female environmental health director at that time in a state of sixty-seven counties.

I incorporated various features of ethnographic field work in the performance of my duties as a public health official. I continued my long habit of participant observation by immersing myself in the community and living by its customs. This increased the residents' acceptance of me and enabled me to acquire immediate knowledge of events impacting on public health. In the specific area of environmental health, it was also important to show residents and my staff that I was not afraid to get my hands dirty, to perform disagreeable tasks, or to work long hours in the sun. By participating in community life, I was able to increase my sensitivity to residents' concerns and gain a more balanced view of the issues important to them versus those important to the state. On the other hand, in the observation mode, impersonal detachment as an outsider allowed me the use of authority in enforcement and other unpopular actions necessary for a public health official.

In addition to participant observation, I employed an open-ended interviewing technique on a daily basis to elicit as complete a contextual framework as possible for the problem or situation at hand. Life histories were particularly helpful in interactions with residents, especially when resolving touchy enforcement situations. Rapid rural assessment was very helpful in crisis situations which demanded the ability to assess the severity and extent of a problem quickly in order to make an informed decision for public health protection. This field technique involves taking time, offsetting biases, detaching oneself from the situation, listening and learning, and using multiple approaches (whichever are most appropriate or effective in a particular situation). (See Michael M. Cernea, ed., *Putting People First: Sociological Variables in Rural Development*, Second Edition [New York: Oxford University Press, 1985].) In all cases, good listening skills facilitated better community relations.

State agency field representatives live and work in this community, but their degree of community participation is limited by where they live and how they spend their spare time. Some live on a nearby barrier island to take advantage of being close to both the beach and the bay. However, this isolates them from most of the local residents whose resources they monitor and regulate. Those state agency field staff who live in one of the two incorporated towns or in any of the settlements in between are also limited by factors of geographic and social isolation. I preferred to make myself more accessible and to participate more by living in the county seat, Apalachicola.

State agency personnel and other neo-locals, such as artisans, tend to congregate at certain local voluntary organizations and certain bars. Permanent, lifelong residents have their own meeting places such as churches, Little League and high school football games, and their usually separate bars. This is not to say that there is no interaction or intermingling, but state agency field workers' perceptions are colored by the fact that their leisure activities are often limited to the safety and comfort of the company of people from similar socioeconomic and occupational backgrounds. If a field person is married and has children, there is added participation in school functions. Church memberships can also help. At first, I did not attend church regularly, but then I decided to go as it made me more familiar and acceptable to the residents and made me feel as though I were more a part of the community.

The level of interaction between locals and neo-locals does increase during large celebrations such as weddings, the annual Florida Seafood Festival, and various fund-raising fish fries, bake sales, and pancake breakfasts or spaghetti suppers. However, though the different occupational and socioeconomic segments of the population participate, the actual intermingling and interaction of people barely scratches the surface of long-held local family, religious, racial, and ethnic boundaries.

Franklin County's primary source of employment is the seafood industry. Many people are self-employed oyster harvesters ("oystermen"), shrimpers, or blue crab or fin fishermen. Others are employed in processing as crab pickers, shrimp headers, and oyster shuckers.

In the Apalachicola bay area, informal political control is provided by a shadowy group of businessmen, attorneys, seafood dealers, and local family members who own large amounts of real estate and sit on the boards of the two local banks. It is a select, informal "club" to which few have any real access; yet locals know whom to contact in an emergency or when a favor is needed. These favors are liberally dispensed, and

197

reciprocity is expected at critical times such as elections or when pressure is needed regarding an issue before the county or city commission. Local political leaders also have a long arm reaching to state government which is periodically used to influence decisions directly affecting the community. Local power to circumvent certain regulations that the state agency field staff are there to enforce is well (though perhaps not consciously) understood. This can make performance of state agency field staff work duties difficult at best.

Because of the need for state agency field representatives to negotiate, mediate, and facilitate constantly with local power brokers over a variety of issues, field representatives tend to ignore less powerful individuals with no less valid concerns, and their possible contributions are underestimated. There is little, if any, effort on the part of federal and state employees to make any but the most cursory of informal contacts with the fishermen, who are perceived to have little knowledge of the bay and its ecological sensitivity and who are considered by some agency staff to be of a lower class. Insensitive jokes abound about incestuous local behavior with resulting dimwitted progeny. The parting gift to a state agency field worker is often a joke gift of a pair of white rubber boots like those worn by fishermen.

I will provide a few brief anecdotes to illustrate the manner in which I used ethnographic techniques to administer environmental health programs and provide service to the public. In general, I emphasized a problem-solving approach with a lot of listening and much explaining of the public health reasons for environmental health requirements. Often health department enforcements are no-win situations where the health official is damned if she does and damned if she doesn't. The job requires the ability to adapt, compromise, and listen to the various nuances of any given event, all day, every day. The job is sensitive, variable, exciting, and sometimes dangerous.

Many times during disputes between neighbors, one of them will call the health department with a false accusation of a sanitary nuisance. (Sanitary nuisance are excessive odors, flies, raw sewage, or other situations causing a public health hazard.) It is easy to find oneself in the middle of neighborhood disputes over which there is no health department jurisdiction. The trick is to investigate and to have an open mind, but also to be sensitive to the elements and

context of the report and to be aware of the ongoing familial, neighborhood, and political relationships in the area. Since this is a small community, I was often able to glean background information from my secretary and the nurses and other health department staff so that I could be better prepared on my arrival at the scene of the complaint.

One example of a valid sanitary nuisance was a phone call complaining about the odor coming from an unburied dead dog. I investigated and verified the complaint, but no one was home. My secretary told me that the resident was a fisherman raising his two sons alone. When I returned, he was repairing a net in his front yard. I explained that I was there because of a complaint about a dog. He said that there was no dead dog and seemed sincere about it. When I showed him where it was, he said he hadn't known it was there and that he would take care of it. The entire conversation was low key. Later on, when his mother died and he could not afford the funeral expenses, I, along with many other community residents, bought a fish dinner at the fund-raising fish fry held at the Catholic church. This fisherman and I always wave to each other despite the history of enforcement.

Another sanitary nuisance involved hunting dogs kept in a pen that had not been cleaned for a long time. I used this particular situation as a teaching experience for a new staff member who tended to use strong-arm tactics. We both wore slacks and shirts and name badges clearly indicating that we were from the county public health unit. We had previously investigated and verified the complaint, but no one had been home. When we returned, a man was tinkering with a lawn mower in the yard. We approached him and chatted a while about machines. Then he said: "I guess you're here about the dogs." I said: "Yes." He said: "I know it's been getting bad. They belong to my son. I'll get him to take care of it when he gets home." In this example, I, as health official, had not had to say anything. The man with the sanitary nuisance did all the talking, and the purpose of eliminating the odors from the pen was accomplished without argument or acrimony.

In the absence of a countywide sewer system, one of the biggest environmental health programs in the county involves the permitting, sizing, and inspection of septic tank systems. Because of concerns that inadequate septic tanks were polluting the bay and its oysters, special septic tank requirements had been imposed on the county by Florida state legislature in the form of a Septic Tank Abatement Program. Inadequate septic tanks had to be retro-fitted or replaced and brought up to current standards. The health department was in charge of notifying residents of their faulty septic tanks. Through a laborious process of first and second notifications, on a schedule established in a county and city septic tank abatement ordinance, residents were given up to six months of extensions before being turned over to the county for enforcement.

The program was extremely unpopular and politically volatile. It had been minimally funded only for people in low-income brackets and did not get much from either the county or the state agency delegated to oversee the program. Furthermore, it was administered in a bureaucratic and culturally insensitive way. Despite my protests to my deputy district administrator for health that the timing was unfortunate, one set of letters was sent out two weeks before Christmas. The use of ethnographic perspectives could have increased the effectiveness of this program and the reputation of the health department.

In retrospect, probably the most important parts of the Septic Tank Abatement Program, in addition to environmental health priorities, were public relations and public education. These were not mentioned in the law nor were they mentioned in the city and county ordinances. Communications and interactions with property owners, local government officials, and staff of the county planning and building department were all very important to the ongoing successes of the program and the completion of repairs. At all times, efforts were made in my office to be courteous and respectful, even in the face of upset property owners and local government officials.

Because of the various political dynamics, and because the programs regulate the practice of some very basic and personal human needs, environmental health field work is very sensitive. This type of work is too often approached in a purely regulatory, police, "I'm-the-boss" and "because-I-say-so" manner. A classic nonanswer by poorly trained and uncaring inspectors is "because it's in the rule." A better approach is to use mediative techniques involving listening to people's feelings and concerns and explaining as clearly as possible the reasons for the environmental health regulations about to be imposed. It also helps to be aware of the cultural context of the community in which one is working and to participate in day-to-day and celebratory community events such as church, school games, dance recitals, weddings, and funerals, as well as local festivals and fund raisers.

The structure of environmental health field work in the state of Florida, both in rural and urban areas, is particularly well suited to perspective derived from anthropology. While I'm sure that differences of gender, socialization, and personality also affected the outcome of my work, my background in anthropology helped me to adjust to a difficult field situation. This involved regulating an isolated, rural community with cultural values far removed from those of the lawmakers in the state capitol and even from my own. While working in the community and doing the field work for my dissertation, I developed my skills in participant observation, interviewing, eliciting life histories, and performing rapid rural assessments. As environmental health director, I move from participant to observer to professional outsider during the course of any working day, depending on the given situation. In environmental health, problem-solving and dispute settlement skills are also very useful.

Anthropologists and anthropology can provide skills and tools for work in many jobs not normally considered anthropological. These skills can be an important addition to the repertoire of environmental health specialists with backgrounds in the natural sciences. Their jobs and the environmental health objectives of safe and sanitary water, sewage disposal, and food hygiene could be accomplished in a more positive and effective manner using these tools. My experience underlines what practicing anthropologists already know: Anthropologists need not limit themselves to traditional academic and research positions; their skills can be applied to a variety of field circumstances.

Questions:

1. What are some of the concerns of people working in the areas of environmental health?

2. What traditional ethnographic techniques did Hammond incorporate into her work as an environmental health specialist?

3. The author feels strongly about the need for understanding the cultural context of the local people. How did she acquire her knowledge of the local cultural context?

The answer section begins on page 243.

32

Not only are applied cultural anthropologists working to solve problems <u>within</u> government bureaucracies, but they can also contribute to bettering relations <u>between</u> governments. The Carter Center, a nonprofit public institute established by former President Jimmy Carter, has conflict resolution between nations as one of its major objectives. Here Honggang Yang describes the role he played as an applied anthropologist at the Carter Center providing timely and culturally relevant data for the third party mediators in international disputes. He raises the vital, but thorny, question of how ethnographic information can be used to supplement the often biased accounts of world events reported in the media.

Practicing Anthropology in the Carter Presidential Center

By Honggang Yang

I first came to the American South from the People's Republic of China in 1986, as a student of applied anthropology. After the completion of my doctoral course work at the University of South Florida (USF), I started an internship that was a part of the training requirements. My internship project took the form of ethnographic fieldwork focusing on the disputing processes involving the management of the commons by a homeowners association in Tampa (Yang 1992a). This research formed the basis for my dissertation.

Upon graduation from USF, I started my job hunting and in the early fall of 1991, I was invited to interview for a position at the Carter Presidential Center in Atlanta. Over the past decade, the Carter Center has received more and more public recognition and has become a symbol of commitment to global peace. I was thrilled when I was hired as a research associate in the conflict resolution program there. Later I learned that it was my cross-cultural knowledge and applied anthropological training in the fields of peacemaking and conflict resolution that had attracted their interest in me.

As an organization, the Carter Center is a nonprofit, nonpartisan public policy institute that former President Jimmy Carter founded in 1982. The Center is home to a group of organizations that unite research and outreach applications. Its core organization is the Carter Center of Emory University (CCEU). Apart from the projects on international health policy, global development, African government, Latin America, and the United States, conflict resolution and human rights are the two principal foci at the Center

(Yang 1993a). In this paper I will draw upon my working experience and observations and reflections at the Center in the past few years to illustrate the challenges now facing anthropologists' involvement in practical issues of peace and conflict resolution.

President Carter's conflict resolution work is based in large part on his experience at the Camp David Peace Talks in 1978 (Babbitt 1994). The resolution of internal, armed conflict is currently his central focus, since the majority of the armed conflicts now are civil wars taking place within national boundaries. Many violent conflicts, Carter believes, are derived from basic human rights violations. But a disservice is done to understanding human rights by constant reference to the United States as the model of a rights-protective society; more reference should be made to the smaller Western social democracies that have longer traditions of protection of civil, political, and economic rights (Howard 1990). Carter recognized this position and initiated his Atlanta Project to address these domestic social issues in 1992.

Disputing parties caught up in costly conflicts had nowhere to turn when they needed assistance in finding nonviolent means to resolve their problems. This lack of recourse was due to the prohibition, restriction, limitation, and constraint of the powers of the international and regional organizations. It was in this complex context that the International Negotiation Network (INN) was developed to fill the identified mediation gap and in which my work was concentrated at the Carter Center.

Yang, Honggang, from Practicing Anthropology in the South, James M. Tim Wallace (ed.) 1997, pp. 155-159. Reprinted by permission of the the University of Georgia Press, Athens, Georgia.

The INN was initiated by Carter, together with other international leaders, in 1987. They envisioned a growing need for a new approach to the resolution the many internal conflicts now found in the world. Overseen by a council of "eminent persons" and a group of experts and practitioners, the INN's approach involves third-party mediation, especially "eminent mediators."

Throughout the implementation of the CCEU programs, the "eminent persons" strategy has been used to get the parties to the table. This strategy has some special characteristics: immediate access to leaders, experts, and data; ability to mobilize resources and borrow infrastructure support without the usual attendant organizational encumbrances; and mass media attention to promote the negotiation environment.

The role of eminent persons in third-party mediation is perhaps the most important characteristic of the INN approach. As a former head of state, Jimmy Carter has access to virtually anyone in the world. His phone calls are always accepted. When he needs assistance, people in various sectors respond (Spencer, Spencer, and Yang 1992). Jimmy Carter has the trustworthiness, credibility, mediation experience and ability, and charismatic authority to persuade the parties to go to the negotiation table. There are very few other world figures who share these attributes. At the same time, the role of an individual is limited by his or her personal, sociocultural, or political background, morality, and acceptability to the parties in a particular context.

In addition, there are some special considerations that shape the CCEU/INN involvement, namely: (1) there should be a mediation gap; (2) duplication or competition with other organizations should be avoided; (3) the invitations have to come from all the parties; and (4) considerations must be given to the timing of third-party assistance. At the Center, we monitored existing and emerging armed conflicts; convened confidential consultations for disputants and mediators; matched disputants' needs with potential third parties, funding sources, and experts; and performed pre-mediation services that included analysis of the issues, generation of options, and building of trust. During my tenure at the Center we held two major consultations to spotlight internal armed conflicts and to set forth action agendas through a strengthened use of nongovernmental and intergovernmental actors (Yang 1993b).

My working role as an applied anthropologist entailed the research and delivery of the third-party assistance (e.g., mediation, facilitation, election monitoring/observing, or convening of the negotiations) based on a cross-cultural understanding of armed conflicts in a complex, international context. In 1993 I also became the coordinator for the internship program on conflict resolution. The collection and provision of information has long been a crucial part of the day-to-day operations at the Center and student interns play important roles in providing the information resources. As director of the internship program, I organized a round table for student interns who gathered the information and provided the weekly updates and encouraged them to think creatively but realistically.

Weekly updates of conflict situations and developments are critical to the Center's work. Compilations of the updates are distributed to the INN Council and core group members, and they cover information on peace attempts, armed conflicts, elections/politics, human rights, humanitarian issues, refugees, and foreign aid. A major source of the information for the updates is the Lexis/Nexis on-line services (Yang 1993a). Ethnographic data were among the things that I took particular care in reviewing and providing. Bias and one-sidedness exist in mass media reports, which therefore need to be balanced with ethnographic holistic, in-depth, field knowledge. There is a problem with straight ethnographic data, as ethnographic documents are often very lengthy and filled with detailed descriptions of everyday life. Nevertheless, many anthropologists did their fieldwork in areas where ethnic disputes and human rights violations now prevail, enhancing the value of those ethnographic documents. It was quite a challenge to make use of these ethnographic materials in a context where rapid developments require quick responses to emerging concerns. In this connection, I suggested (Yang 1992b) that anthropologists pay more attention to the national character studies three years ago, despite the reluctance of many anthropologists to express sociocultural themes beyond particular local or topical boundaries. Of course, empirical generalizations are always defined by their corresponding limitations in concrete contexts. Our research tradition values variations and diversities in conceptualization. Hsu (1983) is right that the anthropologist often has to comment on national societies as wholes, either from scientific or practical reasons, because human issues cannot be understood by descriptions of the marriage customs or age-grading practices in single villages or tribes. From my own experience at the Carter Center, I was often asked to suggest short-term solutions and immediate action steps despite an imperfect understanding of the holistic elements of the culture of the disputing parties (Yang 1994). In my opinion, anthropologists must overcome their reluctance and hesitation to say what they know and what they experienced in the field, regardless of the limitations.

One additional role I fulfilled at the Carter Center was that of an advocate for non-Western, indigenous approaches to addressing the issues of conflict and peace, since the Western mode of dispute settlement dominates (Yang 1993b). I wanted to increase the use of ethnographic knowledge in the field; as a result, I tried to get more anthropologists involved in this work and to make more cross-cultural references in the information gathering and reporting at the Center. There are, however, challenges in advocating the indigenous methods of conflict management, since communally oriented systems of social justice, based on ascribed and differentiated memberships in small-scale pastoral or agricultural societies, unfortunately cannot be, as Howard (1990) points out, transferred to the modern, large-scale state arena. A central, practical question I worked on at the Carter Center was how the indigenous perspectives of peace and grassroots devices of conflict settlement can be better understood within a holistic context and made more applicable, more efficient, and more widespread in peacemaking and conflict resolution.

There are many happy memories for me about my three years at the Center, especially those times when I worked directly with former President Carter. I still remember vividly the time he tried to pronounce my first name when he was visiting Center staff members in their offices. There is a good feeling inside me when I remember the speech I helped to draft that he gave to a United Nations meeting via telecommunication media. And I am filled with pride when I remember when he shook my hand after he had used some briefing materials I had prepared for him prior to a meeting with a Sudanese delegation. He said to me with his warm smile, "Thank you for your help."

I was honored to work for him.

REFERENCES

Babbit, E.F. 1994. Jimmy Carter: The Power of Moral Suasion in International Mediation. In *When Talk Works*, ed. D. M. Kolb and Associates, p. 376. San Francisco: Jossey-Bass.

Howard, R.E. 1990. Group versus Individual Indentity in the African Debate on Human Rights. In *Human Rights in Africa*, ed. A.A.An-Na'im and F.M. Deng, pp. 159-83. Washington , DC: The Brookings Institute.

Hsu, F. L. K. 1983. The Cultural Problem of the Cultural Anthropologist. In *Rugged Individualism Reconsidered: Essays in Psychological Anthropology*, ed. F.L.K. Hsu, pp. 420-38. Knoxville: University of Tennessee Press.

Spencer, D., W. Spencer, and H. Yang. 1992, Closing the Mediation Gap: The Ethiopia/Eritrea Experience. *Security Dialogue* 23(3):89-99.

Yang, Honggang. 1992a Preserving the Commons in Private Cluster-Home Developments. *Practicing Anthropology* 14:2:9-11.

------. 1992b. The Practical Importance of National Character Studies. *Southern Anthropologist* 19:2.

------. 1993a. Operation of the Conflict Resolution Program at the Carter Center. Paper presented at the annual meeting of the Peace Studies Association, University Park, PA.

------. 1993b. The Practical Use of Ethnographic Knowledge: Face-Saving Devices in Conflict Resolution. Paper presented at the National Conference on Peacemaking and Conflict Resolution, Portland, OR.

------. 1994. Keeping the Ethnographic Knowledge Current. Paper presented at the annual meeting of the American Anthropological Association, Atlanta.

Questions:

1. What is the International Negotiation Network (INN) at the Carter Center?

2. How would you describe the role Yang played as an applied anthropologist?

3. In what way does Yang urge some traditional anthropologists to become more bold in their research?

The answer section begins on page 243.

33

While the United States has often been referred to as a "melting pot," some would suggest that a more appropriate metaphor would be a "salad bowl," in which a number of ethnic groups retain a good deal of their cultural distinctiveness. Sometimes these distinct cultural features come into conflict with the large body of civil and criminal statutes that make up our legal system. To illustrate, 19th century Mormons, who valued the practice of having more then one wife at a time, came into conflict with the statutes of the state of Utah requiring monogamous marriage. In this section, applied anthropologist Anne Sutherland discusses a legal case of a Gypsy man arrested for using someone else's social security number when purchasing an automobile. Sutherland served as an expert witness for the defense showing how the accused, owing to certain features of his Gypsy culture, had no intention of defrauding anyone by his actions.

Gypsy Identity, Names and Social Security Numbers

By Anne Sutherland

It is often the case that a law made for one set of purposes has another, unintended impact on a particular group. A recent law making the use of a false social security number a federal felony is intended to help prosecution of major drug crime syndicates, but it has a special impact on Gypsies in the United States. Gypsies, traditionally a nomadic people, frequently borrow each others' "American" names and social security numbers, viewing them as a kind of corporate property of their kin group or *vitsa*. They also often lack birth certificates and must obtain midwife or baptismal certificates to use for identification purposes when they try to obtain credit, enter school, or apply for welfare.

In this article, I shall examine the case of a nineteen-year-old Gypsy man who was convicted under the new social security law and served six months in jail. Arguments for the defense in the case followed three lines of reasoning: 1) that this law unfairly singled out Gypsies for punishment; 2) that there was no intent to commit a crime; and 3) that in using the social security numbers of relatives, Gypsies were following a time-honored tradition to remain anonymous and separate from non-Gypsy society.

Facts of the Case

In the fall of 1991 in St. Paul, Minnesota, a nineteen-year-old Gypsy man was convicted of the crime of using his five-year-old nephew's social security number to obtain credit to purchase a car. When the purchase was questioned by the car dealership, he returned the car and was arrested on a felony charge of using a false social security number. After he was arrested, police searched the apartment where he was staying. They found lists of names, addresses and social security numbers, leading them to suspect an organized crime ring.

In *The United States of America v. S.N,*[1] it was "alleged that the defendant, S.N., while in process of obtaining a new Ford Mustang from a car dealership, used a social security number that was not his own with intent to deceive." Under the statute 42 U.S.C. 408 (g)(2), a person who, with intent to deceive, falsely represents his or her number to obtain something of value or for any other purpose, is a felon.

In Mr. S.N.'s case there is no specific allegation that he intended to deprive another person permanently of property because the focus of the charging statute is false representation of numbers. The underlying purpose which motivates a person to falsely represent his or her number may be an essentially innocent purpose, but the statute, at least as it has been interpreted, does not appear to impose a burden of proof as to wrongful purpose.

The statute punishes the means (false number) which a person may employ to achieve any number of ends and it punishes those means as a felony. The lawyer for the defense argued that the statute's failure to address the nature of the purpose to which false credentials are used is a serious flaw in the law and may punish those who would use the number for petty misconduct as felons. He also argued that there is a potential for discriminatory impact on Gypsies who use false credentials to conceal themselves from mainstream society. A Gypsy household may obtain a telephone by providing a false social security number and even if they pay the telephone bill without fail for years, they are felons under this law. S.N. not only made the payments for his car, but he returned it when the number was questioned. He is still a felon under this law.

The defense lawyer argued that the law is objectionable for two reasons. First, the law's disproportionate impact on the Gypsies is objectionable under the equal protection guarantees in the Fifth Amendment of the U.S. Constitution. He argued that the law denies Gypsies equal protection of the law by irrationally and disproportionately punishing at the felony level certain traditional Gypsy actions which cause no positive injury to anyone. As evidence he used material from my book, *Gypsies: The Hidden Americans*, for testimony that Gypsies routinely use false social security numbers to acquire credit but do pay their bills and are available for repossession in case of default of payment. They get phone service, buy houses and cars and other household items on credit and have a record of payment that is probably better than the general population (*United States v. Sonny Nicholas*, 1991). They do this primarily to remain unknown by mainstream society rather than to cause loss or injury to any person.

Second, as the defense lawyer pointed out, there is a Supreme Court decision that requires the government to prove felonious intent when it seeks to punish a person for wrongful acquisition of another's property. S.N. maintained that he used a false social security number because of a Gypsy tradition to remain anonymous and because his own number had been used by other Gypsies. The government argued that there was a "ring" of Gypsies in the area where S.N. was living. At S.N.'s residence a number of false credentials and social security numbers were found which had been used to obtain cars illegally. Some of these cars are still missing. In other words, there was evidence that false identity had been used recently in the area to steal. In this case, however, S.N. had not stolen anything and was not being accused of stealing, but only of using a false social security number.

Because of the evidence of a ring of car thieves in the area, the prosecution hoped to use the threat of prosecution against S.N., the only Gypsy they had been able to arrest, to plea bargain for information regarding the other people involved in the alleged ring. These other people had disappeared immediately as soon as S.N. was arrested.

One of the problems in the case was that both the prosecution and even the defense had difficulty obtaining complete and accurate information on S.N. For example, they had difficulty determining his "real" name, a moot point for the Gypsies since they have a practice of using many "American" names although they only have one "Gypsy" name (nav romano). The Gypsy name of *o Spiro le Stevanosko* (or Spiro the son of Stevan) uses the noun declension characteristic of the Sanskrit-rooted Rom language and is not immediately translatable into English since it does not employ a surname. Spiro's identity can be pinned down by finding out what *vitsa* (a cognatic descent group) he belongs to so that he will not be confused with any other Spiro le Stevanoskos. The Spiro of our example is a *Kashtare* which is part of a larger "nation" of Gypsies or *natsia* called *Kalderasha* (coppersmith). For his "American" names he may take any of a number used by his relatives such as Spiro Costello, John Costello, John Marks, John Miller, Spiro John or Spiro Miller. His nickname is Rattlesnake Pete.

The Anthropologist as Cultural Broker

S.N.'s defense attorney contacted me after finding that he was less confused about S.N. after reading my book about Gypsies. He sought my help in determining whether S.N. was a Gypsy, what his name was, and any other cultural information (such as the use of social security numbers by Gypsies) that would help him with his case.

Consequently, one cold autumn day I drove to the federal holding prison, one and a half hours from the city, and met S.N. He was a thin young man, perpetually fearful of pollution from contact with non-Gypsies and suffering from the effects of several months of what for him was solitary confinement since he had not seen any of his people since being incarcerated. The telephone was his only link with people to whom he could relate, people from his own culture who spoke his language. His main contact was with a nonGypsy woman who lived with one of his relatives. She was his link with the world he had known and the only "American" household he had been in before prison. Since my primary task was to determine if he was a Gypsy, first I talked to him about his relatives in Los Angeles and his *vitsa* (Yowane) and tried to establish what section of the *vitsa* I personally knew. This exchange of information about vitsa and Gypsies of mutual acquaintance is a normal one between Gypsies. The purpose was to establish a link between us.

Then I asked him about why he was in Minnesota. He talked about a seasonal expedition he and his brothers and cousins make to Minnesota to buy and sell cars and fix fenders before winter sets in. He claimed not to know were his brothers and cousins had gone or how he got into his present predicament.

For S.N., the most immediately effective action I could take was to see that he got the food he needed to stay "clean" in jail. When I met him he had lost fifteen pounds and was suffering demonstrable distress and nervousness. He was upset at being cut off from his culture and people for the first time in his life. In addition, he was distressed at being incarcerated and fearful. for his safety. More importantly, he was worried he would become defiled or *marime*. A major concern of his was that if he ate food prepared by non-Gypsies who did not follow rules of cleanliness considered essential in the Gypsy culture, he would become *marime*, a condition of ritual impurity that would result in his being shunned by his relatives and other Gypsies. To protect himself, he avoided eating prison food in the hopes that when he was released from prison he would be able to return to his family without a period of physical exile, also call *marime* (or "rejected" as the Gypsies translate it into English). I arranged for his lawyer to provide him with money to buy food from the concession because it is packaged and untouched by non-Gypsies and therefore considered clean by Gypsy standards. He bought milk in cartons, candy bars and soft drinks and other packaged foods that, though they may lack in nutrition, at least were not defiling and kept him from starvation.

A further complicating factor for S.N. was that he spoke English as a second language. He had only a rudimentary ability to read, thus straining his grasp of his defense. And his only contact with relatives was by telephone since neither he nor they could write with any ease. Even though his limited English made it difficult for him to follow his own trial, the court did not provide a translator.

The Trial

The trail was held in Federal Court and centered around the constitutionality of a law that unfairly targets a particular ethnic group and the question of intent to commit a crime. My testimony was intended to establish that Gypsies may use false identification for a number of cultural reasons which may have no connection to any intent to commit a crime. For a traditionally nomadic group with pariah status in the wider society and a pattern of secretiveness and autonomy, concealing identity is a long-established pattern.

This pattern is widespread in all Gypsy groups in Eastern Europe, Western Europe, Russia, Latin American and the United States. It is a mechanism they have developed over centuries to protect themselves from a wider society that has persecuted them or driven them away. The recent case of the German government paying large sums to Romania to take back Gypsy refugees is only the latest in an historically established tradition of discrimination against Gypsies. The persecution of Gypsies in the Holocaust, in medieval Europe and in the early part of the 20th century in the United States has been well documented. Current events in Eastern Europe have shown a resurgence of extreme prejudice against Gypsies. Interviews in recent *New York Times* articles have pointed to a hatred of Gypsies so deep that there is talk of extermination.[2] Because of the history of violence against them, Gypsies have developed elaborate mechanisms of secrecy and have hidden their identity in order to survive. It will not be easy to get them to change this pattern that has stood them in good stead for so many centuries.

The purpose of my testimony was to establish that S.N. was a Gypsy and that Gypsies often use false identification without intent to defraud. They do so because as members of a *vitsa*, or cognatic descent group, identification is corporate in nature. Members of the group have corporate access to property owned by other members of the group. That property includes forms of identification.

An additional problem in the S.N. case was the question of identification from photographs. Here we encountered the age-old problem that members of one culture and race have trouble identifying individuals from another culture and race. In simple terms, to many non-Gypsies, all Gypsies look alike. Part of the case involved clearing up erroneous identification of S.N. in photos provided by the prosecution.

I was also asked to testify on my own personal experience with discrimination against Gypsies by the Minneapolis Police Department. One instance of discrimination I related to the court occurred during a talk I gave to some twenty police officers to help them understand Gypsy culture. When I had spoken about the strong sense of family and community among the Gypsies and how much they value their children, a police officer suggested that since the main problem law enforcement officers have is how to detain the Gypsies long enough to prosecute them, removing Gypsy children from their homes on any pretext would be an effective way to keep the parents in town.

Prejudice against Gypsies often goes unrecognized even by culturally and racially sensitive people. The assistant district attorney prosecuting S.N. offered an article that he used to understand the Gypsies, entitled "Gypsies, the People and their Criminal Propensity,"[3] which quotes extensively from my work, including the fact that Gypsies have several names and that the same or similar non-Gypsy names are used over and over. The article concentrates on "criminal" behavior and never mentions the possibility that there are Gypsies who may not engage in criminal activities. In one section, quotations from my book on the ways Gypsies deal with the welfare bureaucracy were placed under the title, "Welfare Fraud," although by far most of the practices I described were legal. These concluding words in Part II are representative of the tone of the article:

> Officers should not be misled into thinking these people are not organized. They are indeed organized and operate under established rules of behavior, including those that govern marriage, living quarters, child rearing, the division of money and participation in criminal acts.

The implication of such statements is inflammatory. Gypsies have a culture, history, language and social structure, but that fact is distorted to imply that their social organization is partly for the purpose of facilitating criminal behavior. Their culture is viewed as a criminal culture. Gypsies have been fighting this view for hundreds of years. It is the view that they still combat in their relations with law enforcement and the criminal justice system. It is the view that was promoted by the prosecution in this case.

In spite of the best efforts of S.N.'s attorney and my testimony that use of a false social security number did not necessarily indicate intent to commit a crime, he was convicted of illegally using a social security number and served about six months in jail.

Conclusions: Anthropology and Cultural Differences in the Courtroom

Anthropologists are often called in as expert witnesses in cases involving cultural difference. Most Native American legal cases, such as the Mashpee case reported by James Clifford,[4] center around Indian status, treaties and land rights. In St. Paul, a number of Hmong legal cases highlighted the conflict between traditional marriage (specifically, the age at which children may marry) and the legal status of minors in American law. With the Gypsies, there is yet another set of cultural issues in their contact with American law.

First is the question of the cultural conflict between a historically nomadic group and the state bureaucracy of settled people. Identification—a serious legal issue in a bureaucratic society composed of people with fixed abodes and a written language—has virtually no meaning for the nomadic Gypsies who consider descent and extended family ties the defining factor for identification.

Second is the conflict between Gypsy religious rules regarding ritual pollution and prison regulations. The Gypsies avoid situations, such as a job or jail, that require them to be in prolonged contact with non-Gypsies. Jail presents special problems for the Gypsies can become *marime*, that is, defiled by unclean food and living conditions. The psychological trauma that results from isolation from their community is compounded if they then emerge from jail and have to undergo a further isolation from relatives because of becoming *marime* in jail.

Finally there is a cultural clash between the Gypsy value of corporate kinship and the American value of individual rights. The rights and status of an individual Gypsy are directly linked to his or her membership in a *vitsa* which is determined by birth. Furthermore, the status of all the members of the *vitsa* is effected by the behavior of each individual *vitsa* member. Since they are so intricately linked, reciprocity between *vitsa* members is expected. Members of a *vitsa* and family share economic resources, stay in each other's homes, help each other in work and preparation of rituals and loan each other cars, information, identification and money. They also share the shame of immoral or incorrect behavior by one member. For the Gypsies, the American idea that each individual has only one name, one social security number, or one medical identification number is contrary to their

207

experience and culture. Unfortunately for the Gypsies in America, it is now a felony to think this way.

Footnotes

1. *United States v. Sonny Nicholas*, U.S. District Court, State of Minnesota, CR 4-91-137 (1991). Quotes from Philip Leavenworth, memorandum in support of a motion to declare 42 U.S.C. 408 (g) (2) unconstitutional.

2. See *New York Times*, November 17 and 28, (1993) for recent accounts of extreme prejudice against Gypsies.

3. Terry Getsay, *Kansas State FOP Journal*, Parts I, II, and III, (1982) pp. 18-30.

4. "Identity in Mashpee," in *The Predicament of Culture*, Cambridge: Harvard University Press (1988) pp. 277-346.

Questions:

1. In the case *United States vs. S.N.*, what three lines of reasoning were used by the defense?

2. Why have Gypsies traditionally wanted to remain anonymous and separate from the non-Gypsy society?

3. What was the defendant's main concern about being kept in jail away from his own culture?

The answer section begins on page 243.

Section V
Economic Development

The term "development anthropology" refers to that area of applied anthropology in which the anthropologist engages in projects that deliberately alter human interaction with the natural or man-made parts of the environment. Such projects involve innovations in agriculture, housing, new energy supplies, the building of schools and clinics, flood control, and the administration of pastures for grazing animals. Often these development projects are initiated from "above" by government bureaucrats and outside development agencies such as the Canadian International Development Agency (CIDA) or the World Bank. In this selection, Inge Bolin describes her role as an applied anthropologist working at the grassroots level in the Peruvian Highlands. She claims that cultural anthropologists—with their intimate knowledge of both local cultures and the outside world—are particularly well suited for working on development projects.

Achieving Reciprocity: Anthropological Research and Development Assistance

By Inge Bolin

In October of 1990 representatives of universities and nongovernmental organizations (NGOs) from different parts of the world participated in a conference in Vancouver, Canada, entitled "Universities and NGOs—International Development at the Crossroads: A New Paradigm in the Making." One of the participants from Belize concluded his speech with the remark: "How can we, the people from the South, reciprocate for the NGO development assistance we receive from the North?" As an anthropologist engaged in field work in various parts of the world, I too have been concerned about reciprocity. My question, however, is diametrically opposed. I have been asking myself: what can anthropologists do for the people in the South whose knowledge, assistance, and patience are crucial to the success of our research?

Anthropologists working at the grass-roots level are well suited to assist in the kind of development advised by most agencies but seldom performed—working with the poorest and most remote villages. Decades of development have shown that "trickle-down" approaches have had little success, as funds that pass between high levels of government too seldom end up where they are most needed. It is also well known that many development projects have failed because the indigenous culture of the people, their modes of conceptualization and their needs, have not been taken into consideration. Furthermore, projects imposed by people from outside the community too often create dependence on materials and/or services from the outside instead of self-sufficiency. Such projects may disintegrate when the developers leave, and they have sometimes destroyed the very fabric of traditional society. Since anthropologists usually get to know the people and their culture better than any other outsider, their participation can substantially improve the probability of successful project implementation.

Yet, whether an anthropologist should actively engage in bringing about change in a society is often questioned. My six years of experience have shown that local people do seek the advice and assistance of anthropologists in the field. This kind of cooperation need not represent any danger to the society involved if the initiative comes from the local populations themselves and the projects proceed under their direction. During my research it became quite clear that local people know how to develop their community and how to organize themselves in accordance with the change that development brings about. On the other hand, villagers often cannot come up with the necessary funds and/or specific technical expertise: these must be acquired from outside the village or district. The following examples illustrate some ways in which the anthropologist in the field can assist in locally initiated development projects.

Reprinted by permission of PRACTICING ANTHROPOLOGY 14(4), Fall, 1992, pp. 12-15.

Securing Funds For Schools

During my doctoral studies in the Peruvian Highlands in 1984-85 my research was focused on the organization of irrigation in several villages, including the village of Chichubamba. Chichubamba is situated on a hillside in the Sacred Valley of the Incas, seventy-six kilometers north of Cusco. Twenty-five years ago the villagers decided to build a school, using their own labor and modest means. The problem, however, was the land. The villagers' small plots were barely large enough to meet the subsistence needs of the 362 families. At that time, and many times subsequently, the villagers approached the church, which owns larger plots of land, and requested to buy a small piece of the centrally located field known as "Señor Pampa." For two and a half decades promises were made and possibilities were evaluated regarding a sale, but the land was never sold to the people of Chichubamba. The children continued to receive sporadic instruction in several small adobe huts, the private residences of peasant families.

Subsistence became more difficult with each year, as the population increased and the repeatedly subdivided fields became too tiny to be divided again among offspring. The people of Chichubamba knew that only education would give their children a chance to find work elsewhere and thus to survive. Another urgent petition was made to the church authorities by the villagers, who were supported by the municipal council of Urubamba (the capital of the district of Urubamba, located in the province of Urubamba) and by the school board. At a meeting in the Archbishopric in Cusco in February 1985, which I attended at the villagers' request, assurances were made again that the land would soon be sold to the community. But in November of the same year it was sold to the highest bidder, someone from outside the village.

The people of Chichubamba were shocked, but they were not willing to give up. They took turns occupying the land by day and night until February 1986, when the new owner consented to sell them the land (although at a price higher than he had paid). The villagers engaged in various fund-raising activities and received some donations, but they knew it would be a long time until they could afford to complete their school.

The people of Chichubamba asked for my advice. Together we devised a proposal consisting of a petition written and signed by the villagers, a budget, photos of the walls that had been constructed out of adobe, and my description of the historic and socioeconomic circumstances in which the villagers live. I presented the proposal to the Lions Club of Leonberg, Germany, which accepted the project and raised the necessary funds for building materials and supplies within six months.

Since at that time I was unable to return to Peru, I put the Lions Club in contact with the honorary consul of Germany residing in Cusco. He accepted the funds and acted as intermediary between the villagers of Chichubamba and the Lions Club in Leonberg. The people of Chichubamba, aided by the students of the technical school of Urubamba, constructed and equipped the building. In memory of the much appreciated cooperation with Leonberg, the villagers of Chichubamba named the school "Leonbamba."

Another school project followed which required less assistance on my part. The subsistence farmers of Chicon, a village situated on the steep hills above Urubamba Valley, had constructed the walls of a school but were unable to finish the project due to lack of funds. The teachers and village elders asked for my assistance. We discussed the project. They then wrote a request including a budget, signed by the villagers at large. I added photos of the state of the building and a description of local circumstances and of my experiences there as an anthropologist. I presented the documents to the Small Project Branch of the Canadian Embassy in Lima. Within four months, villagers received funding from the embassy to build their school. Since I had to leave the field, the project was coordinated by Arariwa, a respected organization of Dominicans who work to improve the agriculture of the region.

In both these projects, my role was mainly that of mediator between the indigenous people and organizations. The knowledge of an anthropologist about the area and his/her contacts with national and international organizations and institutions are important to get a project started. Apart from a final report following inauguration, little work on my part was required once the projects were accepted. Local villagers were in charge of all major planning, implementation, and related matters. Other projects, however, such as the health clinic of Chillihuani described below, have required more input on my part.

Establishing a Health Clinic

In February of 1988 I was invited to participate in community festivities and secret family rituals during *Puqllay* (Carnival) in Chillihuani. No roads lead to this village, close to the perpetual snows of the Andes, and few people from the valley have ever ventured there. Foreigners have never participated in the festivities, I was told. Yet, I was received as a friend and initiated into the many important rituals and to all aspects of everyday life, regardless of the adjustments the people had to make to accommodate me. I left Chillihuani with the desire to reciprocate the hospitality of this society, so generous and elegant despite the harsh circumstances under which the people eke out their existence at an altitude of 4,300 to 5,000 meters.

Six weeks after I left Chillihuani to continue my work in the valley, a typhoid epidemic broke out, killing many people of all ages within a few days of the appearance of the first symptoms. Luckily, a doctor with whom I was working on other health projects at the time, and who was physically fit, agreed to walk the sixteen kilometers to Chillihuani to assess the situation and bring it under control. It became clear that the villagers desperately needed a health station where patients could be isolated and treated. Two years earlier they had started construction of a clinic using adobe blocks they manufactured themselves, but there were no funds to complete the station and equip it.

At the time the epidemic struck, I had just assisted people of Yanahuara in the province of Urubamba to complete a health station, and the experience gained facilitated the preparation of similar project. Together with the elders and health promoters of Chillihuani we discussed the health situation and the steps to be taken to complete the clinic. They devised a proposal to be signed by the villagers describing the health situation, the type of building materials and equipment most urgently required, and the kind of instruction necessary for the two health promoters residing in the village and for the population at large. I translated all documents and added a description of my association with the village.

We discussed the importance of maintaining and/or improving traditional medical practices and herbal medicine which have proven successful in the past. For the local population, traditional medicine is cheaper, more readily available, and often as effective as modern medicine with fewer harmful side effects. Certain traditional medical practices are known only within a restricted region and are disappearing fast. It is important, therefore, to document local practices and to ensure that such knowledge is captured and disseminated.

Back in Canada, friends, relatives, and a school in Red Deer provided the initial funds. The school used the project for its "International Development Week." The NGO Change for Children in Edmonton presented the proposal to the Alberta Agency for International Development, which matched the initial funds. The following year the Canadian International Development Agency doubled that amount, thus returning 4:1 on the initial funds.

In August of 1990 I returned to Peru just as this country was experiencing its worst economic disaster in living memory. Inflation skyrocketed. Prices for virtually every commodity increased between 400 and 3000 percent over-night. This "shock," as the Peruvians called it, paralyzed the country for some time and made survival even more difficult for a large proportion of the population which was already living under desperate conditions. An extensive drought that lasted for several months added to the misery, as it resulted in bad harvests and caused mountain lakes to dry up.

During such dreadful times I would have felt uncomfortable if the sole reason for my presence had been my study of ancient rituals of Chillihuani, while the people themselves desperately tried to survive. It was gratifying, however, to be able to assist the villagers in fulfilling their greatest wish, to build a small health clinic in their mountain wilderness.

It was amazing to see how the herders of Chillihuani, who had until then never received outside assistance, organized themselves to complete the clinic. They called a general meeting in the central plaza. At least one adult member of each family attended, regardless of the distances (up to fifteen kilometers) to be overcome. It was decided that building materials were to be purchased in cooperation with members of the municipal council of the district capital of Cusipata who are more experienced in these matters. Each day about one hundred people went to Cusipata in the valley to carry building materials and equipment some sixteen kilometers up the slopes of the Andes. The Mother's Club of Chillihuani was first to volunteer for this backbreaking activity, carrying some materials and loading others onto their horses and donkeys. Two carpenters were hired from the valley to do the type of work which the villagers were not used to in building their own homes. All able-bodied villagers joined in communal labor in the construction of the health station.

Since the population did not have extensive connections outside the village, I participated in organizing courses in first aid, family planning, preventative medicine, local diseases, and the use of the new equipment. A doctor from Cusco and nurses from the province agreed to teach courses in various subject areas and to hold workshops in the valley for people from surrounding villages. Health promoters from different villages set up a schedule to exchange knowledge among themselves and to educate the population at large. My cooperation was also necessary to acquire medical instruments and equipment that could not be obtained in Cusco, the capital of the department, and had to be brought from Lima and from abroad. The International Red Cross of Stuttgart/Germany provided a large donation of instruments, medication, and supplies.

How Can Anthropologists Assist in Projects?

Since different circumstances prevail in every village, precise guidelines cannot be given regarding the procedures to be taken in assisting a village with a project. Several general principles, however, apply to most situations.

The input that is required depends on the type of project for which the villagers seek assistance and on the villagers' level of expertise in dealing with outside agencies. In some of the villages where I have worked, the people have written a project proposal on their own after a dialogue during which we established possibilities of improvement and funding. Others required some assistance in putting their ideas on paper in such a way that an NGO could understand the social, economic, and ecological conditions; the constraints of the community; and its precise needs. The proposal must include a budget and a letter written by those villagers who are primarily responsible for a project (teachers in a school project; nurses, doctors, or health promoters in a health project), and it must be signed by as many villagers as possible. The proposal should contain photos and perhaps maps of features such as the present state of a facility to be improved. Translation of the documents may be necessary depending on the NGO to be approached. The anthropologist must include a description of his/her association with the village and a description of circumstances relevant to the project.

The anthropologist should ascertain that the proposal meets several essential criteria:

1. The village at large should benefit from the project, not only certain people or groups within the village. In fact, benefits should be fairly evenly distributed among all villagers; unequal distribution causes problems within a society.

2. Appropriate technology should be used in order to avoid dependency of the villagers on outside sources after the project has been implemented. Improving or building on existing technology is most essential in achieving this goal.

3. The project should be sustainable from both a human and an environmental point of view. The villagers must be in control of the project: it must improve their way of life without polluting the environment or jeopardizing its use for future generations.

Once the proposal is complete, the next step is to obtain funding. There are many NGOs such as service clubs, the Red Cross, Save the Children, and church organizations in every city and in many towns. The NGOs I have contacted in North America and Europe were very happy to cooperate on projects that arise directly from the initiative of local communities. A proposal with signatures or thumb prints not only of the village leaders, but of the villagers at large, gives the project the credibility that is necessary to convince contributors that it satisfies the overall needs and wishes of the community. Following the implementation of a project, the final report for the sponsoring NGO and other participants should be written by the villagers and the anthropologist.

The cooperation of an anthropologist can be vital where villagers initiate a project that requires expertise or materials from outside the village, and severe economic constraints often require that some equipment and material be brought from abroad. Long-term research normally brings anthropologists in contact with a variety of regional, national, and international organizations. Villagers usually do not have these contacts. Furthermore, the anthropologist's association with the project and his or her first hand knowledge of the villagers adds to the projects' credibility for potential sponsoring organizations.

When an anthropologist starts to combine anthropological research and development assistance, considerable time may be required in project coordination, finding an appropriate NGO, raising funds, requesting airlines to transport materials in emergency situations, etc. With experience, this becomes much less time consuming. In the above projects, family members, friends, students, and even professionals such as physicians cooperated on a voluntary basis and were ready to take over some of the organization of future projects, while the anthropologist, who has the closest links with the villagers, remained the facilitator. These kinds of projects tend to be exciting and challenging for everyone involved. The anthropologist benefits from a more dynamic relationship with the people and by actually being able to view village activities from inside, as well as being given a chance to reciprocate for the opportunities for research provided by that society.

Self-help at the grass-roots level assumes increasing importance with the unfortunate deterioration of economies in developing countries. For this reason, anthropologists who know the indigenous societies better than other outsiders should take the lead in assisting local development efforts. Material assistance is important, but the villagers appreciate just as much the moral support they receive. In the above projects they were touched by the fact that people who live so far away think about their little Andean villages and assist them in their desperate efforts to survive. One of village elders of Chillihuani stated: "For us, this international cooperation is like an injection with a fresh spirit, a spirit of love, cooperation, and solidarity. We all must learn to cooperate this way. Thank you so much for being with us."

[The initial field work on which this report is based was supported by the Wenner-Gren Foundation for Anthropological Research, the GTZ-German Agency for Technical Cooperation, and the Fund for Support of International Development Activities at the University of Alberta Canada.]

Questions:

1. What role did Bolin play in the two school projects she participated in?

2. Cite three essential criteria that any development project should meet.

3. How does the applied anthropologist benefit from involvement in development projects?

The answer section begins on page 243.

Not only do development anthropologists conduct research that can be used to design overseas development projects, they are also asked to evaluate the effectiveness of such programs. Since anthropologists are skilled at developing rapport quickly with people from culturally different backgrounds, they are in a particularly good position to observe and question people about the effectiveness and consequences of certain development efforts. In this selection, anthropologist Edward Green describes his evaluation of a multidimensional training program for women participating in self-help groups in Swaziland.

Women's Groups and Income Generation in Swaziland

By Edward C. Green

Women's self-help groups known as *zenzele* ("do-it-yourself") have existed in Swaziland since the 1950s, but until recently they received little recognition or support. In 1984 a survey of local-level development organizations showed that zenzele were among the most ubiquitous and self-sufficient local organizations in Swaziland. The survey further discovered a positive statistical correlation between the existence of zenzele groups and the number of other development organizations in the local community.

As a result of these preliminary findings, the United States Agency for International Development (USAID) decided to provide zenzele leaders with training in several areas of development. This was done through an experimental component of the Swaziland Manpower Development Project (SWAMDP) (1985-90) which the author helped design in 1984. Implementation of the project component was the responsibility of anthropologist Robert Hitchcock of the University of Nebraska for the first two years. The author was asked to evaluate the impact of development training on zenzele groups in late 1990.

Zenzele Groups

There are more than two hundred zenzele groups in Swaziland, concerned with a variety of development-related activities. These activities can be grouped under traditional home economics concerns (child care, cooking, nutrition, homestead, sanitation, personal hygiene, sewing, gardening, etc.); general development-related activities (adult literacy, construction of water storage tanks, etc.); and income generation and small business enterprise (produce marketing, handicraft manufacture and sale, school uniform sale and production, pig raising, beekeeping, fish farming, brickmaking, etc.). There has been marked development of income-generating activity in recent years, much of it attributable to SWAMDP.

Zenzele groups average twenty to thirty members, and they meet on a regular basis such as once a week or twice monthly. Members tend to be older women, in their forties and fifties. Widows and others who cannot rely on husbands to provide income, or sufficient income, appear to be attracted to zenzele.

Zenzele organizations are not the only type of rural women's groups concerned with development, but they are the most numerous and widespread, and they have served for years as a link between rural women and the branch of government with the largest cadre of female extension workers, namely the Home Economics (HE) Unit of the Ministry of Agriculture and Cooperatives.

Training of Women Leaders

The Home Economics Unit provided some adult education prior to SWAMDP. Training methods appear to have been essentially didactic, "top-down," and nonparticipatory, and training content focused on traditional areas of home economics such as child care, nutrition, hygiene, sanitation, and cooking. There was little emphasis on imparting income-generating or small business skills.

In the first two years of SWAMDP, Home Economics provided training to leaders of zenzele groups in "organizational skills." This meant how

Reprinted by permission of PRACTICING ANTHROPOLOGY 14(4), Fall, 1992, pp. 19-23.

to form and administer a zenzele group, how to maintain records, and how to raise funds for the group. Another focus was on imparting certain technical skills such as sisal basket making, block making, water jar making, and beekeeping. Here too a didactic, lecture mode of training predominated.

One year into the project (1986), Hitchock's needs assessment documented zenzele women's clear interest in learning more about income generation and small business. The women also expressed preference for learning-by-doing and practical demonstrations rather than formal lectures. Zenzele interest in income generation happened to coincide with a growing interest among donors (the International Labor Organization, the World Bank, and USAID) in assisting the informal or nonformal economic sector.

The contractor implementing the project for USAID (Transcentury Corporation) enlisted the help of African subcontractor, Kenya-based Tototo Home Industries, to develop a business skills training strategy culturally suited to the needs of non- or semiliterate rural Swazi women. Kenyan trainers from Tototo subsequently came to Swaziland, worked out a training plan with HE staff, and conducted the first of a series of training-of-trainers workshops in late 1987. Tototo's approach was to teach "leadership" skills first in order to develop women's self-confidence, group self-reliance, and sense of responsibility. The training content consisted essentially of applied behavioral science, including group dynamics, human relations, and group and personality psychology, as well as practical procedures such as the selection of group leaders who exhibit effective leadership traits. The teaching method was highly participatory, nonformal, and experiential. Zenzele women responded enthusiastically to this method.

After week-long workshops in leadership skills for zenzele group leaders, a pair of two-week workshops known as Business Skills I and II were offered over a period of some three years. It may be useful to think of leadership training and then business skills training as proceeding in waves that swept over Swaziland reaching the most accessible groups first and the least accessible last, if at all. This approach to teaching basic business skills grew out of Tototo's experience in Kenya, and the Home Economics staff in Swaziland, once exposed, quickly came to endorse it.

An important ingredient in the acceptance and eventual success of this approach in Swaziland is the extent to which it was developed and modified by Africans for Africans. In addition to in-country training of Home Economics staff by Kenyan Tototo trainers, a core group of HE staff received more advanced training at Toto headquarters in Mombassa, Kenya. While there, HE trainers were exposed to women's savings clubs that had started with help from Tototo. Upon returning to Swaziland, the HE trainers brought with them training techniques and modules developed in Kenya—including those related to saving clubs—which they redesigned for use in Swaziland.

Impact of Project-Sponsored Training

Following USAID's suggestion, the present evaluation focused more on the period since the project's midterm evaluation (1987) than prior to it; therefore, much of the evaluation is concerned with the Tototo and Tototo-style training that began in late 1987. Evaluation of the project-supported training impact is based on: 1) a survey of 120 zenzele women; 2) group interviews with thirteen zenzele groups from various regions and ecological zones of Swaziland; and 3) in-depth interviews with HE extension workers as well as with other government and donor group representatives. The second method produced by far the most useful findings. Survey findings were useful primarily in quantifying patterns that emerged in group interviews.

To begin with survey findings, 92 percent of respondents claimed they learned something of importance in a project-sponsored workshop; 5 percent said they did not, and 3 percent were not sure. Most of those responding negatively were in fact attending their first HE workshop. When asked what of importance was learned, there was some range and variation of response, as seen in Table 1. It is significant that a plurality of women mentioned traditional home economics subjects such as child care, nutrition, sanitation and the like. This shows that in spite of zenzele women's oft-repeated need to earn income, not to mention HE's emphasis on income generation in its training since 1987, rural women still found topics related to health and basic quality of life both interesting and useful.

In another survey question we asked women if they had become involved in any activity or project as a result of anything learned in a workshop. Fully 95 percent reported they had, and nearly all of the remaining 5 percent happened to be at their first workshop when interviewed. We then asked the 95 percent what activity they had become involved in. Some comparative data are available from a 1987 survey by Hitchcock (Table 2).

Zenzele women have involved themselves in a wide range of activities, and in all cases where comparable data exist, there has been an increase in activity since 1987. It is impossible to factor out the influence of other organizations that train or motivate rural women, except in areas where it is known that HE is the only trainer. The evidence is compelling, however, because the women were asked specifically what activity they had become involved in as a result of something learned in a Home Economics work shop. Almost all reported being engaged in income-generating activities. The "African courtesy response" (telling interviewers what they presumably want to hear) could not account for the range of activities specified nor could it account for the distribution of responses. We can conclude that the project has had an impact in training rural women to become involved in the very activities they themselves identified as desirable at project start-up, namely income generation.

We also asked respondents if workshops could be improved. Every respondent said yes. When asked how, 83 percent suggested more hands-on experience, learning-by-doing, or role playing: 13 percent asked for more workshops or longer workshops. These findings probably should not be interpreted as criticism of training as HE is carrying out now, but rather as an endorsement of participatory training and an expression of heightened "demand" for more training of this sort.

More important findings concerning the impact of the training emerged from the qualitative research methods.

1. *Leadership Training.* Tototo's experience elsewhere in Africa has been that such training must precede any form of business training because rural African women usually lack the self-confidence and, perhaps, the assertiveness to attempt new income-generating and business ventures. Although it is hard to measure, most women who participated in the training felt certain they had gained self-confidence, and this enhanced self-confidence was described as having had significant consequences in their lives generally. They claimed that leadership training: 1) provided them a measure of liberation from traditional constraints facing women; 2) provided them enough self-confidence to attempt

business ventures; 3) had other unforeseen beneficial effects on their lives, such as helping them solve family and community problems; and 4) encouraged them to question information rather than passively accept it.

Such comments suggest that the basics of applied psychology, sociology, and anthropology (usually regarded as advanced academic subjects in Africa) seem to be as teachable and immediately useful and applicable in the lives of semiliterate rural African women as gardening, sewing, or handicrafts. As noted below, women are even willing to pay for training in these subjects.

2. *Small Business and Income Generation.* Group interviews revealed considerable variation in the development of income-generating enterprises. Some such enterprises were small-scale while in other cases zenzele groups had built a 100,000 emalangeni (E) roadside market or had raised nearly E 6,000 toward the down payment for a gas station franchise. (E 1 was approximately $0.35 at time of interviewing.)

One group in Lubombo was typical of the success zenzele women have achieved under SWAMDP. Like many zenzele groups, its first savings went to build what is locally called a worked, in this case along a road some distance from members' homesteads. Women had to commute daily to reach their worked, but they recognized the advantage of the road site for earning income. At the time of the interview the worked had several income-generating functions. Part of it was rented out as a preschool, part as an adult literacy class, and part as a sewing classroom. The worked also served as a wholesale market for handicrafts the women made themselves. Part of the worked was being developed as a restaurant for carry-out snacks.

Women were sufficiently motivated to try a second or third enterprise if the first failed. One zenzele group in Shiselweni was heard singing a song which reminds them of the full range of income-generating possibilities. One phrase went, "if fish farming fails, beekeeping might work." The song was said to combat discouragement.

However uneven the impact of training, it seems evident that an important process had begun—or had been significantly accelerated—under the project: rural women were gaining the requisite self-confidence and business skills to generate income on a scale greater than had been possible before.

3. *Multiplier Effect.* There was also evidence of a multiplier effect in certain areas, notably Shiselweni. In this region, trained zenzele groups

were training other groups unexposed to project workshops, and the recipient groups were paying all associated costs for transportation, accommodation, and subsistence. The zenzele groups themselves were initiating requests for training, and the local HE extension worker was playing an increasingly inactive, supervisory role. This clearly demonstrates the value rural women placed on leadership training. There appears to be a good chance of self-sustained training of trainers continuing well after the end of project support.

4. Savings Clubs. As a result of Home Economics staff training in Kenya savings clubs (SCs) were started on a pilot basis, one in each of Swaziland's four regions. All were in early stages of development at the time of field work.

There are precedents in Swazi culture. Women sometimes pool their savings in a revolving fund and then use this to pay for funerals, weddings, and birthdays. However, individual members of revolving funds are not able to take out personal loans or indeed even handle the money for their direct benefit. Nor does there seem to be a careful accounting of how much money each woman puts in.

Savings clubs, on the other hand, deposit members' joining fees (E 5 to E 20) and monthly subscription fees (E 2 to E 8 monthly) in a business account at a bank, and the account can be used as collateral for a group loan. Individuals or groups of club members can also take out loans for start-up funds or other business-related needs. The maximum amount of a loan is equivalent to the amount the individual or group has contributed up to that point. A treasurer keeps account of individual contributions. If too many women or groups want to withdraw funds at the same time, the SC committee prioritizes the need, and those of lesser priority must wait until earlier borrowers have actually repaid the loans. Note the mechanism of peer pressure on women to repay their loans so that others in their group may have their turns.

At least in the early stage of SC development, loans were being used for personal reasons such as special purchases or emergencies—not for business investment. One woman told us her savings club is "like the National Provident Fund" in that it provides security in times of need, such as when a woman and her family need money for school fees, funeral expenses, or health care. Savings club members said they were more inclined to put money in an SC account than a revolving fund precisely because they are able to

withdraw it for personal emergencies. Members' monthly contributions to SCs seem to be money that individual women had trouble saving in the past. It is money, as more than one woman put it, that their husbands might have used for buying beer.

According to group discussions, rural women had little previous experience with banks. In the past they often hid around their homesteads any money they had earned. Note that Swazi law and custom prevent individual women from being able to take out bank loans without the written consent of their husbands. However, they can open a business account as a zenzele group.

The pilot SCs showed that it is possible for rural women to save considerable amounts in short periods of time. For example, the savings club at Malindza (Lubombo region) had saved E 2,715 ($1,068) in their first three months. There are forty-six members of this SC, meaning that each member contributed an average of E 59.02 in three months, considerably more than the E 100 per year that women are required to contribute as a minimal subscription.

How are "unemployed" rural women able to save such amounts? According to interviews with this SC as well as other zenzele and SC groups, members' husbands rarely contribute their own earnings to women's activities. Instead women make contributions from money they themselves earn. In one area, however, men came to recognize the value of their wives belonging to zenzele, so they allocated part of their cotton fields to their wives from which the women could earn their own money. These women earned additional money making and selling bricks, making maize storage jars, and organizing food bazaars in which they sold their baked goods. Similar accounts were given by other SC groups. It would seem that women find ways to earn money when there are opportunities to invest it in savings clubs or other enterprises controlled by women that directly benefit women.

General Discussion

It is useful to look at SWAMDP in the broader context of women's issues and development. We might well ask, are these efforts really helping women? What do all these elements such as training in leadership, handicrafts, and business skills really add up to?

There is a critical feminist development literature that suggests that a concentration on handicrafts only reinforces Third World women's economic and political marginality. Some studies have concluded that to overcome such marginality it is important to transmit management skills as well as technical skills, so that women are in a position to initiate other activities. Apparently SWAMDP. and Tototo shared this view because management and other human resource skills were taught directly to zenzele groups, and this indeed had the effect of stimulating other valued activities such as savings clubs and day-care centers.

There is also a development literature critical of assisting the informal sector at all. Such assistance is dismissed by critics as romantic, escapist, "evangelistic," and "a panacea for unemployment and poverty." The argument is that donors would do better to address the structural inequities inherent in capitalist economies than to throw a few crumbs of encouragement to handicraft producers or street vendors.

While raising a number of interesting considerations, these viewpoints fail to recognize the importance of small-scale income generation projects in the gradual emancipation of the rural African woman from traditional constraints including total economic dependence on husbands. Part-time handicraft making or commercial vegetable gardening may be all a married woman in a traditional patriarchal, virilocal society can do, given her dependence on her husband and his family and her responsibilities as wife and mother. But in the process, the husband, the mother-in-law, traditional leaders, and others in rural society seem to become used to the woman earning a bit of income outside the homestead,

and controlling that income. Our qualitative findings suggest that husbands and in-laws come to realize that money earned by the wife benefits the whole family: this may outweigh misgivings they may have over the wife's new activities and her growing emancipation from traditional controls. Our findings also show that women are ready to expand their small-scale, home-based income-generating activities to what might be termed "full business enterprises" when given an opportunity, including "formal sector" businesses outside the home that require considerable time and cash investments.

We made no attempt to assess project impact on the political marginality of Swazi women. There should be follow-up research of project-assisted women after several more years of business enterprise development, and this should shed light on the relationship between the growth of independent economic power and political status. In the last generation, formal education has proven a vehicle for Swazi women to move more into the political mainstream. There are now women in parliament, the cabinet, and key civil service positions. I suspect that the growing economic importance of women in the private sector will likewise result in more political power for women. Again, SWAMDP-assisted women entrepreneurs need to be tracked over the next few years to confirm our preliminary findings that they can and do "initiate other activities" once the process of economic empowerment has begun, even if some remain poorly paid handicraft makers.

Table 1
Most Useful Things Learned in Workshop
(Multiple responses recorded)

Topics	Frequency	Percent
Child care, hygiene, sanitation, traditional home economics topics	49	35
Working together, group dynamics, leadership	44	31
Cooking	19	13
Business and marketing	7	5
Handicrafts	5	4
Sewing, knitting	5	4
Jam making	5	4
Miscellaneous	8	6
Total	142	100(rounded)

Table 2
Activities Directly Resulting from Training
(Multiple Responses Recorded)

Activity	Frequency	Percent	1987 Comparison
Sewing/knitting	53	26	16
Handicrafts	50	25	18
Commercial gardening	24	12	5*
Poultry	18	9	7
Beekeeping	18	9	.001
Cooking	14	7	(NA)
Water tank building	13	6	(NA)
Brickmaking	6	3	.06
Candle making	3	1	(NA)
Carpentry	2	1	(NA)
Miscellaneous	2	0	(NA)
Total	203	100	

* The comparable 1987 survey category under income-generating activity was "vegetables." Rural Swazi women tend to think of commercial gardening and vegetable gardening as distinct from fruit tree cultivation or such larger-scale commercial agricultural activities as cotton farming.

Questions:

1. Name the three general types of development activities in which zenzele groups in Swaziland were involved.

2. Why were the Swazi women taught leadership skills?

3. What activities did the Swazi women become involved in as a direct result of the training?

4. What were the four major findings of Green's evaluation research project?

The answer section begins on page 243.

36

The cutting of trees as a source of firewood is one of a number of human activities contributing to the deforestation of many parts of the world. It has been estimated that between forty and sixty percent of all forests have been destroyed in Southeast Asia during the 20th century. Not only is this uncontrolled use of trees depleting a valuable resource, but it causes other problems as well including soil erosion, the loss of many plant and animal species, and potential food shortages. Anthropologist Ben Wallace uses traditional anthropological field methods to observe the cooking and wood-using behavior in four Philippine villages to measure the dimensions of the problem. Only when governments and development agencies have such quantitative data will they be in a position to develop rational programs of agriforestry.

How Many Trees Does It Take to Cook a Pot of Rice?: Fuelwood and Tree Consumption in Four Philippine Communities

By Ben J. Wallace

It is more than environmental or academic rhetoric to note that the planet Earth loses millions of hectares of critically valuable forest each year. Worldwide, around eleven million hectares of forest are being cut down yearly but less than ten percent are returned to forest vegetation (Withington *et al.* 1988). Estimates differ, but in Southeast Asia, somewhere between 40% and 60% of tropical forest have been depleted and replaced with grass over the past 100 years. The rain forests of Southeast Asia have dropped from 250 million hectares in 1900 to less than 60 million hectares in 1989 (Scott 1989). In the Philippines alone, around 200,000 hectares of land are being deforested annually. In Indonesia over 600,000 hectares of forest are being cut each year (Poffenberger 1990). According to United Nations reports, more than half of the population of the Third World will be acutely short of fuelwood, or without fuelwood, by the turn of the century (TFAP 1988). By the year 2000, unless this pattern of deforestation is checked, indigenous people will be displaced and their cultures will disappear, ten to twenty percent of the Earth's plant and animal life may disappear, watersheds will be destroyed leading to the loss of agricultural land and food shortages, and millions of people will lose the economic opportunities derived from timber. In addition, trees protect crops from wind damage and prevent soil erosion; they redistribute nutrients and help protect ground-water stores; they serve as animal fodder; they provide edible leaves, pods, fruits, nuts, honey, insects, and other products for humans; they provide raw materials for constructing houses, boats, ox carts, and other tools; and finally, trees and tree products provide income-generating activities for many people of the world (see FAO 1986).

In the Philippines and other developing nations, the cutting of trees for fuelwood is one of the many human activities contributing to deforestation. In cutting trees for fuelwood, the rural people in these nations are not purposely and maliciously destroying their forests— alternative sources of fuel are generally not available or are too expensive. In an attempt to better understand the processes of deforestation and to initiate a strategy by which stressed ecosystems can be returned to a biodiversity balance, a pioneering cooperative five-year agroforestry research and development project (popularly know in the Philippines as Good Roots—*Ugat ng buhay*) between the academic community (Institute for the Study of Earth and Man at Southern Methodist University), industry (Caltex Philippines Inc.) and government (Philippines Department of Environment and Natural Resources) has begun in the northern Philippines (Wallace 1994). One of the research,

Reprinted by permission of HUMAN ORGANIZATION 54(2), 1995, pp. 182-86.

rather than applied, goals of the Good Roots project is to measure the extent to which human behavior and society, through fuelwood cutting, charcoal making, swidden cultivation, illegal logging and population expansion, contribute to deforestation in the research area. This article, which examines fuelwood use patterns in four Philippine communities, is an initial step in understand the broader issue of deforestation in the region.[1] The non-fuelwood contributors to deforestation will be examined elsewhere. Because rice cooking accounts for a little more than 50% of fuelwood consumption in the study villages, the guiding question stimulating an analysis of the relationships between fuelwood consumption and the number of trees potentially lost to the environment is: How many trees does it take to cook a pot of rice?

The Good Roots Communities

The agroforestry activities of the Good Root project are conducted in and around four villages located along the western foothills of the Cordillera Central in the northern most municipality in the Philippine province of Ilocos Norte. San Isidro, Dampig, Subec (with populations of 641, 768, and 1164, respectively) are typical lowland Ilocano communities. The fourth village, Saliksik, has a population of 165 people, all of whom are members of the ethnic minority Apayao-Esneg, known locally as Yapayao. In 1992, there were 224 households in Subec, 134 households in Dampig, 116 households in San Isidro, and 28 households in Saliksik. The people of these communities were selected for study and development because their agricultural technologies and environmental zones are representative of northern Luzon. The agricultural technology of San Isidro is predominantly one of irrigated paddy rice cultivation. Dampig is mainly a dry field farming community. The people of Subec have a farming technology of both irrigated paddy rice and dry field cultivation. The people of Saliksik exclusively practice slash-and-burn (kaingin) cultivation. Some minor kaingin activity can also be found in all three of the Ilocano communities. Even though these four villages are situated only four to eight kilometers from the South China Sea, the villagers perceive of themselves as agriculturists, the Ilocano identifying with the lowlands and the Yapayao identifying with the mountains.

Species Preference and Consumption

The residents of the four study villages choose different species of trees for fuelwood depending on their perception of the caloric value of the species, species availability, and size of tree. Species used for fuelwood in the four communities are relatively small with the main trunk generally ranging in diameter from 4.5 cm. to 11 cm., with branches ranging from 1.5 cm. to 4.5 cm. For example, a typical ipil-ipil (Leucaena leucocephala, growing to a height of around fourteen meters) has a main trunk diameter of 5.5 cm. and branches ranging from 1.2 to 3 cm.

Based on a complete household survey, informants in the four villages report that in matters of general fuelwood preference, they prefer ipil-ipil, binunga (Macaranga tanarius, growing to a height of eight meters), lagundi (Vitex negundo, growing to a height of about four meters), camachile (Pitchecellobium dulce, growing to a height of ten meters), kakawate (Gliricidian sepium, growing to a height of five meters), and suit (Fraximus griffithii, growing to a height of five meters). Specifically, in Subec and Dampig the preference is first for ipil-ipil and secondly for binunga. In San Isridro, the first preference is camachile and the second preference is lagundi. The people of Saliksik prefer first lagundi and second suit. According to the residents of Subec and Dampig, ipil-ipil is perferred because of its relatively high caloric value. Binunga, even with a lower caloric value than ipil-ipil, is second choice because it is abundant in the area. In addition, farmers say that because it is light-weight, a larger bundle can be carried on a single trip. The people in San Isidro say they prefer camachile and lagundi because of its high caloric value. Finally, lagundi and suit are preferred in Saliksik because of their abundance and accessibility.

By actual measurement of household fuelwood stockpiles, the people of subec use binunga, kakawate, suit, and ipil-ipil as their main tree-based fuelwood over a period of a year. The residents of Subec prefer ipil-ipil and binunga. Because the range of variation among the four major species used, however, is only fourteen trees per household per year, the difference between preference and actual use is insignificant. The consumption pattern of fuelwood trees in Dampig, in order of importance, is ipil-ipil, lagundi, binunga, and bignai (Antidesma bunius, growing to height of about six meters). The people of Dampig prefer ipil-ipil and binunga. They are able to secure sufficient *ipil-ipil* because of a nearby communal tree farm which is primarily planted to *ipil-ipil*. The residents say their second choice is *binunga* and even though it is relatively abundant in the area, they actually consume more *lagundi* than *binunga*. Since the difference between the number of *lagundi* and *binunga* consumed is only seven trees per household per year (50 as opposed to 43), there is not a significant difference between preference and actual use. In matters of use, the people of San Isidro consume, in order of importance, *camachile, lagundi, ipil-ipil,* and *kakawate*. Species preference and species used in San Isidro are the same; 200 *camachile* per household per year and 86 *lagundi* per household per year. In Saliksik, the residents consume, in order of importance, *lagundi, suit,* and *binunga*. Again, species preference and species use are the same. The first two preferences are *lagundi* and *suit* and this reflects actual consumption.

In the four villages under consideration here, there is no significant difference between species preference for fuelwood and the actual fuelwood species consumed. In general, villagers prefer species with a relatively high caloric value, but in reality, are dependent upon species that are readily accessible to them. A few of the villagers in Dampig and Subec have access to a communal tree farm but most fuelwood comes from primary forest areas, secondary forest areas, and abandoned *kaingins*, all located within one to two hours walking from the village. Distance, in time, has not yet become a significant factor affecting the cutting and/or gathering of fuelwood as is sometimes the case (see Subhadhira *et al.* 1987). In general, men cut trees for fuelwood and either men, women or older children carry it back to the village. While there is some variation in fuelwood consumption because of seasonal temperatures and special celebrations, on average, the variation is not significant.

As part of a Farming Systems Research and Development approach (CGIAR 1978, De Walt 1985, Jones and Wallace 1986, Shaner *et al.* 1982, Sukmana *et al.* 1989, Wallace 1989) and during a complete household survey of the four communities and Rapid Rural Appraisal (see F/FRED n.d., Kohn Kaen University 1987) early in the research, farmers were asked "How many sticks of fuelwood are used daily?" to cook rice, other foods, for animal food and for heating. These responses were then verified by the research team through random measurements, by diameter and length, of fuelwood sticks used over a period of a year. The research team also went to a sample of the households and measured the different species of fuelwood sticks by length and by diameter in the household fuelwood stockpile. Care was taken to measure only fuelwood. These measurements, representing different species of sticks used for fuelwood, were converted into volume in cubic meters. The percentage of the volume of each species in a woodpile was determined by dividing it by the total volume of the woodpile. This percentage was then multiplied by the average daily fuelwood consumption in the household to determine the volume of species being consumed each day. An average, for all species of fuelwood consumed by households per day in the four villages is, as follows: Subec, 0.022 cubic meters; Dampig, 0.030 cubic meters; San Isidro, 0.020 cubic meters; and Saliksik, 0.019 cubic meters.

The village of Subec consumes 1801 cubic meters of fuelwood per year; in Dampig, 1467 cubic meters per year; in San Isidro, 848 cubic meters per year; and in Saliksik, 194 cubic meters of fuelwood per year. The variance here is primarily a function of population size: in a per capita basis, Subec consumes 1.5 cubic meters of fuelwood each year; In Dampic, 1.9 cubic meters; In San Isidro, 1.3 cubic meters; and Saliksik, 1.2 cubic meters. Why individuals in Dampic consume more fuelwood each year than other villagers is unclear at this time.

Different species of trees vary in size and shape and in total cubic volume of material available for fuelwood use. To determine the actual volume of wood available for fuelwood use from a tree, the research team cut average size fuelwood tree species and measured the length and diameter of each cut piece. Sections of the trunk and branches were cut into fuelwood-length pieces. From these measurements, actual volume of wood available for fuelwood use by species was determined. For example, a small but commonly used, native *ipil-ipil* tree, when cut, provides only 0.014 cubic meters of fuelwood. This is because at two to three years, at about seven to eight meters tall, the main trunk is only four to seven centimeters in diameter and the branches are only one to three centimeters in diameter. At four to five years, a *suit* tree is ten meters tall but has a main trunk of only four to five centimeters in diameter and branches only two to three centimeters in diameter and provides only 0.009 cubic meters of fuelwood. All of the tree species used for fuelwood by the participants in the Good Roots project are relatively small. Large, hardwood trees such as those in the mahogany (e.g., *Swietenia macrophylla*) or teak (e.g., *Tectona grandis*) families are reserved for use in construction.

To determine the equivalency of the number of trees cut for use as fuelwood the research team converted the actual cubic meters of fuelwood consumed to the measured cubic meters of volume in the different tree species. In the case of the four villages considered here, Subec consumes as fuelwood the equivalent of 57.1 trees per year per capita; Dampig, 49.2; San Isidro, 60.0; and Saliksik, 105.7. The significant difference in number of trees consumed between the three Ilocano lowland communities and the Yapayao in the mountain village of Saliksik is primarily a function of the fact that trees are smaller, they are more readily available in Saliksik and there is a greater need for use of fuelwood because of a longer cold season.

Although each person in the Good Roots communities consumes on average 68 trees each year as fuelwood, it should be remembered that trees may be a renewable resource. Except for *binunga* and *suit*, the other important fuelwood trees in the areas have a sufficiently fast regeneration cycle that they may be recut every twelve months. *Suit* will re-grow and can be cut again after two years; *bununga* after four years. *Suit* and *binunga* constitute about 37% of the total trees cut for use as fuelwood. Or, 63% may be re-cut after one year and 37% may be re-cut in two to four years. Observations by both farmers and researchers of selected forest and fallow field areas over a period of a year suggest that approximately fifteen percent of all the trees cut for fuelwood will never re-grow, i.e. tree stocks are being slightly reduced yearly. While each of the Good Roots villages cuts down 68 trees per capita each year for fuelwood, the actual measurement of the extent to which fuelwood consumption contributes to deforestation in the area remains a part of the on-going research effort of the Good Roots project. FAO reported over a decade ago that acute fuelwood scarcities were being encountered in eighteen African countries, three Asian countries, and six Latin American countries (de Montalembert and Clement 1983). It is clear that fuelwood consumption is a contributing factor to deforestation in the Good Roots research area but until fuelwood use can be measured against other factors such as charcoal making, illegal logging, swidden cultivation, and population expansion, the extent of its impact will remain unknown. If, however, observations by researchers and farmers are correct that all but

fifteen percent of the fuelwood trees species in the area regenerate and can be cut again within one to four years, the loss to the environment is not as important as it might initially appear. Nonetheless, this constitutes a loss of about ten trees per person per year. This becomes a significant loss, if calculated to include the total population of Subec, Dampig, San Isidro and Saliksik or if projected to the total rural population of the Philippines.

To cook a pot of rice, usually twice a day, for five to seven persons requires, by actual measurement, with minor variation due to species, an average of 0.009 cubic meters of fuelwood. A fuelwood tree in the Good Roots communities provides an average of 0.049 cubic meters of wood for use in cooking. Consequently, each time a family cooks a pot of rice they burn around eighteen percent of a tree, depending on the species, or a little more than one tree is used every three days by each household to cook rice. Approximately 56% of the fuelwood is Subec, Dampig, San Isidro, and Saliksik is used for cooking rice and the remainder is used to cook other foods, in preparing food for animals, and to keep warm during the nights of the cold season. Since cooking rice is a major activity involving the consumption of fuelwood, the process is undoubtedly a contributor to the depletion of the natural resources in the area even if most of the trees regenerate and can be cut again in a few years.

Conclusion

At the rate of cutting thousands of trees per year for use as fuelwood, even if only fifteen percent of the trees fail to regenerate, it will only be a matter of a few years before the forest covered hills around the Good Roots project area, as well as around other villages in the Philippines and the rest of Southeast Asia, become even further denuded. The situation is rendered even more acute if the factors of over-population, logging, and agricultural and industrial expansion are considered. The results of this human intervention into nature is a predictable tragedy. Until alternative fuel sources become available and affordable, farmers in Subec, Dampig, San Isidro, and Saliksik, as well as farmers throughout Southeast Asia, will have no option but to go farther and farther into the forests for fuelwood. Although there is no single nor obvious answer to the complexities of deforestation, one partial solution is that promoted by the Good Roots project: farmers and people from science, industry, and government can pool their respective talents and resources to insure that, at least in the short term, trees can be grown and harvested as a renewable resource. Until alternative sources of fuel become available, each village family in areas like the northern Philippines will continue to burn another tree every three days to cook their twice-daily pot of rice.

Notes

[1] The aim here is to present an analysis of original data and no attempt is made to review the critiques and many activities of agroforestry. For a general review of agroforestry see FAO 1986 and Steppler and Nair 1987. Specifically for the Philippines see Fujisaka, Sajise and del Castillo 1986 and for Southeast Asia see Poffenberger 1990.

REFERENCES CITED

CGIAR. 1978 Farming Systems Research at the International Agricultural Research Centers. Consultative Group on International Agricultural Research. Washington, D.C.

de Montalembert, M.R. and J. Clement. 1983 Fuelwood Supplies in the Developing Countries. FAO Forestry Paper 42. Food and Agriculture Organization of the United Nations. Rome.

De Walt, B. R.. 1985 Anthropology, Sociology, and Farming Systems Research. Human Organization 44:106-114.

FAO . 1986 Tree Growing by Rural People. FAO Forestry Paper 64. Food and Agriculture Organization of the United Nations. Rome.

F/FRED. n.d. Handbook on Data Collection and Research Methods for the Regional Study of On Farm and Village Forest and Land Use Practices. Winrock: Bangkok.

Fujisaka. S., P. Sajise and R. del Castillo, eds.. 1986 Man, Agriculture and the Tropical Forest: Change and Development in the Philippine Uplands. Winrock International Institute for Agricultural Development. Bankok.

Jones J.R. and B.J. Wallace, eds.. 1986 Social Sciences and Farming Systems Research: Methodological Perspectives on Agricultural Development. Westview Press. Boulder and London.

Kohn Kaen University. 1987 Proceedings of the 1985 International Conference on Rapid Rural Appraisal. Rural Systems Research and Farming Systems Research Project. Thailand.

Poffenberger, M., ed.. 1990 Keepers of the Forest: Land Management Alternatives in Southeast Asia. Kumarian Press. West Hartford.

Scott, M.. 1988 The Disappearing Forests. Far Eastern Economic Review. Jan:32.

Shaner, W.W., P.F. Philipp, and W.R. Schmehl. 1982 Farming Systems Research and Development: Guidelines for Developing Countries. Westview Press. Boulder.

Steppler, H.A. and P.K.R. Nair, eds.. 1987 Agroforestry: A Decade of Development. International Council for Research in Agroforestry. Nairobi.

Subhadhira, S., et al. 1987 Fuelwood Situation and Farmer's Adjustment in Northeastern Thai Villages. Proceedings of the 1985 International Conference of Rapid Rural Appraisal. Kohn Kaen, Thailand:Kohn Kaen University.

Sukmana, S., P. Amir and D.M. Mulyadi, eds.. 1988 Development in Procedures for Farming Systems Research: Proceedings of an International Workshop, Bogor, Indonesia. Agency for Agricultural Research and Development. Jakarta.

TFAP. 1989 Tropical Forestry Action Plan. Summary of FAO, World Bank and UNDP report. Bangkok Post. Thailand.

Wallace, B.J.. 1990 Multipurpose Tree Species: A Perspective on On-Farm Research Priority and Design. In Development in Procedures for Farming Systems Research, Proceedings of an International Workshop, Bogor: 146-157. Agency for Agricultural Research and Development. Jakarta.

1994 Multipurpose Research and the Multipurpose Research Team: The Philippine Good Roots—Ugart ng Buhay—Project. Bulletin of the Culture and Agriculture Group No. 48, Winter, American Anthropological Association (Forthcoming).

Withington, D., K.G. MacDicken, C.B. Sastry, and N.R. Adams, eds.. 1989 Multipurpose Tree Species for Small-Farm Use. Winrock International Institute for Agricultural Development, USA and International Development Research Center of Canada.

Questions:

1. In addition to the loss of a precious natural resource, what other negative consequences are brought about by deforestation?

2. In addition to fuelwood cutting, what other human activities are threatening the existence of forests in Southeast Asia?

3. How many trees does it take to cook a pot of rice in the Philippines?

The answer section begins on page 243.

Development anthropologists have long been interested in the area of agricultural development, owing in large part to their experience in working closely with small scale farming communities. This interest often coincides with national interests of improving agricultural productivity, alleviating food shortages, and decreasing rural poverty. In this selection, anthropologist William Loker discusses his work in the area of pastures research in the Peruvian Amazon. Specifically, his research on cattle raising practices and their impact on the environment can have far reaching implications for the type of government assistance farmers receive in the future.

Pastures Research in the Peruvian Amazon

By William Loker

There are few places on earth hotter than an Amazonian pasture at midday. With the canopy of the rainforest trees removed, the sun beats down relentlessly on unbroken fields of grass and weedy shrubs, baking plants, animals, and anthropologist alike. The forest is cool by comparison. Yet in pastures is where I found myself repeatedly while studying the role of cattle in the agricultural production systems of colonist farmers in the Peruvian Amazon.

I got involved in the project as a postdoctoral fellow in the Rockefeller Foundation's Social Science Research Fellowship in Agriculture Program. This fellowship, which is open to members of all social science disciplines, places recent Ph.D.s in one of eighteen International Agricultural Research Centers scattered mostly throughout the developing world. Anthropologists have figured prominently in the postdoctoral program, which provides an unparalleled opportunity to get quickly on the inside of international agricultural research.

My experience with the Rockefeller program took me to the Centro International deAgricultura Tropical (CIAT), headquartered in Cali, Colombia. There I was attached to the Economics Unit of the Tropical Pastures Program (TPP)—a group of animal scientists, range scientists, plant breeders, pathologists, and entomologists charged with developing improved pastures for the acid, infertile soils of the tropics. Within Latin America, the principal regions of interest for the TPP were the Colombian and Venezuelan Llanos, the Brazilian cerrado, and Amazonia. The first two regions were relatively uncontroversial research sites; as they are characterized by savannah-type vegetation, improved pastures simply represent replacing one type of grassland with another. But, as nearly everyone knows, the issue of cattle production in the Amazon is highly controversial. There was considerable debate, within and outside CIAT, regarding the wisdom of pursuing pastures research in this region.

I was familiar with the broad outlines of the debate. Cattle raising was condemned for being ecologically destructive, economically unprofitable (without subsidies), and a weak generator of employment opportunities, and for favoring big capital and contributing to the frontier expansion that threatened the lives and lifeways of indigenous peoples. Proponents of cattle raising (when they could be found) claimed that pastures were an appropriate use of the acid, infertile soils of the region (of marginal productivity for annual crops) for small-to-medium farms as well as extensive ranches. Given the expanding frontier, pastures, they argue, are a rational use of land and can contribute to raising beef and milk production in countries with chronic deficits in these products. Working with the TPP would place my research squarely within this debate.

There is no doubt where anthropologists come down on this issue. Most can be found in the anti-cattle camp, reflecting our historical tradition of working with indigenous peoples and advocating their cultural survival. In this project, I found myself working with the "cowboys" instead of the "Indians."

I was to be "outposted" by the TPP to the Peruvian Amazon to work with a multidisciplinary team on pastures development.

Reprinted by permission of PRACTICING ANTHROPOLOGY 16(2) Spring, 1994, pp. 3-6.

My work would have two specific goals. One was to study the farming systems in the region and try to understand why cattle raising was such a popular activity even among small-to-medium farmers. (A small-to-medium farm in the Amazonian context is 25-300 hectares.) It had been noted by casual observers that many farmers plant pasture even when they have few or no animals. This seemed like decidedly "irrational" behavior.

The second specific goal was to conduct on-farm testing of promising improved forage species. These forage species, mostly legumes, had been identified through agronomic trials on experiment stations as candidates for widespread diffusion to farmers in the region. My work was to test these species under the more demanding and variable conditions obtaining on farms, assess farmer reaction to the new forage species, and measure the impact of the new forage species on animal performance. Carrying out these research objectives involved many of the traditional anthropological methods of participant observation, formal and informal interviews, and administration of questionnaires.

In addition to these two goals, I had another research agenda I wished to pursue. I was interested in measuring the ecological impact of farmer practices, specifically of cattle raising. One of the goals of the TPP was to enhance the sustainability of cattle-based farming systems in Amazonia. Program scientists claimed that forage legumes would enhance both the ecological sustainability of farming systems (by contributing nitrogen to the soil) and their productivity by improving animal nutrition. This was hard to prove because of the difficulty in operationalizing the concept of sustainability and measuring either negative or positive ecological impacts of a given farming system. An additional difficulty was that such research would necessarily be of a long-term nature; ecological processes associated with agricultural activities work themselves out over a period of years—much longer than the two-year period of the postdoc.

I decided to focus my attention on measures of environmental variables that would reflect the putative negative ecological impacts of cattle raising in the Amazon and that could be gathered with a cross-sectional methodology. Once identified, these same variables might also prove to be useful in measuring the sustainability of grass-legume pastures some time in the future.

Perhaps most important from an anthropological point of view would be to understand the implications of these findings for the welfare of small-to-medium farmers in the Amazon and the long-term economic viability of such operations in the region. There were hints in the ecological and agronomic literature regarding appropriate variables to measure the ecological impact of cattle raising in general and grazing in particular. What the biological and agronomic scientists failed to do was to trace out the logical implications of their data for farmer survival and the policy implications of their research. I felt my role as an anthropologist was to keep the focus on people—in this case on the farmers involved as well as the wider society which must bear the ecological and social consequences of activities carried out on farms.

These were the concerns that placed me in hot Amazonian pastures, often at midday. But first I had to find appropriate farmers willing to collaborate on a relatively long-term project (two or more years) testing a relatively risky technology. Selection of farmers involved a few other criteria as well: I wanted to work with small-to-medium producers, preferably resident on their farms, who had a certain minimum herd size (ten cattle), and who milked their animals on a daily or near-daily basis. This last criteria was one of the more difficult to fulfill. "Dual-purpose" (milk and beef) cattle production in the region was common. However, for many producers, the dairy part of their operation was secondary, sporadic, and more of a sideline than a principal activity. Fortunately, milk production was stimulated by the formation of a dairy marketing association by the local veterinary research institute IVITA (Instituto Veterinario de Investigacion in Trópico y Altura), associated with the Universidad Mayor de San Marcos. The services provided by the IVITA veterinarians included artificial insemination, technical advice, and (most importantly) daily milk pick-up and transport to the local urban market.

Finding committed dual-purpose producers was important because the project proposed to measure milk production as the primary means of assessing the impact of the technology on animal production, and by derivation on farmer incomes. Presumably, better nourished cows will produce more milk (raising the average milk production from around 2.5 liters/animal/day). Measuring milk production is decidedly easier than measuring changes in liveweight, reproductive performance, the nutritional status of calves, or any other indicator of animal production.

I, like the farmers, also often found myself in forests that would be cleared for pasture. In virtually every case this meant secondary regrowth (not "virgin forest") that had lain fallow for some time. The typical cropping sequence in this region involved the planting of annual crops (usually maize, rice, or manioc) followed by the planting of pasture. The planted pasture would be grazed for two to ten years, until productivity declined. Then the plot would be left fallow to allow the soil and vegetation to regenerate.

One of the key variables chosen to gauge the ecological impact of grazing was the rate of vegetation regeneration. The method was to collect land-use histories of plots that would be cleared for agriculture, determine the nature and extent of grazing, get an estimate of the length of fallow, measure biomass of the plot, and estimate the rate of biomass accumulation per year. If grazing significantly depressed the rate. of vegetation regeneration, this would constitute a clear negative ecological effect of grazing and one with profound implications for the viability of the overall farm enterprise.

The results indicated that indeed there was a significant difference in the rate of vegetation regeneration between grazed and ungrazed plots. Ungrazed plots accumulate biomass at a rate of about 10,400 kilograms/hectare/year, while grazed plots accumulate biomass at a rate of about 4,634 kilograms/hectare/year. Thus biomass accumulation in plots that have been grazed is about 44 percent that of ungrazed plots. To farmers, this means they must wait twice as long for a grazed plot to accumulate the same amount of biomass as an ungrazed plot. This can lead to a significant "crunch" in terms of land availability as the farmer rotates his fields through the crop-fallow cycle. When land is needed for planting of crops and pastures, it may not have regenerated sufficiently (as measured in accumulated biomass) to produce adequate yields (See William Loker, "The Human Ecology of Cattle Raising in the Peruvian Amazon: The View from the Farm," *Human Organization* 52,1 [1993]: 14-24).

The anthropological contribution was to document this situation of ecological instability and raise this issue before agricultural and biological researchers. Their reaction has been mixed. There is still considerable controversy over whether, in fact, grazing is necessarily harmful in the humid tropic context. Some researchers simply reject the results outright, criticizing the methodology employed. While not airtight, the results of my research do closely replicate those of a similar project in Paragominas in the Brazilian Amazon. (See Christopher Uhl, Robert Buschbacher, and E. Adilson Sarrrao, "Abandoned Pastures in Amazonia, I: Patterns of Plant Succession," *Ecology* 76 [1988]: 663-681.) Other agronomically oriented agricultural researchers blame the farmer for the trends noted. They insist that "rational management" would avoid the problems generated by "traditional" (read "rustic," "untutored," "peasant") management.

Those who do accept the validity of the results differ concerning the implications of the findings. To many pastures researchers, the conclusion that grazing induces a process of land degradation in the humid tropics through inhibiting biomass regeneration is very worrisome. The information could be interpreted to mean that grazing in this ecosystem should cease, and that, by extension, pastures research in the region should also be terminated. There are critics of cattle raising in the Amazon who would like to see the region declared a "cattle-free zone" and cattle-raising activity simply banned.

The "cattle-free" advocates fail to consider the role of cattle in the adaptive strategies of Amazonian farmers. Cattle fulfill multiple economic objectives for farmers in a frontier situation. For one, they serve as a "bank account" or insurance function. Farmers invest profits from other activities in cattle because they are both capital goods and productive assets; they retain their value in inflationary economies and can be cashed in at any time to meet family financial necessities. Cattle are a high-value commodity with a ready market year round, are nonperishable (on the hoof), and can walk to market when road linkages are weak (as in the rainy season). In addition, in contrast to the production of many other high-value commodities, cattle raising requires relatively little labor, another important asset among farmers who are often labor-constrained. (Since this is a frontier region with additional land available for cultivation, farms are large relative to the family labor supply and there are few landless laborers available for wage work.) Finally, cattle are valued for their dual-purpose production; economic output in the form of milk or cheese can provide a steady income stream, while the cattle retain their "stored value" as beef that can be sold to obtain a large sum of cash. Until critics can find alternative economic activities that fulfill many of these same roles in household economies based on diversified production of food crops and varied sources of income, cattle raising will continue to be a popular activity among Amazonian farmers.

Thus, even though cattle raising does not appear to be a sustainable activity compatible with ecological conditions in many portions of the Amazon Basin, a strong argument can be made that research on improved pastures for the Amazon region should go forward. One of the principal goals of such research should be to enhance the sustainability and productivity of planted pastures.

Unfortunately, the jury is still out regarding the improved pastures tested as part of this project. Preliminary evidence indicates that the improved pastures raise milk production slightly compared to the best local control (that is, the best widely used, local alternative to the improved technology). The increment of improved production is not as great as hoped, however, and it remains to be seen if farmers can be induced to adopt a technology based on a 7 to 15 percent increase in milk production. Nor is it clear whether improved pastures are more sustainable than the best local control. Preliminary data indicate that soil conditions under grass-legume pastures are stable, which is a good (though not the only) indicator of sustainability. But it is not clear whether improved pastures will persist longer than grass-only pastures, nor whether improved pastures will solve the problem of grazing-induced inhibition of biomass regeneration during the fallow period.

These questions can only be answered with long-term research. Such research is difficult for several reasons: (1) farmer fatigue—farmers get tired of working with researchers on problems whose solution does not yield immediate tangible benefits; (2) institutional fatigue—research organizations lose interest and patience in long-term experiments as the value of results appears to decline over time; and (3) economic and political instability—the Peruvian Amazon has undergone significant social and economic upheaval, and investigators often work in situations that expose them to considerable personal danger.

My role in the long-term research project was to get it started and turn it over to national researchers who would carry out the long-term monitoring. I initiated this research, in collaboration with national research institutions (IVITA and INIAA, the Instituto Nacional de Ivestigación Agraria Y Agroindustrial) in 1987, and I remained on the project full time in 1988. After turning it over to a Peruvian agronomist, my involvement continued on a part-time basis in 1989 and as a consultant periodically since then.

It has been difficult to keep the focus on farmers. There is a tendency on the part of agronomic researchers to intervene too actively in on-farm research, incorporating inputs and techniques not generally used by farmers and thus making research results less representative of actual on-farm conditions. It has also been difficult to maintain enthusiasm for long-term agro-ecological research, given the difficulties mentioned above. But long-term agro-ecological research that systematically includes people—as active agents in the transformation and manipulation of ecosystems—is necessary to answer many questions regarding agricultural sustainability in the Amazon and elsewhere. Anthropologists have a key role to play in issues of agricultural sustainability if they are willing to tackle the difficult methodological and intellectual issues involved, if they are willing to communicate their results to nonanthropologists, and if they have the staying power, institutionally and financially, for long-term research.

Questions:

1. What were the goals of Loker's research?

2. What did Loker find to be the effect of grazing on the regeneration of vegetation?

3. What were several of the multiple economic functions of cattle for farmers living in the Peruvian Amazon?

The answer section begins on page 243.

When we hear the term "economic development," we usually imagine the transfer of technology and expertise from the wealthy, industrialized nations to the LDCs (less developed countries). But, as anthropologists have often demonstrated, cultural diffusion is a two way process. As with the case of Europeans and the Native Americans they "discovered" in 1492, we can see that Native Americans have made a number of contributions to European cultures, including many food items, medicine, smoking tobacco, clothing items, and musical styles to name a few. It should come as no surprise, then, to learn that certain economic development strategies developed in the LDCs have relevance in the more industrialized world. In this article anthropologist Maurine Huang describes how "microenterprise loans," first developed by an economist in Bangladesh, are now being used to enable refugee populations in California to develop economic self sufficiency by starting their own small businesses.

Sacramento Learns from Bangladesh: A New Twist on Economic Development

By Maurine Huang

Church bulletins often carry inserts describing various development projects in Third World nations which church members can assist. Favored projects include cooperative ventures such as village-owned wells or farms in sub-Saharan Africa or craft co-ops for oppressed women in South Asia. By making generous contributions to special denominational offerings, church members, sitting in their pews in their most developed of countries, can help poor unfortunate individuals in some backward Third World country.

Public support for U.S. government aid is based on similar motives. We are the richest and most developed country in the world, we have an abundance, and it is our moral duty to share with those less fortunate. We assume the position of giver, providing hand-outs and education which may or many not be appropriate.

In both instances, material aid and technical assistance flow from *us* to *them*. Seldom is any thought given to the possibility of anything flowing in the other direction, with the occasional exception of such things as the crafts made by the South Asia women's Craft Co-op which the offering dollars have funded. The presumption is that there is very little which *we* can learn from *them*.

This is not always true. Anthropologists are familiar with the many nonmaterial ways in which lives of dispossessed Third World people are infinitely richer than those of middle-class Americans. In the area of economic development, also, there are lessons which can flow from the Third World to the United States, as I have discovered during the last three years.

I have resettled refugees in Sacramento, California, since 1990. Because two-thirds of my clients are from the former Soviet Union, I hired a Ukrainian man who interprets, provides case management for Russian-speaking cases, and gives me an insider perspective on starting life in a new country. Some three years ago, he announced to me, "People want to start businesses and they don't know how." He added with great emphasis, *"We have to help them."* That pronouncement was the start of the Microenterprise Assistance Program.

I was determined not to reinvent the wheel, and so I began by investigating the kinds of technical and financial assistance available to people such as my clients—people who have faulty English, few resources, no credit ratings, and little basic business literacy. I approached widely publicized resources such as the Sacramento office of the Small Business Administration (SBA), the Service Corps of Retired Executives (SCORE), and the Greater Sacramento Small Business Development Center. When I asked the Small Business Administration about loans for start-up businesses, I was informed

Reprinted by permission of PRACTICING ANTHROPOLOGY 18 (1), Winter, 1996, pp. 10-14.

that their version of a small loan was in the range of $100,000. Our clients were on welfare and had no credit history. The president of SCORE asked me with some disdain, "What does the retired CEO of Proctor and Gamble (referring to himself) have in common with *those people*?" It was obvious that SCORE and SBA programs would not be of much help.

While I was researching possible sources of technical and financial assistance, my interpreter was investigating Slavic community needs. He and I had many conversations about what kind of assistance would be best. We eventually decided to pursue a three-pronged approach: formal education in basic business literacy, individualized technical assistance, and a loan fund with underwriting criteria designed to meet our clients' unique circumstances.

My search for resources led eventually to an organization in Sacramento named California Capital Small Business Development Corporation. Offering direct loans and loan guarantees to individuals not usually considered eligible for conventional loans, California Capital provides innovative economic development programs. Its president, Clarence Williams, introduced me to an area of banking and economic development which I had not known existed.

I had long known of the kinds of economic development project which churches love to sponsor in Africa and Asia, and I had heard of Grameen Bank in Bangladesh, which makes small business loans to poor people. What I did not know was that the Grameen Bank model was one of those too-few instances in which rich countries were finding something of value to borrow from a Third World country.

Grameen Bank was founded in Bangladesh in 1976 by Muhammad Yunus, an economist at Chittagong University. Yunus was convinced that business ownership would provide a means by which desperately poor people could become financially self-sufficient. Unable to find financing for his unconventional ideas, he used his own resources to open the bank. People who borrow from Grameen Bank must abide by sixteen practices designed to provide a better life-style. These range from building and using pit latrines to refusing to tolerate injustice.

Grameen Bank engages in a practice known as "peer lending," in which a loan is given to a group of individuals who are then responsible for deciding among themselves who should receive it. In the peer-lending model, peer pressure and support provide what in conventional lending is provided through credit history and collateral—some assurance that the loan will be repaid. Commonly, after the first few payments are made on an outstanding loan, the peer group can apply for a second loan which then goes to another person in the group. In the nineteen years since its founding, Grameen Bank has loaned $400 million and boasts a repayment rate of 98 percent, well above average. Because each loan is so small and the businesses so financed are very often home-based sole proprietorships, the term "microenterprise loan" is commonly used to refer to them.

About a decade ago, the U.S. Agency for International Development began experimenting with microenterprise development. In 1988, Congress allocated $50 million for this purpose, and in 1991, $112 million was allocated. When U.S. foundations discovered how successful microenterprise development was overseas, they began backing the idea at home. A wide variety of microenterprise development projects have subsequently sprung up in the United States.

Microenterprise development projects in the U.S. serve clients who are desperately poor and have been, for whatever reasons, bypassed by other means to economic self-sufficiency. As in Bangladesh, many of the businesses started are home-based sole proprietorships, such as day care centers, catering businesses, hair care salons, and jewelry design studios. A number of programs, such as Women's Self-Employment Project in Chicago or Women's Initiative for Self-Employment in San Francisco, serve only women; others, such as Good Faith Fund in Arkansas or Lakota Fund in South Dakota, provide equal assess to men. (Tellingly, Lakota Fund has found that women more than men are interested in the project; 76 percent of their borrowers are women.) Some funds enforce a peer-lending model; others utilize an individual-lending model, reasoning that their clients are so marginal that guaranteeing someone else's loan would be too much of a burden, both financially in case of default and emotionally.

A few years ago the federal Office of Refugee Resettlement, which is part of the Department of Health and Human Services, decided to encourage microenterprise development among refugee populations by providing funding for this purpose to nonprofit agencies serving refugees. A number of nonprofit agencies, such as the Immigrant Center in Honolulu, Hawaii; Church Avenue Merchants Association, Inc., in Brooklyn, New York; and the Center for Southeast Asian Refugee Resettlement in San Francisco, have created microenterprise development projects and loan funds. Many have opted for individual rather than peer lending, finding their clients resistant to participation in peer lending. Most projects provide technical as well as financial assistance.

With the blessing of Clarence Williams, who introduced me to the many domestic varieties of the Grameen Bank model and gave me the Biblical injunction, "Go thou and do likewise," and with the promise of backing from my church deacons, I began talking about my ideas to more people. Two summers ago a group of interested individuals representing four local churches and the Slavic community began an intensive series of meetings. These meetings accomplished three things: 1) a name, Microenterprise Assistance Program; 2) an agreement as to the advisability of the three-pronged approach (basic business education, technical assistance, and loans); and 3) a determination to proceed.

With no financial backing, we approached Sacramento's Regional Occupational Programs, which, through the auspices of the County Office of Education, provides various classes in technical fields, including one in small business basics. The instructors agreed to offer a class for our clients. After great deliberation, we decided to charge a nonrefundable registration fee of $50, reasoning that his was low enough that people serious about going into business could afford it, but high enough to screen out those individuals who might sign up simply out of curiosity. Of the thirty-six applicants, twenty-five were chosen for our first class, and eighteen completed the course. From this group, four had already started business, and four others have subsequently opened businesses.

In reviewing the results of our first class it became apparent that the instructors, despite numerous requests that they tailor their curriculum to meet our students' needs, were happy with their time-honored way of doing things. The instructors had perfected their teaching techniques on American youth, not Slavic adults. As a result, they gave few real-life examples and emphasized certain elementary aspects of retail trade such as giving correct change rather than trying to present general business principles. The instructors also lacked experience teaching with an interpreter and presented information in larger segments than the interpreter could reasonably be expected to remember and translate into Russian.

In May 1994 Laura Leonelli, then program coordinator for Sacramento Lao Family Community, Inc., suggested we combine forces. Together we wrote funding proposals to various sources, and we received a positive response from Sacramento Employment and Training Agency, the local government organization which oversees and funds most refugee programs.

With funding, we have been able to do two things. One is to extend services to the Laotian community as well as to Slavic refugees. The other is to experiment with creating a curriculum more specifically tailored to the needs of our clientele. Students from both Slavic and Hmong communities lack an understanding of such terms as "collateral," "liability," and "corporation," and of the associated concepts and ramifications. We decided to focus on very basic business literacy, helping the students develop a practical working understanding of such concepts. We also decided to utilize the same basic curriculum for each community, but provide separate classes for the two groups. Each class would have a bilingual tutor.

We had earlier found that several individuals wanted substantial amounts of money based on "a good idea," the feasibility of which had not been investigated. With that in mind, our second class, which began in December 1994, started with a five-week feasibility study. Each student was expected to present a written feasibility study for a specific business at the end of the five-week period. We found with both groups that this task was too difficult. While the students were obviously interested in learning how to do a feasibility study, many did not have a prospective business in mind. Nonetheless, the feasibility study provided a basis for what followed.

We then moved into a ten-week series of seminars taught by guest experts, each of whom targeted a specific topic such as business banking or marketing. The third phase of the course was a four-week lecture, discussion, and writing laboratory. For this phase, students formed small groups and worked together with Americans in the preparation of their business plans, which they presented us in written form at the conclusion of the course. In order to successfully complete the formal coursework, students had to have attended at least twelve classes, of which at least seven must have been seminars, as well as submitting the business plan.

Evaluating our first attempt at developing a curriculum, we decided that we were providing a Cadillac when a well-tuned bicycle was needed. Our instructor, a communications specialist, found that the students seemed confused about what was to be included in the business plan. He proposed that we design an eight-session course using a workbook approach and emphasizing only the preparation of a business plan. Because both groups of students had complained that the weekly four-hour classes were too long and too far apart, we decided to offer two two-hour classes a week. We also decided to experiment with teaching both ethnic groups in the same classroom. Despite the potential for cultural misunderstanding, this worked quite well, and it gave the two groups of students a chance to learn something about each other. We are also developing other courses on other aspects of business, such as taxes, accounting, and marketing.

Business education and technical assistance are very important; often what appears to be a financial problem is really a management problem. But still, there must be money to manage.

Recently we received a $15,000 grant from Pacific Telesis Foundation to provide loans for our clients. We have drawn up loan underwriting criteria for our program, formed a loan committee, and decided how loans will be approved and the loan fund administered.

Since our loans will be based on clients' potential rather than prior credit history, we adopted the following loan underwriting criteria:

1. Evidence of successful completion of the educational component, as verified by the instructor and by the program manager. This will include submission of a business plan and records of attendance and promptness in arriving at the teaching site.
2. Personal resume, including background and work experience.
3. If available, credit history.
4. Evidence of having paid rent and utility bills.
5. Written evidence from a voluntary agency of having repaid the travel loan or made satisfactory progress toward repayment.
6. Written character reference from a community leader.*
7. Written character reference from at least three friends who have loaned money to the applicant and been repaid.*
8. Collateral—a list of business property, family autos, and attachment to any real property, if available.
9. Proof of income—receipts of welfare checks, and income tax forms, if available.
10. A copy of the family budget showing the impact of projected business income and expenses.

11. A copy of an I-94 visa, permanent resident card, or citizenship papers, as appropriate.
12. A copy of signed legal disclaimers, privacy act notices, or releases which Microenterprise Assistance Program will provide.

(*The references may be in a language other than English, but an English translation must be provided).

To our delight, Clarence Williams offered to assist us in developing the loan program. Prospective borrowers will apply at California Capital, which will assume responsibility for assembling the loan package, interviewing the applicant, and making a recommendation to our loan committee. As presently constituted, the loan committee is comprised of a member of the Microenterprise Assistance Program board, a small business owner, and a bank officer. This committee will make the final determination concerning each loan application. Because of resistance from both ethnic communities to the idea of peer lending, we have decided to utilize an individual-lending approach initially. Since the total amount available is small, loans will range from $500 to $3,000.

The Hmong find it easy to borrow from within the extended family for amounts ranging up to several thousand dollars. Many of them also have credit cards. One Hmong man asked me pointedly why he should come to me, since he can easily get $3,000 or more from relatives or as a cash advance on a credit card. I replied that borrowing from us would help him establish a credit history. While I am not sure my answer satisfied him, he did not drop out of the class. In general, however, our discussion about the advisability of using our loan fund to develop a credit history has fallen on deaf ears among the Hmong.

The Slavs, on the other hand, find relatives reluctant to loan money for unproven business ventures. They want a credit history, but are unsure how to get one, and find the loan application process confusing and burdensome. Mike, a tailor who opened an alterations business six weeks after class ended, told me it was very easy to borrow money in his country and implied that we were making it unduly difficult. He was not entirely reassured when I told him he needed to regard our loan process as a kind of school.

Our program has not been without its problems. The problem we had with our first attempts at formal education was corrected when we received funding and were able to begin developing our own curriculum. Another issue occurred during the feasibility study when many people dropped out of the class. In my view, this is not all bad; far too many individuals open businesses without good investigation or proper planning, and then wonder why they fail.

One of our prominent clients is a Ukrainian who three years ago was convinced of easy riches through pizza parlor ownership. The easy riches have not materialized, and Yaroslav has learned some difficult lessons about business success in the United States, which he has freely shared with others.

Yaroslav had been approached by someone looking for a partner. This person had told Yaroslav how much his initial investment would need to be and how someone on welfare could finance such a venture. He neglected, however, to tell Yaroslav of the frustrations of pizza ovens breaking down with clockwork regularity, customers paying with bad checks or stolen credit cards, or employees finding ways to get paid without accomplishing the work. Nor had he adequately prepared Yaroslav to work an entire year before beginning to realize a return on his investment.

Yaroslav's experience provides an example of how refugees and immigrants, strange to American ways, can become easy targets. While Yaroslav's partner perhaps did not intend to mislead, he succeeded in giving Yaroslav an incomplete picture of the American dream of success through business ownership. Had Yaroslav realized in advance all that would be involved, he may well have decided against pizza parlor ownership.

Since one of our goals is to steer people without the necessary background and determination away from business ownership, we counted as a success the decision Petr made. Petr entered our program intent on learning all he could about business and then opening a restaurant. During the last four weeks of class, the instructor and American mentors questioned the students intensively about their plans. Petr participated once. The following week, when his turn to be questioned came, he announced that he had discovered that he didn't know enough to start a business and that he had therefore decided to go to school first. We felt gratified that Petr made this discovery before investing

considerable time, energy, and scarce resources into a venture for which he was ill-prepared.

As our loan program develops, we face other problems. Despite all our talk about the importance of starting small and growing, the students' version of "small" is considerably larger than ours. Lo wants to go from being a college student to being the proprietor of a noodle shop. Chua is investigating the feasibility of buying a donut shop. Yuriy, a beekeeper, wants at least 500 beehives at $65 per hive. Viktor would like a real auto body repair shop.

In each instance, the jump from where they are to where they want to be is large enough that the term "microenterprise" is inappropriate. With $15,000 we cannot hope to provide a noodle shop for Lo, a donut shop for Chua, 500 beehives for Yuriy, and an auto body shop for Viktor—but we can provide some equipment for each of them. I am hopeful that, when they can begin serious work on their business plans and discuss with each other and the Americans who will be there the feasibility of their dreams, they will find that they must focus on building ladders, rather than taking quantum leaps.

Interest in the Microenterprise Assistance Program is high, both in the refugee communities and among lenders and development specialists. I can foresee the day when we will offer, for instance, one-day seminars in safety requirements for proprietors of auto body shops or in health requirements for restaurants; when our loan fund has enough in it to provide more substantial loans to refugees; when refugees throughout Sacramento come to us for basic business literacy; and when our graduates will be able to walk into First Interstate or the Bank of America and be treated with respect and given a fair hearing.

From Bangladesh to Sacramento. There are many lessons we in the rich countries of the world can learn from impoverished countries. Microenterprise development for the dispossessed should rank high among these lessons.

And yes, I donate generously to my church's special offerings. Besides funding Third World development projects, they provide funding for work here at home, including my work with refugees. I support this in any way I can, and I try to be open to the lessons which come from participating in it.

Questions:

1. What is the major purpose of this article?

2. What is the Grameen Bank?

3. What is meant by the term "peer lending"?

The answer section begins on page 243.

With extensive experience as an applied anthropologist in Indonesia and Pakistan, anthropologist Michael Dove concentrates on how indigenous knowledge and resource-use patterns can be integrated into national systems of development. In this selection Dove discusses his work on a development project in Pakistan in which his job as an applied anthropologist was to help the Pakistan Forest Service assist small farmers to grow more trees. Not only did Dove study the "target population" of the project (i.e., the farmers,) but he found that it was also vital to the project's success to study the attitudes and behaviors of the government bureaucrats (the foresters). In this article, Dove makes the very important point that anthropologists must not only study the local indigenous populations, but must also turn their critical analysis on the very process in which they are engaged, namely the <u>development process</u> itself.

Anthropology Development vs. Development Anthropology: Mediating the Forester-Farmer Relationship in Pakistan

By Michael R. Dove

The Forest Service of Pakistan has concerned itself since colonial times largely with the production, protection, and extraction of trees in the nation's state forests. The only contact that its officers had with most farmers (except large land-owners, with whom they had traditional patron-client relations) was to levy punishments for violations of forest laws or gather fees for the use of forest resources. In recent years, the state forests have declined in area and importance, and the need to increase on-farm supplies of tree products and halt resource degradation has increased. As a result, the Government of Pakistan, with the assistance of the U.S. Agency for International Development (USAID), decided to change the basic direction of the Forest Service—away from state lands to private lands, away from commercial to subsistence or mixed subsistence/commercial production, and thus away from the rural elite to the small farmer. The vehicle chosen to accomplish this was the bilaterally funded Forestry Planning and Development Project, Pakistan's first major social forestry project.

The mission assigned me as project anthropologist was to assist the Forest Service to make this transition to a public service agency by helping it to identify and communicate with its intended clientele, the small farmers of Pakistan.

It was initially assumed that my work would focus on ways of "motivating" the farmers, based on the then-widespread belief within the Forest Service and USAID that small farmers were inherently ill-disposed towards trees and tree cultivation. My field research soon revealed that this was largely a myth, and that the real constraint to the development of farm forestry was that many foresters were ill-disposed towards working with small farmers. A large part of my mission shifted, therefore, from motivating farmers to plant trees to motivating foresters to help farmers plant trees, and from communicating forestry technology to farmers to communicating farmers' attitudes and needs to foresters.

The Role of the Project Anthropologist

As the project anthropologist I was one of four long-term, expatriate experts on a technical assistance team assembled by the Windrock International Institute for Agricultural Development under contract to USAID. The other expatriate experts were a farm forester, a research forester, and a training expert. On the Government of Pakistan's side, a special project cell was established in the federal office of the Inspector General of Forests to provide overall supervision and guidance, and individual project

Reprinted by permission of PRACTICING ANTHROPOLOGY, 13 (2), Spring 1991, pp. 21-25.

offices were established in each of the country's four provinces to carry out field operations. My direct counterpart in all activities was a Deputy Inspector General of Forests in the federal project cell. I was assisted in my work by one full-time and eight part-time Pakistani sociologists and by thirteen farmers hired to keep daily records.

The specific goals of the project anthropologist were (1) to carry out a national program of research to establish a base line for farm forestry in Pakistan, monitor farmer response to the project, and promote research relevant to farmers' needs within the Forest Service; (2) to assist in developing practical extension strategies based on this research, with special attention to the involvement of women and the landless; and (3) to assist in the development of socially relevant curricula at the Pakistan Forest Institute and to develop in the forest service generally an appreciation of the utility of a social science perspective. A project-wide goal, to which I also devoted a good deal of my time, was to develop a national policy to better manage the forest and tree resources of Pakistan.

My approach to the first goal, involving a national program of research, was to carry out a series of surveys in the three project provinces of Baluchistan, the Northwest Frontier Province, and the Punjab. There were five stages to this research, each more focused than—and to some extent based on the results of—the previous stages: (1) group interviews on basic village characteristics (in 118 villages); (2) interviews on basic household characteristics in 1132 households; (3) in-depth interviews on farm ecology and economics in 589 households; (4) in-depth interviews on village ecology with 40 village groups and village religious leaders; and, finally, (5) daily monitoring of farm dynamics for 18 months in 13 households.

I adapted anthropological techniques for analyzing and reporting on these data to the time constraints, pragmatic interests, and expository style of government forest officers. Ten timely, succinct reports were issued, focused on identifying the proper clientele for project services, describing their needs, and predicting their responses. Highlights of these reports were the presentation of complex data in easily-understood, computer generated graphs which show that interest in planting trees for use as fuel is essentially uniform among Pakistani farmers, regardless of farm size. This finding refuted the widely held belief in social forestry that farmers (especially better-off farmers) are not interested in planting trees for

use as fuel. Another highlight of the reports (for me, if not my intended audience) was the use of the prose of the biological sciences (for the benefit of the Pakistani foresters) and the U.S. government (for the benefit of USAID). This expository style differs from that of anthropology in its emphasis on brevity, use of numbers rather than prose, and implications of authoritativeness.

I used these reports as the basis for developing extension strategies, which was another goal of the project anthropologist. This involved, among other efforts, preparation with my Forest Service counterpart of a manual on social forestry extension in Pakistan, emphasizing simple techniques for contacting and communicating with common farmers. These techniques were lacking among many forest service officers, in part because the social and political structure of Pakistani society normally rules out any contact between visiting government officers and common villagers. Many foresters initially regarded meetings with local officials as the beginning and end of their "extension" activities, with the focus of these meetings being on what the Forest Service could do for the officials. In contrast, in our manual we emphasized that meetings with local officials are just the beginning and that their focus should be on what the officials can do for the project. One thing that local officials can not do for the project, however, is be responsible for contacting local farmers. The initial impulse of most foresters was to rely upon local officials to set up all farmer meetings. In our manual we strongly encouraged the foresters to do this themselves on the grounds that meetings arranged by local officials are invariably limited to a tiny minority of economically and politically influential farmers, who have the least need of extension services.

With the same counterpart, I established an Urdu-language quarterly, *Farm Forestry Newsletter*, for farmers, focusing not only on communication to farmers of simple, useful information, but also on communication to foresters on the farmers' own skills and knowledge. Foresters tended to be slow to appreciate this knowledge because of a cognitive block against the perception of tree cultivation in non-conventional patterns, locations, and strategies. For example, the most common farm forestry system in Pakistan, the thorn fence—incorporating a wide variety of trees, bushes, and grasses; some wild, some managed, and some planted; and variously used for fuel, fencing, fodder and timber—is invisible to most foresters. In each issue of the newsletter we

239

accordingly highlighted traditional practices of tree cultivation and implicitly made the point that the farmers knew how to cultivate trees before the Forest Service came along, that some of this knowledge is unknown to the Service, and that there are things that the forest officers could learn from—as well as teach to—the farmers.

A notable example is the traditional system of lopping and pruning, which is part of a sophisticated management system for maximizing desired impacts and products of trees and minimizing undesired impacts and products. One widespread custom is lopping trees just before the winter wheat planting in order to reduce shading of the wheat seedlings and energize the soil and at the same time ameliorate a seasonal shortage of fuel and fodder. I discovered that this management system is based on an indigenous system of humoral classification of trees and tree shade, the understanding of which should offer promising new perspectives on research and extension concerning the critical tree-crop interface. (See M. Dove, "The 'Humor' of Shade: The Peasant Epistemology of Tree Shade in Pakistan," *Human Ecology*, forthcoming.)

These efforts to stimulate a flow of knowledge from farmer to forester reflected my concern for institutional development, the third goal assigned to the project anthropologist. My efforts in this regard included co-sponsoring an international seminar (with the Office of the Inspector General of Forests) on the need for a more people-oriented forestry policy in Pakistan. I also co-authored with this same office a review of past national forest policies and a draft of the new policy. In our review of past policies, I used anthropological techniques of textual analysis to reveal the implicit structure of past policies, which produced some novel and useful perspectives for policy revision. For example, Table 1 shows that past forestry policies in Pakistan have relied most heavily on planning or organizational changes to attain policy goals and least heavily on study or research.

For the Pakistan Forest Institute, I developed a syllabus for a course (in the M.Sc. curriculum) in "Rural Sociology/Anthropology" based on South Asian case studies of the use of anthropology and rural sociology to solve extension problems in natural resource use. I subsequently co-edited a textbook (*The Sociology of Natural Resources in Pakistan and Adjoining Countries*. M. Dove and C. Carpenter, eds. Lahore: Vanguard Press for the Mashal Foundation, forthcoming) for this course.

Use and Impact of Anthropology in the Project

As an ecological anthropologist, with eight years prior field experience studying indigenous use of forests and grasslands in Indonesia, I drew on ecological anthropology and ethnoscience to analyze Pakistan's farming systems, recommend directions for forestry extension, and prepare extension tools like the farmer newsletter. I looked at what tree species the farmers were already cultivating; how, where, and why they were cultivating them; and what the principal perceived constraints were. One finding, for example, was that farmers decide when to plant trees based not only on climatic conditions, but also on the availability of labor, a constraint that the foresters had not previously had to consider (when planting trees with hired labor in state forests). The times preferred for tree planting are when farmers are least busy in the fields with food crops.

I drew on the traditional tools of social and economic anthropology to correlate variables of interest to the Forest Service, such as willingness to plant seedlings, with important differentiating variables in rural Pakistani society, like land tenure or access to irrigation. I then identified for the Forest Service the household types likely to be most receptive to extension efforts, as well as those where the net impact of these efforts would likely be greatest. I established that landless tenants possess some traditional rights to trees, and that rural women play a major role in the production and consumption of tree products, and I accordingly recommended an increased extension focus on both groups.

I attempted to meld the anthropological focus on local-level dynamics and perceptions—which I believe is essential to revealing farmer needs—with the short time-frame and broad scope of a national development project. I did this through use of open-ended questionnaires emphasizing local perceptions and knowledge, and strategic mixing of sample size and interview focus. I also utilized the novel method of having farmers keep records of their own activities to provide the in-depth and long-term data normally used by anthropologists but typically missing from development projects. The application of anthropological methods was not limited to farmers alone: I utilized techniques of unstructured interviewing, with senior officials as my expert informants, to produce the first draft of the new national forestry policy. This proved to be a very successful exercise and suggests a new avenue for contributions by anthropologists— drawing on our special skills in eliciting and structuring informants' beliefs—to the formation of development policy.

Of most importance, perhaps, I drew on anthropological tools for institutional analysis to help mediate a conflict over the basic philosophy of the project. The explicit design of the project— to assist small farmers to cultivate trees to meet household needs—initially met with resistance from some forest officers who contended that there were no small farmers in Pakistan, and if there were, they would not be interested in planting trees. These officers pressured for a redirection of the project to cultivation by large farmers of block tree plantations for the market. Drawing on our base line study data, I was able to demonstrate not only that small farmers exist in Pakistan, but that they are very interested in tree cultivation. I determined that small farmers were invisible to some members of the Forest Service because they defined "farmer" as big land-owner, a definition that I traced to traditional patron-client ties between forest service officers and rural elites. My documentation of the interest of small farmers in tree cultivation, and hence of the practicality of the project design, contributed to a subsequent decision by the Forest Service to discourage efforts to redirect the project towards a market-oriented project for large farmer and refocus attention on improving implementation of the existing project.

After three and one-half years there was considerable evidence that the value of these anthropological inputs was appreciated within the Pakistan Forestry Service. The sample and methodology of the base line study was adopted for use in two major Forest Service research projects; reports on the results of the base line study were accepted for publication in the *Pakistan Journal of Forestry* (the foremost publication of forestry research in Pakistan), the first ever by an anthropologist; in the revision of the national forestry policy in which I participated, social forestry was elevated to a position equal to traditional commercial or protection forestry; and the Federal Government unilaterally requested USAID to extend the involvement of the project anthropologist beyond the original commitment. This represented an about-face from the start of my appointment, which one provincial forestry office had attempted to block and which the USAID project officer had called an "experiment." (This starting position—not at "go," but at some point

considerably behind it—is, unfortunately, still the norm rather than the exception for anthropologists working in international development).

Anthropology of Development vs. Development Anthropology

The most stimulating work that I did in Pakistan, and the work that drew most heavily on my anthropological training, involved the analysis not of peasant behavior and beliefs, but the behavior and beliefs of government officials. It was not small farmers, but government officials that posed the principal development challenge in my project. This is often the case in rural development, yet the belief systems of government officials in developing countries are rarely studied by anthropologists (or, indeed, by any other discipline). Why is this?

I suggest that anthropologists do not study government officials (at least not in developmental contexts), do not treat them as the anthropological "other," because to do so is to call into question the conventional perceptions of development. To treat the *object* of development, the farmer, as "other" is fine; but to treat the administering official as "other," to study (and hence implicitly question the basis for) his perceptions, is to acknowledge that there is a subjective element in the management of development programs. Institutional and personal aversion to making this acknowledgment has contributed to a tradition of study in which the anthropological "other" is firmly located outside of government, development, and aid offices.

This positioning of the "other" in non-governmental contexts is part of a more general effort in post-World War II anthropology to draw a boundary between research and application, selecting non-applied topics for basic research, and then attempting to apply the insights gained to development problems. The result is a theoretical anthropological literature that has little to say about development, and a (grey) development literature that has little to say about anthropological theory.

The conclusion to be drawn from this unfortunate schism is that relevance and theory are mutually developed not by the application of research findings to relevant topics, but by the selection, in the first instance, of relevant topics for research. An "applied anthropology" is good for neither application nor theory (recognition of which is reflected in the use of "practicing" instead of "applied" in this journal's title). Many of the most relevant topics involve the development process itself; the use of anthropology within development must not, therefore, preclude the study *of* development by anthropology.

The development process itself should be one of the foremost topics of anthropological study. This is one of three lessons that any anthropologist with an interest in "praxis" should bear in mind. The second is that a sincere commitment to the first lesson will inevitably, as in any such self-reflective exercise, create conflict with some colleagues and counterparts. The third lesson is that the practicing anthropologist must be willing to assist in any activity, whether strictly anthropological in nature or not; this will provide the data needed to honor lesson number one, and it will provide the political capital needed to survive lesson two.

The study of development process (as opposed to the study of the objects of this process) implies that the anthropologist has an agenda of his or her own, over and above the particular tasks assigned within the context of the development project. The existence of a personal agenda raises a number of problematic ethical issues, *but so does the absence of a personal agenda*. To bring one's own agenda to a development project is to bring one's own moral conscience. There is nothing in recent development history to suggest that this is not needed, and much to suggest that it is.

Table 1 Methods Proposed to Attain Forestry Policy Objectives

% of All Methods Proposed:	Type of Method Proposed to Attain Announced Objectives of 1955/1962/1980 Forestry Policies			
	Study & Research	Extension	Field Activity	Planning & Organization
	11%	23%	26%	39%

Questions:

1. How did Dove's basic mission shift during his work with foresters and farmers in Pakistan?

2. What were the goals of the project anthropologist?

3. What does the author mean by "Anthropology of Development"?

The answer section begins on page 243.

Answers

Chapter One

1. "Disease" refers to the biomedical model which emphasizes physiological evidence while "illness" refers to the more subjective experiences of the patient.
2. Since mothers considered infant diarrhea to be normal, they saw no reason for treatment.
3. Attitudes toward contraception, mother's recognition of infant malnutrition and the training of local community health workers.

Chapter Two

1. Many African-Americans, particularly older ones, lacked both trust and rapport with the community health facilities.
2. They wanted information about employment opportunities and public safety.
3. Bailey recommended the use of more African-American health care and social services personnel, promoting the event in African-American media, and using more culturally appropriate teaching techniques.

Chapter Three

1. She served on the hospital's Internal Review Board, lunched with physicians and other hospital personnel, met with the Mayor's Blue Ribbon Committee on Infant Mortality, and consulted with officials at other health facilities that specialized in programs for pregnant women.
2. Interviews and in-depth review of medical records.
3. Boone was able to redefine maternal and infant health problems as sociomedical rather than strictly medical.

Chapter Four

1. She worked as a nurse for a Cuban physician and then served in the Peace Corps in India for two and a half years.
2. She was able to make recommendations to other staff members about his diet, his communication patterns, and how best to support him while he was dying.
3. Anthropologists are sensitive to general dietary habits found in the Hispanic woman's culture.

Chapter Five

1. The concept of community and the importance of having a global perspective which regards domestic and international research as being relevant for each other.
2. Shortages of condoms, poor treatment by the clinic staff, and fear of threats by neighbors who want them to work elsewhere.
3. Educating women at a convenient place and time, conducting open dialogues with the women, recognizing the importance of protecting children from infection, and using videos of communities that failed to acknowledge the problem of AIDS.

Chapter Six

1. The need for translation and special care for refugees is costly in terms of both time and money.
2. These outreach teams allow caseworkers and sponsors to be more active and better informed of their clients' health needs.
3. They can help with dealing with landlords who provide substandard housing and they can serve as translators in certain situations.

Chapter Seven

1. High stress (relocation, living in poverty), poor diets, and bad habits such as smoking, alcohol consumption, and drug use.
2. Owing to the extreme modesty of Mexican women, husbands typically do not see their wives until after the delivery is over.
3. In many Asian countries women are seen as a "wasted investment" and consequently receive less food, education, and medical attention.

Chapter Eight

1. First, in-depth cultural training has not been given high priority in education of dietitians, and second, the scientific (biological) aspects of dietetics has been given much more attention than how to deliver nutritional services.
2. Participant-observation and informant interviewing.
3. The availability of new foods, the desire to fit into the new culture, and a desire to associate with the foods of higher status people.

Chapter Nine

1. The DSM-IV refers to the fourth edition of the Diagnostic and Statistical Manual of Mental Disorders published by the American Psychiatric Association. It has been criticized by the more culturally sensitive clinicians because the culture-related syndromes were relegated to an appendix rather than playing a central role in the manual itself.
2. Only in North America and European cultures is so much cultural emphasis placed on the equation of thinness and attractiveness.
3. Worry sickness, unhappiness, heartbroken, drunkenlike craziness, and disappointment and pouting.

Chapter Ten

1. The psychiatrist neither prescribed a treatment or admitted the girl to the hospital.
2. Applied medical anthropology can provide information on the patient's own illness experiences, their views on sickness and health, and the cultural context in which these beliefs are embedded.
3. California "New Age" theories, neurolinguistic programming, acupuncture, chiropractic, and hypnotherapy.

Chapter Eleven

1. From on-the-job training.
2. The belief that one will be successful in a different culture if they are successful in their own environment.
3. People who return from overseas assignments before the end of their contracts.

Chapter Twelve

1. It builds a common language skill for communication between people who speak English as a second language, and it builds an awareness of each culture's unique approach to business encounters.
2. It helps the company's staff and managers become more aware of multicultural diversity issues and how the behaviors are affecting their business interactions.
3. Each person wanted to take individual credit for their own ideas despite the fact that group interaction generates the best ideas. Thus, they were stuck on how to generate ideas effectively.
4. All humans try to create meanings in their lives.

Chapter Thirteen

1. In a wide range of professional settings rather than in academia.
2. Kin, occupational groups, and recreational associations.
3. Learning material took too long to arrive, materials arrived in incorrect quantities, books arrived in poor condition, and materials would sit in ground-level lobbies in large heavy boxes, forcing employees to carry them up in pieces due to the weight.

Chapter Fourteen

1. To help companies change their organizational cultures to make better use of each employee's contributions and talents.
2. 85% of those joining the workforce between 1985 and 2000 will be minorities and women. White males will only count for 15% of new additions to labor.
3. Training managers and implementing awareness workshops for employees.
4. Timing and defining who exactly was the client.

Chapter Fifteen

1. North Americans need to be liked while Germans need to establish credibility and position in the hierarchy.
2. Germans want to establish hierarchy while North Americans want to dissolve it.
3. Problem solving and being liked.

Chapter Sixteen

1. It puts them in a one-down position.
2. Men are more focused on information and women are more sensitive to the feelings of the person with whom they are speaking.
3. For men- banter, joking, teasing, playful put-downs, avoiding one-down positions. For women- maintaining equality, taking the other person's reactions into account, down-playing authority.

Chapter Seventeen

1. The Sapir-Whorf hypothesis is the linguistic hypothesis that suggests that language is more than a mechanism for sending and receiving messages, but rather it also affects the way people perceive because it sets linguistic categories in their heads.
2. The author suggested that this reflected the cultural value of individualism.
3. Japanese language is used to create consensus and harmony while in the United States the goal is to demonstrate eloquence.
4. "Rapport-talk," associated with women, seeks to establish agreement and social relationships; "report-talk," on the other hand, is a male mode of discourse and seeks to maintain personal independence and establish a place in the competitive hierarchy.

Chapter Eighteen

1. HBO hired an ethnic marketing director, one marketing agency developed a direct campaign targeting Hispanics and African-Americans, and a cable operator in San Diego developed an in-house research and marketing campaign directed at Hispanic nonsubscribers.
2. Anthropological research is exploratory, fieldwork is done on informants' "home turf," and it allows researchers to tune into consumers' conceptual systems.
3. In the city where Hispanics were fluent in English, the people opted for Spanish programming. In the city where Hispanics had recently arrived in the U.S., they tended to favor bilingual programming.

Chapter Nineteen

1. Movies, music, software programs, electronic communication, medical and biotechnical products, financial services, and research and development.
2. To understand the way in which a particular culture operates.
3. The nature of the brand personality, its appeal and relevance, the consistency of a brand's communication, and the integrity of its identity.

Chapter Twenty

1. E-Lab bases its marketing recommendations on what customers actually do rather than what they think or say they do.
2. Disposable cameras were given to potential customers who were asked to photograph their audio equipment whenever they listened to it.
3. "Anthropump" was a technique used by E-Lab researchers which involved asking customers to view the videos they were in and explain their behavior.

Chapter Twenty One

1. –Strong sense of community and cooperation.
   –Use of oral history and story telling as a teaching device
   –Avoidance of confrontation
   –Journey (process) is more important than the destination (product)
   –Choice in learning
2. –Emphasizes process over product.
   –Emphasizes the group, cooperation, and collaborative learning.
   –Suggests that learning to read and write parallel learning oral language.
   –Places value on quality literature.
   –Taught through content area themes.
   –Includes qualitative assessments.
   –Incorporates student initiated projects.
3. First, Native American cultures emphasize the journey rather than the destination and the focus of whole language learning is on the process rather than the product or outcome. Second., the use of themes in whole language teaching makes the process more integrated and Native Americans generally believe that all areas of life are interrelated. And third, the opportunity for self selection of literature in whole language learning supports the idea of choice prevalent in Native American learning styles.

Chapter Twenty Two

1. A major theme is their perception about their dual roles as (1) adults with head-of-household responsibilities outside of school and as (2) adolescents required to follow rules meant for minors within school.
2. Generally, the students had positive feelings about the alternative school they were attending because the teachers cared, the education was more challenging, and they were learning.
3. This study suggests that there should be some rethinking of the goals of high schools so as to make them more relevant to the demands of today's society and marketplace.

Chapter Twenty Three

1. Reflective practice and the application of anthropological perspectives.
2. Culture, context, social structure, and power.
3. Observation, open-ended interviews, and examination of artifacts.

Chapter Twenty Four

1. The Bell Curve suggested that intelligence is a biologically based entity, fixed at birth, that can be measured by so-called IQ Tests; that various races have either more or less of this thing called intelligence; that IQ is associated with economic success, morality, and criminality; that attempts to educationally enrich those with low intelligence is a waste of time and money.
2. Our cultural blinders keep us from seeing cultural alternatives.
3. It is vital that we try to understand culturally different people within their cultural context; and we need to recognize the limits and biases of our own cultural assumptions.

Chapter Twenty Five

1. Why does the literacy rate among the Toto remain so low relative to other groups? What can be learned that will help improve the educational situation?
2. The Toto need their children to help with farming, particularly during harvest season; there are numerous holidays and feast days that Toto children are expected to observe; Toto children cannot be taught in the native language because it lacks a written form; educational materials are irrelevant to the lifeways of Toto children; and inadequate teaching staff.
3. The hiring of more qualified and caring teachers; financial compensation to families for the loss of labor of their children; the use of more culturally relevant teaching materials; encouragement of female children to attend school; and the provision for secondary schools in the region.

Chapter Twenty Six

1. Training in participant-observation and generally dealing with cross cultural situations.
2. Green brokered between the two worlds of typical and atypical children as well as between children and teachers.
3. Three themes running through both adult learning principles and current research in educational anthropology are (1) empowerment, (2) collaboration, and (3) critical reflection.

Chapter Twenty Seven

1. Since 1969 the cost of living has increased 300 percent in New York City while basic welfare grants have risen only 56 percent.
2. Participant-observation and systematic interviewing.
3. Press-releases, sending the findings to public and private agencies, presentation of findings at legislative and public hearings, and expert witness testimony

Chapter Twenty Eight

1. She played the roles of teacher, consultant, trainer, and expert witness.
2. The consultant affords legitimacy by saying that certain Native American religious traditions do exist outside of prison.
3. When the clients are exclusively Native American.
4. The bond which results can be misinterpreted by prisoners as personal affection or willingness to do favors.

Chapter Twenty Nine

1. Security needs, medical needs, and program needs.
2. One must systematically apply the accumulated knowledge of the discipline of anthropology to practical problems.
3. Statistical analysis is imperative; the goal should be simplicity, not complexity; the need to work collaboratively with a number of people rather than being an academic loner.

Chapter Thirty

1. Dash is the Nigerian term for a "bribe."
2. Legal domination is characterized by authority residing in the office, not the individual person, and that authority is validated by a universally applied set of rules and regulations. Patrimonial domination, on the other hand, is characterized by rulers who create and maintain personal social relationships with their subjects.
3. The Nigerian bureaucratic system is not irrational but rather is built on a different set of cultural assumptions as compared to western bureaucratic systems. The Nigerian system is base on the values of strong social relationships emanating from kinship and clientship while western systems are based on the value of efficiency, precision, speed, and fairness.

Chapter Thirty One

1. The area of environment health deals with providing a safe and sanitary environment and deals with such issues as sewage disposal, maintaining adequate supplies of drinking water, food hygiene, rabies surveillance, and the sanitary inspection of group care facilities, mobile home parks, and other institutions.
2. Participant-observation, open-ended interviewing, collection of life histories, rapid rural assessment, and good listening skills.
3. Hammond participated in the day to day community events such as church affairs, school games, dance recitals, weddings, funerals, festivals, and fund raisers.

Chapter Thirty Two

1. INN was a network of eminent people in the field of international negotiations and mediation who served as third party negotiators in international conflict situations.
2. Yang supplied culturally relevant information for the third party mediators which could help facilitate the negotiation process.
3. Yang urges anthropologists to be less reluctant in expressing general sociocultural themes that extend beyond the boundaries of their local studies.

Chapter Thirty Three

1. The law unjustly singled out Gypsies for punishment; there was no intent to defraud; and the Gypsies were simply practicing a traditional strategy for maintaining their anonymity.
2. To minimize the persecution they have experienced over the centuries.
3. He was afraid to eat food prepared by non-Gypsies who did not follow Gypsy rules of cleanliness, and thus, he feared he would become ritually impure.

Chapter Thirty Four

1. She mediated between the local people and the national and international organizations that provided various types of assistance.
2. The village as a whole should benefit, not just certain individuals or segments of the community; appropriate technology should be used; the project should be sustainable.
3. The anthropologist benefits by establishing more dynamic relationships with the indigenous people and by being able to view village life from inside.

Chapter Thirty Five

1. Home economic activities (i.e., nutrition, child care, cooking), general development related activities (i.e., literacy, water storage), and income-generating activities.
2. The women were taught leadership skills for the purpose of developing their self -confidence, self reliance, and sense of responsibility.
3. Sewing, knitting, handicrafts, commercial gardening, and poultry keeping.
4. The four major findings of the evaluation research included:
   –Leadership training must precede training in specific business skills.
   –While the income generating activities stemming from this project varied, it seems clear that the training positively affected the women's ability to enter into entrepreneurial activities.
   –There was a "multiplier effect," whereby women who received the training were passing on their newly learned skills to other women.
   –The introduction of savings clubs from Kenya proved to be an effective mechanism for women's self-help groups to raise needed capital for new businesses.

Chapter Thirty Six

1. Indigenous peoples will be replaced and their cultures lost; loss of agricultural land due to soil erosion; the loss of watersheds; and the disappearance of other plant and animal life.
2. Charcoal making, swidden cultivation, illegal logging, and population expansion.
3. According to Wallace's calculations, it takes approximately 18% of a tree to cook a pot of rice.

Chapter Thirty Seven

1. Loker wanted to (1) learn why cattle raising was so popular among local farmers, (2) conduct on-farm testing on promising forage species, and (3) measuring the ecological impact of cattle raising.
2. Grazed plots of land regenerate only about 44 percent of the biomass that ungrazed land regenerate.
3. –Cattle are a real economic asset in that they are both capital goods (can be sold for cash) and productive assets (they produce milk).
   –Cattle require relatively little labor.

Chapter Thirty Eight

1. The major purpose of this article is to demonstrate that there are lessons to be learned about economic development that can flow from the LDCs to the more industrialized nations.
2. Started in 1976 by Muhammad Yunus, a Bangladesh economist, the Grameen Bank made small loans to desperately poor people in Bangladesh to enable them to start their own small businesses.
3. A practice used by the Grameen Bank, "peer lending" refers to the process of making a loan to a group of individuals who are then responsible for deciding as a group who should receive a loan.

Chapter Thirty Nine

1. Dove's task or mission shifted from motivating farmers to plant trees to motivating foresters to help farmers plant trees.
2. Conduct base-line research, develop extension strategies based on that research, and develop a socially relevant curriculum for the Forest Institute.
3. "Anthropology of development" refers to the anthropological study of the development process, including not only the attitudes and behaviors of the local people, but also the attitudes and behaviors of the government officials.